Southern
Illinois
Birds

Southern Illinois Birds

An Annotated List and Site Guide

W. Douglas Robinson

Southern Illinois University Press
Carbondale and Edwardsville

Frontispiece: Carolina Wren, New Burnside, Johnson Co., 3 August 1991.
Photo by Todd Fink.

Cover illustrations: front, Mississippi Kite, photo by Todd Fink;
spine, Blue Jay, photo by Richard Day, Daybreak Imagery.

Library of Congress Cataloging-in-Publication Data

Robinson, W. Douglas.
    Southern Illinois birds : an annotated list and site guide / W. Douglas
Robinson.
        p. cm.
    Includes bibliographical references and index.
    1. Birds—Illinois. 2. Bird watching—Illinois—Guidebooks.
    3. Birding sites—Illinois—Guidebooks. 4. Illinois—Guidebooks. I. Title.
QL684.I3R63 1996
598.29773′9—dc20   95-14767
ISBN 0-8093-2032-0   CIP

The paper used in this publication meets the minimum requirements
of American National Standard for Information Sciences—Permanence
of Paper for Printed Library Materials, ANSI Z39.48-1984. ♾

For the next generation of naturalists,
and
in fond memory of
Todd Fink,
a true friend and colleague

Contents

Maps

Acknowledgments

Without the gracious assistance of many birders, this book would have suffered greatly. If it even approaches being comprehensive and complete, it is a result of the cooperation of many good friends. Bob Danley, Todd Fink, Jeff Hardt, Steve Olson, and John Robinson reviewed the first draft of this book in 1989; their comments encouraged me to expand the scope and detail of the book into its present form. The records included here come from no less than 125 observers, some of whom supplied me with copies of their original field notes or summaries of the highlights from them. In particular, Richard Brewer, Todd Fink, Vernon Kleen, Steve Olson, and Bruce Peterjohn were exceptionally helpful in providing details on their observations of many of the region's species. Numerous others helped me with specific records and provided advice on problematic records; special thanks to Steve Bailey, H. David Bohlen, Judy DeNeal, Ron Goetz, Vernon Kleen, and Terry Walsh. Lee Drickamer suggested that I include page references to field guides in each species account. Scott Robinson reviewed the section on forest fragmentation and shared unpublished data on nest parasitism and predation rates. Todd Fink and Tara Robinson patiently read the revised manuscript and offered many helpful suggestions for improvement.

Probably the greatest challenge to completing a work of this sort is realizing that it cannot be done quickly. Even projects of moderate size like this one require years to complete, and they seem to create more questions than they provide answers. My family, especially my mother, Betty, and my wife, Tara, were instrumental in encouraging me to finish this book. Todd Fink, whose encouragement, interest, and critical assistance sustained me, was patient and always willing to take time to discuss his impressions of seasonal or regional patterns; his company in the field as we tried to fill in various obvious gaps in our knowledge about southern Illinois birds was always a delight. Todd also generously shared his many excellent photos of birds in southern Illinois; their inclusion here has added a wonderful touch to the book.

The enthusiasm, professionalism, and dedication of the people at Southern Illinois University Press has been a joy to experience. In particular, Rick Stetter, Susan Wilson, Jill Butler-Wilson, and John Wilson were instrumental in smoothly guiding this project to its completion.

Finally, thanks to the birders and naturalists of the future. I have often daydreamed about the days when the sky was darkened by Passenger Pigeons, when chattering flocks of parakeets coursed along river banks, and when shadows of Ivory-billed Woodpeckers disappeared into the still, dim forest. I hope these pages provide you with daydreams about what it is like in these days.

Introduction

Southern Illinois is a unique and wonderful place to find birds, particularly when it is compared with the rest of Illinois. Unlike most of central and northern Illinois, the south has extensive tracts of upland and lowland forest, has dramatic topographic relief in the unglaciated Shawnee Hills, and is surrounded on three sides by two of the continent's major rivers. Consequently, southern Illinois offers a wide variety of habitats and birds that are unusual in Illinois. Comparing the habitats and birdlife in the southern tip of the state with those in the entirety of Illinois has been referred to as being analagous to comparing the habitats and birdlife of the southern tip of Texas with those of the remainder of the lower forty-eight states. Southern Illinois has much to offer to anyone interested in the birds of Illinois, or in the birds of the midwestern United States for that matter.

In writing this book, I had several objectives. First, my primary goal was to document the current knowledge of the avifauna of the region based on a survey of the published literature and the unpublished field notes of active observers. My survey of unpublished notes is probably the most important component, because it summarizes many important observations that would likely not otherwise be made available. Second, by compiling the information included in this book, I wished to show that there is actually quite a lot known about the birds of this comparatively little-studied section of the state. In comparison with central and northern Illinois, there have been few active field observers in southern Illinois in the past, but the contributions of those who have worked there have been considerable. I hope that their efforts are convincingly displayed in these pages. Third, I wanted to indicate the gaps in current knowledge. Throughout the species accounts, comments are made concerning pieces of information that are lacking or unclear regarding the status, migratory dates, and so on of some species. Hopefully, this book will stimulate other researchers to fill in these gaps in our knowledge. Fourth, I designed the book to be used by birders in the field and at home. The book includes information on early arrival and late departure dates of migrants, highest reported single-day counts in each season, and records of vagrants, all of which may be of interest to birders who wish to determine the importance of their observations after a day in the field. In addition, guides to some of the best birding areas are included to encourage birders and others to explore the many birding and scenic attractions in southern Illinois. Fifth, and finally, I designed this book to be a reference for conservation and government agencies, college students in biology courses, and future researchers who wish to determine the status and abundance of southern Illinois's birds. Toward this end, I have not refrained from including pertinent conservation information, general locations for important populations of rare bird species, and a guide to the pages on which each bird species is illustrated in popular field guides so that those just learning their birds may work through this book and a field guide together.

COVERAGE AREA. Throughout this book, southern Illinois refers to the southernmost seventeen counties of the state, including a small portion of an eighteenth county, St. Clair, where the north portion of Baldwin Lake occurs (see map 1).

In most instances, the name of the county is included with any reference to a particular location, but sometimes it is not, particularly in references to some of the most heavily visited sites. Map 2 is a map of the coverage area with many of the site names commonly referred to in the text.

PHYSICAL FEATURES AND TOPOGRAPHIC DIVISIONS. The southern Illinois landscape is divided into several physiographically distinct regions, each of which tends to have some species of plants and animals that are not found in the other regions (Mohlenbrock 1986). The regions are called Natural Divisions. Six divisions occur in the seventeen southernmost counties of Illinois. Each of these divisions is divided into two or three subunits called sections, which are

Map 1. County map of Illinois. The outlined counties comprise the southern Illinois region covered in this text.

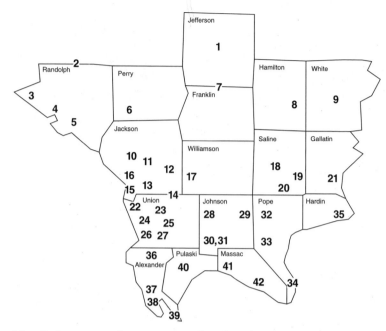

Map 2. Location of sites commonly referred to in the text: *1* = Mt. Vernon; *2* = Baldwin Lake; *3* = Prairie du Rocher; *4* = Fort Kaskaskia State Park; *5* = Randolph County Conservation Area; *6* = Pyramid State Park; *7* = Rend Lake; *8* = Hamilton County Conservation Area; *9* = Carmi; *10* = Lake Murphysboro State Park; *11* = Murphysboro; *12* = Carbondale; *13* = Pomona and Cave Creek Valley; *14* = Giant City State Park; *15* = Grand Tower; *16* = Oakwood Bottoms; *17* = Crab Orchard National Wildlife Refuge; *18* = Harrisburg; *19* = Garden of the Gods; *20* = Saline County Conservation Area; *21* = Shawneetown; *22* = Pine Hills; *23* = Trail of Tears State Forest; *24* = Wolf Lake; *25* = Anna-Jonesboro; *26* = Union County Conservation Area; *27* = Dutch Creek; *28* = Ferne Clyffe State Park; *29* = Ozark; *30* = Little Black Slough; *31* = Heron Pond; *32* = Bell Smith Springs; *33* = Dixon Springs State Park; *34* = Smithland Lock and Dam; *35* = Cave-in-Rock State Park; *36* = South Ripple Hollow; *37* = Horseshoe Lake Conservation Area; *38* = Willard; *39* = Cairo; *40* = Cypress Creek National Wildlife Refuge; *41* = Mermet Lake; *42* = Fort Massac State Park.

distinguished by differences in soil types and historical events, such as glaciation (Schwegman et al. 1973). Unlike many plants, birds tend not to be as particular in their selection of sections. The differences among birds tend instead to occur at the division level or even higher. For this reason, throughout this book I have differentiated among only three physiographic regions: the Floodplains, the Shawnee Hills, and the Till Plain (see map 3).

The Floodplains region includes the bottomland drainages of, in the west, the Mississippi River and its major tributaries; in the south, the Ohio and Cache Rivers; and in the east, the Ohio and Wabash Rivers. The terrain tends to be rather flat in the Flood-

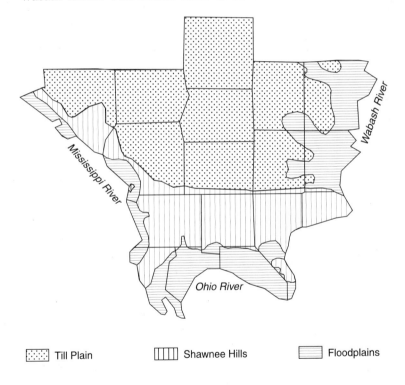

::::: Till Plain |||| Shawnee Hills   Floodplains

Map 3. Three physiographic regions in southern Illinois: *stippling*, the Till Plain; *vertical hatching*, the Shawnee Hills; *horizontal hatching*, the Floodplains.

plains, with well-developed soils. Consequently, much of this region has been deforested and converted to agricultural row crops. The patches of bottomland forest that remain are dominated by pin oak, overcup oak, swamp white oak, cottonwood, silver maple, shagbark hickory, and sweet gum trees among others. The bottomland swamps, such as Heron Pond and Horseshoe Lake, occur in this region; they are dominated by tupelo gum and bald cypress trees. Many of southern Illinois's best marshes are located in the Floodplains, so this is often the region to find marsh birds, such as rails, herons, egrets, and gallinules.

The Shawnee Hills stretch across southern Illinois from Fountain Bluff in the west to the Shawneetown Hills in Gallatin County in the east. It is the most extensively forested region in southern Illinois, with large tracts of oak, hickory, beech, and maple forest. The topographic relief is much greater in the extreme west than it is in the east. A narrow strip of especially steep terrain runs from central Alexander County through western Union County, western Jackson County, and western Randolph County. Within the Shawnee Hills, ravines tend to be much moister than ridgetops and thus to support different plant and bird communities. In the eastern Shawnee Hills, extensive plantations of loblolly pine still remain; these sites attract Pine Warblers. Populations of breeding birds tend to be greater in the far western Shawnee Hills than in the eastern Shawnee Hills. Some species show the reverse pattern, however, such as the Black Vulture, which is conspicuously more numerous in the east.

The Till Plain is an area of gently rolling, hilly topography. Formerly, it was primarily covered with forest, especially with post oak flatwoods. Much of it has been cleared for agriculture, however, so a large proportion of the Till Plain is now under cultivation. Ravines surrounding drainages tend to have small patches of mesic forest that may sometimes be rich in birdlife. Southern Illinois's two largest lakes occur in this region: Crab Orchard Lake and Rend Lake. It is also the region where strip-mining for coal occurs. Some reclaimed strip mines provide extensive areas of grassland that are used by such species as Upland Sandpipers and Barn Owls and by several sparrow species. Where there are ponds left by the mining operations, small populations of Least Bitterns, Blue-winged Teal, Pied-billed Grebes, and American Coots may breed. On older mines that were not reclaimed after abandonment, scattered trees form a savanna-like habitat that attracts Bell's Vireos and Willow Flycatchers.

The climate of southern Illinois as a whole is rather mild. The average winter temperature is 36°F (2°C), and the average July temperature is 80°F (27°C), which gives a year-round average temperature of about 59°F (15°C). The mean annual precipitation is about 47 inches (119 centimeters), much of it coming between November and April.

Format of Text

Species Accounts

SPECIES NAMES. Each species account begins with the common name and the scientific name currently accepted by the American Ornithologists' Union (1983 and supplements). The order in which the species are presented also follows the A.O.U. (1983) *Check-list*. Names of species considered to be of hypothetical occurrence in the region are enclosed in brackets.

MIGRATION DATES. For species with distinct periods of migration, the span of typical dates in which the species is engaged in migratory movements is given immediately below the name of the species. Many year-round residents also migrate, so the migratory dates are often given for those species as well. Some residents, however, have such large breeding and wintering populations that it is very difficult to discern when migration is occurring. In such cases, the dates of migration are not given, but some comment regarding the suspected span of dates is made in the records and remarks section. Studies of the migratory movements of year-round residents would be especially useful.

STATUS AND ABUNDANCE. Information regarding the regularity with which each species is encountered in the region and the approximate numerical abundance is provided in this section. Abundances often vary between seasons and physiographic regions, so comments are made about each season and region whenever differences in status or abundance occur. For definitions of the terms used in the text, see the Definition of Terms section following this introduction.

HABITAT. A brief description of the principal habitat types in which a species can be found is given for most species. Generally, these habitats are listed from most preferred to least preferred. In cases of very rare or hypothetical species, the habitat section is sometimes omitted because too little information is available on habitat selection.

RECORDS AND REMARKS. In this section, comments are made about each species' ecology, behavior, former status (if it differs from the current status), and other items of interest, particularly those specifically relevant to southern Illinois. Furthermore, a summary of significant and representative records for each season is given. The sequence in which this information is presented varies among species; typically the account begins with the first season in the calendar year immediately following a season in which the species is not regularly found in the region. Accounts of species that occur as migrants and winter residents but do not breed in southern Illinois, for example, begin with the autumn season. When species are year-round residents, the accounts begin with spring. Information on patterns of migrational movements, breeding success, and current population trends are often given. Records representing early arrival and late departure dates of migrants and highest counts for each season are provided for most species. Surprisingly, some of the most common species in the region have the least information available, so the accounts are sometimes rather brief for those species. Indeed, sometimes there is little or no information available even for entire seasons. Clearly, an emphasis on studying populations of the common year-round residents would be useful. Also included in the records and remarks section are all records for unusual species and for common species occurring at unusual times of the year.

Most of the records included in this book come from the observations of individual birders. Some of the records have been published in state or regional ornithological journals, but most have not. To give credit to the individuals responsible for each record, either a literature citation or the initials of the observers present at a particular sighting are provided at the end of each record included in this book. There is, however, one exception to this treatment; this exception regards Christmas Bird Counts. Every winter during the last three weeks of the year, thousands of birders across the world participate in Christmas Bird Counts. From one to more than two hundred participants attempt to count and identify all species of birds they see or hear during one day within a circle that is fifteen miles in diameter. Usually these counts are located to include a local refuge or wildlife area known to have interesting populations of wintering birds. When they include a familiar area, they are often named after that area (e.g., the Horseshoe Lake Christmas Bird Count in southern Illinois); but in some cases these counts are given less precise names, and thus the count names are not always completely informative. Consequently, when records from southern Illinois Christmas Bird Counts are included in this book, the name of the Christmas Bird Count is provided as the locality of the observation. Persons interested in discovering the exact location of count circles should consult the relevant Christmas Bird Count issue (published every November) of the journal *American Birds* (now called *Field Notes*). Furthermore, in this book no initials are provided to credit observers for records obtained during Christmas Bird Counts, because that information is typically not readily available and multiple observers are often responsible for these records.

Christmas Bird Counts differ from Spring Bird Counts. Unlike the worldwide Christmas Bird Counts, Spring Bird Counts are held only in Illinois. On the Saturday between 4 and 10 May (the peak of spring migration), birders all across Illinois venture out to count and identify all bird species they see or hear within a county they have volunteered to cover. Attempts are made to have volunteers cover all of Illinois's 102 counties. From one to one hundred or more observers spend the day scouring the countryside and counting birds within their county. Spring Bird Counts usually uncover some interesting observations, many of which are included in this book. In contrast to the treatment of Christmas Bird Count records, however, it is possible to identify a specific county as the locality for a Spring Bird Count record. As with the Christmas Bird Counts, it is often not possible to identify which particular individual birder is responsible for a record. Thus, for Spring Bird Count records, the abbreviation "SBC" is used to designate who was responsible for a record. Persons interested in acquiring further information on such records should consult past issues of the journals *Illinois Birds and Birding* and *Meadowlark* to obtain the addresses for the county compilers; the compilers may be able to provide additional details. Alternatively, queries may be directed to the Avian Ecology Program, Illinois Department of Conservation, 524 South Second Street, Springfield, Illinois, 62701, where all Spring Bird Count data are archived.

DOCUMENTATION. Not all bird species reported from the region have been included in this book. A certain level of rigorous review is required to keep a regional list of species free from erroneous reports, such as accidental misidentifications. To this end, all species officially accepted for the regional list have at least one of four types of evidence preserved that can be independently reviewed by any interested party. The key point here is that some sort of hard evidence of a particular sighting or report has been saved that can be studied by observers who were not present at the time of the sighting. This evidence can then be used to verify the correctness of the record or to dismiss it if it appears to be incorrect.

The most convincing form of documentary evidence is a specimen. A specimen is the actual bird seen in the field, which has been collected for scientific purposes. Few observers have the appropriate permits, however, to collect specimens, so this form of documentation of unusual sightings is rare. If a specimen is obtained, it should be deposited immediately at an approved scientific depository, such as the Department of Zoology at Southern Illinois University at Carbondale (SIUC). Detailed information should be deposited with each specimen, including the place of collection (including the county name), the date of collection, and the name of the collector. The museum curator then prepares the specimen for permanent storage and adds information on the species' name, sex, weight, and gonadal status to a label that is permanently attached to the specimen.

The second type of documentary evidence is a photograph. The most useful photographs show a diagnostic view of the species that leaves no question regarding the identity of the species. Photographs that are taken from a distance or are slightly blurry can be used as supporting evidence in combination with a written description (see the discussion that follows) but are not diagnostic by themselves. All documentary photographs should be labeled with the species' name, the locality where the photograph was taken, the date the photograph was taken, and the name of photographer. Photographs may be deposited at the Department of Zoology, SIUC, where they will be permanently stored in the bird collection with other photographs of birds.

The third type of supporting evidence is a voice recording. Some species are so similar in appearance (e.g., *Empidonax* flycatchers and some hummingbirds) that a photograph, even a very good one, is not sufficient evidence to prove that an identification was correct. In these cases, a recording of the call notes or song of the species can often be very helpful. Experts can differentiate between two species similar in appearance just by their voices, so a tape recording is an excellent form of documentation. Of course, it is necessary to supplement the voice recording with a detailed written description of the fieldmarks seen in the field. Cassette tapes of voice recordings may also be deposited at the Department of Zoology, SIUC. The outside of the tapes should be labeled with the species' name, the locality where the recordings were made, the date the recordings were made, and the observer's name; the same information should also be verbally recorded onto the tapes.

The final type of documentary evidence is the written description. It is the most commonly obtained type of evidence, but it is also in many respects the most difficult to do correctly. Written documentations must accurately portray what was actually seen in the field, and they must do so in thorough enough detail to convince a reviewer that the correct identification was made. It must be stressed here that the only fieldmarks to be included on a written documentation are those that were observed on the bird in question, not those that should have been seen or that appear in the illustrations of that species in a field guide. It is critical that the written description reflect only what was clearly seen in the field. Other details to be included in a written description are the species' name, the number of birds seen, the age and sex of the birds (if known), a description of the vocalizations (if they were heard), a description of the habitat in which the species was found, a summary of how species similar in appearance were eliminated from consideration, the names of other observers present at the time, and a description of the viewing conditions. It is especially important to discuss details of the viewing conditions, such as distance between the observer and the bird, type of optics used, weather conditions, position of the sun relative to you and the bird, and so on. In short, any information that will aid a reviewer in accurately determining the circumstances of the observation will be extremely helpful. It is far better to include too much information than too little.

Standardized documentation forms for written descriptions are available for free from the Avian Ecology Program, Illinois Department of Conservation, 524 South Second Street, Springfield, Illinois, 62701. Completed forms should be mailed to the same address (be sure to keep a copy for yourself). They are then routed to a review committee, the Illinois Ornithological Records Committee, which is composed of seven expert birders. These committee members independently review the documentation forms and then submit their opinions regarding the accuracy of the identifications to the secretary of the committee. The secretary then officially accepts or rejects each record if most of the committee members have the same opinion. If opinions differ, the secretary recirculates the record until a final decision is made. The documentations are then archived for permanent storage so that future researchers may have access to them. The details of the workings of the I.O.R.C. are discussed by Robinson and Goetz (1988). Written descriptions must be completed by two or more observers to be considered sufficient evidence for the species to be accepted onto the official southern Illinois list (but see the discussion of provisional acceptance that follows); records reported by only one observer are regarded as hypothetical.

Within this book, the highest form of documentary evidence available for each species is listed in the documentation section. Generally, the locality (including the county) and the date of the record are given. For specimens, the age and sex are often given, and the location of the specimen is always given. Each specimen has a unique specimen number given by the museum in which it is housed. For the abbreviations of the museum names, see the list of abbreviations following this introduction.

Two final clarifications regarding evidence of documentation must be made. First, some species are of regular occurrence in southern

Illinois, yet there is no documentary evidence of them available (e.g., Canvasback). In these cases, it would be silly to consider the species hypothetical. I have, therefore, listed such species as being accepted on the regional list by provisional acceptance. This is intended to make the official list realistic and to indicate to observers the species for which we still need written or photographic evidence. In addition, several rare species have been seen multiple times but were seen by a single observer each time (e.g., Swainson's Hawk). When the documentations were all convincing, I accepted the species onto the official regional list. Normally, however, species seen by just one observer are regarded as hypothetical until either more observers submit written descriptions or a voice recording, photo, or specimen is obtained. Thus, no documentary evidence is provided in the species accounts for those species considered to be hypothetical.

The final tally of bird species for the southern Illinois coverage area includes 361 species. Of these, 28 are regarded as hypothetical; one has been extirpated (Greater Prairie-Chicken); and three are extinct (Passenger Pigeon, Carolina Parakeet, and Ivory-billed Woodpecker).

FIELD GUIDES. This final section of each species account provides the page numbers on which that particular species is illustrated in each of the three most popular North American field guides: the Golden guide (G; Robbins et al. 1966, 1983); the National Geographic Society guide (N; National Geographic Society 1983, 1987); and the Peterson eastern guide (P; Peterson 1980). Hopefully, this section will be particularly useful to those readers who are learning their birds as they read through this book.

Site Guides

Descriptions of twenty-six of the best birding sites in southern Illinois are included in part 2 of this book. Directions concerning the easiest access to each area are given, sometimes in combination with a map when finer details about specific sites are offered. The most interesting rarities reported at each site are also included; this ploy is directed at luring even the most skeptical birder to visit a site. There is substantial seasonal variation in the number of birds and number of species that occur at each site, so suggestions regarding the better times to visit are also provided. Finally, some practical hints and advice are offered regarding hazards—such as poisonous snakes and ticks—and the availability of camping and picnicking sites. There are a multitude of places worthy of a birding trip, just a few of which are described here. So grab a map and go exploring!

A History of Southern Illinois Bird Study

Southern Illinois has a long and rather underappreciated history of bird study. The earliest information on the avifauna of the region comes from deposits uncovered at archaeological sites in Carrier Mills, Saline County; north of Prairie du Rocher, Randolph County; and near Thebes, Alexander County. The site near Thebes, named the Pettit Site, provides the most information on the remains of birds found in the camps of Native Americans (Breitburg 1990). The bone and tissue fragments at the Pettit Site have been dated at between 800 and 1000 A.D. Bones of at least twenty different bird species have been identified, including bones of Wild Turkey, ducks, and Northern Bobwhite, and many bones from Passenger Pigeons, which were presumably an important food source, because a large proportion of the bones had been burned.

Although the Native Americans clearly used the avifauna of southern Illinois as a source of food, they did not preserve written accounts of any kind to document the patterns of bird species distribution or abundance. Apparently the first written report of a bird observation from southern Illinois was by John Heckenwelder of Kentucky, who reported seeing a large flight of Passenger Pigeons at the mouth of the Wabash River on 2 December 1792 (Wright 1911). No subsequent reports came from Heckenwelder or anyone else until the winter of 1810–1811, when John James Audubon traveled along the Ohio River from Louisville, Kentucky, then up the Mississippi River to Cape Girardeau, Missouri (Audubon

1868); this particular trip yielded only a few reports of birds. More productive visits by Audubon were in 1819 and 1820 (Audubon 1929). In 1819, he found a nest of a Sharp-shinned Hawk on the bluff at Cave-in-Rock, Hardin County, and collected the female to use as a model for his painting of the species. During the fall of 1820, he reported seeing Carolina Parakeets, Passenger Pigeons, swans that may have been trumpeters, an Ivory-billed Woodpecker, and a Sandhill Crane along the Ohio River. He also saw a Whooping Crane at the mouth of the Tennessee River in Kentucky, just across from Massac County. Another competent ornithologist of the early 1800s was Maximilian, Prince of Weid. He visited New Harmony, Indiana, just across the Wabash River from White County, during the winter of 1832. His journals contain reports of Passenger Pigeons and Carolina Parakeets (Thwaites 1906).

There was little ornithological work accomplished from the time of Maximilian until the early 1870s, but then there was a burst of research activity. E. W. Nelson of the U.S. Bureau of Biological Survey made a collecting trip to Cairo, Alexander County, from 17 July to 31 August 1875 (Nelson 1877). He remarked on the surprising number of birds in the area, including hundreds of herons and egrets and swarming kettles of Swallow-tailed Kites and Mississippi Kites. He even collected the region's first record of Swainson's Warbler. Interestingly, he did not record a single Passenger Pigeon or Carolina Parakeet during his stay. The research of Robert Ridgway, who worked with the U.S. National Museum, overlapped Nelson's. Ridgway studied birds in southern Illinois, primarily near Mt. Carmel, Wabash County, from the early 1870s through about 1915 (Ridgway 1873, 1874, 1878, 1889, 1895, 1914, 1915). Although most of his observations are from outside the coverage area of this book, many are directly relevant. Two other observers also worked in nearby areas during the late 1800s and made observations that are useful in characterizing the birdlife in southern Illinois: Cooke (1888) commented on the migration of birds in the Mississippi River Valley, and Otto Widmann (1895, 1907) made extensive observations in southeastern Missouri.

After the surge of activity in the late nineteenth century, there was a paucity of interest until the late 1940s. Beginning about 1945, several dedicated observers contributed many hours to studying southern Illinois birds, especially in Jackson County and around Crab Orchard Lake in Williamson County. Lee Bush, a technician at the Crab Orchard refuge office had actually been observing birds in the area since the 1930s, but he began to keep good records much later. Unfortunately, his field notes were lost after he died, but he contributed records via letters to the "bird woman" of the 1940s and 1950s, Esther Bennett, and to a young Murphysboro high school student, Richard Brewer. Bennett synthesized the information from her own work and that from Bush, Brewer, and their colleagues and wrote the first "Checklist of Birds of Southern Illinois," which she mimeographed at SIUC in 1952. Brewer and his college friend, J. W. Hardy, were constant companions in the field, striving to keep Bennett's checklist out-of-date. Brewer kept extensive field notes and had several drafts of the regional checklist, which he was continually revising, but he never published any of it. Instead, he and Hardy published several papers in ornithological journals, writing on Least Terns, Swainson's Warbler, summer territory sizes of swamp-thicket birds, and other miscellaneous observations.

Brewer and Hardy's excitement and interest in southern Illinois birds was contagious, spreading to many students and faculty at SIUC before the two left the region to pursue their educations elsewhere. Others picked up the torch and continued studying the region's birdlife. One faculty member at SIUC was particularly active, William G. George. George was very fond of the Cave Creek Valley near Pomona and did most of his fieldwork there. He collected hundreds of specimens, many from Pomona, but an equal number from his home near Cobden, Union County. George was also very interested in the ecology of Cerulean Warblers, the molt patterns of White-eyed Vireos and Downy and Hairy Woodpeckers, and Illinois endangered species. He compiled the second official "Check List of Birds of Southern Illinois" in 1968, when he mimeographed the list at SIUC as material to be distributed to members of the Wilson Ornithological Society, who were having their annual meeting in Carbondale that year.

Most of the fieldwork done by Brewer, Hardy, George, and those who preceded them was casual; birding was simply a fun and interesting pastime. The advent of systematic surveys of bird populations in southern Illinois came when Richard and Jean Graber of the Illinois Natural History Survey began their censuses of birds all across the state (Graber et al. 1971, 1972, 1973, 1974, 1977, 1978, 1979, 1983, 1985, 1987). Their intensive surveys were designed to provide quantitative population estimates of all birds encountered, especially the songbirds. They surveyed birds in each season along long transect routes through many different habitat types. The primary censuses were completed in 1967, when they studied areas in Pope, Massac, Johnson, and Saline Counties, and in 1970, when they worked in Alexander, Union, Pulaski, southern Jackson, and southwestern Williamson Counties. Their work provided a valuable record of bird distribution and abundance patterns with which future surveys may be compared. These sorts of systematic survey will prove to be the most valuable contribution to the study of regional bird populations.

Recently, especially since 1970, the activities of faculty and students at SIUC increased dramatically. Beginning with the compilation of the region's third bird list (Kleen and Bush 1972), concentrated birding efforts were expended by many observers. In fact, activity became so vigorous that a special birding organization, Southern Illinois Bird Observatory, was established in the late 1970s. Unfortunately, when its organizers departed the region, the club dissolved. Nevertheless, the birding activity in the 1970s contributed much to the knowledge of the region's birds. Some of the most active contributors were Bruce Peterjohn and Vernon Kleen. Peterjohn was a careful observer who added several species to the regional list. Kleen had the gift to invigorate and excite others, and he had the drive to organize the efforts of the many birders in southern Illinois and throughout the state. He organized the statewide Spring Bird Count, and after taking the Avian Ecologist position in the Illinois Department of Conservation, he began soliciting observers from throughout Illinois to submit their field notes to him at the end of each season. He then compiled them and distributed the highlights in seasonal reports. This effort was an important step in the history of southern Illinois birds, because it provided an outlet for the many bits of information on bird occurrences gathered in a casual way; these records could then easily find their way into the literature from which future researchers could access them.

The 1980s and early 1990s brought further intensive fieldwork, mostly from students at SIUC and from a handful of other dedicated people. It was an active period of filling in gaps in knowledge, trying to find species that should occur in the region but had not yet been recorded, and trying to thoroughly cover the entirety of the seventeen-county region. Beginning in 1989, Scott Robinson, the ornithologist at the Illinois Natural History Survey, began intensive summer fieldwork in Union and Alexander Counties. His research interests focused on the effects of forest fragmentation and nest parasitism by cowbirds on forest songbird populations. He and his crew of fifteen to twenty-five undergraduate and graduate students censused and searched for bird nests in many different study sites; the primary focus, however, was on Pine Hills, Trail of Tears, Dutch Creek Camp near Jonesboro, and South Ripple Hollow in northern Alexander County. In 1993, the research expanded to include the Cache River Valley. Robinson established dozens of permanent census transects, which he and some of his students censused each summer. These census data, like those of the Grabers, provide an important base for comparison with future studies. In addition, Robinson's group collected data on hundreds of songbird nests and documented the patterns of brood parasitism by cowbirds and of predation by nest predators. These data sets are equally valuable and may aid us in understanding how human activities directly and indirectly influence bird populations by creating opportunities for populations of nest parasites and nest predators to increase.

Looking to the future, we must acknowledge that, despite the long and impressive history of work, we know very little about the dynamics of bird populations in the region. The casual, everyday bird observations of weekend birders are useful contributions to the study of southern Illinois birds, as long as the observers keep in mind that accuracy (both in species identification and in counting numbers of individuals) is absolutely essential. At the same time, these sorts of observations do not provide the necessary information from which we can understand changes in bird populations. Because human-caused disturbance of the environment is proceeding at an ever-increasing pace, we need to obtain measurements of bird populations and regional distribution patterns in ways that can be repeated exactly by future researchers. Without such standardization of methods, there is no way to make any sort of confident statement about population increases or decreases of any species. Our contributions need to go further than just recording new species for the region and further than participation in Spring and Christmas Bird Counts. Through censusing birds along regular routes using standardized methodologies, we will obtain the necessary information. I am not encouraging abandonment of "normal" birding; I am merely indicating that many birders who have the necessary skills to make these kinds of contributions to the study of bird populations do not attempt to do so. We need an effort to inform observers on the methods that are appropriate to addressing questions about bird populations; for the time being, I refer the interested reader to Verner (1985) and Hutto et al. (1986). Let us make the best of the present, so that observers in the future will have the necessary information to try to better understand the changes in distribution and abundance patterns of southern Illinois birds.

Effects of Forest Fragmentation on Songbird Reproductive Success in Southern Illinois

Forest fragmentation is the phenomenon of dividing formerly contiguous expanses of forest into smaller isolated patches (Harris 1984). Today, most fragmentation is caused by humans. The process also occurs naturally, but natural fragmentation events occur on a much more sporadic and local scale. Human-caused fragmentation is of growing concern to conservation biologists because of its effects on plant and animal communities (Soule and Wilcox 1980). The primary effect of fragmentation is the increase of forest edge relative to forest interior. As forest tract size decreases, the ratio of edge length to interior area increases; that is, smaller forest tracts have proportionally much more edge than do larger tracts. The biological effect is that animal communities that normally occur only along edges penetrate much more deeply into the interior of small forest tracts than of larger ones (Brittingham and Temple 1983). Edge animal communities are often composed of species that negatively affect interior animal communities (Whitcomb et al. 1981). When the edge communities grow larger, they have larger effects on the interior communities. The negative impacts are realized primarily in two ways: through higher predation on the interior communities and, among birds, through higher rates of nest parasitism by Brown-headed Cowbirds.

Because predator populations may be much larger along edges, birds nesting nearer to edges may have less nesting success (Wilcove 1985). Some species seem to require forest interior in which to breed if they are to successfully escape predation (Blake and Karr 1984; Robbins et al. 1989). These species are called area sensitive, and in addition to being sensitive to nest predation, they are also highly susceptible to parasitism by cowbirds (Brittingham and Temple 1983). In contrast to bird species that normally nest along edges and have evolved defenses against cowbird parasitism, interior species are unlikely to recognize that their nests have been parasitized, and they tend to naively accept the foreign egg (Mayfield 1965; Rothstein 1982). Unfortunately, most nests that are successfully parasitized by cowbirds produce mostly cowbird young, so parasitism is in some ways just as bad as having the nest contents eaten by a predator (Payne 1977). In short, parasitism and predation tend to be much greater near forest edges, so as fragmentation increases, the negative impacts associated with edges also increase.

Southern Illinois was formerly mostly continuous forest, but much of the forest has been cleared for row crops, pasturing, and other types of human development. Consequently, the once extensive, unbroken forest has been reduced to hundreds of small patches ranging in size from less than 1 acre (.4 hectares) to more than 12,000 acres (4,900 hectares). Hence, southern Illinois has plenty of edges. Even within the largest tracts, there are openings for roads, wildlife openings, and horse trails; very little of southern Illinois's forest is truly interior.

The extreme heterogeneity of the southern Illinois landscape has undoubtedly contributed to the extremely high rates of nest predation and parasitism found throughout the region. In extensive fieldwork conducted primarily in the Shawnee National Forest since 1989, Scott Robinson and his field crews from the Illinois Natural History Survey have found staggeringly high rates of nest predation and parasitism for most songbird species. Even more surprisingly, they found that nests built as far as 1,100 yards (1,000 meters) from the forest edge still suffered rates of nest predation and parasitism as high as nests built within just a few yards of the edge. In fact, the impacts were sometimes even higher in the interior than on the edge.

Robinson and his crews worked in four of the largest tracts in the Shawnee to try to determine if there are any truly interior sites remaining where songbirds might escape the effects of predation and parasitism. They worked in Pine Hills (4,500 acres, 1,820 hectares), Dutch Creek (300 acres, 120 hectares; a study plot within otherwise extensive forest), South Ripple Hollow (3,000 acres, 1,215 hectares), and Trail of Tears State Forest (5,000 acres, 2,000 hectares); and in 1993, they added many of the forest tracts in the Cache River Valley to their list of study plots. Within each forest, they censused breeding birds by song counts and netting and marking techniques, and they searched for nests. When nests were found, they were checked to determine if cowbirds had parasitized them, and then they were visited until the nests fledged young or failed because of predation or weather damage. Overall, Robinson's study group found that there was considerable variation among bird species in rates of nest predation and parasitism and between years and sites as well. The overwhelming pattern, however, was that songbirds in the Shawnee National Forest do not produce very many of their own young—probably not enough to replace themselves and keep the regional populations stable. Paradoxically, though, the census data do not show the dramatic population declines we might expect based on the very poor nesting success.

Robinson hypothesized that the Shawnee is a population sink—that is, that the high rates of nest predation and parasitism act as a strong drain that siphons off the songbird population because reproductive output is far below the presumed adult mortality rates. To keep a population stable, reproductive output must equal adult mortality, but Robinson and his crews found that output is extremely low in the Shawnee. Populations, however, are not regulated only by their reproductive output and mortality rates. Other nearby populations may critically influence the size of a given population (Pulliam 1988). If, for example, neighboring populations, such as those in Missouri or Indiana, produce an excess of young, then those surplus young may immigrate into the Shawnee. In other words, the neighboring populations act as a source of new individuals that become part of the Shawnee population and thus help prevent it from collapsing despite its own reproductive failures.

The source-sink idea, as it is called, is a plausible story, but it is difficult to prove. First, to demonstrate the occurrence of immigration in bird populations is difficult, especially when the sources are a hundred or more miles away. Birds banded in the source region would have to be recaptured in the sink, a highly improbable event even if immigration were occurring. Second, immigration could be unimportant if our estimates of adult mortality are wrong. Measuring lifespan of wild birds is about as difficult as capturing a banded immigrant. If birds live much longer than we think they do, they may have far more opportunities to breed and replace themselves; eventually they will probably get lucky and breed successfully. Third, it is also possible that there is a cryptic breeding population out there that researchers, predators, and cowbirds overlook simply because the nests are difficult to find. This cryptic population could be highly successful and could essentially support the entire regional population. In short, there are many alternative explanations for the source-sink model, and teasing them apart will be difficult.

Forestry in Southern Illinois

There is heated controversy and debate about whether forest harvesting should be permitted in southern Illinois, especially in the Shawnee National Forest. Robinson's data on the effect of fragmentation on forest birds has been used by both sides to fuel the fanatical fire. Those opposing logging use the data to suggest that further fragmentation will negatively impact bird populations, whereas those in favor of logging could justifiably argue that the forest is already fragmented and that further harvest will not really add insult to current injury. On the one hand, forest birds currently appear to have no escape from high predation or parasitism rates, even if they attempt to breed in the region's largest forest tracts. Thus, it could be argued that additional logging is unlikely to cause further harm. On the other hand, many forest bird species are area sensitive and will not breed in small forest tracts. This tendency to avoid small habitat patches is undoubtedly related, at least in part, to high predation and parasitism in smaller patches. One could reasonably argue, therefore, that harvesting in the largest tracts could reduce their size to a point that area-sensitive forest species would be eliminated from them. So what should we do?

There is no easy answer, but one conclusion is quite clear: extreme actions are unlikely to provide positive results. On the one hand, allowing harvesting without regard for the significance of a forest block to the songbird populations that are breeding there is shortsighted. Some large forest tracts should be protected to allow breeding populations of area-sensitive species to persist within the region. These few large tracts could conceivably act as the regional source, despite their own high populations of predators and cowbirds; relative to very small forest tracts, they are clearly more productive. On the other hand, completely eliminating all harvesting is unrealistic. Done properly, some harvesting methods actually provide habitats that increase populations of forest bird species. Selective harvest techniques, for example, may mimic natural treefall gaps and thus provide breeding habitat for Hooded Warblers, Rufous-sided Towhees, and Carolina Wrens. Hence, a decision to completely eliminate harvesting is a bit shortsighted as well. A balanced, carefully considered decision is necessary.

Robinson has offered several suggestions that could help minimize the negative effects of forest fragmentation on songbird populations in the Shawnee:

1. Ownership should be consolidated. One of the primary reasons for the highly fragmented nature of the Shawnee is that so many privately owned parcels of land are intermixed among the federal lands. Much of the fragmentation problem is a direct result of private landowners clearing forest on their properties. It would be useful to attempt to create large unfragmented tracts of forest by purchasing private lands near the largest extant Shawnee tracts. Patches of greater than fifteen thousand acres could be created, which might give some interior species a respite from the predation and parasitism.

2. Internal openings, such as wildlife openings, should be eliminated. The Shawnee is riddled with thousands of forest openings created for game management purposes. Considering that it is one of the most fragmented sites in the country, it makes

little sense to intentionally add edge within the larger forests. Allowing these openings to regrow would close the canopy and minimize the impacts of edge effects from within the forest.

3. Logging practices to be used should be carefully considered. Selective harvesting techniques where single or small groups of trees are removed should be preferred over clear-cutting. Selective harvesting can actually create necessary habitat for some forest species, whereas clear-cutting creates large clearings that may give increased access to cowbirds and predators.

4. Rotation periods should be increased. Some forest interior species, such as Cerulean Warblers, require huge trees and mature forest in which to breed. Increasing the length of the rotation periods may help make more of this rare habitat available.

5. Canopy breaks should be minimized. Within the larger forest tracts, it would be beneficial to minimize the creation of logging roads and other canopy-breaking sites, such as campgrounds. Such sites not only create forest openings but also provide foraging areas within the forest for cowbirds, thus giving them easier access to nests of bird species living in the forest interior.

Clearly, the impacts of fragmentation on southern Illinois's bird populations have been severe, but there is still much to learn about the impacts of predators and brood parasites on each bird species. It will require time and careful collection and analysis of pertinent data before any firm recommendations can be made regarding the best strategies for managing the forests of southern Illinois.

Definition of Terms

Definitions of terms used throughout this book to describe species status and abundance follow. Examples of species that fall into each category are provided in parentheses.

Status

Escaped
: Species normally maintained only in captivity and unable to maintain a wild breeding population in the region (Black Swan).

Extinct
: Species whose entire world population no longer exists (Carolina Parakeet).

Extirpated
: Species whose regional population no longer exists but that may still occur elsewhere (Greater Prairie-Chicken).

Hypothetical
: Species reported from the region but for which there is no convincing documentary evidence (Vermilion Flycatcher).

Introduced
: Species whose natural range does not include the region but that has been released directly into the region (Ring-necked Pheasant). Does not include species that have expanded into the region after introduction into other parts of the U.S. (e.g., House Sparrow).

Migrant
: Species whose breeding range is north of the region and whose wintering range is south of the region and that occurs here

only in transit between the two ranges (Blackburnian Warbler).

Summer resident   Species known to breed in the region (Wood Thrush).

Summer visitor   Species occurring in the region during the summer but not known to breed in the region (Lesser Yellowlegs).

Winter resident   Species with an established pattern of wintering within the region (Dark-eyed Junco).

Winter visitor   Species that has been recorded during the winter but that has not established a pattern of repeated occurrence (Orchard Oriole).

Year-round resident Species that is present throughout the entire year. Some may have seasons of migratory movement (American Robin); others may not (Northern Bobwhite).

Abundance

Common   Easily detected in appropriate habitat; may occur in large flocks (Red-winged Blackbird) or in a dominant habitat (Indigo Bunting). Perhaps a dozen or so to many thousands may be counted in a day.

Fairly common   Usually easily recorded in appropriate habitat but occurs in smaller numbers than common species (Semipalmated Plover in spring). Typically less than a dozen are seen in a day.

Uncommon   Sometimes difficult to locate, even in appropriate habitat. Usually less than six are seen in a day, but this number may vary widely (Ruby-crowned Kinglet in winter).

Occasional   Usually difficult to locate but typically present in appropriate habitat. Most often recorded as single individuals, although high counts of five or more may sometimes occur (Mourning Warbler in spring).

Rare   Always difficult to locate. May be recorded only once or twice or not at all in an entire season. High counts are nearly always only one individual (Connecticut Warbler in spring).

Very rare   A highly unusual occurrence. Usually applies to species that have not yet established a discernible pattern of occurrence in the region (Swainson's Hawk) or in a certain season (Indigo Bunting in winter).

Abbreviations

The following abbreviations are used frequently in the species accounts in this book. Abbreviations of museum names are used in the documentation section of species accounts and are usually followed immediately by a specimen number. Publication abbreviations are typically followed by a volume number (where applicable) and a page number where the reference to a specific record or the illustration of a specific species can be found.

Museums and Museum Collections

CAS	Chicago Academy of Sciences, Chicago, Ill.
FMNH	Field Museum of Natural History, Chicago, Ill.
INHS	Illinois Natural History Survey, Champaign, Ill.
ISM	Illinois State Museum, Springfield, Ill.
ISU	Illinois State University, Bloomington-Normal, Ill.
NIU	Northern Illinois University, DeKalb, Ill.
NMNH	National Museum of Natural History, Washington, D.C.
SIU	Southern Illinois University at Carbondale, Carbondale, Ill.
A-#	refers to specimens at SIU
AP-#	refers to photographs at SIU
USNM	United States National Museum, Washington, D.C.

WGG   William G. George Collection, SIU

Publications
AB   *American Birds*
AFN   *Audubon Field Notes*
G   Golden guide (Robbins et al. 1966, 1983)
IAB   *Illinois Audubon Bulletin*
IBB   *Illinois Birds and Birding*
N   National Geographic Society guide
                    (National Geographic Society 1983, 1987)
P   Peterson eastern guide (Peterson 1980)
SR   *Seasonal Report,* Illinois Department
                    of Conservation

Place names
CA   conservation area
Co./Cos.   county/counties
NP   nature preserve
NWR   national wildlife refuge
SF   state forest
SP   state park

Other
e.   east
n.   north
n.e.   northeast
n.w.   northwest
s.   south
s.e.   southeast
s.w.   southwest
w.   west
ad.   adult/adults
imm.   immature/immatures

juv.	juvenile/juveniles
subad.	subadult/subadults
yg.	young
IDOC	Illinois Department of Conservation
IORC	Illinois Ornithological Records Committee

Observers and Observation Sources

The following abbreviations for individual observers and other observation sources are used throughout the species accounts. This list does not include observation sources listed in the Literature Cited.

Individual Observers

ABa	Al Balliet
AW	Andy West
BAM	B. and A. Minkler
BC	B. Coleman
BD	Bob Danley
BG	Ben Gelman
BL	Bob Lindsay
BM	Betty Millard
BP	Bruce Peterjohn
BR	Bill Rudden
BW	B. Wood
CC	Charlie Clark
CCu	Calvin Cummings
CM	C. Marbut
CMc	Chris McGinnis
CP	Carlos Perralta
CPa	Charles Paine
CS	Cody Smout
CT	Cheri Trine

CW	Cindy Watkins
DB	D. Baumgartner
DBe	Dave Becher
DC	Dave Cooper
DDR	Daniel D. Roby
DF	David Fletcher
DH	David Hayward
DJ	Denny Jones
DJa	Deborah Jacques
DK	Dan Klem
DKa	Dan Kasselbaum
DKe	Dave Kennedy
DR	D. Rowe
DT	Dennis Thornburg
DTe	Diane Telschow
DY	Dick Young
EC	Elizabeth Chato
EW	Eric Walters
FG	F. Glass
FR	Frank Reuter
GB	Gary Bowman
GBi	G. Biggs
GC	Glen Cooper
GCD	G. and C. DeNeal
GF	George Feldhamer
GP	Gene Pope
GS	G. Smout
GSa	G. Sanford
GSm	G. Small
GSma	Glen Smart
GV	Glendy Vanderah

GW	George Waring
HC	H. Crenshaw
HD	Henry Detwiler
HDB	H. David Bohlen
HP	Harvey Pitt
HW	Houstoun Waring
ID	Ida Domazlicky
IM	I. McClure
JCR	John C. Robinson
JD	Judy DeNeal
JE	J. Eades
JEW	J. and E. Ward
JG	Jim Garver
JGr	Jean Graber
JGre	J. Greenberg
JH	Jeff Hardt
JHa	J. Haw
JHe	Jim Herkert
JJ	Judith Joyner
JJa	J. Janacek
JK	Jerry Keller
JL	Jim Landing
JM	Joe Milosevich
JN	Jack Nawrot
JP	J. Priest
JS	Jim Smith
JW	Jack White
JWH	J. W. Hardy
KA	K. Arhos
KB	Kris Bruner
KM	Keith McMullen

KP	Kathy Phelps
KPi	Ken Pierson
KR	Kevin Richmond
KRu	Ken Rushing
KS	K. Stewart
LA	Louise Augustine
LB	Lee Bush
LBa	Larry Balch
LH	Leroy Harrison
LHo	Larry Hood
LJ	Leslie Jette
LM	Lonny Morse
LMc	Lynn McKeown
LN	Lloyd Nelson
LS	Leonard Stanley
Ma	Maginel
MC	M. Carter
MCo	Maggie Cole
MD	Myrna Deaton
MF	Mike Flieg
MH	Mike Homoya
MHa	M. Harris
MJM	M. J. McNerney
MMl	Mike Mlodinow
MMo	Mike Morrison
MO	M. O'Leary
MP	Mark Peters
MS	Mike Sweet
MSe	Mark Seifert
MSw	Mark Swayne
MSwa	Mark Swan

MT	Mike Tove
MW	Mel Warren
OK	O. Kettlecamp
PB	Paul Biggers
PG	Paul Gurn
PH	Paul Heye
PHu	Pat Hughes
PK	Paul Kittle
PM	Patti Malmborg
PW	Pat Ward
RA	Richard Anderson
RB	Richard Brewer
RBr	Ron Bradley
RBu	Robin Butler
RC	Robert Chapel
RCo	R. Coles
RCr	R. Crompton
RG	Ron Goetz
RGr	Richard Graber
Ri	Rice
RJ	Rhetta Jack
RK	Randy Korotev
RKl	Ron Klann
RM	R. Madding
RMo	Robert Montgomery
RMW	R. and M. Woods
Ro	Rose
RP	Richard Palmer
RR	R. Russell
RS	Richard Sandburg
RZ	Ray Zoanetti

SA	Steve Amundsen
SB	Steve Bailey
SE	Sherri Evans
SH	Steve Hossler
SKR	Scott K. Robinson
SO	Steve Olson
SRu	Skip Russell
SS	Sue Stroyls
SV	S. Vasse
SVa	Steve Varsa
TC	Terry Chesser
TE	Tracy Evans
TF	Todd Fink
TG	Tony Girard
TM	Tim Merriman
TRR	Tara R. Robinson
VB	Valerie Blakely
VH	V. Hamer
VK	Vernon Kleen
VS	V. Shaw
WDR	W. Douglas Robinson
WGG	William G. George
WO	William O'Brien
WS	William Southern

Other Observation Sources

CBC	Christmas Bird Count
INHS	Illinois Natural History Survey
m.ob.	many observers
SBC	Spring Bird Count
SIU	Southern Illinois University at Carbondale

Part One

Species Accounts:
The Past and Present Status
of Birds in Southern Illinois

Order Gaviiformes: Loons

Family Gaviidae: Loons

Red-throated Loon *Gavia stellata*

Late October–Late November

STATUS AND ABUNDANCE: Very rare fall migrant.

HABITAT: Large reservoirs.

RECORDS AND REMARKS: Tend to stay in deeper water near the center of reservoirs; this habit, in combination with close plumage similarities to other fall-plumaged loons, can make identification difficult. See Appleby et al. (1986) and Kaufman (1990) for discussion of field-marks.

1, Rend Lake, 27 Oct 1985 (LH)
1, Crab Orchard NWR, 10–11 Nov 1984 (TF et al.)
1, Carbondale, 16 Nov 1989 (BD)
2 imm., Crab Orchard NWR, 19–23 Nov 1990 (BD et al.)
1, Rend Lake, 15 Dec 1991 (WDR)

DOCUMENTATION: Written description—Crab Orchard NWR, 10–11 Nov 1984.

FIELD GUIDES: G=18; N=20; P=32.

Pacific Loon *Gavia pacifica*

STATUS AND ABUNDANCE: Very rare visitor.

HABITAT: Large reservoirs.

RECORDS AND REMARKS: Presently there are only two records, so it is difficult to determine any particular pattern of occurrence. Both records, however, probably represent fall migrants. Pacific Loons were once considered conspecific with the species now named Arctic Loon (G. *arctica*), which occurs primarily in the Old World.

1, Rend Lake, Franklin Co., 25–26 Nov 1992 (TF, JD)
1, Rend Lake, Franklin Co., 24–27 Dec 1991 (TF, WDR)

3

DOCUMENTATION: Written description—Rend Lake, Franklin Co., 24–27 Dec 1991.

FIELD GUIDES: G=18; N=18; P=32.

Common Loon *Gavia immer*

Late March–Mid-May
Late October–Mid-December

STATUS AND ABUNDANCE: Uncommon spring migrant. Rare summer visitor. Fairly common fall migrant. Rare winter resident.

HABITAT: Large reservoirs and rivers.

RECORDS AND REMARKS: The most common loon in the region. Usually stay in the middle of large reservoirs, though sometimes they enter bays and feed near the shore. Sometimes loons land on small ponds and become stranded there because they do not have sufficient room to gain the running speed necessary to allow them to become airborne.

AUTUMN—Loons return in good numbers by late October, but a few may arrive as soon as early October. Maximum single day counts are normally fifteen to twenty-five birds, but occasionally large concentrations occur at Rend Lake or Crab Orchard Lake.

3, Crab Orchard NWR, 19 Oct 1985 (TF)
113, Rend Lake, 28 Oct 1985 (TF)
34, Rend Lake, 6 Nov 1990 (TF, JD)
5, Rend Lake, 1 Jan 1992 (TF, JD)

WINTER—Some loons will linger late into winter until freezing water forces them south. In some years, a few may attempt to overwinter on warm-water lakes. February records may represent birds that have initiated spring migration early in response to warming spells.

1, Crab Orchard NWR, 18 Jan 1985 (JCR)
1, Baldwin Lake, 30 Jan 1983 (HDB)
3, Baldwin Lake, 17 Feb 1985 (JCR)
1, Harrisburg, Saline Co., 17 Feb 1991 (KP)

SPRING—Most birds are still in nonbreeding plumage during spring migration, but the majority of individuals seen in late April and May have molted into breeding plumage. Concentrations are much smaller in spring than during autumn; maximum daily counts usually do not exceed fifteen birds.

1, Crab Orchard NWR, 7 Mar 1976 (BP)
1, Crab Orchard NWR, 12 Mar 1986 (WDR)
2, Union Co., 5 May 1984 (SBC)
1, Ferne Clyffe SP, Johnson Co., 24 May 1981 (MSwa)

SUMMER—Individuals present during summer are probably very late migrants or wandering nonbreeding birds; most are in non-breeding plumage. There is no evidence that any have attempted to spend the entire summer here.

1, Baldwin Lake, 10 June 1977 (MMo)
1, Crab Orchard NWR, 13 June 1983 (JCR)
1, Lake of Egypt, Williamson Co., 30 June 1985 (JCR)
1, Rend Lake, 8 July 1985 (KM)

DOCUMENTATION: Photograph—Crab Orchard NWR, Williamson Co., Nov 1985 (SIU AP-1).

FIELD GUIDES: G=18; N=20; P=32.

Order Podicipediformes: Grebes

Family Podicipedidae: Grebes

Pied-billed Grebe *Podilymbus podiceps*

Late February–Late May
Early September–Late December

STATUS AND ABUNDANCE: Common spring and fall migrant. Uncommon winter resident. Rare summer visitor, very rarely breeding.

HABITAT: Ponds, lakes, and marshes.

RECORDS AND REMARKS: Although they sometimes are found in the middle of large lakes, they seem to prefer foraging and resting in the shallow bays of lakes. A running start is required for take-off into flight, so they tend to occur more frequently on fairly large ponds than on small farm ponds. These grebes can disappear from view by slowly sinking into the water without making any splash.

SPRING—Grebes return very early in spring, soon after the first thaw. High counts are usually small, typically not more than twenty to thirty birds.

1, Carbondale, 17 Feb 1986 (KM)
1, Saline Co. CA, 21 Feb 1987 (KP)
1, Crab Orchard NWR, 24 May 1984 (TF)

SUMMER—Nesting occurs only very rarely. Summer records are associated with swamps, strip-mine ponds, or flooded wheat fields.

brood of 7 yg., Cypress Creek NWR, 17 May 1992 (TF)
2 juv., Carbondale, 13 and 20 June, with one still present 18 July 1991 (PM)
3 nests, s.w. Jackson Co., 20 June 1973 (DH, VK)
2 imm., Union Co. CA, 21 June 1982 (PK)
1, Horseshoe Lake CA, 29 June 1985 (SO)
3, n. Randolph Co., 3 July 1985 (TF, JCR)

AUTUMN—A few grebes appear each year during July or August, before the typical fall migration period; these early birds may be postbreeding wanderers that bred somewhere in or near Illinois.

ad., s.w. Jackson Co., 12 July 1986 (WDR)
2 ad., Carbondale, 19 July 1988 (WDR)
imm., Union Co. CA, 30 July 1983 (JCR)
2 ad. and 1 imm., Saline Co. CA, 18 Aug 1987 (WDR)
1, Mermet Lake CA, 3 Sep 1983 (JCR)
80, Saline Co., 17 Sep 1994 (JD)
43, Carbondale, 9 Oct 1971 (VK)
53, Crab Orchard NWR, 23 Oct 1985 (TF)
72, Crab Orchard NWR CBC, 17 Dec 1983

WINTER—As long as there is open water available, some grebes will linger into winter, but counts of more than ten or so are unusual. Several attempt to overwinter each year on warm-water lakes.

1, Harrisburg, Saline Co., 16 Jan 1991 (TF)
18, Lake of Egypt, Williamson Co., 28 Jan 1984 (JCR)
25, Crab Orchard NWR, 8 Feb 1989 (WDR)

DOCUMENTATION: Specimen—Marion, Williamson Co., 1937 (SIU A-1939).

FIELD GUIDES: G=20; N=22; P=34.

Horned Grebe *Podiceps auritus*
Early March–Very Late April
Mid-October–Late December

STATUS AND ABUNDANCE: Uncommon spring migrant. Very rare summer visitor. Fairly common fall migrant. Rare winter resident.

HABITAT: Large reservoirs; also found on some smaller lakes and ponds.

RECORDS AND REMARKS: Identification can be tricky, especially during spring, because many individuals are molting into breeding plumage during northward migration. Many have smudgy faces and necks, making them appear similar to the much less numerous Eared Grebe. During fall the identification is more straightforward because the cheeks and neck of most Horned Grebes are distinctly white. Another good fieldmark to use is the size of the bill and the way it is held relative to the water surface; Horned Grebes have a thicker, straighter bill that is usually held horizontal to the water surface, whereas Eared Grebes have a thinner bill with a slightly upturned lower mandible that causes the appearance of the bill to look as though it is held at an upward angle from the horizontal of the water surface.
SPRING—A few arrive just after the first spring thaw in late February, but migration is not really fully underway until March. High counts are distinctly lower in spring than in fall; fifteen to twenty-five birds is a good single-day count.
2, Crab Orchard NWR, 20 Feb 1984 (SS)
2, Crab Orchard NWR, 29 Apr 1984 (TF, KR)
1, Sparta, Randolph Co., 3 May 1986 (TF et al.)
3, Jackson Co., 7 May 1977 (SBC)
SUMMER—ad., near Prairie du Rocher, Randolph Co., 13 June 1971 (HDB)
AUTUMN—Large concentrations sometimes occur at Rend Lake

and Crab Orchard Lake during November. A few will linger late into December as long as open water is available.

1, Crab Orchard NWR, 24 Sep 1988 (BD, WDR)
60, Crab Orchard NWR, 1 Nov 1985 (SO)
260, Crab Orchard NWR, 24 Nov 1982 (JCR)
1, Crab Orchard NWR CBC, 19 Dec 1987
WINTER—Recent concentrations at the warm-water Baldwin Lake are remarkable. Winter records from other sites in the region are very unusual.
80, Baldwin Lake, 3 Jan 1989 (RG)
76, Baldwin Lake, 9 Jan 1988 (SRu, MP), with 25 still there on 7 Feb 1988 (RG)
60, Baldwin Lake, 21 Jan 1992 (TF, JD)
1, Lake of Egypt, Williamson Co., 28 Jan 1984 (JCR)
1, Rend Lake, 9 Feb 1991 (WDR)

DOCUMENTATION: Specimen—Crab Orchard NWR, Williamson Co., 19 Oct 1955 (SIU A-2).

FIELD GUIDES: G=20; N=22; P=34.

Red-necked Grebe *Podiceps grisegena*
Late March–Early April
Late October–Late November

STATUS AND ABUNDANCE: Very rare migrant and winter visitor.

HABITAT: Reservoirs.

RECORDS AND REMARKS: This species has a diagonal (northwest to southeast) migration route that passes well north of southern Illinois; it breeds in central Canada and winters on the U.S. Atlantic Coast. Consequently, there are few records.
SPRING—2, Crab Orchard NWR, 6–19 Mar 1994 (KM)
4, Crab Orchard NWR, 20 Mar–9 Apr 1971 (GC, VK)
1, Lake Murphysboro, 7 Apr 1954 (RB)
AUTUMN—1, Rend Lake, 27 Oct 1985 (LH)
3, Lake Glendale, Pope Co., 28 Oct 1967 (VS)
6, near Murphysboro, Jackson Co., 26 Oct–7 Nov 1946 (JWH)
1, Crab Orchard NWR, 10–17 Nov 1984 (JCR et al.)
1, Rend Lake, 22 Nov 1975 (MMo)

WINTER—4, Baldwin Lake, 1 Jan 1994 (TF)
DOCUMENTATION: Photograph—Crab Orchard NWR, 20 Mar–9 Apr 1971 (on file at ISM).
FIELD GUIDES: G=20; N=20; P=34.

Eared Grebe *Podiceps nigricollis*
Mid-March–Mid-April
Late November–Mid-December

STATUS AND ABUNDANCE: Rare spring and fall migrant. Very rare winter visitor.

HABITAT: Small to large lakes, especially lakes with extensive shallow areas.

RECORDS AND REMARKS: Probably more numerous in fall than in spring. May be overlooked because it is similar in appearance to the Horned Grebe, with which it sometimes associates. For this reason, observers should use care when identifying an Eared Grebe, especially in spring, when molting individuals can closely resemble Horned Grebes.

SPRING—Not encountered every spring. Most records seem to occur from late March through mid-April.
1, Crab Orchard NWR, 15 Mar 1987 (WDR)
1, Crab Orchard NWR, 29 Mar and 3 Apr 1986 (WDR)
1, Carbondale, 19 Apr 1976 (BP)
2, Union Co. CA, 4 May 1992 (TF et al.)

AUTUMN—All autumn records are from rather late in the season, but a few could occur as early as late September in some years.
1, Crab Orchard NWR, 24 Nov 1985 (TF, SO)
1, Rend Lake, 28 Nov 1987 (TF)
1, Crab Orchard NWR, 28–30 Nov and 5 Dec 1983 (JCR)
3, Rend Lake, Franklin Co., 17–19 Dec 1993 (TF)
5, Crab Orchard NWR, 18 Dec 1983 (TF)

WINTER—There are three early-winter records of birds from the warm-water Baldwin Lake; these records may be very late fall migrants.
1, Baldwin Lake, 9–16 Jan 1988 (SRu et al.)
1, Baldwin Lake, 10–11 Jan 1986 (WDR, TF, RG)

2, Baldwin Lake, 8 Feb 93 (TF, JD)

DOCUMENTATION: Photograph—Crab Orchard NWR, Williamson Co., 18 Dec 1983 (SIU AP-4).

FIELD GUIDES: G=20; N=22; P=34.

Western Grebe *Aechmophorus occidentalis*
Mid-October–Late November

STATUS AND ABUNDANCE: Very rare fall migrant.

HABITAT: Reservoirs.

RECORDS AND REMARKS: Although there are four records for the genus *Aechmophorus*, only two (the 1993 and 1994 records) have been documented with enough detail to make a confident identification to species level. Western and Clark's Grebes are extremely similar in appearance, so very close views are usually required to identify birds to species. The identification problems are further complicated by the occurrence of natural hybrids, which are usually intermediate between the two species in plumage characteristics. The Western Grebe (*A. occidentalis*) is considered a rare, but regular, fall migrant in Illinois, and it may likewise occur regularly in southern Illinois. Frequent checks of Rend and Crab Orchard Lakes during November may produce more records. There is only one definite record of Clark's Grebe (*A. clarkii*) from Illinois (Bohlen 1989), so it is probably reasonable to assume that Clark's is just as rare in our region. All observations of this genus should be thoroughly documented with written descriptions and photos whenever possible.
1, Crab Orchard NWR, 8–31 Oct 1941 (LB)
1, Crab Orchard NWR, 22 Oct 1994 (TF)
1, Crab Orchard NWR, 10–28 Nov 1993 (BD, m.ob.)
2, Rend Lake, 15 Nov 1975 (BP, MMo)
1, Crab Orchard NWR, 23 Nov 1970 (GC, VK)

DOCUMENTATION: Written descriptions—Crab Orchard NWR, Williamson Co., 10–28 Nov 1993.

FIELD GUIDES: G=20; N=20; P=34.

Order Pelecaniformes: Totipalmate Swimmers

Family Pelecanidae: Pelicans

American White Pelican *Pelecanus erythrorhynchos*
Early May
Late August–Late November

STATUS AND ABUNDANCE: Very rare spring migrant and summer visitor. Rare fall migrant.

HABITAT: Mudflats and shallow rivers and lakes.

RECORDS AND REMARKS: Pelicans can occur at nearly any time of year. There are apparently only two records from the eastern part of southern Illinois: a record from Brookport, Massac Co., on the Ohio River and the Mermet Lake record below.
SPRING—29, Rend Lake, Jefferson Co., 1–6 Apr 1994 (DR)
1, East Cape Girardeau, Alexander Co., 7–11 May 1983 (PK)
SUMMER—Birds present during June and July are probably non-breeding wanderers, although they could conceivably be either very late spring migrants or very early autumn migrants.
16, Baldwin Lake, 11 June 1975 (AB 29:979)
20, Fort Kaskaskia SP, Randolph Co., 14 June–4 July 1963 (MF, RA)
1, Ware, Union Co., 24–30 June 1992 (TF, m.ob.)
AUTUMN—Fall encounters generally involve single birds, some of which linger at a location for several weeks. Most records are from the period of mid-September to mid-November.
1, Crab Orchard NWR, 11 Aug–17 Oct 1954 (LB)
1, Rend Lake, Jefferson Co., 19 Aug 1989 (BD, TF, WDR)
1, Crab Orchard NWR, 17 Sep–16 Nov 1971 (VK et al.)
1, Carbondale, 25 Sep.–23 Nov 1990 (BD et al.)
1, Carbondale, 15 Oct 1985 (CP)
1, Horseshoe Lake CA, 1 Nov 1974 (DKe)
1, Mermet Lake CA, Massac Co., 5 Nov 1991 (TF et al.)
3, Crab Orchard NWR, late Nov 1979 (BG)

DOCUMENTATION: Specimen—Crab Orchard NWR, Williamson Co., 14 Oct 1955 (SIU A-353).

FIELD GUIDES: G=32; N=40; P=78.

Family *Phalacrocoracidae*: Cormorants

Double-crested Cormorant *Phalacrocorax auritus*
Mid-March–Mid-May
Early September–Late December

STATUS AND ABUNDANCE: Common migrant in the west. Uncommon migrant in the east. Rare summer visitor. Rare summer resident at Rend Lake. Rare winter resident.

HABITAT: Frequents large lakes, rivers, and sloughs, especially those with numerous standing dead trees or stumps.

RECORDS AND REMARKS: These gregarious birds dive from the water's surface for fish. When a cormorant is swimming, its body rides low in the water, so sometimes only the snakelike neck can be seen from a distance. Cormorants also frequently perch in trees and spread their wings to air-dry their feathers. Adults are all black, whereas immatures are dull brown. They routinely fly in V-formations, but their long tails and deep wing beats distinguish them from geese, even at a distance.

SPRING—Spring migration may begin during February in response to false springs. More typically, the first arrivals do not appear until mid-March or later. Numbers peak during April and then decrease until mid-May, when most migrants have departed.

1, Williamson Co., 13 Feb 1985 (JCR)
1, Union Co. CA, 19 Feb 1989 (TF, JH, WDR)
2, Rend Lake, 6 Mar 1987 (TF)
2,500, Rend Lake, 4 Apr 1993 (TF)
14, Pomona, 3 May 1988 (TF, JCR, LA, WDR)
25, Pope Co., 4 May 1985 (SBC)
10, Crab Orchard NWR, 4 June 1984 (EC)
imm., s. Alexander Co., 7 June 1984 (VK)
SUMMER—Breeding may occur regularly at Rend Lake. As Illinois's breeding population increases, it is likely that more breeding will occur at Rend Lake and perhaps at other southern Illinois locations.
5, Rend Lake, 14 June 1989 (WDR)
nest with 2 yg., Rend Lake, July 1980 (RZ)
3 ad. and 1 imm., Rend Lake, 8 July 1986 (WDR)
2 nests, each with 2 yg., Rend Lake, 2 Oct 1994 (TF)

AUTUMN—A few wandering individuals are detected during July and August, but substantial migration does not begin until mid- or late September. Very large concentrations have been noted recently at Rend Lake, and the numbers continue to increase each year. Cormorants will linger very late into December as long as open water is available.

imm., w. Alexander Co., 5 July 1988 (WDR)
1, Crab Orchard NWR, 1 Aug 1987 (WDR)
1, Mermet Lake CA, 18 Aug 1988 (WDR)
3,000, Rend Lake, 7 Oct 1990 (TF, JD)
400, Rend Lake, 21 Dec 1990 (WDR)
5, Rend Lake, 31 Dec 1988 (TF, WDR et al.)
WINTER—Some hardy individuals periodically attempt to over-winter. Some of the region's January records involve injured birds.
2, Crab Orchard NWR, 17 Dec–1 Feb 1989 (SO, WDR)
1–3, Rend Lake, 17–23 Jan 1992 (TF, JD)
1, Baldwin Lake, 21 Jan 1991 (TF, JD)
1, Rend Lake, 26 Jan 1987 (TF)
1, Rend Lake, 1 Feb 1989 (WDR)

DOCUMENTATION: Specimen—Crab Orchard NWR, Williamson Co., 27 Nov 1955 (SIU A-11).

FIELD GUIDES: G=36; N=46; P=40.

Neotropic Cormorant *Phalacrocorax olivaceus*

STATUS AND ABUNDANCE: Very rare visitor.

RECORDS AND REMARKS: There is one record of a bird found dead along the Ohio River near Cairo, Alexander Co., on 10 July 1878 (ISU 12). That specimen is the only specimen evidence for Illinois, but there have been a few recent records of sightings and photograph records from northern Illinois. Observers in southern Illinois should carefully search all Double-crested Cormorant flocks for small cormorants with relatively long tails (and white neck plumes if seen during the breeding season).

DOCUMENTATION: Specimen—1878 record.

FIELD GUIDES: G=36; N=44; P=40.

Family Anhingidae: Anhingas

Anhinga *Anhinga anhinga*

STATUS AND ABUNDANCE: Very rare visitor.

HABITAT: Sloughs, swampy lakes, and rivers.

RECORDS AND REMARKS: Formerly more numerous (Ridgway 1881). Anhingas nested at least as close as Fulton Co., Kentucky, in the past (Ganier 1937:43); they are again nesting at Reelfoot, Tennessee, providing the opportunity for postbreeding wanderers to be detected in southern Illinois more often (Monroe et al. 1988). Anhingas often soar on heat thermals during midday.
SPRING—There is one recent spring record that may be classified as an overmigrant.
male, Union Co. CA, 28 Apr 1985 (JCR, BD)
SUMMER—1, Oakwood Bottoms, Jackson Co., 4 June 1977 (MMo), and possibly the same bird at Cedar Lake, Jackson Co., 24–26 July 1977 (JG)
1, s. Alexander Co., 5 July 1986 (WDR)

DOCUMENTATION: Photograph—Alexander Co., 5 July 1986 (*IBB* 3:34).

FIELD GUIDES: G=36; N=44; P=40.

Family Fregatidae: Frigatebirds

[Magnificent Frigatebird *Fregata magnificens*]

STATUS AND ABUNDANCE: Hypothetical.

HABITAT: The only record was of a bird seen flying over the Mississippi River. This is a species of the open ocean, so vagrants will most likely occur near water.

RECORDS AND REMARKS: An adult female was in southern Alexander Co., on 19 July 1986 (WDR), but it was seen and described by only one observer.

FIELD GUIDES: G=34; N=38; P=78.

Order Ciconiiformes: Herons and Allies

Family Ardeidae: Herons

American Bittern *Botaurus lentiginosus*

Late March–Early May
Mid-September–Mid-November

STATUS AND ABUNDANCE: Uncommon spring migrant. Former rare summer resident. Rare fall migrant. Very rare winter visitor.

HABITAT: Marshes, especially where cattails are common.

RECORDS AND REMARKS: This species is undoubtedly more common than records indicate, but it is very secretive and is usually not seen without much searching in its appropriate marshy habitat. The many records from Oakwood Bottoms indicate, at least in part, the past quality of the habitat there; the area is now very overgrown with trees and probably does not attract as many bitterns as it did during the 1970s and early 1980s.
SPRING—Most birds arrive during April. Peak numbers are encountered from mid-April through the first few days of May. Numbers quickly decline after the first week of May.
3, Oakwood Bottoms, Jackson Co., 25 Mar 1984 (JCR)
1, Perry Co., 1 Apr 1986 (TF)
10, Oakwood Bottoms, Jackson Co., 27 Apr 1979 (HD)
10, Jackson Co., 5 May 1973 (SBC)
2, Black Bottoms, Massac Co., 9 May 1986 (WDR)
1, Mermet Lake CA, Massac Co., 13 May 1988 (RP, MD)
SUMMER—Bennett (1957) found young at Crab Orchard NWR in 1950–1952, plus four nests in 1952. There are no known breeding records since then. It is possible, however, that nesting could still occur in dense cattail habitat along the margins of reclaimed strip-mine ponds, or at other marshes.
AUTUMN—Not often encountered during fall, perhaps because of a lack of searching effort in the appropriate habitats. Apparently some bitterns will stopover in hay fields during fall migration, perhaps in response to the general lack of extensive wet, marshy habitats at this usually dry time of year.
1 found dead, Crab Orchard NWR, 26 Sep 1993 (TF)

1, Lovett's Pond, Jackson Co., 9 Oct 1993 (TF)
1, Crab Orchard NWR, 20 Oct 1983 (JCR)
1, Carbondale, 30 Oct 1949 (RB)
1 found shot, Oakwood Bottoms, Jackson Co., 14 Nov 1972 (MS)
WINTER—Formerly a winter visitor, and perhaps a winter resident
during warm winters. Ice cover should force these birds to move
south for the winter.
1 shot, Crab Orchard NWR, 17 Dec 1949 (verified by RB)
1 heard, Crab Orchard NWR, 1 Feb 1950 (JWH)

DOCUMENTATION: Provisional acceptance.

FIELD GUIDES: G=98; N=48; P=104.

Least Bittern *Ixobrychus exilis*

Early May–Early October

STATUS AND ABUNDANCE: Uncommon migrant. Locally uncommon summer resident.

HABITAT: Cattail and *Phragmites* marshes.

RECORDS AND REMARKS: As with the American Bittern, this species may be more numerous than realized. Secretive habits probably limit the number encountered by birders, particularly in fall, when few are detected after mid-August. May breed annually in the excellent cattail marsh at Mermet Lake (Robinson 1988).
SPRING—Typically arrives after the fifth of May. Most birds are encountered as they are flushed up from cattail marshes by the persistent observer. These bitterns are also quite vocal during spring and will respond to playbacks of their call. High counts are usually less than three birds per day, even in excellent habitat. The presence of the breeding population obscures detection of spring departure dates for migrants.
1, Rend Lake, 7 May 1988 (TF)
1, n. Randolph Co., 15 May 1988 (WDR)
1, Pope Co., 22 May 1982 (RBr)
SUMMER—Breeding occurs during midsummer. On 3 July 1990, six nests at Mermet Lake were at the following stages: five had eggs (one set of eggs was hatching) and one had young (TF). Fledglings were noted at Mermet Lake on 20 July 1991 (TF).
8 nests, Crab Orchard NWR, summer 1952 (Bennett 1957)

Least Bittern nest with nestlings, Mermet lake, Massac Co., 6 July 1990

3 nests, Mermet Lake CA, summers 1973 and 1974 (DH, VK)
8 (including some yg.), n. Randolph Co., 16 June 1985 (JCR)
4, e. of Herrin, Williamson Co., 9 July 1983 (JCR)
3 nests, Union Co. CA, 30 July 1993 (MO)
AUTUMN—These birds just seem to disappear after breeding. Very few are detected after mid-August.
1, Rend Lake, 12 Oct 1987 (TF)

DOCUMENTATION: Specimen—ad., n. Randolph Co., 15 May 1988 (SIU A-2163).

FIELD GUIDES: G=98; N=48; P=104.

Great Blue Heron *Ardea herodias*
Mid-February–Late December

STATUS AND ABUNDANCE: Common migrant and summer resident. Fairly common winter resident.

HABITAT: Marshes, swamps, rivers, and reservoirs.

RECORDS AND REMARKS: Migration occurs, but dates are difficult to assess because of summer and winter populations. More detailed data are needed to understand movements of this species in the region. In particular, regular counts throughout February and

March might provide information on spring arrivals of birds that wintered south of the region.

SPRING—Spring migration probably occurs between mid-February and mid-April in most years.

2 migrants, Johnson Co., 20 Mar 1990 (TF)

SUMMER—Nests are placed near the canopy of bottomland forest trees, often within large forest tracts (Graber et al. 1978). Breeding may begin as early as March and may continue until late July. Kleen (1987) indicated five active nesting colonies in southern Illinois: Rend Lake, Jefferson Co. (400 nests); Black Bottoms, Massac Co. (500 nests); Reevesville, Pope Co. (100 nests); Ware, Union Co. (25 nests); and Little Black Slough, Johnson Co. (350 nests). In addition, there are smaller colonies at Horseshoe Lake CA; Grantsburg, Johnson Co.; and LaRue Pine Hills, Union Co.

AUTUMN—Fall migration begins with the arrival of postbreeding wanderers from south of Illinois in late July or early August; it peaks between mid-September and mid-October, and it ends by late November in most years.

112, Crab Orchard NWR, 12 Oct 1983 (JCR)

WINTER—Many linger into winter as long as open water is available. They can sometimes be seen fishing from the edges of holes in the ice in the center of large lakes.

179, Crab Orchard NWR CBC, 19 Dec 1987

DOCUMENTATION: Photograph—Mermet Lake CA, 18 Aug 1988 (SIU AP-227).

FIELD GUIDES: G=96; N=54; P=100.

Great Egret *Casmerodius albus*

Late March–Early May
Mid-July–Late October

STATUS AND ABUNDANCE: Fairly common spring migrant in the west; uncommon spring migrant in the east. Locally uncommon summer resident. Common fall migrant in the west; uncommon fall migrant in the east. Rare winter visitor.

HABITAT: Marshes, lakes, sloughs, and rivers.

RECORDS AND REMARKS: Formerly known as the American Egret

and the Common Egret, this large white heron is difficult to over-look. They are less numerous in spring than in fall, probably because birds present during fall are postbreeding wanderers from the large heronries in the southern United States.

SPRING—Spring numbers vary widely from year to year. Most first arrivals are present by the last week of March, occasionally sooner. Numbers peak in April and then taper off to breeding population levels by early May.

1, Rend Lake, 11 Mar 1981 (RZ)

SUMMER—Associates with colonies of Great Blue Herons. Recent nesting attempts have involved less than ten pairs. Formerly more numerous, one colony near Ware, Union Co., had one hundred nests in 1973 (Graber et al. 1978). Now breeds only in very wet years when floodplains have many sloughs and flooded pools: for example, a breeding colony was recorded near Gale, Alexander Co., in summer 1985 (TF, JCR). Some midsummer sightings in Alexander and Union Cos. are of birds dispersing into Illinois to forage from nearby colonies in s.e. Missouri. A few pairs nested with Great Blue Herons at Little Black Slough in 1991 (TF).

AUTUMN—Postbreeding wanderers begin arriving from south of Illinois by mid-July, usually peak during August, and then retreat back south by the end of October.

1, near DeSoto, Jackson Co., 1 July 1972 (VK)
41, w. Alexander Co., 26 July 1986 (WDR)
200, s.w. Jackson Co., 29 Aug 1974 (VK, HDB, CC)
71, Union Co. CA, 16 Sep 1989 (WDR)
53, Rend Lake, 24 Sep 1985 (LH)
88, Crab Orchard NWR, 26 Sep 1993 (TF)
1, Oakwood Bottoms, Jackson Co., 28 Nov 1984 (JCR)

WINTER—Some birds linger very late into early winter, but only one record suggests that Great Egrets may on occasion overwinter.

1, Crab Orchard NWR, 14 Dec 1983 (JCR)
1, Union Co., 19 Dec 1971 (VK)
1, LaRue Pine Hills, Union Co., 23 Dec 1981 (DH)
1, Pine Hills, Union Co., 30 Jan–20 Feb 1994 (DKa)

DOCUMENTATION: Photograph—Union Co., 19 Dec 1971 (VK collection).

FIELD GUIDES: G=94; N=52; P=102.

Snowy Egret *Egretta thula*

Late April–Mid-May
Mid-July–Early September

STATUS AND ABUNDANCE: Locally uncommon spring migrant and fairly common fall migrant in the floodplains of Alexander, Union, and Jackson Cos. Rare fall migrant in the rest of the region. Uncommon summer resident in the Alexander Co. floodplains.

HABITAT: Sloughs, flooded fields, and marshes.

RECORDS AND REMARKS: Snowy Egrets are generally more numerous during fall than in spring, but numbers vary in both seasons from year to year. They are conspicuously more numerous in the western Floodplains. They should be recorded in Randolph Co. every year, because the birds migrating to and from the St. Louis area colonies should pass through that county, but there are no available records.
SPRING—The first arrivals are most typically encountered in the last few days of April. Daily high counts rarely exceed one to three birds. A few birds are present all summer, so it is difficult to confidently identify average spring departure dates.
1, s.e. Saline Co., 14 Apr 1994 (JD)
5, Union Co., 19 Apr 1993 (KM)
1, Ware, Union Co., 22 Apr 1984 (DJ)
SUMMER—A few Snowy Egrets breed in Alexander Co. in some years. In most years, however, it is likely that sightings during June are of birds from the small colony in nearby s.e. Missouri.
11, w. Alexander Co., 26 May 1985 (JCR)
18, Alexander Co., 6 June 1977 (MMo)
15, s. Alexander Co., 26 June 1978 (MMo)
AUTUMN—Postbreeding wanderers begin appearing during mid-July, and numbers peak from late July through mid-August. Most have departed by the end of the first week in September.
28, s. Alexander Co., 12 July 1990 (TF, WDR)
44, Pulaski Co., 13 July 1994 (TF)
1 ad. and 1 imm., Mermet Lake CA, 23 July 1988 (TF, WDR)
imm., Rend Lake, 13–20 Aug 1988 (TF, WDR)
151, w. Jackson Co., 21 Aug 1993 (CS)

1, Rend Lake, 15–27 Aug 1987 (TF)
1, Rend Lake, 8 Sep 1985 (LH)
1, Crab Orchard NWR, 26 Sep 1993 (TF)
DOCUMENTATION: Written description—Alexander Co., 20 Apr 1985.
FIELD GUIDES: G=94; N=52; P=102.

Little Blue Heron *Egretta caerulea*
Early April–Late May
Early July–Late September

STATUS AND ABUNDANCE: Uncommon spring migrant, locally uncommon summer resident, and common fall migrant in western Floodplains. Rare spring migrant and uncommon fall migrant in remainder of region.

HABITAT: Marshes, sloughs, rivers, and reservoirs.

RECORDS AND REMARKS: This medium-sized heron has three distinctive plumages: adults are all dark blue and maroon; immatures are all white except for dusky wingtips; and subadults are a piebald mix of gray blotches on white plumage. All ages have greenish legs. Distinctly more numerous in the west; many birds pass through the western Floodplains en route to and from colonies in the St. Louis area and elsewhere.
SPRING—During unusually warm springs, a few birds arrive in late March, but more typically the first birds arrive in early April. Daily high counts rarely exceed ten birds. Late-spring sightings may represent late migrants or birds that have wandered in from nearby colonies in neighboring states to forage.
ad., Crab Orchard NWR, 26 Mar 1988 (WDR)
ad., Union Co. CA, 29 Mar 1986 (TF, WDR)
4, Crab Orchard NWR, 12 Apr 1984 (TF)
SUMMER—In years when there are many flooded fields in the Alexander Co. floodplains, some birds remain to breed. Some nests near Gale, Alexander Co., in the late 1960s were placed in young cottonwood trees (Graber et al. 1978).
108, n.w. Alexander Co., 3 June 1985 (KR, TF)

25 nests, n.w. Alexander Co., summer 1985 (JCR)
1, Crab Orchard NWR, 22 and 29 June 1984 (JCR)
AUTUMN—An influx of postbreeding wanderers occurs in early
July; many of these birds are the white immatures. They sometimes
congregate in fairly large flocks in flooded fields and ditches.
1 ad. and 1 imm., Johnson Co., 10 July 1988 (TF)
160, s. Alexander Co., 19 July 1990 (WDR)
20, Rend Lake, 22 July 1986 (LH)
40, Mermet Lake CA, 23 July 1988 (TF, WDR)
176, s.w. Jackson Co., 29 July 1951 (JWH, RB)
29, Crab Orchard NWR, 3 Aug 1972 (VK)
51, Rend Lake, 24 Aug 1976 (BP)
200, s.w. Jackson Co., 29 Aug 1974 (VK, HDB, CC)
3 imm., Ware, Union Co., and s.w. Jackson Co., 10 Oct 1970
(RGr, PH)
1, s.w. Jackson Co., 7–15 Oct 1984 (JCR)
imm., Crab Orchard NWR, 21 Oct 1993 (TF)

DOCUMENTATION: Specimen—Miller City, Alexander Co., 26 Apr
1969 (SIU A-2108).

FIELD GUIDES: G=96; N=50; P=100.

Tricolored Heron *Egretta tricolor*

STATUS AND ABUNDANCE: Very rare visitor.

HABITAT: Marshes, sloughs, and rivers.

RECORDS AND REMARKS: Formerly known as the Louisiana Heron,
this distinctively patterned southern species occurs as an overmigrant
during spring and as a postbreeding wanderer during late summer and
autumn. Currently, there are only three documented records.
SPRING—1, near Ware, Union Co., 28 Apr 1974 (RM)
SUMMER—1, near East Cape Girardeau, Alexander Co., 28 June
1969 (Anderson 1971)
1, Rend Lake, Jefferson Co., 9 July 1994 (TF, BD, JD)

DOCUMENTATION: Photograph—1, near Ware, Union Co., 28 Apr
1974.

FIELD GUIDES: G=96; N=50; P=100.

[Reddish Egret *Egretta rufescens*]

STATUS AND ABUNDANCE: Hypothetical.

HABITAT: In its normal range, occurs in tidal pools, sloughs, and shallow-water areas.

RECORDS AND REMARKS: Nelson (1877) called this species "common" near Cairo, Alexander Co., in late August 1875. Bohlen (1978) is likely correct in stating that Nelson confused this species with Little Blue Herons, which would be truly common near Cairo in late August. Without documentary evidence, the Reddish Egret cannot be placed on the region's list of accepted species.

FIELD GUIDES: G=96; N=50; P=100.

Cattle Egret *Bubulcus ibis*

Early April–Late May
Mid-July–Mid-October

STATUS AND ABUNDANCE: Fairly common to common migrant in the western Floodplains. Uncommon migrant elsewhere. Locally uncommon summer resident in the Alexander Co. floodplains.

HABITAT: Marshes, sloughs, rivers, and reservoirs. Also forages in pastures.

RECORDS AND REMARKS: The first Illinois record for this species is from the Chicago area in 1952 (Bohlen 1978); there were few records after that until the 1960s. The earliest record located so far for southern Illinois is a notation on an old Mermet Lake checklist of the sighting of two individuals there in May 1966. As with the other heron species, numbers vary wildly from year to year, probably depending on water conditions. In fall 1993, when thousands of acres of agricultural floodplain fields were flooded in Alexander, Union, and Jackson Cos., a huge roost was located along the Big Muddy River in Jackson Co.

SPRING—First arrivals are usually encountered near 1 April. Peak numbers are present from late April through mid-May and then decline quickly.

1, near Carbondale, 30 Mar 1981 (WDR)
1, Carbondale, 30 Mar 1985 (KM)

12, Ina, Jefferson Co., 3 Apr 1986 (KPi)
91, near Heron Pond, Johnson Co., 28 Apr 1974 (VK)
300, Union Co., 4 May 1993 (TF)
50, Crab Orchard NWR, 1 June 1983 (JCR)
15, Trail of Tears SF, Union Co., 2 June 1981 (MMl)
SUMMER—Breeds in the region (especially in Alexander Co.), but irregularly, depending on water conditions. Few birds can be found during dry years. A colony of three hundred nests was present on Billings Island in the Mississippi River near Willard, Alexander Co., in 1975 (Graber et al. 1978).
100+ nests, n.w. Alexander Co., summer 1985 (JCR)
1,082, Alexander Co., 3 June 1985 (TF, KR)
AUTUMN—Postbreeding wanderers begin arriving by mid-July, peak in late August and early September, and typically depart by mid-October. Some, however, may linger quite late.
10,000, s.w. Jackson Co., 23–30 Aug 1993 (CS, TF, BD et al.)
145, Pulaski Co., 4 Sep 1982 (PK)
7, Union Co. CA, 12 Nov 1977 (IM)
1, s.w. Jackson Co., 23 Nov 1986 (KRu)
1, Ozark, Johnson Co., 23 Nov 1990 (TF)
3, Union Co. CA, 4 Dec 1984 (TF, JCR)
1, Waltonville, Jefferson Co., 9 Dec 1990 (TF)

DOCUMENTATION: Photograph—Ozark, Johnson Co., 23 Nov 1990 (TF).

FIELD GUIDES: G=94; N=52; P=102.

Green-backed Heron *Butorides striatus*
Mid-April–Mid-October

STATUS AND ABUNDANCE: Common migrant and summer resident. Very rare winter visitor.

HABITAT: Ponds, creeks, marshes, lakes, and rivers.

RECORDS AND REMARKS: Generally more solitary than most other herons. This is the heron most frequently encountered around farm ponds and along wooded creeks.
SPRING—First arrivals are back by 10 April. Daily counts usually

Green-backed Heron, Mermet Lake, Massac Co., 30 July 1990

range from one to ten birds. Because there is a substantial breeding population, it is difficult to discern departure dates.

1, Carbondale, 30 Mar 1949 (RB)

1, Carbondale, 31 Mar 1979 (HD)

1, Crab Orchard NWR, 3 Apr 1985 (JCR)

1, Alexander Co., 5 Apr 1991 (TF, JD)

SUMMER—Surprisingly little information is available about nesting habits or success in the region. These birds are very quiet around their nests, however, which may explain the lack of information.

nest with 3 eggs, DeSoto, Jackson Co., 1 July 1972 (VK)

AUTUMN—Postbreeding movements have begun by early July, when birds begin to gather at roadside ditches and along lake margins. These early-summer aggregations may consist primarily of local breeders and juveniles. Later in July and in August, there is probably an influx of postbreeding wanderers from the south and migrants from the north. Most have departed the region by 15 October, but a few may linger later, even into winter.

25, Alexander Co., 7 July 1984 (TF, JCR)
50, s.w. Jackson Co., 29 Aug 1974 (VK, HDB, CC)
1, Oakwood Bottoms, Jackson Co., 18 Nov 1973 (MS)
1, Alexander Co., 2 Dec 1983 (RBr)
WINTER—1, Crab Orchard NWR, 17 Jan 1983 (TF)

DOCUMENTATION: Specimen—2 miles n. of Cobden, Union Co., 6 June 1969 (SIU).

FIELD GUIDES: G=96; N=50; P=104.

Black-crowned Night-Heron *Nycticorax nycticorax*

Early April–Early May
Early July–Late October

STATUS AND ABUNDANCE: Uncommon migrant in the Floodplains and the Till Plain. Rare migrant in the Shawnee Hills. Locally uncommon summer visitor. Rare summer resident. Very rare winter visitor.

HABITAT: Marshes, sloughs, rivers, reservoirs, and wooded swamps.

RECORDS AND REMARKS: Apparently more numerous in the west than in the east, this heron frequents dense vegetation and can be difficult to detect. They may come out into the open to forage in the early morning and in the late afternoon and evening. Adults are strikingly patterned with black, white, and gray; immatures are brown with whitish spots. The immatures closely resemble immature Yellow-crowned Night-Herons but have larger spots (especially on the back), shorter legs, a chunkier head, and a longer, thinner bill.

SPRING—Often difficult to find during spring. A few may arrive during March, but most often the first birds are reported during April. Most migrants have departed by 10 May; birds encountered later may be breeders or wanderers from colonies in nearby states.

1 ad., Rend Lake, 11 Mar 1989 (WDR)
1, Rend Lake, 28 Mar 1988 (TF)
1, Dixon Springs SP, Pope Co., 4 Apr 1985 (TF)
SUMMER—Breeds across from Alexander Co. in s.e. Missouri; therefore, sightings in Alexander Co. during late May and June may be of individuals dispersing from that colony. May also breed at Rend Lake. A few nests were found at Crab Orchard NWR during the 1960s.
2 ad., Klondike, Alexander Co., 26 May 1988 (WDR)
20, Alexander Co., 26 June 1978 (MMo)
AUTUMN—As with other heron species, postbreeding wanderers begin appearing in mid- to late summer; but Black-crowneds generally do not form large foraging groups.
11, Alexander Co., 16 July 1983 (JCR)
10, Rend Lake, 24 Aug 1985 (RP)
20, w. Jackson Co., 30 Aug 1993 (CS)
WINTER—imm., Union Co. CA, 19 Dec 1984 (JS et al.)
1, Crab Orchard NWR, 23 Dec 1985 (WDR)
DOCUMENTATION: Provisional acceptance.
FIELD GUIDES: G=98; N=48; P=104.

Yellow-crowned Night-Heron *Nyctanassa violacea*
Mid-April–Late August

STATUS AND ABUNDANCE: Uncommon migrant and locally uncommon summer resident in the Floodplains. Rare migrant in the Till Plain and the Shawnee Hills.

HABITAT: Swamps, marshes, sloughs, and reservoirs. Breeds in bottomland forest.

RECORDS AND REMARKS: Generally solitary, but sometimes forms small groups in appropriate habitat. Very few records from the east, perhaps because of a general lack of coverage by observers.
SPRING—First arrivals are usually detected in mid-April, but sometimes a few appear in late March. Daily high counts are low, typically not exceeding three to five birds, except in areas near breeding colonies, where up to fourteen birds have been counted.
1, Oakwood Bottoms, Jackson Co., 22 Mar 1986 (TF, WDR)
1, Rend Lake, Jefferson Co., 17 Apr 1987 (TF)

9, s.w. Jackson Co., 1 May 1985 (VK)
14, Jackson Co., 7 May 1977 (SBC)
imm., Mermet Lake CA, 10 May 1986 (WDR)
2, Rend Lake, 30 May 1987 (TF)
SUMMER—Probably breed at Oakwood Bottoms, Jackson Co.,
every year. Nests have also been discovered at Crab Orchard NWR
(3 nests, spring 1950 [LB]); Belle Pond, Johnson Co. (June 1991
[TF]); and Rend Lake (Graber et al. 1978).
4 nests, Buttonland Swamp, Pulaski Co., 30 Apr 1983 (MMl, MS)
14, Oakwood Bottoms, Jackson Co., 7 June 1975 (HDB)
7 ad., Union Co. CA, 22 June 1982 (PK)
AUTUMN—There is not really any obvious influx of postbreeding
wanderers. The few small concentrations observed in the past have
been near summer breeding areas. Some birds may linger into September or early October (there are several similar records from central and northern Illinois), but no such records are available from
southern Illinois.
21, s.w. Jackson Co., 24 July 1986 (WDR)
imm., Mt. Vernon, Jefferson Co., 15 Aug 1988 (TF)
15, s.w. Jackson Co., 29 Aug 1974 (VK, HDB, CC)
1, Alexander Co., 9 Sep 1993 (TF)

DOCUMENTATION: Photograph—Mt. Vernon, Jefferson Co., 15
Aug 1988 (SIU AP-173).

FIELD GUIDES: G=98; N=48; P=104.

Family *Threskiornithidae: Ibises*

White Ibis *Eudocimus albus*

STATUS AND ABUNDANCE: Very rare fall visitor.

HABITAT: Sloughs, swampy thickets, and marshes.

RECORDS AND REMARKS: This distinctive wading bird has occurred
at least five times since 1963, all during fall. Interestingly, with the
exception of the 1986 record, exactly ten years passed between each
record. They forage in relatively shallow water by probing into the
sediment in flooded fields and marshes. They often associate with
other herons.

AUTUMN—1, Fort Kaskaskia SP, Randolph Co., 4 July 1963 (Anderson 1964)
imm., Willard, Alexander Co., 5 July 1986 (WDR)
1, Union Co., 13 July 1973 (MH)
imm., w. Jackson Co., 26–28 Aug 1993 (TF, CS)
imm., s.w. Jackson Co., 29 Oct 1983 (JN)

DOCUMENTATION: Written description—Willard, Alexander Co., 5 July 1986.

FIELD GUIDES: G=100; N=56; P=108.

Glossy Ibis *Plegadis falcinellus*

STATUS AND ABUNDANCE: Very rare spring and fall visitor.

HABITAT: Sloughs, flooded fields, and swamps.

RECORDS AND REMARKS: The two North American *Plegadis* ibises pose a difficult identification problem. Close views are needed to see the appropriate fieldmarks well enough to confidently separate the Glossy Ibis *(P. falcinellus)* from the White-faced Ibis *(P. chihi)*. During spring, adults can be separated by differences in iris and facial skin color and in the amount of white feathering around the edge of the facial skin (see Pratt 1976 for discussion of fieldmarks). During fall it is extremely difficult to separate these two species, because facial skin color fades, age determination must be made before iris color can be used correctly, and the white feathers along the edge of the facial skin are molted out. Consequently, most birds observed in the region, in either spring or fall, lack sufficient detail to determine specific identity. There is, however, one record of two birds positively identified as Glossy Ibises at Cypress Creek NWR, Pulaski Co., on 8 May 1993 (Fink 1993b). Other *Plegadis* ibis records include the following:
SPRING—1, s.w. Jackson Co., 6 May 1972 (MJM)
1, Rend Lake, Franklin Co., 7 May 1994 (BD)
AUTUMN—1, s.w. Jackson Co., 7–8 Oct 1984 (SO et al.)
1, Crab Orchard NWR, 19 Oct 1980 (HD, BG; photo in *IAB* 196:39)
1, Crab Orchard NWR, 23 Oct 1972 (GC)
1, Crab Orchard NWR, 28 Oct 1993 (BD)

DOCUMENTATION: Written description—2, Cypress Creek NWR, Pulaski Co., 8 May 1993.

FIELD GUIDES: G=100; N=56; P=108.

Family Ciconiidae: Storks

Wood Stork *Mycteria americana*

STATUS AND ABUNDANCE: Very rare visitor.

HABITAT: Sloughs and marshes. Oxbow swamps along the Mississippi River should be ideal habitat.

RECORDS AND REMARKS: No recent records. Nelson (1877) collected some from sandbars in the Ohio River near Mound City, Pulaski Co., but the disposition of the specimens is unknown. He also reported that they occurred at Cairo, Alexander Co., from 1 August to 30 September 1875, being "numerous" from 11 August to 4 September. There are no reports since 1960.
AUTUMN—50, Jefferson Co., 30 July–23 Aug 1925 (Carson 1926)
12, Neunert, Jackson Co., 3 Sep 1949 (JWH)
1, Horseshoe Lake CA, Sep 1941 (George 1968)
1, DuQuoin, Perry Co., early fall 1945 (George 1968)
40, Union Co., fall 1960 (Comfort 1961)

DOCUMENTATION: Provisional acceptance.

FIELD GUIDES: G=100; N=54; P=106.

Order Anseriformes: Swans, Geese, and Ducks

Family Anatidae: Swans, Geese, and Ducks

Fulvous Whistling-Duck *Dendrocygna bicolor*

STATUS AND ABUNDANCE: Very rare visitor.

HABITAT: Flooded fields, swampy wetlands, and shallow lake borders.

RECORDS AND REMARKS: Currently there are two records of this southern species. The Jackson Co. bird associated with Mallards in flooded fields and mudflats near and on the Big Muddy River. The Jefferson Co. birds kept to themselves and foraged in shallow water in a flooded agricultural field along the edge of Rend Lake; they were observed from the Nason waterfowl observation deck.

SPRING—2, Rend Lake, Jefferson Co., 13–14 May 1990 (BD et al.)

AUTUMN—1, s.w. Jackson Co., 24–31 Aug 1974 (Madding and Bell 1975)

DOCUMENTATION: Photograph—2, Rend Lake, 13–14 May 1990 (SIU, uncatalogued).

FIELD GUIDES: G=52; N=76; P=48.

[Black Swan *Cygnus atratus*]

STATUS AND ABUNDANCE: Hypothetical.

RECORDS AND REMARKS: Two well-flighted individuals of this Australian species were viewed as they foraged at Rend Lake, Jefferson Co., on 19 September 1993 (TF). One, probably one of the same pair, was at Crab Orchard NWR, from 2 to 9 October 1993 (TF). There is insufficient evidence to conclude that these were wild vagrants.

FIELD GUIDES: G=not pictured; N=90; P=302.

[Egyptian Goose *Alopochen aegyptiacus*]

STATUS AND ABUNDANCE: Hypothetical.

RECORDS AND REMARKS: One bird that wintered with Canada Geese at Union Co. CA from 23 December 1993 to 20 February 1994 was well-flighted but was almost undoubtedly an escapee. This species of the African tropics migrates very little, so the occurrence of a bird in the United States by natural vagrancy is highly unlikely.

FIELD GUIDES: Not pictured. See Madge and Burn (1988).

Tundra Swan *Cygnus columbianus*

Early November–Mid-February

STATUS AND ABUNDANCE: Occasional migrant and winter resident.

HABITAT: Shallow-water areas of lakes; sometimes roosts on ice with flocks of geese.

RECORDS AND REMARKS: Most migrate north of our region; they winter on the central Atlantic coast and breed in north-central Canada. They are generally observed every year in the west, where they associate with Canada Geese. There are very few records from the east. Immatures pose difficult identification problems because they can be confused with immature Mute Swans. Formerly called the Whistling Swan.

AUTUMN—A few sometimes appear during October, but most early arrivals do not appear until November. Most records involve one or two birds. The departure of fall migrants is difficult to determine, because many birds that arrive during fall tend to linger very late into winter.

1, Horseshoe Lake CA, 15 Oct 1979 (DT)

3 ad. and 2 imm., Crab Orchard NWR, 13–15 Nov 1984 (JCR)

2, Union Co. CA, 4–6 Dec 1979 (DT)

WINTER—A few, usually in groups of two to five, sometimes winter with flocks of Canada Geese.

2, Saline Co., 18 Nov 1991–17 Jan 1992 (JD, TF)

3–5, Crab Orchard NWR, 17 Dec 1988–11 Feb 1989 (SO, WDR et al.)

2 ad., Horseshoe Lake CA, 18 Dec 1985–7 Jan 1986 (VK, WDR et al.)

12, Horseshoe Lake CA CBC, 28 Dec 1978

5, Rend Lake, 6 Jan 1982 (RZ)

1 imm., Bay City, Pope Co., 4–6 Jan 1991 (TF, JD)

2, Pankeyville, Saline Co., 7 Jan 1990 (KP)

1 imm., Baldwin Lake, 13 Jan 1985 (SRu)

SPRING—Northward movements begin as soon as the first warm spell of the year arrives. Occurrence in the region peaks during late January and early February. Some should occur through about mid-March, but apparently no such records are as yet available.

5, Mermet Lake CA, 27 Jan–6 Feb 1992 (CMc, TF)

12, Alexander Co., and 5, Union Co. CA, 27 Jan 1983 (RCr)

3, s.w. Jackson Co., 13 Feb 1983 (PK)

4, Ullin, Pulaski Co., 19 Feb 1987 (SO)

DOCUMENTATION: Written description—Crab Orchard NWR, 17 Dec 1988.

FIELD GUIDES: G=40; N=60; P=42.

[Trumpeter Swan *Cygnus buccinator*]

STATUS AND ABUNDANCE: Hypothetical.

RECORDS AND REMARKS: Extirpated. Formerly a migrant and winter resident, possibly bred. The University of Illinois obtained a specimen from W. N. Butler of Anna in 1880 (Coale 1915), but it lacked data, so the bird may have been collected elsewhere. Audubon (1838, 1929) recorded Trumpeter Swans along the Ohio River from late October through early March, including a specific record of 2, near Little America, Pulaski Co., on 15 November 1820. Spring migrants were seen at Shawneetown, Gallatin Co., on 19 March 1885 (Cooke 1888). Only one summer record exists: some at the mouth of the Kaskaskia River, Randolph Co., 4 or 5 June 1819 (Peale 1946–1947).

Because of this swan's similarity with the Tundra Swan, early records may be considered dubious. Bent (1925), however, thought that trumpeters were "the more numerous species" at that time. With the advent of reintroductions in northern states, some migrants have begun to occur in Illinois again. A 20 February 1994 record of a flock of eight first-year birds at Burning Star Mine in Jackson Co. (GS) may be just the beginning of the reoccurrence of this species in southern Illinois; all eight swans had neck collars.

FIELD GUIDES: G=38; N=60; P=not pictured.

Mute Swan *Cygnus olor*

STATUS AND ABUNDANCE: Very rare migrant.

HABITAT: Ponds and shallow lakes.

RECORDS AND REMARKS: Occurs more often as a feral species mixed in with barnyard geese on farm ponds or at golf courses or park lakes. Some published records from Lake Murphysboro SP,

Jackson Co., are of feral birds. Genuinely wild individuals have been recorded, however. There is definite migration by wild individuals, but there are too few records to define accurately the migration periods. It is likely, for example, that most of spring migration is over by mid-March, rarely extending into mid-April. Although it is possible that some may attempt to overwinter, there are no such records at present. Immatures can closely resemble immature Tundra Swans.

AUTUMN—1, Horseshoe Lake CA, 19 Dec 1989 (SB, WDR)
2, Union Co. CBC, 20 Dec 1989
1, s.e. Saline Co., 10 Jan 1994 (JD)
SPRING—1, Union Co. CA, 12 Feb 1991 (TF)
1, Carbondale, 15 Feb–3 Mar 1985 (SO et al.)
2 ad. (one with black-and-yellow neck collar), Pinckneyville, Perry Co., 11 Mar 1986 (TF)
1 imm., near Cutler, Perry Co., 18 Apr 1986 (TF)

DOCUMENTATION: Written description—Horseshoe Lake CA, Alexander Co., 19 Dec 1989.

FIELD GUIDES: G=40; N=60; P=42.

Greater White-fronted Goose *Anser albifrons*
Early October–Mid-November
Mid-February–Mid-April

STATUS AND ABUNDANCE: Occasional migrant. Rare winter resident.

HABITAT: Grassy fields and agricultural areas.

RECORDS AND REMARKS: With effort, a few can be found each year during migration, especially at the goose refuges in the western portions of the region. "Specklebellies" often associate with Canada or Snow Geese. Most encounters are with groups of only a few birds, especially during winter, though flocks may be larger during migration. From below when in flight, these geese look like small Canada Geese, but their double-noted, barking honk is distinctively different from the calls of all other regional geese species.

AUTUMN—October is the month when peak numbers of whitefronts are present. The first migrants tend to arrive around the first of October, but sometimes a few will arrive even earlier. The majority of migrants passed south by mid-November, but some usually linger later and may attempt to overwinter.

1, Crab Orchard NWR, 16 Sep 1982 (JCR)
ad., Union Co. CA, 1 Oct 1972 (VK)
27, Rend Lake, 8 Oct 1990 (TF, JD)
24, Rend Lake, 25 Oct 1991 (TF)
3, Crab Orchard NWR, 4 Nov 1984 (JCR)

WINTER—At least a few probably attempt to overwinter each year, but they can be difficult to find amid the masses of Canada Geese.

1, Union Co. CA, 18 Dec 1983 (JCR, SS)
1, Crab Orchard NWR, 24 Dec 1991 (WDR)
4, Union Co. CBC, 29 Dec 1978 and 31 Dec 1987
3, Union Co. CA, all winter 1971–1972 (VK)
2–10, Rend Lake, all winter 1991–1992 (TF, BD)
180, Union Co. CA, 9 Jan 1995 (TF)
1, Rend Lake, 19 Jan 1985 and 30 Jan 1983 (JCR)

SPRING—During mild winters, spring migrants may begin arriving as early as mid- or late January. Flocks are often larger (on average) during spring than at other seasons. Numbers peak during February and early March and decline slowly until mid-April; most birds have departed by 15 April.

14, Union Co. CA, 2 Feb 1991 (TF, JD)
25, Horseshoe Lake CA, 15 Feb 1976 (BP)
1, Baldwin Lake, 19–20 Feb 1983 (JL, JM)
20, Perry Co., 6 Mar 1986 (TF)
5, Alexander Co., 16 Mar 1985 (JCR)
11, near Carrier Mills, Saline Co., 6 Apr 1989 (TF)
1, Union Co. CA, 6 May 1972 (VK)
1, Perry Co., 19–21 May 1986 (TF)

DOCUMENTATION: Written description—Horseshoe Lake CA, Alexander Co., 16 Dec 1989.

FIELD GUIDES: G=44; N=62; P=44.

[Bar-headed Goose *Anser indicus*]

STATUS AND ABUNDANCE: Hypothetical.

RECORDS AND REMARKS: A probable escape represents the only re-

gional record of this Asian species. Often raised domestically, so the probability that one encountered in the United States is an escapee is much greater than the chance that it is a true vagrant. Found with other flocks of geese near agricultural fields or reservoirs.
1, Crab Orchard NWR, 22 Dec 1961 (LB)

FIELD GUIDES: G=not pictured; N=90; P=302.

Snow Goose *Chen caerulescens*
Early October–Mid-December
Early February–Mid-April

STATUS AND ABUNDANCE: Fairly common migrant in the west; uncommon migrant in the east. Uncommon winter resident in the west; rare winter resident in the east. Locally common migrant and winter resident at Baldwin Lake.

HABITAT: Grazes in large grassy fields. Also forages on agricultural fields. Roosts on large lakes.

RECORDS AND REMARKS: The blue phase is usually more common than the white phase; ratios typically range from 1 blue:1 white to 2 blues:1 white. One white phase bird that had been tagged and dyed pink was present at Crab Orchard NWR on 12 October 1974; it had been captured and marked in August 1974 on Wrangel Island, Siberia (Frey 1975).
AUTUMN—The first Snow Geese arrive with the official onset of autumn, usually just after 20 September. Numbers build up for several weeks and then peak during November. Departure dates are difficult to discern because so many linger into early winter, and the timing of mass departure usually depends strongly on weather patterns.
1 (blue phase), Rend Lake, Jefferson Co., 26 Aug 1994 (TF)
1, Rend Lake, 17 Sep 1990 (LH)
3, Crab Orchard NWR, 26 Sep 1989 (BD)
3,100, Crab Orchard NWR, 18 Nov 1955 (LB)
WINTER—A sizable flock often winters at Baldwin Lake each year. A few may winter at other regional locations, with flocks of Canada Geese, but most depart for at least a few weeks.

1,000, Baldwin Lake, all winter 1983–1984 (RG)
3,000, Baldwin Lake, 11 Jan 1986 (RG)
SPRING—Large numbers stage at Ballard Co., Kentucky, during late January and early February; they often fly into Pulaski or Massac Cos. to forage. The majority depart northward by the end of February or early March.
2,500, Massac Co., 28 Jan 1989 (WDR)
6,000, Massac Co., 1 Feb 1986 (JCR)
2,000, Pulaski Co., 4 Feb 1991 (TF)
20,000 migrating, Ozark, Johnson Co., 13 Feb 1993 (TF)
2, Union Co. CA, 8 May 1971 (VK)
1, Sparta, Randolph Co., 21 May 1986 (TF)

DOCUMENTATION: Photograph—Union Co. CA, Union Co., 1 Nov 1980 (SIU AP-15).

FIELD GUIDES: G=44; N=64; P=42, 44.

Ross' Goose *Chen rossii*

Early November–Mid-December
Early February–Early April

STATUS AND ABUNDANCE: Rare migrant and winter resident.

HABITAT: Found in large fields, usually near reservoirs, with Snow Geese.

RECORDS AND REMARKS: This small goose species has been reported annually since 1983 at Baldwin Lake. Its occurrence there has prompted observers to carefully scrutinize all flocks of Snow Geese. Identification marks include its small size; the lack of a grin patch on the bill; the presence of a purplish, warty area at the base of the bill; the small, rounded head on a short, thick neck; and the lack of an ocher patch on the nape and hind neck. All records (more than thirty for the region) are of white-phase birds. Movement patterns closely follow those of Snow Geese, because Ross' Geese are almost always associated with them.
AUTUMN—2, Baldwin Lake, 3 Nov 1985 (DBe, m.ob.)
1–2, Baldwin Lake, 12–23 Nov 1984 (JCR, m.ob.)
imm., Rend Lake, Jefferson Co., 25 Nov 1988 (TF, WDR)
ad. and juv., Horseshoe Lake CA, 26 Nov 1956 (Smart 1960)

WINTER—ad., Baldwin Lake, 27 Nov 1986–22 Jan 1987 (TF, m.ob.)
imm., Union Co. CA, 20–23 Dec 1992 (TF, VK et al.)
1, Rend Lake, Jefferson Co., 23 Dec 1987 (TF, WDR)
3 ad., Baldwin Lake, 4 Jan 1986 (RG)
1–2, Baldwin Lake, 22 Jan–11 Feb 1983 (RG, m.ob.)
SPRING—ad., near Mermet, Massac Co., 28–29 Jan 1989 (WDR, BD)
2 ad., near Mermet, Massac Co., 1 Feb 1986 (JCR)
1, Pulaski Co., 4 Feb 1991 (TF)
1, Union Co. CA, 12 Feb 1991 (TF, JD, CW)
1 ad. blue phase, Union Co. CA, 12 Feb 1994 (TF)
1, Waltonville, Jefferson Co., 2 Mar 1988 (TF)
1, Alexander Co., 16–17 Mar 1985 (JCR)
2, near Carrier Mills, Saline Co., 6 Apr 1989 (TF)

DOCUMENTATION: Specimen—ad., Horseshoe Lake CA, Alexander Co., 26 Nov 1956 (GSma collection).

FIELD GUIDES: G=44; N=64; P=42.

Brant *Branta bernicla*

STATUS AND ABUNDANCE: Very rare visitor.

HABITAT: Usually found grazing in fields with other geese.

RECORDS AND REMARKS: This "sea goose" has occurred at least five times in the region within the last thirty years. It may occur more often than thought, but the combination of its physical similarity to and association with Canada Geese may make it quite difficult to detect.
AUTUMN—ad., Union Co. CA, 15 Oct 1976 (DT)
1, Crab Orchard NWR, 16 Dec 1985 (TF)
WINTER—1, Crab Orchard NWR, 19 and 31 Dec 1963 (Montgomery and Rice 1967)
ad., Union Co. CA, 23–24 Dec 1992 (VK, m.ob.)
SPRING—1, Baldwin Lake, 30 Mar–5 Apr 1987 (VH et al.)

DOCUMENTATION: Photograph—1, Crab Orchard NWR, Williamson Co., 16 Dec 1985 (SIU AP-17).

FIELD GUIDES: G=42; N=66; P=44.

Brant, Crab Orchard NWR, 16 December 1985

[Barnacle Goose *Branta leucopsis*]

STATUS AND ABUNDANCE: Hypothetical.

RECORDS AND REMARKS: One present at the Union Co. CA, on 3 Jan 1981 (VK et al.) associated with a flock of Snow Geese. This Old World species is unlikely to occur as a natural vagrant; most North American records are treated as probable escapes from captivity.

FIELD GUIDES: G=42; N=66; P=44.

Canada Goose *Branta canadensis*

Mid-September–Early April

STATUS AND ABUNDANCE: Common migrant and winter resident. Uncommon summer resident.

HABITAT: Reservoirs and agricultural areas, including grassy fields and pastures.

RECORDS AND REMARKS: Amasses in large flocks at the refuges at Rend Lake, Crab Orchard Lake, and Horseshoe Lake, and at the refuge in Union Co. Smaller flocks occur throughout the region, especially during migration. Migrant and winter flocks are composed principally of three subspecies: *B. c. interior* comprise 97 percent, *B. c. maxima* comprise 2.8 percent, and *B. c. hutchinsii* comprise 0.2 percent (Spitzkeit and Tacha 1986).

AUTUMN—First arrivals regularly occur in mid-September, but peak numbers do not move into the region until December. Weather strongly influences movements of these geese. During mild winters, many geese stay north, never reaching southern Illinois.

WINTER—Highest counts come from aerial surveys made by the IDOC. One of the highest counts was 515,000 in the southern Illinois quota zone during the winter of 1985–1986 (DT).

135,000, Crab Orchard NWR CBC, 19 Dec 1987
155,000, Horseshoe Lake CBC, 29 Dec 1977
132,000, Union Co. CBC, 30 Dec 1987

SPRING—Northward movements are dependent on weather and may begin as early as late January. Because of the large wintering population and daily, local movements to and from foraging areas, it is often difficult to detect truly migrational departures. Flocks flying at very high altitudes are probably migrants.

20,000, Sesser, Franklin Co., 1 Feb 1991 (WDR)

SUMMER—Canada Geese now breed in small numbers throughout the region. The subspecies is *B. c. maxima*. At least a few can be found on most reservoirs and on many strip-mine ponds. Bennett (1957) found seventeen nests and eighty-three young at Crab Orchard Lake between 1949 and 1952.

120, Baldwin Lake, 16 June 1985 (JCR)
98, s.e. Williamson Co., 14 July 1985 (JCR)

DOCUMENTATION: Specimen—ad. female, Crab Orchard NWR, Williamson Co., 29 Jan 1955 (SIU A-20).

FIELD GUIDES: G=42; N=66; P=44.

Wood Duck *Aix sponsa*

Late February–Mid-December

STATUS AND ABUNDANCE: Common migrant and summer resident. Rare winter resident.

HABITAT: Reservoirs, large wooded creeks, flooded bottomland forest, and swamps.

RECORDS AND REMARKS: The duck most likely to be encountered in forests. Woodies also forage in open water along the edges of reservoirs, where fairly sizable congregations may occur, especially during late summer and fall. In flight, these birds have a distinctive profile because of their long, rounded tail; they also give a distinctive *whoo-eek* call.

SPRING—Migration begins as soon as creeks and rivers thaw in February and continues into April, but departure dates are obscured by the large breeding population. Wood Ducks do not concentrate in large numbers like many other duck species; groups of less than fifty or so birds are commonplace.

6, Union Co. CA, 19 Feb 1989 (TF, JH, WDR)

SUMMER—Because this species nests in tree cavities, largest breeding populations occur in mature bottomland forests and swamps. Many also breed at lakes where artificial nest boxes have been erected. Nesting begins as early as March and extends into August.

158, Union Co. CA, 8 June 1982 (PK)

AUTUMN—Somewhat larger concentrations than those that occur in spring are noted during fall. Some August and early-September high counts are of local birds congregating in good habitat, not migrants. Migrants begin arriving by late September, and the majority of birds have passed through by late November; during warm Decembers, many may stay later.

200, Rend Lake, 25 Oct 1975 (BP)

613, Horseshoe Lake CBC, 18 Dec 1985

121, Union Co. CBC, 19 Dec 1985

WINTER—Few Wood Ducks overwinter in southern Illinois, but at least some are present each year. Some midwinter records may be of crippled birds.

pair, Rend Lake, 1 Jan 1992 (TF)

female, Carbondale, 22 Jan 1984 (JCR)

DOCUMENTATION: Specimen—ad. male, Crab Orchard NWR, Williamson Co., 1 Oct 1980 (SIU, uncatalogued).

FIELD GUIDES: G=52; N=78; P=50.

Green-winged Teal *Anas crecca*

Mid-August–Mid-December
Late February–Mid-April

STATUS AND ABUNDANCE: Fairly common migrant. Uncommon winter resident.

HABITAT: Mudflats and shallow-water areas of lakes and marshes.

RECORDS AND REMARKS: Forms tight flocks in flight, moving quickly and erratically, like shorebirds. Often walks on mudflats, also like shorebirds. Males in eclipse plumage and females resemble the Blue-winged Teal. Early-fall records, therefore, should be identified with care.

AUTUMN—A few early arrivals appear during August and September, but they do not become numerous until October. Numbers peak from mid-October to mid-November. Most have moved south by late December.

2, Carbondale, 11 Aug 1988 (WDR)
120, Rend Lake, 12 Oct 1987 (TF)
500, Crab Orchard NWR, 5 Nov 1989 (WDR)
1,000, Rend Lake, 12 Nov 1990 (TF)
700, Union Co. CA, 19 Dec 1990 (TF, WDR)
28, Crab Orchard NWR, 1 Jan 1985 (JCR)

WINTER—Most depart the region during winter, but in mild winters a few may overwinter on refuges with other ducks. Warm-water lakes attract some in most years.

17, Crab Orchard NWR, all winter 1986–1987 (WDR)
12, Baldwin Lake, all winter 1982–1983 (RG)

SPRING—Date of first arrivals depends on weather; some migrants begin appearing soon after the first thaw. Flocks are smaller, on average, in spring than during fall.

50, Union Co. CA, 12 Feb 1991 (TF, JD)
400, Rend Lake, 20 Mar 1976 (BP)
78, Crab Orchard NWR, 21 Mar 1984 (JCR)
7, Alexander Co., 1 May 1971 (VK, DH)
1, Rend Lake, 13 May 1987 (TF)

DOCUMENTATION: Specimen—female, Union Co., 6 Nov 1950 (SIU A-372).

FIELD GUIDES: G=50; N=70; P=52.

American Black Duck *Anas rubripes*
Early September–Early April

STATUS AND ABUNDANCE: Common migrant and winter resident. Very rare summer resident.

HABITAT: Shallow-water areas of reservoirs and marshes.

RECORDS AND REMARKS: Usually associated with Mallards, but may form small monospecific flocks. Far less numerous than Mallards, but still present in good numbers.
AUTUMN—Migration peaks late, usually in November and December, and extends into early January in some years.
1, Rend Lake, 24 Aug 1976 (BP)
1, Rend Lake, 24 Aug 1985 (RP)
558, Union Co. CBC, 19 Dec 1985
3,289, Crab Orchard NWR CBC, 27 Dec 1956
1,950, Rend Lake CBC, 31 Dec 1988
WINTER—Although regularly encountered throughout the region during winter, very few large aggregations have been reported.
150, Bay City, Pope Co., 7 Jan 1991 (TF)
160, Baldwin Lake, 10 Jan 1986 (WDR)
SPRING—Northward migration begins by mid-February in most years, but the presence of a winter population obscures detection of first arrivals. Apparently no high counts have been made for spring.
2, Rend Lake, 3 May 1988 (TF)
2, Union Co. CA, 8 May 1987 (VK)
1, Rend Lake, 18 May 1987 (TF)
SUMMER—Bennett (1952) found a nest at Crab Orchard NWR in 1952 and four young in 1950. Bennett's are the only breeding records for the region.
1, Union Co. CA, 15 June 1982 (PK)
3, Rend Lake, Franklin Co., 10 July 1971 (VK)
2, Union Co. CA, 17 July 1972 (VK, DH)

DOCUMENTATION: Specimen—female, Crab Orchard NWR, Williamson Co., 6 Nov 1957 (SIU A-543).

FIELD GUIDES: G=46; N=68; P=48.

Mallard *Anas platyrhynchos*
Early September–Late March

STATUS AND ABUNDANCE: Common migrant and winter resident. Uncommon summer resident.

HABITAT: Ponds, lakes, marshes, rivers, swamps, and flooded bottomland forest.

RECORDS AND REMARKS: The most numerous duck species in the region. It is often domesticated, and various hybrid forms and varieties can be found in parks and around farms; sometimes these odd ducks get mixed in with wild flocks as well. A Mallard and Northern Pintail hybrid was noted at Crab Orchard NWR on 1 February 1986 (SO). There are also several records of Mallard and American Black Duck hybrids, most of them bagged by hunters.

AUTUMN—Detection of fall arrivals is obscured by a breeding population. Sometimes occurs in huge flocks, especially where extensive shallow-water areas exist for resting and foraging. May also be seen foraging in agricultural fields on waste grains.
98,000, Crab Orchard NWR, 27–28 Nov 1955 (LB)
9,000, Crab Orchard NWR, 30 Nov 1983 (JCR)
8,957, Horseshoe Lake CBC, 18 Dec 1985
8,621, Union Co. CBC, 19 Dec 1985
30,000, Rend Lake CBC, 31 Dec 1988
5,000, Bay City, Pope Co., 7 Jan 1991 (TF)

WINTER—Large numbers may be present well into winter, but the majority of birds do not overwinter. The winter population depends on the severity of weather and availability of open water. Nevertheless, Mallards are commonly encountered throughout the entire region in a wide variety of wetland habitats.

SPRING—Migration begins by mid-February and extends into March. Apparently does not form flocks quite as large as those characteristic of fall migration.

SUMMER—Regularly breeds throughout the region at lakes, rivers, farm ponds, and even golf courses. Egg laying begins by early April (or sooner), and nesting continues at least through early August.

DOCUMENTATION: Specimen—ad. female, Crab Orchard NWR, Williamson Co., 5 Nov 1955 (SIU A-26).

FIELD GUIDES: G=46; N=68; P=48.

Northern Pintail *Anas acuta*
Mid-February–Mid-April
Mid-September–Late December

STATUS AND ABUNDANCE: Fairly common migrant. Uncommon winter resident. Very rare summer visitor.

HABITAT: Lakes, marshes, and flooded fields.

RECORDS AND REMARKS: Graceful, slender ducks that may fly in V-formations high in the sky when migrating. They are generally found in shallow water, but migrants may rest in deep water. They also sometimes forage for waste corn in harvested fields.

AUTUMN—Fall migration peaks during November and December; largest concentrations have been reported from Christmas Bird Counts.

1, Rend Lake, 15 Aug 1976 (BP)
10, Crab Orchard NWR, 22 Aug 1970 (VK)
7, Crab Orchard NWR, 16 Sep 1983 (JCR)
1,654, Horseshoe Lake CBC, 18 Dec 1985
450, Union Co. CBC, 19 Dec 1985
WINTER—As with other dabblers, the winter pintail population is influenced by weather and availability of open water. A few occur at warm-water lakes or sewage lagoons in most years.
200, Bay City, Pope Co., 9 Jan 1991 (TF)
30, Crab Orchard NWR, 15 Jan 1987 (WDR)
SPRING—Very early migrants, pintails may arrive as early as late January, but mid-February is more typical. Although few high counts have been published for the region, the northern pintail is one of the few duck species that is generally more numerous in spring than in fall.
14, Crab Orchard NWR, 12 Feb 1983 (JCR)
100, Union Co. CA, 19 Feb 1989 (TF, JH, WDR)
1, Union Co. CA, 11 May 1987 (VK)
SUMMER—female, Crab Orchard NWR, June 1950 (JWH)
eclipse male, s. Alexander Co., 12 July 1986 (TF, WDR)

DOCUMENTATION: Specimen—male, Crab Orchard NWR, Williamson Co., 19 Oct 1958 (SIU A-731).

FIELD GUIDES: G=48; N=72; P=50.

Blue-winged Teal *Anas discors*

Early March–Mid-May
Early August–Late November

STATUS AND ABUNDANCE: Common migrant. Rare winter visitor.
Rare summer resident.

HABITAT: Marshes, mudflats, shallow lakes, and ponds.

RECORDS AND REMARKS: When in flight, this small dabbler forms
tight flocks that twist and turn like flocks of shorebirds. The blue
wing patches of the males are conspicuous. The males lose their
white facial crescent during summer and fall, which can make
identification of resting birds somewhat difficult. The whistled call
note is distinctive.
SPRING—Arrives later than most dabblers, well after the first
spring thaw. Numbers peak during late March and April. Some
regularly linger into mid-May.
4, Carbondale, 27 Feb 1986 (WDR)
2, Rend Lake, 2 Mar 1988 (TF)
275, Rend Lake, 20 Mar 1976 (BP)
225, Alexander Co., 24 Apr 1984 (TF)
6, Sparta, Randolph Co., 21 May 1986 (TF)
SUMMER—Breeding records come from shallow ponds, such as
some strip-mine ponds, where emergent vegetation is present. Some
summer records are probably of nonbreeding birds.
pair with yg., Oakwood Bottoms, 3–4 June 1977 (MMo)
pair, Rend Lake, Jefferson Co., 7 June 1986 (WDR)
2 males, East Cape Girardeau, Alexander Co., 8 June 1985 (JCR)
ad. and 5 yg., s.w. Jackson Co., 20 June 1973 (VK, DH)
ad. and 4 yg., n. Randolph Co., 24 June 1989 (WDR)
male, s.w. Jackson Co., 29 June 1985 (JCR)
3 ad. and 8 yg., n. Randolph Co., 3 July 1985 (TF, JCR)
2 broods, s.w. Jackson Co., June/July 1993 (TF)
AUTUMN—A few early migrants characteristically appear during
July, but good numbers of birds do not begin arriving until August.
Seems to occur in larger groups in fall than during spring. Tight
flocks sometimes rest in deep water of large lakes, especially during
inclement weather.
eclipse male, Willard, Alexander Co., 8 July 1989 (WDR, JH, EW)
1, Jackson Co., 11 July 1976 (BP)

1, Rend Lake, 28 July 1987 (KM)
1, Alexander Co., 30 July 1983 (JCR)
400, Crab Orchard NWR, 31 Aug 1950 (LB)
3,000, Crab Orchard NWR, late Sep 1954 (LB)
450, Crab Orchard NWR, 1 Oct 1976 (BP)
3, Crab Orchard NWR, 30 Nov 1983 (JCR)
WINTER—Nearly all Blue-wings have departed for their wintering grounds by 1 December. There are some later departure records, however, mostly from Christmas Bird Counts. Overwintering has not been confirmed.
female, Union Co. CA, 19 Dec 1984 (VK)
2, Horseshoe Lake CBC, 30 Dec 1974
4, Union Co., 3 Jan 1987 (VK, TF, WDR)
1, Union Co. CA, 7 Jan 1986 (WDR)
DOCUMENTATION: Specimen—ad. female, 6.5 miles w. of Murphysboro, Jackson Co., 11 Apr 1957 (SIU A-44).
FIELD GUIDES: G=50; N=74; P=52.

Cinnamon Teal *Anas cyanoptera*

STATUS AND ABUNDANCE: Very rare visitor.

HABITAT: Occurs in shallow water with other dabbling ducks.

RECORDS AND REMARKS: There are two records. An adult male was at Horseshoe Lake CA on 23 March 1970 (HDB; *AFN* 24:614). Another was photographed at Rend Lake, Jefferson Co., on 5 April 1994 (TF). This species from western North America occurs as a vagrant, often with flocks of Blue-winged Teal in shallow marshy habitats.

FIELD GUIDES: G=48; N=74; P=52.

Northern Shoveler *Anas clypeata*

Late August–Late December
Late February–Very Early May

STATUS AND ABUNDANCE: Common migrant. Uncommon winter resident.

HABITAT: Marshes and shallow lakes.

RECORDS AND REMARKS: The spatulate bill of these ducks makes them truly unmistakable. The males are boldly patterned in green, white, and chestnut when in their breeding colors, but their plumage resembles the brown plumage of the female at other times. Shovelers have blue wing patches, like Blue-winged Teal, so identification of flying birds should be made with care. Shovelers often forage in social groups, bunching together and whisking their heads from side to side in the water, and sometimes even spinning in circles like phalaropes.
AUTUMN—Migrants arrive early, with peak numbers passing through from mid-October to mid-November. Some linger each year until freeze-up forces them south.
3, Rend Lake, 16 Aug 1989 (WDR)
2, Crab Orchard NWR, 21 Aug 1987 (WDR)
120, Horseshoe Lake CA, 23 Nov 1993 (KM)
200, Union Co. CBC, 30 Dec 1977
WINTER—As long as shallow-water areas are unfrozen, at least a few try to overwinter each year, but groups are generally small and locally distributed.
55, Crab Orchard NWR, 1–7 Jan 1989 (BD, WDR)
25, Crab Orchard NWR, 20 Jan 1989 (WDR)
SPRING—First arrivals appear soon after the first February thaw. Numbers peak from late March through the first few days of May. Some birds regularly linger past the Spring Bird Count period of early May.
125, Horseshoe Lake CA, 8 Feb 1975 (BP)
2, Crab Orchard NWR, 12 Feb 1984 (SS)
500, Rend Lake, 20 Mar 1976 (BP)
142, Crab Orchard NWR, 5 Apr 1984 (JCR)
100, Crab Orchard NWR, 11 May 1954 (LB)
1, Rend Lake, 14 May 1976 (BP)
1, Crab Orchard NWR, 14 May 1984 (JCR)

DOCUMENTATION: Specimen—male, 3 miles e. of Carbondale, Jackson Co., 15 Apr 1957 (SIU A-378).
FIELD GUIDES: G=50; N=74; P=52.

Gadwall *Anas strepera*
Late September–Mid-December
Mid-February–Early May

STATUS AND ABUNDANCE: Common migrant. Fairly common winter resident.

HABITAT: Ponds, lakes, marshes, and other shallow-water areas.

RECORDS AND REMARKS: One of the most beautiful of all ducks; the male's breeding plumage can be truly appreciated only at close distances. It is intricately patterned with black, gray, and white and has chestnut wing coverts and white secondaries. The white secondary patch is a distinctive fieldmark for flying birds of both sexes. Gadwalls often associate with other dabbler species. They are a common migrant, but flocks generally do not exceed a few hundred individuals in size.

AUTUMN—Migration is not fully underway until late September, but a few individuals may arrive as early as August. They usually aggregate in shallow water for foraging, but they sometimes rest in large flocks on deep water of large lakes.

1, Rend Lake, Jefferson Co., 13 Aug 1987 (TF)
female, Carbondale, 15 Aug 1988 (WDR)
2, Crab Orchard NWR, 10 Sep 1982 (JCR)
195, Crab Orchard NWR, 17 Oct 1984 (JCR)
150, Rend Lake, 30 Oct 1987 (TF)
400, Union Co. CA, 16 Nov 1975 (BP)
398, Horseshoe Lake CBC, 18 Dec 1990

WINTER—Present nearly every winter in good numbers, as long as open water is available. Especially often found on warm-water lakes and sewage treatment ponds that do not freeze.

178, Union Co. CBC, 31 Dec 1987
88, Horseshoe Lake CA, 7 Jan 1972 (VK, DH)

SPRING—The influx of spring migrants is obscured by the wintering population. Some individuals linger late into the period of the Spring Bird Count period or later.

150, Carbondale, 10 Feb 1989 (WDR)
62, Crab Orchard NWR, 21 Mar 1983 (JCR)
5, Unionville, Massac Co., 7 May 1988 (WDR)
1, Rend Lake, 14 May 1987 (TF)
2, Crab Orchard NWR, 23 May 1983 (JCR)
1, Crab Orchard NWR, 26 May 1987 (WDR)

DOCUMENTATION: Specimen—ad. female, near Carrier Mills, Saline Co., 28 Oct 1955 (SIU A-37).

FIELD GUIDES: G=48; N=70; P=48.

American Wigeon *Anas americana*
Mid-September–Mid-December
Mid-February–Late April

STATUS AND ABUNDANCE: Fairly common migrant. Uncommon winter resident.

HABITAT: Shallow lakes and ponds.

RECORDS AND REMARKS: Often called Baldpate by hunters because of the male's white crown patch. Wigeon are usually found in small groups of two to twenty birds, although flocks may reach into the hundreds on some occasions, especially during autumn. In flight they are easily recognized by the large white patches on the leading edge of their wings. They utter a distinctive, whistled call note.
AUTUMN—A few arrive during August in some years, but a more typical arrival date is during mid-September. Numbers peak during November and slowly diminish as winter sets in. Most birds depart for the winter, but many will stay as long as open, shallow water is available.
3, Rend Lake, 14 Aug 1976 (BP)
3, Rend Lake, Jefferson Co., 19 Aug 1989 (TF, BD, WDR)
100, Rend Lake, Jefferson Co., 30 Oct 1987 (TF)
450, Baldwin Lake, 5 Dec 1981 (RK)
210, Union Co. CBC, 19 Dec 1984
WINTER—Winter concentrations are usually small, but many may gather at warm-water lakes and sewage treatment ponds.
100, Baldwin Lake, all winter 1983–1984 (RG)
SPRING—The arrival of the earliest migrants is obscured by a small winter population. Wigeon often associate with other species of dabblers; they do not usually occur in large, pure flocks.
30, Crab Orchard NWR, 7 Feb 1987 (WDR)
49, Jackson Co., 25 Mar 1984 (TF, JCR)
4, Rend Lake, Jefferson Co., 8 May 1987 (TF)
male, Union Co. CA, 11 May 1987 (VK)
2, Rend Lake, 14 May 1976 (BP)

DOCUMENTATION: Specimen—ad. male, Crab Orchard NWR, Williamson Co., 28 Jan 1955 (SIU, uncatalogued).

FIELD GUIDES: G=48; N=72; P=50.

Canvasback *Aythya valisineria*
Early November–Late December
Mid-February–Early April

STATUS AND ABUNDANCE: Fairly common migrant. Uncommon winter resident. Very rare summer visitor.

HABITAT: Lakes and rivers.

RECORDS AND REMARKS: A diving duck with a long, sloping forehead that lends it a distinctive profile even when viewed from great distances. "Cans" have experienced recent population declines, which have warranted special attention from conservation groups. They may forage and rest in the middle of deep-water lakes or come in close to shore.

AUTUMN—Often form large, tightly packed flocks (rafts) in the middle of large lakes, where they rest and forage.
1, Crab Orchard NWR, 29 Oct 1983 (JCR)
376, Crab Orchard NWR CBC, 17 Dec 1983
1,000, Rend Lake, 18 Dec 1976 (MMo)
1,300, Rend Lake, 31 Dec 1975 (BP)
701, Crab Orchard NWR CBC, 31 Dec 1977

WINTER—In many years, there are only two or three weeks between the departure of the latest fall migrants and the arrival of the earliest spring migrants. During mild winters, it is sometimes difficult to tell whether birds are northbound, southbound, or wintering.

SPRING—A few migrants appear during the first thaw (or "false spring") of January, but migration is not typically fully underway until February.
10, Carbondale, 12 Jan 1990, but 175 there on 19 Jan 1990 (BD)
1, Harrisburg, Saline Co., 21 Jan 1991 (JD)
500, Crab Orchard NWR, 20 Feb 1983 (JCR)
1, East Cape Girardeau, Alexander Co., 8 May 1972 (PK)
male, Union Co. CA, 11 May 1987 (VK)
1, Carbondale, 13 May 1984 (TF)
SUMMER—male, s.w. Jackson Co., 3 July 1973 (DH)

DOCUMENTATION: Provisional acceptance.

FIELD GUIDES: G=54; N=78; P=58.

Redhead *Aythya americana*

Late October–Late December
Mid-February–Early April

STATUS AND ABUNDANCE: Fairly common migrant. Rare winter resident. Very rare summer visitor.

HABITAT: Lakes and rivers.

RECORDS AND REMARKS: Similar in plumage to the Canvasback, this diver has a very rounded head and a two-tone (black-and-gray) bill. Small groups mingle with Canvasbacks and scaup. Populations have apparently declined dramatically in recent years.

AUTUMN—Generally do not occur in large numbers during fall migration. The first arrivals appear late in the season, usually after 20 October. A few may linger into early January, but most have departed by the end of December.

9, Crab Orchard NWR, 14 Oct 1983 (JCR)
60, Rend Lake, 30 Dec 1986 (WDR)

WINTER—Very few are present during the first three weeks of January, even on warm-water lakes. Because spring migration can begin very early, there often seems to be a few present all winter, but only a handful of individuals actually overwinter.

SPRING—Northbound migrants arrive very early in some years, right after the first January thaw. They appear in much larger flocks in spring than during fall. Peak numbers pass through during March. Most have departed by 10 April, but a few typically straggle behind.

2, Rend Lake, 19 Jan 1986 (SO)
70, Rend Lake, 12 Feb 1984 (JCR)
115, Crab Orchard NWR, 20 Feb 1983 (JCR)
800, Carbondale, 26 Feb 1949 (RB)
240, Carbondale, 2 Mar 1973 (VK)
250, Rend Lake, 5 Mar 1988 (TF)
1, Crab Orchard NWR, 14 May 1984 (JCR)
1, Crab Orchard NWR, 19 May 1970 (VK, DH)
SUMMER—male, s.w. Jackson Co., 1 June 1973 (DH)
male, Rend Lake, Jefferson Co., 27 June 1994 (TF)

DOCUMENTATION: Specimen—male, Crab Orchard NWR, Williamson Co., 11 Oct 1957 (SIU A-721).

FIELD GUIDES: G=54; N=78; P=58.

Ring-necked Duck *Aythya collaris*
Early October–Late December
Mid-February–Early May

STATUS AND ABUNDANCE: Common migrant. Uncommon winter resident. Very rare summer visitor.

HABITAT: Ponds, lakes, marshes, swamps, and rivers.

RECORDS AND REMARKS: Occurs in deep, open water of lakes and rivers, with other diving ducks, but also frequents shallow areas where stumps and standing trees are present. Frequently visits small ponds, especially those in grasslands or pastures.
AUTUMN—Arrives earlier than most other divers. Lingers well into winter when water conditions are favorable. The departure of migrants is difficult to detect because of the presence of wintering birds.
4, Crab Orchard NWR, 1 Oct 1984 (JCR)
625, Rend Lake, 18 Nov 1989 (BD, WDR)
500, Crab Orchard NWR, 23 Nov 1983 (JCR)
3,065, Rend Lake CBC, 18 Dec 1993
400, Rend Lake, 23 Dec 1987 (TF, WDR)
312, Union Co. CBC, 3 Jan 1987
WINTER—Overwinters in moderate numbers, especially on warm-water lakes and sewage treatment ponds and in unfrozen swamps, such as Horseshoe Lake CA. Less numerous in the Till Plain and east than elsewhere.
SPRING—Migration normally begins in mid-February, but a few birds appear as early as late January in some years. Some linger into the period of the Spring Bird Count period each year.
86, Horseshoe Lake CA, 25 Jan 1973 (VK)
300, Rend Lake, 10 Feb 1991 (TF, m.ob.)
250, Crab Orchard NWR, 17 Feb 1984 (PH)
400 on 1 pond, Crab Orchard NWR, 27 Feb–1 Mar 1986 (WDR)
2,000, Rend Lake, 5 Mar 1988 (TF)
male, Mermet Lake CA, 7–13 May 1988 (WDR, RP)
male, Union Co. CA, 11 May 1987 (VK)
male, Carbondale, 22 May 1989 (WDR)
SUMMER—There are at least four records of individual males or pairs lingering into the summer, but there is no definite evidence of breeding.

2 males, Crab Orchard NWR, 20 May–30 June 1987 (WDR)
2 pairs, s.w. Jackson Co., 1 June 1973 (DH)
pair, East Cape Girardeau, Alexander Co., 4 and 14 June 1975 (VK)
male, Union Co. CA, 28 July 1990 (WDR)

Documentation: Specimen—imm. female, Crab Orchard NWR,
Williamson Co., 30 Oct 1957 (SIU, uncatalogued).

Field Guides: G=54; N=80; P=58.

Greater Scaup *Aythya marila*
Early November–Mid-December
Late February–Late March

Status and abundance: Occasional migrant. Rare winter resident.

Habitat: Large lakes and rivers.

Records and remarks: Sometimes associates with the more common and very similar Lesser Scaup, but usually acts independently with its own species. Identification can be difficult at a distance but is straightforward in good light and at close range. See Kaufman (1990) for a discussion of fieldmarks. Recorded nearly every year now, they may be increasing in numbers; although increased observer confidence in separating Greaters from Lessers may better explain the recent surge in reports.
AUTUMN—First arrivals appear with the early November influx of diving ducks. They tend to be present in small, usually irregular numbers throughout the fall and winter.
2, Crab Orchard NWR, 31 Oct 1984 (JCR)
1, Carbondale, 5–17 Nov 1984 (TF)
1, Crab Orchard NWR, 12 Nov 1975 (BP)
5, Rend Lake, 15 Dec 1991 (WDR)
1, Union Co. CA, 18 Dec 1983 (JCR)
WINTER—Wintering birds are difficult to distinguish from migrants. Fall migration may extend even into early January in some years, and northbound spring migrants may appear during late January.
1, Lake Murphysboro, 26 Dec 1953–3 Jan 1954 (RB)
2–7, Crab Orchard NWR, 24 Dec 1986–24 Jan 1987 (WDR)

female, Union Co. CA, 5 Jan 1987 (WDR)

2, Carbondale, 10–12 Jan 1985 (SO, TF)

SPRING—The appearance of small flocks from late January to early March indicates that spring migration is underway. Some small flocks appear as soon as the first patches of open water become available in January. Recent sightings have involved flocks of unprecedented size.

10, Rend Lake, 17 Jan–1 Feb 1976 (BP, MMo)

63, Crab Orchard NWR, 21–22 Jan 1989 (TF, WDR)

85, Rend Lake, Franklin Co., 9 Feb 1992 (TF, JD)

92, Rend Lake, Franklin Co., 10 Feb 1991 (TF, BD, WDR)

5, Crab Orchard NWR, 21 Feb 1987 (WDR)

31, Crab Orchard NWR, 1 Mar 1986 (WDR)

3 females, Crab Orchard NWR, 27 Apr 1985 (JCR)

female, s.w. Jackson Co., 29 Apr 1985 (KR)

DOCUMENTATION: Written description—63, Crab Orchard NWR, Williamson Co., 21–22 Jan 1989.

FIELD GUIDES: G=54; N=80; P=58.

Lesser Scaup *Aythya affinis*

Early October–Mid-December

Mid-February–Late April

STATUS AND ABUNDANCE: Common migrant. Fairly common winter resident. Very rare summer visitor.

HABITAT: Lakes and ponds.

RECORDS AND REMARKS: Forms large flocks in the middle of large lakes during migration. Also occurs in smaller numbers on ponds and marshes.

AUTUMN—Tends to arrive somewhat earlier than most other divers, usually beginning in the first few days of October. Numbers peak from late October through mid-November and then decline rapidly. The winter population obscures the departure of the last migrants.

50, Rend Lake, 29 Sep 1987 (TF)

3,730, Crab Orchard NWR, 28 Oct 1984 (JCR)

3,000, Rend Lake, Franklin Co., 29 Oct 1988 (JH, WDR)

4,650, Crab Orchard NWR, 4 Nov 1960 (LB)
68, Horseshoe Lake CBC, 18 Dec 1985
WINTER—Present on warm-water lakes each year in variable numbers. Can be very scarce at times.
128, Murphysboro CBC, 27 Dec 1948
52, Union Co. CBC, 2 Jan 1976
75, Baldwin Lake, 10 Jan 1986 (WDR)
SPRING—The first northbound migrants appear early, right after the first thaw, but migration is not really into full swing until February. Peak numbers occur during March, and a few birds linger into May each year.
30, Rend Lake, 17 Jan 1991 (TF, JD)
125, Crab Orchard NWR, 20 Feb 1983 (JCR)
1,000, Rend Lake, 6 Mar 1987 (TF)
14,000, Crab Orchard NWR, 16 Mar 1955 (LB)
2,630, Crab Orchard NWR, 11 Apr 1985 (JCR)
male, Union Co. CA, 11 May 1987 (VK)
18, Rend Lake, 14 May 1976 (BP)
SUMMER—There are at least four records of one to two birds lingering into summer.
male, Union Co. CA, 3 June 1992 (TRR, WDR)
2 males, near Gorham, Jackson Co., 20 June 1973 (DH)
male, Mermet Lake CA, 4 July 1988 (WDR)
1 (possibly crippled), Rend Lake, 16 July 1976 (BP)

DOCUMENTATION: Specimen—male, Crab Orchard NWR, Williamson Co., 23 Oct 1958 (SIU A-712).

FIELD GUIDES: G=54; N=80; P=58.

King Eider *Somateria spectabilis*

STATUS AND ABUNDANCE: Very rare visitor.

RECORDS AND REMARKS: Two females and an immature male were taken at Rend Lake, Jefferson Co., in November 1973 (HP).

DOCUMENTATION: Specimen—imm. male, Rend Lake, Jefferson Co., Nov 1973 (HP collection).

FIELD GUIDES: G=58; N=82; P=56.

Oldsquaw *Clangula hyemalis*

Early November–Early April

STATUS AND ABUNDANCE: Rare migrant and winter resident.

HABITAT: Large reservoirs.

RECORDS AND REMARKS: This diver sometimes associates with flocks of Common Goldeneye, but just as often it seems to act independently of any nearby ducks. All records come from western portions of the region, at the large lakes. There is apparently considerable movement even during the middle of winter, so designation of some records to particular seasons can be difficult. Most records are distributed from mid-December to mid-January, which suggests that a few birds wander through the region in search of open water ahead of advancing cold weather. Records from late January through early April have been considered spring migrants.
AUTUMN—2, Crab Orchard NWR, 31 Oct 1959 (LB)
male found dead, Cairo, Alexander Co., 11 Dec 1961 (SIU, uncatalogued specimen)
1, Horseshoe Lake CA, 17 Dec 1991 (SKR)
female, Crab Orchard NWR, 18 Dec 1983 (TF)
1, Crab Orchard NWR, 28 Dec 1970 (DH)
WINTER—pair, Crab Orchard NWR, 20 Dec 1985–4 Mar 1986 (TF, WDR)
1–2, Rend Lake, Franklin Co., 31 Dec 1988–15 Jan 1989 (DY, m.ob.)
female, Crab Orchard NWR, 13 Jan 1990 (BD)
SPRING—2, Crab Orchard NWR, 31 Jan 1993 (TF)
7, Baldwin Lake, 19 Feb 1983 (*SR* 36:5)
pair, Crab Orchard NWR, 25 Mar–2 Apr 1951 (LB)
female, Crab Orchard NWR, 29 Mar 1990 (BD)

DOCUMENTATION: Specimen—ad. female, Crab Orchard NWR, Williamson Co., 10 Nov 1959 (SIU A-859).

FIELD GUIDES: G=60; N=86; P=56.

Black Scoter *Melanitta nigra*

Late October–Mid-December

STATUS AND ABUNDANCE: Very rare fall migrant.

HABITAT: Large lakes and ponds.

RECORDS AND REMARKS: This distinctive diving duck typically winters on the Atlantic and Pacific Coasts of North America; it migrates to and from the coasts well to the north of southern Illinois. Some regularly pass through the Great Lakes region. There are at least seven records for the southern Illinois region, all from fall.

AUTUMN—imm. male, Crab Orchard NWR, 23 Oct 1958 (SIU)
female, Rend Lake, 4 Nov 1974 (HP)
female, Waltonville, Jefferson Co., 12 Nov–2 Dec 1990 (TF, m.ob.)
2, Rend Lake, Franklin Co., 19 Nov 1993 (TF)
2, Crab Orchard NWR, 2 Dec 1984 (JCR)
1, Rend Lake, 5–13 Dec 1975 (BP)
1, Rend Lake, Franklin Co., 18 Dec 1993 (WDR)

DOCUMENTATION: Specimen—imm. male, Crab Orchard NWR, Williamson Co., 23 Oct 1958 (SIU A-722).

FIELD GUIDES: G=60; N=84; P=54.

Surf Scoter *Melanitta perspicillata*

Late October–Mid-November
Late April–Late May

STATUS AND ABUNDANCE: Rare fall migrant. Very rare winter visitor and spring migrant.

HABITAT: Large lakes, ponds.

RECORDS AND REMARKS: Sometimes associates with flocks of other divers, such as Lesser Scaup. All records except those for spring are of immatures or females. This scoter migrates mostly north of Illinois to winter on the ocean coasts, so very few pass through the region.

AUTUMN—Most regional records are from autumn, and they tend to be highly clumped in the four weeks between 15 October and 15 November.

5, Carbondale, 18 Oct 1989 (BD)
1, Carbondale, 21 Oct 1985 (SO)
4, Rend Lake, Jefferson Co., 26 Oct 1987 (TF)
1, Crab Orchard NWR, 30 Oct 1957 (LB)

1, Carbondale, 6–7 Nov 1988 (WDR, m.ob.)
1, Crab Orchard NWR, 11 Nov 1990 (BD)
14, Rend Lake, Franklin Co., 19 Nov 1993 (TF)
WINTER—December records may be late migrants, but more records are needed to clarify the patterns.
3, Crab Orchard NWR, 2 Dec 1984 (JCR)
1, Crab Orchard NWR, 19–24 Dec 1987 (TF, WDR)
1, Union Co. CA, 22 Dec 1994 (HDB et al.)
SPRING—Very few records; pass through unusually late for a duck.
male, Carbondale, 21–26 Apr 1991 (BD)
1, Carbondale, 23–31 May 1977 (MMo)

DOCUMENTATION: Photograph—Carbondale, Jackson Co., 21 Apr 1991 (TF).

FIELD GUIDES: G=60; N=84; P=54.

White-winged Scoter *Melanitta fusca*

Early November–Early December
Late January–Mid-March

STATUS AND ABUNDANCE: Rare migrant.

HABITAT: Lakes and large ponds.

RECORDS AND REMARKS: Seem to act independently of other ducks, but may associate with divers or dabblers in good habitat or when resting in the middle of large lakes. The white wing patch helps identify this duck in flight, even at a long distance. Like the other two scoter species, White-wings winter on the ocean coasts and breed at high latitudes, so migration takes these birds far north of southern Illinois. At present, there are no winter records; spring migrants begin arriving during late winter, just after the first warming spell.
AUTUMN—1, Rend Lake, Franklin Co., 29 Oct 1988 (TF)
1 shot, Crab Orchard NWR, 3 Nov 1950 (verified by LB)
2, Carbondale, 10–13 Nov 1984 (TF)
1, Crab Orchard NWR, 26 Nov 1986 (WDR)
SPRING—imm., Rend Lake, Franklin Co., 17 Jan 1992 (TF, BD, JD)
1, Crab Orchard NWR, 19–25 Jan 1986 (TF)

1–4, Crab Orchard NWR, 29 Jan–16 Feb 1971 (DH)
4, Crab Orchard NWR, 24 Feb 1986 (SO)
1, Crab Orchard NWR, 25 Feb–17 Mar 1989 (BD)

DOCUMENTATION: Photograph—Carbondale, Jackson Co., 13 Nov 1984 (SIU AP-24).

FIELD GUIDES: G=60; N=84; P=54.

Common Goldeneye *Bucephala clangula*

Mid-November–Early April

STATUS AND ABUNDANCE: Common migrant and winter resident.

HABITAT: Large lakes, ponds, and rivers.

RECORDS AND REMARKS: These strikingly patterned diving ducks are highly gregarious. Next to Mallards, they are the most likely duck to occur on a body of water, small or large, during winter. As they fly overhead, their wings make a characteristic whirring sound. The male performs a humorous courting display for the female by suddenly extending his neck upward and then quickly throwing his head back until it touches his back.

AUTUMN—Arrives late in fall, rarely forming large groups. Movement occurs all winter, but the bulk of migration seems to end by mid- or late December.
1, Rend Lake, Franklin Co., 29 Oct 1988 (WDR)
15, Carbondale, 30 Oct 1970 (VK)
65, Crab Orchard NWR, 26 Nov 1986 (WDR)
160, Crab Orchard NWR CBC, 17 Dec 1983

WINTER—During many winters, there are only two or three weeks when the winter goldeneye population is relatively stable. At other times, there are constant arrivals and departures, which can be difficult to ascribe to a particular season. Warm-water lakes often have the largest winter numbers.
299, Rend Lake CBC, 31 Dec 1988
200, Baldwin Lake, 2 Jan 1984 (TF)

SPRING—Because many birds stay as far north as possible during the winter, the passage of birds that wintered south of our region peaks very early. As soon as lakes begin thawing, goldeneyes move in. Peak regional counts are probably of northbound migrants at

the southern edge of the freeze line, "waiting" for lakes to the north to thaw.
1,000, Rend Lake, Franklin Co., 15 Jan 1989 (TF, BD, WDR)
2,200, Rend Lake, 17 Jan 1991 (TF, JD)
female, near Gorham, Jackson Co., 9 Apr 1972 (VK)
imm. male, Rend Lake, Jefferson Co., 6 May 1988 (TF)
ad. male, Mermet Lake CA, 6 May 1989 (WDR)
SUMMER—injured female, Cache River, Alexander Co., 22 June 1973 (VK, DH)

DOCUMENTATION: Specimen—ad. male, Crab Orchard NWR, Williamson Co., 28 Jan 1955 (SIU A-85).

FIELD GUIDES: G=56; N=86; P=60.

[Barrow's Goldeneye *Bucephala islandica*]

STATUS AND ABUNDANCE: Hypothetical.

RECORDS AND REMARKS: Two records from Crab Orchard NWR have been reported: 1 male, 10 Mar 1967; and 1 male, 11 Mar 1957 (George 1968). Although the records are probably correct, no documentary evidence was obtained. See Tobish (1986) for identification details.

FIELD GUIDES: G=56; N=86; P=60.

Bufflehead *Bucephala albeola*

Early November–Mid-December
Mid-February–Mid-April

STATUS AND ABUNDANCE: Common migrant. Uncommon winter resident.

HABITAT: Ponds and lakes.

RECORDS AND REMARKS: Small divers, these ducks are found in groups of up to one hundred birds. Typical flock size, however, is usually two to thirty birds. The males have a striking black-and-white plumage; the head has a large white ear patch that extends all the way to the back of the head. Males are superficially similar to Hooded Mergansers, but they lack the black border to the white head patch and the rusty barring on the sides of the merganser.

AUTUMN—The first migrants usually arrive during the first few days of November, occasionally earlier. Numbers peak from mid-November to early December. Most fall migrants have departed the region by mid-December, but some regularly linger later.

5, Crab Orchard NWR, 30 Oct 1985 (TF)
81, Crab Orchard NWR, 30 Nov 1983 (JCR)
80, Crab Orchard NWR, 6 Dec 1984 (JCR)
30, Crab Orchard NWR CBC, 17 Dec 1983

WINTER—Occurs locally in small numbers throughout winter, especially at warm-water lakes and sewage ponds.

2, Baldwin Lake, 2 Jan 1984 (TF)
42, Carbondale, 12 Jan 1985 (JCR)

SPRING—Some arrive after the first significant spring thaw, but migration does not peak until late March. Most have departed by 15 April. Seem to use ponds, even small farm ponds, more often during spring than in fall.

30, Crab Orchard NWR, 7 Feb 1987 (WDR)
95, Crab Orchard NWR, 5 Apr 1984 (JCR)
2, Carbondale, 23 Apr 1986 (WDR)
2, Sparta, Randolph Co., 29 Apr 1986 (TF)

DOCUMENTATION: Specimen—female, Carbondale, Jackson Co., 23 Nov 1937 (SIU A-1929).

FIELD GUIDES: G=56; N=86; P=60.

Hooded Merganser *Lophodytes cucullatus*
Early November–Late March

STATUS AND ABUNDANCE: Common migrant. Fairly common winter resident. Rare summer resident.

HABITAT: Lakes, rivers, swamps, wooded ponds, and creeks.

RECORDS AND REMARKS: Generally the mergansers that occur in small flocks, Hoodeds are unusually common at some localities in southern Illinois. They regularly occur in big numbers at Crab Orchard Lake. "Hoodies" form large, loose flocks; they usually spread out along the shore of a bay and forage in shallow water for small fish.

AUTUMN—First arrivals appear around 1 November, sometimes during the last few days of October. Numbers peak during November. Because of the presence of a winter population, latest departure of migrants is difficult to assess. Most of the southbound migrants are probably gone by late December, but some may linger as long as open water is available.

155, Crab Orchard NWR, 29 Oct 1988 (JH, WDR)
750, Crab Orchard NWR, 18 Nov 1989 (BD, WDR)
400, Crab Orchard NWR, 30 Nov 1960 (LB)
240, Crab Orchard NWR, 24 Dec 1987 (WDR)

WINTER—At some sites, winter numbers can be as high as the numbers during migration.

50, Baldwin Lake, 2 Jan 1984 (TF)
310, Crab Orchard NWR, 10 Jan 1989 (BD, WDR)
100, Crab Orchard NWR, 24 Jan 1987 (WDR)

SPRING—Migrants arrive soon after the first thaw. Large groups are not common, because many birds are paired and ready to begin breeding. Some northbound migrants may occur as late as mid-April, but the presence of a breeding population obscures the status of sightings in spring.

13, Crab Orchard NWR, 3 Feb 1984 (JCR)
36, Crab Orchard NWR, 11 Mar 1986 (WDR)

SUMMER—Breeding begins early, probably in April, so May sightings in appropriate habitat may indicate breeding. At least a few pairs may be double-brooded, as indicated by the sighting of a female with 2 young from a first brood and seven from a second brood at Little Black Slough, Johnson Co., on 24 May–7 June 1989 (TF, WDR).

1, Horseshoe Lake CA, 10 May 1986 (JCR)
11 yg., Union Co. CA, 26 May 1984 (VK)
5 yg., Massac Co., 1 June 1974 (VK)
female, Heron Pond, Johnson Co., 10 June 1973 (HDB)
imm., s.e. Jackson Co., 12 June 1985 (WDR)
8 yg., Union Co. CA, 15 June 1982 (PK)
imm., s.w. Jackson Co., 20 June 1973 (VK)
male collected, Crab Orchard NWR, 30 June 1966 (SIU)
female, East Cape Girardeau, 12 July 1990 (TF, WDR)

1, Crab Orchard NWR, 3 Aug 1983 (JCR)

DOCUMENTATION: Specimen—ad. female, Crab Orchard NWR, Williamson Co., 2 Dec 1955 (SIU A-99).

FIELD GUIDES: G=62; N=88; P=62.

Common Merganser *Mergus merganser*

Mid-November–Late March

STATUS AND ABUNDANCE: Common migrant and winter resident. Very rare summer visitor.

HABITAT: Lakes and rivers.

RECORDS AND REMARKS: The most common midwinter duck, this merganser sometimes packs by the hundreds into the last remaining patch of open water on an otherwise frozen lake. The males have bright red-orange bills and legs, and their breast feathers sometimes have a pinkish tint. The females resemble female Red-breasted Mergansers but have a cleaner white throat, bulkier head when viewed in profile, and a clean contrast between the reddish sides of the neck and the grayish back and breast.

AUTUMN—Females and immatures arrive earliest, followed very late by males. Peak numbers may not appear until December or January. Migrates diurnally, especially along rivers.

8, Carbondale, 8 Nov 1986 (WDR)

1, Rend Lake, Jefferson Co., 11 Nov 1987 (TF)

1,390, Crab Orchard NWR, 30 Nov 1960 (LB)

5,000, Rend Lake, 1 Jan 1978 (BP)

WINTER—There is substantial local movement during winter in response to water and ice conditions, so determining whether birds are wintering or migrating is difficult.

750, Crab Orchard NWR, 29 Jan 1984 (JCR)

SPRING—Spring migration closely follows the freeze line northward as more northerly lakes begin to thaw. Peak numbers occur very early after the thaw, and then only modest numbers are recorded until the last departures in April.

1,900, Crab Orchard NWR, 13–15 Feb 1988 (WDR)

300, Rend Lake, 6 Mar 1987 (TF)

2, Crab Orchard NWR, 8 Apr 1988 (WDR)

2, Pine Hills, Union Co., 12 Apr 1987 (TF)

SUMMER—1, Rend Lake, 20 June 1986 (KM)

DOCUMENTATION: Specimen—ad. male, Crab Orchard NWR, Williamson Co., 5 Feb 1957 (SIU A-93).

FIELD GUIDES: G=62; N=88; P=62.

Red-breasted Merganser *Mergus serrator*
Early November–Mid-December
Mid-February–Mid-April

STATUS AND ABUNDANCE: Common migrant. Rare winter resident. Very rare summer visitor.

HABITAT: Lakes and rivers.

RECORDS AND REMARKS: Closely resembles the Common Merganser, but males have a rusty pattern on the chest and grayish sides, and females have a more diffuse blending of the rusty hood and gray neck than do female Commons. Red-breasts appear to have a thinner neck and head and a shaggier crest as well.

AUTUMN—Fall migrants arrive near 1 November in most years. Numbers peak during November and early December but decline quickly during December. Occasionally, a few linger into early winter.

imm. female, w. Jackson Co., 8 Sep 1993 (CS, BD)

10, Crab Orchard NWR, 1 Nov 1985 (SO)

300, Crab Orchard NWR, 24 Nov 1982 (JCR)

400, along Ohio River, Hardin Co., 4 Dec 1992 (JD)

3, Crab Orchard NWR CBC, 17 Dec 1983

20, Rend Lake, Franklin Co., 27 Dec 1991 (TF, WDR)

WINTER—Some winter season records may be of fall stragglers lingering until freeze-up; few birds seem to stay at one place for more than a few days. Occasionally, one will be mixed in with a group of Common Mergansers holed up in the last unfrozen waters.

2 females, Rend Lake, Franklin Co., 31 Dec 1988 (WDR)

female, Crab Orchard NWR, 1–5 Jan 1986 (TF, WDR)

9, Rend Lake, Jefferson Co., 5 Jan 1987 (TF)

male, Lake of Egypt, Williamson Co., 21 Jan 1984 (JCR)

SPRING—Migrants may arrive as early as January, soon after the

first thaw. Numbers peak during March and then decline rapidly until mid-April; most birds have departed by 15 April.
pair, Crab Orchard NWR, 22 Jan 1989 (WDR)
5, Crab Orchard NWR, 9 Feb 1986 (SO)
6, Crab Orchard NWR, 15 Feb 1984 (JCR)
800, Crab Orchard NWR, 25 Mar 1987 (WDR)
1, Crab Orchard NWR, 16 May 1984 (TF)
1, Rend Lake, 25 May 1986 (TF)
SUMMER—ad. male, Little Grassy Lake, Williamson Co., 1–27 June 1985 (WDR, JCR)
female, Rend Lake, Jefferson Co., 3 July 1993 (TF)

DOCUMENTATION: Written description—male, Little Grassy Lake, Williamson Co., 1–27 June 1985.

FIELD GUIDES: G=62; N=88; P=62.

Ruddy Duck *Oxyura jamaicensis*
Early October–Mid-December
Mid-February–Mid-April

STATUS AND ABUNDANCE: Common migrant. Uncommon winter resident. Rare summer resident.

HABITAT: Lakes and marshes.

RECORDS AND REMARKS: Large numbers are regularly found at Carbondale Reservoir (Evergreen Park). Most other concentrations occur on large lakes, where tight rafts rest near the middle of the lake. The pale cheek patch and stiff, upwardly tilted tail are distinctive fieldmarks.
AUTUMN—Fall arrivals typically follow the first cold front in early October. Numbers peak during November and early December and then decline.
4, Carbondale, 12 Sep 1989 (WDR)
1, Union Co. CA, 3 Oct 1976 (BP)
1, Crab Orchard NWR, 5 Oct 1983 (JCR)
432, Carbondale, 8 Nov 1986 (WDR)
436, Rend Lake, 18 Nov 1989 (BD, WDR)
WINTER—Generally scarce during winter; typical encounters are

of less than a dozen birds. They stay until severe cold forces them south, and even then a few hold over on warm-water lakes.

127, Union Co. CA, 5 Jan 1987 (WDR)

SPRING—Migrants arrive after the first February thaw, with peak numbers recorded during March.

6, Carbondale, 13 Feb 1984 (TF)

2, Union Co. CA, 19 Feb 1989 (TF, JH, WDR)

340, Carbondale, 10 Mar 1986 (WDR)

1, Carbondale, 19 May 1987 (WDR)

2 males, Crab Orchard NWR, 26 May 1987 (WDR)

SUMMER—The only confirmed evidence of breeding is a record of two broods and one female in a flooded wheat field in s.w. Jackson Co., 18 July 1973 (DH). One other summer record may have been a nonbreeding individual:

female, Carbondale, 19 July 1988 (WDR)

DOCUMENTATION: Specimen—male, Williamson Co., 6 Nov 1950 (SIU A-373).

FIELD GUIDES: G=62; N=76; P=60.

Order Falconiformes: Diurnal Birds of Prey

Family Cathartidae: Vultures

Black Vulture *Coragyps atratus*

STATUS AND ABUNDANCE: Uncommon year-round resident in the Shawnee Hills. Rare to uncommon year-round resident in the Ohio River floodplain from Massac Co. to Shawneetown, Gallatin Co. Rare migrant in the remainder of the Floodplains and in the Till Plain.

HABITAT: Soars high over hilly areas. Nests in bluffs, hollow trees, and isolated, abandoned barns or houses. Roosts on high-tension power poles and in trees.

RECORDS AND REMARKS: Most numerous in Johnson, Pope, Mas-

Black Vulture on nest, Ozark, Johnson Co., 23 April 1988

sac, and southern Saline Cos. Often associates with Turkey Vultures, particularly at roost sites.

SPRING—The initiation of northward movement varies annually. In some winters, nearly all Black Vultures retreat south of the region, so their arrival after the first warming period in January or February can be conspicuous. In milder years, a thin winter population can obscure detection of first spring arrivals. The length of the migratory period is uncertain. Most begin breeding during April, and southern Illinois is at the northern edge of the breeding range, so it is likely that the entire breeding population has arrived by sometime in February.

50, Grantsburg, Johnson Co., 22 Jan 1989 (TF)

99, Johnson Co., 31 Jan 1992 (TF)

30, Heron Pond, Johnson Co., 6 Mar 1974 (VK, HDB)

SUMMER—They typically nest on bare ground in a sheltered cove in a bluff. They may also sometimes nest in large hollow tree stumps or in abandoned buildings.

nest with 2 eggs, Pine Hills, Union Co., 17 Mar 1952 (Bennett 1952)

nest with 2 eggs, Panther's Den, Union Co., 9 Apr 1990 (RKl)
nest, Ozark, Johnson Co., Apr–June 1988 (TF)
1, s.w. Williamson Co., 25 Apr 1987 (WDR)
26, Pope Co., 10 May 1980 (SBC)
1, Harrisburg, Saline Co., 1 June 1986 (SO)
1, Union Co. CA, 3 June 1976 (BP)
1, near Murphysboro, Jackson Co., 25 June 1981 (MMl)
AUTUMN—After breeding, communal roosts form again. There seems to be a limited postbreeding dispersal that is revealed by some late-autumn records from northern and western sections of the region.
60, Vienna, Johnson Co., 21 Aug 1989 (TF)
1, Giant City SP, 23 Sep 1989 (BD)
2, s. Randolph Co., 6 Nov 1991 (TF)
1, Crab Orchard NWR, 7 Dec 1984 (TF)
WINTER—Some Black Vultures stay until severe weather forces them south. There are at least five records from Christmas Bird Counts: 6, Horseshoe Lake, 1950; 2, Murphysboro, 1954; 1, Mermet Lake, 1965; 1, Union Co., 1980; and 1, Union Co., 1991.
31, Vienna, Johnson Co., 4 Jan 1987 (TF)

DOCUMENTATION: Photograph—Ozark, Johnson Co., 23 Apr 1988 (SIU AP-26).

FIELD GUIDES: G=66; N=182; P=160.

Turkey Vulture *Cathartes aura*

Late January–Early May
Mid-August–Early November

STATUS AND ABUNDANCE: Common migrant and summer resident in the Shawnee Hills. Uncommon winter resident in the Shawnee Hills. Fairly common migrant and summer resident in the Floodplains and the Till Plain. Rare winter resident in the Floodplains and the Till Plain.

HABITAT: Soars relatively low over hilly areas as well as flat agricultural lands. Perches in dead trees and on high-tension power poles.

RECORDS AND REMARKS: Usually soars low over forest treetops, though may ascend considerably higher on warm days when strong thermals form. After a rain, these vultures sometimes perch high in dead trees or on exposed bluffs and hold their wings out to dry. They commonly roost in groups, often in wooded swamps or on high-tension power poles (especially in Johnson Co.).

SPRING—After the first warming spell in January, there is a noticeable influx of birds. The length of the migratory period is uncertain because of a substantial summer population. Some northbound birds, however, are probably still passing through in early May. Large aggregations are not necessarily indicative of migratory movement but may indicate presence of a food source or a roost site.

1, Harrisburg, Saline Co., 11 Jan 1986 (KP)

163, Heron Pond, Johnson Co., 31 Jan 1992 (TF)

1, White Co., 25 Jan 1987 (SS, TF, WDR)

18, Johnson and Hardin Cos., 1 Feb 1984 (JCR)

90, Pope Co., 7 May 1977 (SBC)

SUMMER—Nests are placed in bluffs, hollow trees, and abandoned buildings and on the ground in forests. Breeding begins during April and extends through July and sometimes through August. Juvenile Turkey Vultures have blackish heads, which makes them look like Black Vultures. The longer, slimmer body, longer neck, and lack of white bases to the underside of the primaries are important fieldmarks to note. Groups may form after breeding and roost together for several days or weeks before beginning the southward migration.

32, Union Co. CA, 29 July 1988 (WDR)

AUTUMN—The arrival of fall migrants is obscured by the presence of the breeding population. Normally, migration continues through early November, but some birds remain as long as the weather is favorable.

60, Johnson Co., 14 Oct 1984 (TF)

143, Glendale, Pope Co., 25 Oct 1990 (TF)

1, Crab Orchard NWR, 11 Nov 1989 (BD)

WINTER—Most of the winter population is in the Shawnee Hills and the Ohio River floodplains south of Shawneetown. In winters with severe weather, the entire population may move south out of the region for a few weeks.

17, Crab Orchard NWR CBC, 15 Dec 1984

2, Union Co. CBC, 19 Dec 1971
60, Horseshoe Lake CBC, 21 Dec 1982
9, Horseshoe Lake CBC, 28 Dec 1978

DOCUMENTATION: Photograph—near Simpson, Johnson Co., 14 Oct 1984 (SIU AP-27).

FIELD GUIDES: G=66; N=182; P=160.

Family Accipitridae: Accipiters, Hawks, and Eagles

Osprey *Pandion haliaetus*
Late March–Mid-May
Late August–Early November

STATUS AND ABUNDANCE: Uncommon migrant. Very rare summer resident; rare summer visitor.

HABITAT: Lakes and rivers.

RECORDS AND REMARKS: This fish-eating raptor has a distinctive flight profile because it holds its wings with the wrists higher than the rest of the wing, which gives it a shallow M-shape when viewed from in front or behind. Sometimes they perch on dead branches along lake or river margins between their foraging flights.
SPRING—Usually only single birds are encountered, but sometimes more than one can be seen around an excellent habitat. During the peak of migration (April and early May), individuals can even be encountered foraging at small ponds.
1, Rend Lake, 13 Mar 1986 (KPi)
1, Rend Lake, Jefferson Co., 19 May 1986 (WDR)
1, Williams Hill, Pope Co., 27 May 1989 (SKR)
SUMMER—Most summer sightings are of nonbreeding birds. The last definite nest record for the region is from Crab Orchard NWR where one to two nests were active from 1949 to 1955 (LB). There was apparently a nest at Mermet Lake between 1978 and 1982, but definite details are unavailable. In 1986, a pair built a nest and raised at least one young on a high-tension power pole across the Ohio River from Bay City, Pope Co. The adults foraged along the

Ohio River regularly. Nesting occurred there at least through 1991. Several recent summer records may involve nonbreeding individuals.

1, s.w. Jackson Co., 14 June 1980 (MSw)
1, Crab Orchard NWR, 23 and 29 June 1984 (JCR)
1, s.w. Jackson Co., 19 July 1975 (BP)
3, Rend Lake, 20–21 July 1985 (TF, JCR)
1, Rend Lake, 27 July 1986 (LH)

AUTUMN—Southward movements begin during August but do not peak until late September. Generally, only a few individuals are seen each day, even during the peak of migration. Late-fall and winter records should be carefully documented; immature Bald Eagles have sometimes been misidentified as Ospreys.

1, Crab Orchard NWR, 10 Aug 1983 (JCR)
1, s.e. Saline Co., 21 Sep 1986 (SO)
3, Rend Lake, Franklin Co., 23 Sep 1989 (TF)
3, Crab Orchard NWR, 4 Oct 1986 (TF)
2, Baldwin Lake, 11 Nov 1981 (RK)
1, Mermet Lake CA, 12 Nov 1992 (TF)

DOCUMENTATION: Specimen—male, Ewing, Franklin Co., 17 Oct 1962 (SIU A-1632).

FIELD GUIDES: G=78; N=200; P=158.

[American Swallow-tailed Kite *Elanoides forficatus*]

STATUS AND ABUNDANCE: Hypothetical.

RECORDS AND REMARKS: This graceful kite was apparently formerly quite common in the Floodplains of our region. Nelson (1877) stated that is was "numerous in the immediate vicinity of Cairo, where I was informed it had been abundant the week previous to my arrival." Slightly northeast of our region, Ridgway (1873:201) mentioned seeing "hundreds" in Richland Co. in 1871. By the 1890s the species had completely disappeared from our region; the latest record from the general vicinity of southern Illinois is a May 1894 record from the Missouri bootheel (Widmann 1895). Serious population declines have continued to the present, and swallowtails are now restricted to the southeastern states. There are a few recent midwestern records of overmigrants, however.

DOCUMENTATION: No documentary evidence has been preserved from our region. Ridgway obtained a specimen, however, from nearby Mt. Carmel, Wabash Co., on 1 Aug 1870 (USNM).

FIELD GUIDES: G=68; N=186; P=150.

Mississippi Kite *Ictinia mississippiensis*

Early May–Late August

STATUS AND ABUNDANCE: Locally common summer resident in the Mississippi River floodplain south of Jackson Co. Locally uncommon summer resident in the Mississippi River floodplains of Jackson and Randolph Cos. and in the Ohio River floodplains of Alexander and Pulaski Cos. Rare summer visitor to the Cache River floodplains and Cave Creek Valley. Very rare visitor throughout the remainder of the region.

HABITAT: Forages over grassy fields near mature bottomland forest; usually near water.

RECORDS AND REMARKS: Nelson (1877) described this kite as abundant near Cairo and present also in Mound City. Cahn and Hyde (1929) recorded some in Union Co. in 1929, but the species seemed to undergo a precipitous decline between 1910 and about 1955, when only very few were encountered. By the early 1970s, a sizable population was breeding in Union and Alexander Cos. Hardin et al. (1977) found thirteen pairs in Union Co., twelve pairs in Alexander Co., and two pairs in Randolph Co.; they saw a foraging flock of thirty-six over one field in Union Co. during late June. Currently, the population still seems to be growing. They can be easily overlooked, even in areas where they are numerous, because they soar very high in the air during midday and often perch amid fairly dense foliage in the understory or canopy of trees. SPRING—First spring arrivals are not usually detected until the first week of May, but in some warm springs, a few arrive in April. Records from the Till Plain represent overmigrants; there is an additional Till Plain record from Crab Orchard NWR in "early spring" 1949 (LB).

1, Union Co. CA, 20 Apr 1984 (DJa)
1, Union Co. CA, 22 Apr 1988 (WDR)
2, Ft. Massac SP, Massac Co., 6 May 1989 (WDR, SO)
3, Heron Pond, Johnson Co., 8 May 1983 (JW)
1, Ferne Clyffe SP, Johnson Co., 31 May 1983 (PK)
1, Crab Orchard NWR, 31 May–1 June 1986 (TF, JCR)
subad., Little Black Slough, Johnson Co., 7 June 1989 (TF)
subad., Crab Orchard NWR, 13 June 1976 (BP)
SUMMER—Breeding begins immediately after arrival. Incubation (thirty-one days) begins during late May, and fledglings are present by late July (Hardin et al. 1977). Nests are usually placed high in cottonwood or other high-canopy trees.
6, Fort Kaskaskia SP, Randolph Co., 5 June 1980 (RA et al.)
1, Grand Tower, Jackson Co., summer 1961 (LHo)
nest, Fort Kaskaskia SP, Randolph Co., summer 1972 (RA)
12 nesting pairs, Bumgard Island, Alexander Co., summer 1982 (SE)
39, Union Co. CA, 26 June 1977 (MMo, MT)
pair, Pomona, summer 1988 (WDR, m.ob.)
AUTUMN—Fall migration is almost imperceptible, because very few pairs of kites breed north of southern Illinois. Most of the breeders have departed by the end of August, but a few juveniles linger into September.
5 juv., Union Co. CA, 16 Sep 1989 (WDR)

DOCUMENTATION: Photograph—5 miles s. of Thebes, Alexander Co., 5 May 1984 (SIU AP-151).

FIELD GUIDES: G=68; N=186; P=150.

Bald Eagle *Haliaeetus leucocephalus*

Late September–Early April

STATUS AND ABUNDANCE: Fairly common migrant and winter resident in the western portions of southern Illinois. Uncommon migrant and winter resident in the eastern portions. Locally uncommon summer resident.

HABITAT: Large reservoirs and rivers, especially those with large wintering flocks of waterfowl.

RECORDS AND REMARKS: A very large raptor, this eagle takes four years or more to reach the full adult plumage with the white head and tail. Immatures pass through various plumages that are mostly dark brownish, with obscured whitish mottling that occurs especially on the underwings. They will take fish while in flight, and they also eat injured or dead waterfowl. Sometimes during winter they can be seen perched on the ice in the middle of large lakes.

AUTUMN—Fall migration peaks late in October and November, but some begin arriving by mid-September. Because a substantial winter population is present, latest departure dates are difficult to detect.

1, Jefferson Co., 8 Sep 1985 (JCR)

WINTER—Most of the wintering population congregates at the waterfowl refuges and along the Mississippi and Ohio Rivers.

imm., s.e. Saline Co., 16 Dec 1986 (SO)

95, Horseshoe Lake CBC, 3 Jan 1976

78, Union Co. CBC, 3 Jan 1987

35, Crab Orchard NWR CBC, 18 Dec 1982

SPRING—Northward movements begin during February, and most migrants have passed through the region by early April; some stragglers may occur later, but most birds seen after mid-April are probably breeders.

imm., Pulaski Co., 16 Feb 1984 (AW)

4, Saline Co. CA, 24 Feb 1984 (KP)

SUMMER—Eagles formerly nested in many parts of the region—for example, in Gallatin and Hamilton Cos. and along the Mississippi River (Grier et al. 1983)—but they were extirpated as breeding residents by the late 1940s. In 1943, before the extirpation, nests were found along the Mississippi River, near Horseshoe Lake CA (Bellrose 1944); and several nests were found at Crab Orchard NWR and Horseshoe Lake CA from 1946 to 1949 (RB). After many forms of pesticides were banned, the population began to recover, and eagles were found nesting again during the early 1970s. Nest-building was observed at Crab Orchard NWR in 1973 (Staff 1981) and at Union Co. CA in 1974 (Robinson 1985). The first successful nest fledged two young from near Horseshoe Lake CA in 1978 (Robinson 1985). Eagles were found incubating at Crab Orchard NWR the next year (Staff 1981). Since then, the regional breeding population has continued to grow, with confirmed breeding at Crab Orchard NWR (1980–1991), Union Co. CA (1991–1992), Horseshoe Lake CA (1987, 1990–1992), and Pope Co. (1989). Nest-building has also been observed at Rend Lake. Robinson (1985) lists the average date for start of incubation as 16 March; the average hatch date as 16 April; and the average fledging date as 2 July.

ad., Rend Lake, 1 June 1987 (TF)

ad., s.w. Jackson Co., 6 June 1980 (JG, DT)

imm., Santa Fe Chute, Alexander Co., 8 July 1989 (WDR, JH, EW)

DOCUMENTATION: Photograph—ad., Crab Orchard NWR, Williamson Co., 6 Dec 1981 (SIU AP-150).

FIELD GUIDES: G=78; N=184; P=158.

Northern Harrier *Circus cyaneus*

Mid-September–Early May

STATUS AND ABUNDANCE: Uncommon migrant and winter resident. Rare summer visitor; very rare summer resident.

HABITAT: Extensive grasslands and agricultural areas.

RECORDS AND REMARKS: Harriers are typically encountered as single individuals or in small groups teetering as they fly a few meters above grassy fields, where they hunt for rodents and small birds.

AUTUMN—Although southward migration does not fully begin until September, a few very early migrants or wandering birds have been detected in mid- and late summer. Passage of migrants seems to peak during October. Because of the wintering population, latest fall departure dates are difficult to determine.

1, Crab Orchard NWR, 6 July 1983 (JCR)

3, Rend Lake, Franklin Co., 26 July 1972 (VK)

male, Rend Lake, Jefferson Co., 15 Aug 1987 (TF)

1, Rend Lake, 5 Sep 1985 (KM)

WINTER—Highest winter counts come from Christmas Bird Counts and from roosting sites. Harriers aggregate in fallow fields to roost and hunt.

5, Crab Orchard NWR CBC, 18 Dec 1985

12, Horseshoe Lake CBC, 20 Dec 1983

8, Union Co. CBC, 22 Dec 1982

64 in roost, Perks, Pulaski Co., 10 Jan 1993 (TF)

SPRING—The presence of wintering individuals obscures the onset of spring migration, but northward movement begins by late February in most years. Latest spring departures occur during early May, so encounters after then may represent breeding individuals.

6 in roost, Carrier Mills, Saline Co., 7 Mar 1992 (TF)

SUMMER—Breeding may begin as early as late April in ideal habitat, so observers should make special searches for nests in areas where pairs of harriers are noted during late spring; there is only one recent confirmed breeding record for the region.

1, near Ellis Grove, Randolph Co., 16 May 1975 (BP)

pair, Pope Co., 1 June 1986 (TF)

2, n. Randolph Co., 16 June 1985 (JCR)

successful nest in wheat field, near Eldorado, Saline Co., June–July 1990 (TF, m.ob.)

DOCUMENTATION: Specimen—female, near Gorham, Jackson Co., 5 Jan 1964 (SIU A-1631).

FIELD GUIDES: G=70; N=188; P=152.

Sharp-shinned Hawk *Accipiter striatus*

Mid-September–Early May

STATUS AND ABUNDANCE: Uncommon migrant and winter resident. Very rare summer resident.

HABITAT: Woodland and woodland edge.

RECORDS AND REMARKS: This bird-eating hawk can be confused with the larger Cooper's Hawk; see Kaufman (1990) for identification criteria.

AUTUMN—Fall migration begins during September and peaks late in that month and during October. Sometimes small flocks can be seen migrating together ahead of an advancing cold front. Latest departures are difficult to determine, because of the winter population, but southward movement is essentially over by late November.

8, s.e. Saline Co., 28 Sep 1986 (SO)

WINTER—Typically encountered as singles during winter. May be a "guest" at bird feeders, where it ambushes flocks of small passerines.

6, Horseshoe Lake CBC, 30 Dec 1987

7, Rend Lake CBC, 31 Dec 1988

SPRING—The onset of spring migration is obscured by the winter population but probably begins during mid-March. "Sharpies" do not usually migrate in groups at this season. Some mid-May records could represent breeding birds.

1, Ft. Massac SP, Massac Co., 6 May 1989 (SO, WDR)

1, Pomona, 12 May 1984 (JCR)

SUMMER—A proliferation of recent summer records suggests that a small breeding population may be present in the Shawnee National Forest. All three recent nests have been placed in loblolly pine plantations. The nest Audubon found was on a cliff ledge over the Ohio River.

1, Williams Hill, Pope Co., 27 May 1989 (SKR)

ad., Trail of Tears SF, 31 May 1991 (WDR)

ad. carrying food, Atwood Ridge, Union Co., 14 June 1991 (WDR)

ad. male, Ozark, Johnson Co., 8 June 1989 (TF)

pair, Pine Hills, Union Co., 16 June 1989 (SB)

nest, Cave-in-Rock, Hardin Co., spring 1819 (Audubon 1840)

successful nest, Pope Co., summer 1980 (JGr, RGr)

unsuccessful nest, near Raum, Pope Co., June 1987 (WDR, TF)

nest, Carterville, Williamson Co., June 1988 (JK)

DOCUMENTATION: Specimen—ad. female, Crab Orchard NWR, Williamson Co., 13 Nov 1953 (SIU A-240).

FIELD GUIDES: G=70; N=190; P=152.

Cooper's Hawk *Accipiter cooperii*

Mid-September–Mid-April

STATUS AND ABUNDANCE: Uncommon migrant and winter resident. Locally uncommon summer resident.

HABITAT: Woods and woodland edge. Breeds in isolated woods, particularly in pines.

RECORDS AND REMARKS: This medium-sized bird hawk can be

separated from the similar Sharp-shinned Hawk by its generally larger size, rounded tail, darker cap (in adult plumage), and relatively larger head (which makes the eye appear rather small). They hunt for small birds (thrushes to woodpeckers and Blue Jays is the typical size range) by ambush and aerial pursuit.

AUTUMN—Fall migrants sometimes travel in small groups ahead of cold fronts, but not in numbers as great as do Sharp-shinned Hawks. They are most often detected as single birds flying across open fields away from the observer; accipiters almost always seem to detect the birder before the birder detects them. The winter population makes determination of latest departures difficult.

imm., Rend Lake, 19 Aug 1989 (TF, WDR)

WINTER—Typically, at most one or two are seen per day. Cooper's will sometimes attack birds at feeders.

4, Union Co. CBC, 19 Dec 1984

4, Rend Lake CBC, 31 Dec 1988

3, Crab Orchard NWR, 31 Jan 1986 (TF)

SPRING—Northward migration is difficult to detect because of the presence of both winter and summer populations in the region. Northward movements probably begin by mid-March, however, and are essentially over by mid-April. Birds encountered in late spring are probably breeders.

SUMMER—Cooper's Hawks tend to place their nests in mature pine plantations; there are a couple records of nests in deciduous trees, however; but these are always in very large unfragmented forest tracts. Eggs are laid in April; young fledge during June and July. Some nonbreeding immatures are detected each summer throughout the region. Ehrlich (1990) provided data on sixteen nests found in southern Illinois between 1988 and 1990; fourteen nests were in pines, and two were in deciduous trees. Average clutch size was four. Ehrlich estimated thirty to sixty breeding pairs in southern Illinois.

nest, Pomona, Apr 1971 (WGG)

nest with 3 yg., Pomona, Apr–June 1986 (TF, WDR)

unsuccessful nest, Pope Co., 27 May 1991 (TF)

nest, Giant City SP, June 1986 (TF)

nest with 2 yg., Atwood Ridge, Union Co., May–July 1989 (INHS)

ad. female and dependent juv., Hamburg Hill, Union Co., 28 June 1990 (WDR) ad. female, Ozark, Johnson Co., 30 June 1989 (TF)

DOCUMENTATION: Specimen—ad. male, near Cave-in-Rock, Hardin Co., 27 June 1954 (ISM 603664).

FIELD GUIDES: G=70; N=190; P=152.

Northern Goshawk *Accipiter gentilis*

Mid-November–Early April

STATUS AND ABUNDANCE: Rare migrant and winter resident.

HABITAT: Woodland and woodland edge.

RECORDS AND REMARKS: Occurs irregularly; most numerous during invasion years, when a majority of records involve adults. Invasion winters occurred in 1972–1973 and 1982–1983. Adults are unmistakable, but immatures must be identified with care because they closely resemble immature Cooper's Hawks; immature Red-shouldered Hawks and perched Northern Harriers can be misidentified as goshawks, too.

AUTUMN—Most goshawks are not detected until December, but during invasion years, they may arrive earlier. Migration patterns are not well known, so latest fall departure dates are unclear. It is possible that migration is continuing even throughout December.

ad., Carbondale, 14 Nov 1982 (TF)

ad., n. of Sparta, Randolph Co., 1 Dec 1972 (VK)

ad., Carbondale, 4 Dec 1982 (TF)

WINTER—ad., Ozark, Johnson Co., 13 Dec 1985 (TF)

ad., Crab Orchard NWR, 16 Dec 1985 (TF)

2, Horseshoe Lake CBC, 18 Dec 1985

ad., Crab Orchard NWR CBC, 18 Dec 1982

imm., Crab Orchard NWR, 19 Dec 1989 (BD)

1, Horseshoe Lake CBC, 20 Dec 1983

3 ad., Horseshoe Lake CBC, 21 Dec 1982

ad., Rudement, Saline Co., 1 Jan 1993 (JD)

imm., Colp, Williamson Co., 7 Jan 1987 (WDR)

1, Lusk Creek Canyon, Pope Co., 7 Jan 1973 (LBa, CC)

SPRING—Migrational movements begin in February. There are very few spring records.

ad., Union Co. CA, 7 Feb 1986 (WDR)

ad., Crab Orchard NWR, 12 Feb 1983 (JCR)
ad., Giant City SP, 21 Feb 1983 (JCR)
ad., Pine Hills, 12 Apr 1987 (TF, SO, BD)
The latter record was not accepted by the Illinois Ornithological
Records Committee (*IBB* 5:9). Nondocumenting observers argued
that the bird, which was viewed from below as it migrated northward along Pine Hills Bluff, was a Northern Harrier based on a
brief look at what appeared to be a white rump when the bird
banked. Because goshawks have very loose, white undertail coverts
(crissum) that often curl up over the base of the tail, they can appear to have a rump patch (even some Cooper's Hawks exhibit
this). The experience of the documenting observers and the lack
of experience of the nondocumenting observers persuade me to accept this report as a valid and valuable record.

DOCUMENTATION: Written description—3, Horseshoe Lake, Alexander Co., 21 Dec 1982.

FIELD GUIDES: G=70; N=190; P=152.

Red-shouldered Hawk *Buteo lineatus*

Mid-February–Late March
Mid-August–Mid-November

STATUS AND ABUNDANCE: Uncommon migrant and summer resident. Fairly common winter resident in the Shawnee Hills and the
Floodplains; uncommon winter resident in the Till Plain.

HABITAT: Bottomland and upland woods, primarily near open or
semiopen areas.

RECORDS AND REMARKS: Formerly described as "one of our most
common hawks, equally as common in winter as in summer"
(JWH, personal field notes, 1947); the regional population seems
to have declined dramatically in recent years. The reason for this
apparent decline is unclear but demands serious attention.
SPRING—Migration begins during February but is difficult to discern, because of the winter population. The breeding population
obscures the departure of migrants. Migrating birds can sometimes
be seen with groups of migrating Red-tailed Hawks.
SUMMER—Breeding begins very early; some pairs begin nest

building in early March. Egg laying regularly occurs during April, and young are present by May. Red-shoulders normally require large unfragmented tracts of bottomland forest in which to nest, but they will occasionally breed in smaller tracts like those along river courses in the Till Plain.

2 at nest, Carbondale, 5 Mar 1949 (RB, JWH)

2 nests, Pomona, 11 Apr 1986 (KM)

nest with 3 yg., Pomona, 3 May 1989 (TF)

4, Pope Co., 12 June 1986 (WDR)

AUTUMN—Fall migration is not well defined. Wandering or migrating birds can occur from August through November. Small groups are sometimes seen circling high overhead with other *Buteo* species.

5, s. Alexander Co., 16 Aug 1986 (WDR)

3, Crab Orchard NWR, 4 Sep 1983 (JCR)

WINTER—The largest winter concentrations occur in bottomland forests of the Floodplains.

33, Horseshoe Lake CBC, 21 Dec 1982

17, Union Co. CBC, 22 Dec 1982

11, Crab Orchard NWR CBC, 31 Dec 1977

11, Oakwood Bottoms, Jackson Co., 16 Feb 1975 (BP)

DOCUMENTATION: Photograph—imm., Horseshoe Lake CA, Alexander Co., 14 Feb 1981 (SIU AP-147).

FIELD GUIDES: G=74; N=192; P=156.

Broad-winged Hawk *Buteo platypterus*

Early April–Late October

STATUS AND ABUNDANCE: Uncommon migrant and summer resident.

HABITAT: Deciduous woods.

RECORDS AND REMARKS: Requires large forest tracts for breeding. Occurs in nearly any wooded habitat during migration.

Reports of this species from winter must be substantiated with complete details, preferably including photographs; past reports may have been misidentifications of Red-shouldered Hawks.

SPRING—No large flocks have been reported during spring. Most are detected by their shrill, distinctive whistle, *pe teeee*. Migrants may be present through early May, but the substantial breeding population obscures departure dates.

female found dead, Crab Orchard NWR, 14 Mar 1972 (SIU)

1, Heron Pond, Johnson Co., 27 Mar 1976 (BP)

1, Giant City SP, 2 Apr 1989 (WDR)

SUMMER—Breeding begins soon after arrival. Nests can be found by following birds that just finished copulating back to their nests. Copulating birds give a distinctive whistling call; and then one of the pair carries a stick back to the nest. Nests are placed fifteen to twenty-five meters up in deciduous trees, usually oaks.

2 nests, Giant City SP, 20 Apr 1989 (WDR)

nest fledged 3 yg., Dixon Springs SP, Pope Co., Apr–June 1992 (TF)

nest, Trail of Tears SF, May–June 1990 (WDR)

AUTUMN—Forms large flocks during migration, especially ahead of advancing cold fronts; flocks often pass overhead at very great heights. Peak numbers pass through the region between 20 September and 7 October. Very few are seen past 25 October. There is one record of a dark morph, from Ozark, Johnson Co., on 17 September 1989 (TF).

166, Crab Orchard NWR, 22 Sep 1983 (JCR)

2,000, Rend Lake, Jefferson Co., 23 Sep 1987 (TF)

300, Carbondale, 5 Oct 1986 (TF)

93, Pine Hills, Union Co., 5 Oct 1986 (WDR)

1, Crab Orchard NWR, 2 Nov 1986 (WDR)

DOCUMENTATION: Specimen—female, Crab Orchard NWR, Williamson Co., 14 Mar 1972 (SIU, uncatalogued).

FIELD GUIDES: G=74; N=192; P=156.

Swainson's Hawk *Buteo swainsoni*

STATUS AND ABUNDANCE: Very rare visitor.

HABITAT: Perches in isolated trees, on telephone poles, or along a woodland edge near open areas, such as agricultural fields.

RECORDS AND REMARKS: There are only three records, all from autumn, of this typically western raptor.

AUTUMN—imm., Willard, Alexander Co., 16 Aug 1986 (WDR)
ad., Crab Orchard NWR, 13 Oct 1982 (JCR)
1, Carbondale, 30 Nov 1980 (JJa; AB 35:189)

DOCUMENTATION: Provisional acceptance.

FIELD GUIDES: G=74; N=194; P=154.

Red-tailed Hawk *Buteo jamaicensis*
Mid-February–Late March
Mid-September–Early November

STATUS AND ABUNDANCE: Common migrant and winter resident. Fairly common summer resident.

HABITAT: Perches in isolated trees, on telephone poles, or along a woodland edge near open or semiopen areas. Nests in woodlots and forests. Soars frequently, passing over nearly every habitat.

RECORDS AND REMARKS: Highly variable in plumage. At least four subspecies occur in the region. Most birds belong to *B. j. borealis*. Other subspecific records include the following:
Krider's *(B. j. krideri)*—Jackson Co., 8 Mar 1975, 5 Apr 1975 and 6 Jan 1976 (BP); Rend Lake, 18 Nov 1989 (BD, WDR)
Harlan's *(B. j. harlani)*—ad., Alexander Co., 3 Apr 1971 (VK et al.); ad. dark phase, Randolph Co., 3 Jan 1988 (RG); Horseshoe Lake CA, 2 Jan 1987 (HDB); melanistic, Union Co. CA, 16 Nov 1975 (BP)
B. j. calurus, a western subspecies, should also occur, but apparently no published records are available.
SPRING—Sometimes Red-tails migrate in groups, riding thermals high up into the air before traveling northward. Although both winter and summer populations make the beginning and end of spring migration difficult to discern, when migration peaks during March, it sometimes seems as though every other telephone pole has a Red-tailed Hawk perched on it.
31, Crab Orchard NWR, 6 Mar 1985 (JCR)
SUMMER—Pairs begin breeding as early as late February. Incubating birds can sometimes be seen sitting on their bulky nests well before the trees have begun to leaf out. Fledglings are present from May through July.

AUTUMN—Migration begins during September and peaks in October. The end of the southward migration is obscured by a large winter population.

49, Crab Orchard NWR, 25 Oct 1983 (JCR)

WINTER—The winter distribution seems to be determined by food supply. Red-tails can be remarkably numerous around a good habitat where rodent and rabbit populations are high.

70, Crab Orchard NWR CBC, 18 Dec 1982
90, Horseshoe Lake CBC, 21 Dec 1982
56, Wayne-Fitzgerrell SP, Franklin Co., 1 Jan 1988 (WDR)
74, Union Co. CBC, 3 Jan 1987

DOCUMENTATION: Specimen—imm., 4 miles n.w. of Alto Pass, Union Co., 14 Mar 1955 (SIU A-111).

FIELD GUIDES: G=72; N=194; P=154.

[Ferruginous Hawk *Buteo regalis*]

STATUS AND ABUNDANCE: Hypothetical.

RECORDS AND REMARKS: One was reported from Olive Branch, Alexander Co., 2 Jan 1981. However, Bohlen (1986) indicated the possibility that this sighting may have been a Krider's Red-tailed Hawk. A specimen, diagnostic photograph, or detailed written description is needed to confirm the species for our area. See Bohlen (1986) for important fieldmarks to note.

FIELD GUIDES: G=72; N=196; P=154.

Rough-legged Hawk *Buteo lagopus*

Early November–Early April

STATUS AND ABUNDANCE: Uncommon migrant and winter resident.

HABITAT: Woodland edge and open fields.

RECORDS AND REMARKS: Often perches at tips of trees along hedgerows bordering grassy fields or agricultural areas. Commonly hovers while hunting. Marked annual variation in numbers; may be virtually absent in some years, but at least a few can always be found in the Till Plain and in central Pope Co., near the Dixon Springs Agricultural Station. Both the dark and light phases have been observed, but there are no data available on the ratios of the two in our region.

AUTUMN—Fall migrants arrive in late autumn and are usually encountered as single individuals. Some migrants may still be arriving during December.

1, s. Perry Co., 28 Oct 1983 (TF)

WINTER—10, Pope Co., 8 Dec 1989 (TF)

3, Crab Orchard NWR CBC, 18 Dec 1971

4, Horseshoe Lake CBC, 20 Dec 1983

7, Union Co. CBC, 2 Jan 1976

5, Pope Co., 3 Feb 1984 (TF)

SPRING—Because southern Illinois lies at the southern edge of the winter range, spring migration is not very noticeable. It basically involves the departure of the winter population. Northward movement begins soon after the first warm spell in February.

4, n.w. Gallatin Co., 27 Feb 1971 (VK, DH)

11, Jackson Co., 13 Mar 1949 (RB)

1, Union Co. CA, 14 Apr 1988 (WDR)

1, Red Bud, Randolph Co., 16 Apr 1983 (RG)

DOCUMENTATION: Photograph—Dixon Springs Agricultural Station, Pope Co., 15 Jan 1989 (SIU AP-277).

FIELD GUIDES: G=72; N=196; P=156.

Golden Eagle *Aquila chrysaetos*
Late October–Mid-April

STATUS AND ABUNDANCE: Locally uncommon migrant and winter resident in the west. Rare migrant and winter resident in the east.

HABITAT: Frequents open and semiopen areas, particularly near concentrations of waterfowl.

RECORDS AND REMARKS: This eagle of open country is found annually at the waterfowl refuges of southern Illinois. It is sometimes found in other sections of the region, especially during migration. Recent improved coverage of southeastern Illinois has provided several records from that area. Immature Bald Eagles are sometimes misidentified as Golden Eagles; see Clark and Wheeler (1987) for identification criteria.

AUTUMN—Most birds do not arrive until November, and migration probably extends well into December.

imm., Crab Orchard NWR, 21 Sep 1982 (JCR)

imm., Rend Lake, Jefferson Co., 30 Oct 1987 (TF)

WINTER—Golden Eagles are found nearly every year during the Christmas Bird Counts at Union Co. and Horseshoe Lake. They are extremely mobile, however, and can cover many miles in a few hours. Additionally, they often soar very high, and because they are so large, they can be seen for many miles. It is possible that some of the highest counts from Christmas Bird Counts actually involve only one or two birds that were seen by more than one party.

1, Horseshoe Lake CA, 27 Dec 1949 (RB)

4, Union Co. CBC, 31 Dec 1972 and 30 Dec 1976

3, Horseshoe Lake CBC, 2 Jan 1987

3, Union Co. CA, 8 Jan 1994 (TF)

imm., Crab Orchard NWR, 21–22 Jan 1989 (TF, WDR)

ad., Hardin Co., 25 Jan 1988 (TF)

ad., Rend Lake, Franklin Co., 3 Feb 1991 (BD)

SPRING—Migration seems to begin during February, following the first warm spell and the northward departure of the flocks of Canada Geese.

ad., Pulaski Co., 15 Feb 1991 (TF)

imm., Saline Co., 16 Feb 1991 (JD)

ad., near Sandusky, in Pulaski Co., 19 Feb 1989 (TF, JH, WDR)

imm., East Cape Girardeau, Alexander Co., 21 Feb 1984 (TF)

7, Union Co., 18 Mar 1990 (BD)

2 imm., near Stoneface, Saline Co., 19 Mar 1989 (TF, JD)

2 imm., Union Co. CA, 24 Mar 1972 (VK)

2 imm., Oakwood Bottoms, Jackson Co., 25 Mar 1972 (DH)

imm., Grand Tower, Jackson Co., 25 Mar 1989 (WDR)

imm., Union Co. CA, 19 Apr 1975 (BP)

imm. found freshly dead, South Ripple Hollow, Alexander Co., 16 May 1989 (RJ)

DOCUMENTATION: Photograph—Crab Orchard NWR, Williamson Co., 23 Dec 1986 (SIU AP-270).

FIELD GUIDES: G=78; N=184; P=158.

Family Falconidae: Falcons

American Kestrel *Falco sparverius*

STATUS AND ABUNDANCE: Common migrant and winter resident. Fairly common summer resident.

HABITAT: Open and semiopen areas, like roadsides, pastures, and cultivated lands; also occurs in towns.

RECORDS AND REMARKS: Often perches on telephone wires and poles. Well-known for its habit of hovering for extended periods of time over one spot and then either pouncing on prey or flying off and hunting elsewhere.

AUTUMN—Fall migration begins during September and peaks during October. Flocks of these falcons sometimes occur ahead of advancing cold fronts, especially in early and mid-October. Most of the winter population is probably here by late November.
18, Johnson and Union Cos., 26 Oct 1986 (TF)

WINTER—Sex can be determined by wing color: males have blue wings, whereas females have brown. A sample of one hundred kestrels in the Till Plain during the winter of 1990 showed that 60 percent were males and 40 percent were females.
56, Crab Orchard NWR CBC, 28 Dec 1974
69, Horseshoe Lake CBC, 2 Jan 1987
67, Union Co. CBC, 22 Dec 1994

SPRING—Dates of northward movement are difficult to determine, because of the presence of both winter and summer populations. Migration may begin as soon as early February and may extend into late April or May (Enderson 1960).
17, Perry Co., 15 Feb 1986 (WDR)

SUMMER—Nests in old woodpecker holes, in nest boxes, and even in cavities in the sides of buildings. Egg laying occurs principally in April and May, with fledglings present by late June.
9, Alexander Co., 16 July 1983 (JCR)

DOCUMENTATION: Specimen—ad. female, 5 miles n.e. of Cobden, Union Co., 8 Dec 1955 (SIU A-120).

FIELD GUIDES: G=80; N=202; P=162.

Merlin *Falco columbarius*

Mid-September–Late October
Late March–Early May

STATUS AND ABUNDANCE: Occasional migrant. Rare winter resident.

HABITAT: Open and semiopen areas, like grassy fields and forest edge.

RECORDS AND REMARKS: Nearly all records of this small falcon involve single individuals. They are somewhat more numerous in fall than in spring, but the available records are rather evenly distributed between autumn, winter, and spring. Because Merlins are most often detected as flybys, they are sometimes confused with kestrels; special attention should be given to the tail pattern and body proportions. See Clark and Wheeler (1987) for identification details.
AUTUMN—The first birds arrive in the third week of September. Peak passage occurs from 20 September to 10 October, when raptor migration as a whole is peaking. Most have departed by the end of October, but a few remain throughout late fall and winter in at least some years.
1, Crab Orchard NWR, 15 Sep 1989 (WDR)
1, Pine Hills, Union Co., 20 Sep 1975 (BP)
1, Rend Lake, Jefferson Co., 24 Sep 1989 (WDR)
1, Giant City SP, 6 Oct 1984 (TF)
1, Horseshoe Lake CA, 8 Oct 1984 (JCR)
1, Crab Orchard NWR, 12 and 18 Oct 1983 (JCR)
WINTER—An irregular visitor during winter, though recent overwintering records from Pope Co. have been established.
1, Crab Orchard NWR CBC, 18 Dec 1971
1, Horseshoe Lake CBC, 29 Dec 1976
1, Nason, Jefferson Co., 31 Dec 1988 (TF, SO)
male, Belknap, Johnson Co., 8 Jan 1993 (TF)
male, Johnson Co., 20 Jan–4 Feb 1995 (TF)
1, Crab Orchard NWR, 15 Feb 1971 (HDB)
1, near Dixon Springs SP, Pope Co., 26 Feb–10 Mar 1991, and possibly the same bird there 26 Jan–8 Mar 1992 (TF)
SPRING—Migrants arrive by late March and are present into early May, but few are detected each year.

1, Oakwood Bottoms, Jackson Co., 25 Mar 1989 (WDR)
1, Golconda, Pope Co., 27 Apr 1984 (SO)
1, Murphysboro, Jackson Co., 30 Apr 1988 (VK, LH)
1, Union Co. CA, 10 May 1977 (VK, HDB)

DOCUMENTATION: Specimen—female, 2 miles e. of Carbondale, Jackson Co., 14 Oct 1958 (SIU A-622).

FIELD GUIDES: G=80; N=202; P=162.

Peregrine Falcon *Falco peregrinus*
Late September–Mid-October
Early April–Early May

STATUS AND ABUNDANCE: Rare migrant. Very rare winter visitor. Formerly a rare summer resident.

HABITAT: Typically found in open or semiopen areas, often near rivers or lakes.

RECORDS AND REMARKS: This majestic falcon experienced a dramatic population decline in the mid-1900s, in large part because of negative responses to toxic chemicals, such as DDT. With the banning of many of the worst chemicals, the Peregrine population is slowly recovering. Breeding programs have established nesting populations in some large cities, such as Chicago. Peregrines once nested on the high bluffs overlooking the Mississippi River floodplain in Jackson Co., but now the species occurs almost exclusively as a migrant.
AUTUMN—Peak numbers occur between 22 September and 5 October. Most sightings are from refuges where ducks concentrate in large numbers. These falcons are often among the raptors seen during the "fallout" days that occur when birds are migrating ahead of strong cold fronts.
1, Rend Lake, Jefferson Co., 23 Sep 1989 (BD)
1, Crab Orchard NWR, 25 Sep 1985 (TF)
1, s.w. Jackson Co., 26 Sep 1985 (TF)
1, Jefferson Co., 3 Oct 1986 (TF)
1, Crab Orchard NWR, 4 Oct 1986 (TF)
1, Rend Lake, 14 Oct 1984 (LH)

1, Crab Orchard NWR, 15 Oct 1984 (JCR)
WINTER—imm., Horseshoe Lake CBC, 2 Jan 1987
1, Jackson Co., 25 Jan 1947 (JWH)
1, Jackson Co., 15 Feb 1946 (JWH)
SPRING—Occurrence during spring may be strongly affected by weather. Many of the records are from days when sudden storms and heavy overcast situations appear. Migrating falcons may often land and wait out the storm; on clear days, they may simply fly over the region, never stopping.
breeding pair returned to eyrie, Jackson Co., 14 Mar 1951 (RB)
ad., Union Co. CA, 6 Apr 1986 (WDR)
1, Rend Lake, Jefferson Co., 19 Apr 1986 (WDR, TF, SS)
1, Crab Orchard NWR, 28 Apr 1984 (TF, KR)
1, Union Co., 7 May 1983 (VK et al.)
1, Union Co., 9 May 1987 (KM et al.)
1, Johnson Co., 13 May 1992 (TF)
SUMMER—Nested on the bluffs over the Mississippi River near Grand Tower, Jackson Co., in the 1880s and 1890s (Widmann 1907). The last nest was at Hickory Ridge, Jackson Co., in 1950 (when 2 young were raised) and 1951 (George 1968). There is one other summer record:
1, Union Co., 17 July 1955 (RB)

DOCUMENTATION: Specimen—imm. male, near Murphysboro, Jackson Co., 5 Oct 1959 (SIU A-862).

FIELD GUIDES: G=80; N=204; P=162.

Prairie Falcon *Falco mexicanus*

STATUS AND ABUNDANCE: Very rare visitor.

HABITAT: Found in extensive agricultural areas, where it often perches in isolated trees. Usually occurs near rivers.

RECORDS AND REMARKS: Occurrences of this large falcon seem to be increasing in Illinois and, therefore, could increase in southern Illinois. They should be searched for in extensive agricultural areas

and around reclaimed strip mines during November, February, and March, when most of the migratory movements are occurring.
WINTER—1, near Ware, Union Co., 31 Dec 1987 (RG, WDR)
SPRING—1, Union Co. CA, 20 Mar 1992 (TF, JD)
1, Alexander Co., 31 Mar 1984 (JCR)

DOCUMENTATION: Written description—1, Union Co., 31 Dec 1987.

FIELD GUIDES: G=80; N=204; P=162.

Order Galliformes: Gallinaceous Birds

Family Phasianidae: Gallinaceous Birds

[Ring-necked Pheasant *Phasianus colchicus*]

STATUS AND ABUNDANCE: Hypothetical. Locally uncommon year-round resident at sites where it has been introduced.

HABITAT: Brushy fields and hedgerows near agricultural lands where waste grain is present.

RECORDS AND REMARKS: This Asian species was first introduced into the United States about 1890 but has never been able to sustain populations in southern Illinois. Many are released annually at regional hunt clubs and at Wayne Fitzgerrell SP, Franklin Co. Some that escape hunters may breed, but without annual supplementation from release programs, the population would certainly go extinct. Occasionally a pheasant can be seen at other sites in the region; these are presumably escapes from local farms or hunt clubs. The only counts available are those from the Rend Lake Christmas Bird Counts, where they are recorded each year; the highest count was seventeen on 31 December 1988.

DOCUMENTATION: Specimen—ad. male, Union Co., Apr 1988 (SIU, uncatalogued).

FIELD GUIDES: G=92; N=222; P=144.

Ruffed Grouse *Bonasa umbellus*

STATUS AND ABUNDANCE: Locally uncommon year-round resident near release sites.

HABITAT: Forests intermixed with gaps that provide dense cover.

RECORDS AND REMARKS: Formerly an uncommon year-round resident, but extirpated sometime around the late 1890s or 1900. The IDOC reintroduced some into Pope Co. in 1953–1958 and 1967 and into Alexander Co. in 1972, but the populations did not survive. More recently, introductions into Union Co. and northern Alexander Co. seem to be having more success. Breeding has been confirmed at Atwood Ridge in Union Co. (in 1989 and 1990). A few can be heard drumming in that area each spring. Apparently, a few still occur in northern Pope Co. (e.g., 1 drumming, Delwood, 3 Apr 1987 [TF]), but the population is very small. One was seen as far north as Stoneface, Saline Co., on 15 March 1989 (TF). A few are reported some years from the Union Co. Christmas Bird Counts; the highest count was four on 3 January 1987.

DOCUMENTATION: Specimen—ad., Alexander Co., fall 1973 (IDOC).

FIELD GUIDES: G=86; N=210; P=144.

Greater Prairie-Chicken *Tympanuchus cupido*

STATUS AND ABUNDANCE: Extirpated.

RECORDS AND REMARKS: Formerly a locally uncommon year-round resident in prairie grasslands. Colonies in Perry and Jefferson Cos. were last recorded in the early 1950s (Bennett 1952); fourteen, for example, were seen in one soybean field near DuQuoin in fall 1991 (GSa, JWH, RB). Some long-distance dispersal events—for example, one at Crab Orchard NWR on 20 Dec 1940 (Bennett 1952)—periodically accounted for extralimital records.

DOCUMENTATION: Specimen—juv., Jefferson Co., June 1951 (SIU A-136).

FIELD GUIDES: G=88; N=214; P=146.

Wild Turkey *Meleagris gallopavo*

STATUS AND ABUNDANCE: Locally uncommon year-round resident in the Shawnee Hills and the Floodplains. Rare year-round resident in the Till Plain.

HABITAT: Mature forests.

RECORDS AND REMARKS: Turkeys were formerly common throughout the region. They were common food items among the archaeological excavations at the Pettit Site in northern Alexander Co. dated from 800 to 1,000 A.D. (Breitburg 1990). By 1900, however, turkeys had been overhunted and were nearly extirpated. One flock was seen near Olive Branch in 1907 (Cory 1909), and some were thought to be present in Union Co. until about 1935 (Smith and Parmalee 1955). Reintroductions by the IDOC from 1954 to 1958 were unsuccessful, but those introduced in 1959–1967 again established a viable breeding population in southern Illinois (Calhoun and Garver 1974). The population has grown to the point that turkeys are now hunted in most counties in the region.

Breeding begins early in the spring; males can especially be heard gobbling during April and early May. Nests are placed on the ground under treefalls or in thick vegetation. Poults are frequently seen during June.

60, s.e. Saline Co., 9 Dec 1986 (SO)
89, Union Co. CBC, 29 Dec 1988
33, Crab Orchard NWR, 30 Jan 1985 (JCR)

DOCUMENTATION: Specimen—male, n. end of Possum Trot Trail, Alexander Co., 17 Sep 1970 (ISM 604592).

FIELD GUIDES: G=84; N=222; P=144.

Northern Bobwhite *Colinus virginianus*

STATUS AND ABUNDANCE: Common year-round resident.

HABITAT: Weedy fields and hedgerows, often near agricultural areas.

RECORDS AND REMARKS: Bobwhites are conspicuous inhabitants of southern Illinois during spring and summer, when their distinctive whistle, *bob white*, can be heard. They are usually seen as singles or pairs then, and sometimes an adult will be seen with a parade of chicks following it. At other seasons, they form coveys and are less conspicuous. They are typically encountered by walking through weedy fields and flushing up a flock that bursts into flight with a noisy whir of wings. Most counts made by birders come from organized bird counts:

51, Union Co., 4 May 1991 (SBC)
52, Horseshoe Lake CBC, 21 Dec 1982
116, Union Co. CBC, 2 Jan 1976
229, Crab Orchard NWR CBC, 4 Jan 1976

DOCUMENTATION: Specimen—ad. male, Carbondale, Jackson Co., 10 Sep 1954 (SIU A-126).

FIELD GUIDES: G=92; N=216; P=148.

Order Gruiformes: Cranes, Rails, and Allies

Family Rallidae: Rails

Yellow Rail *Coturnicops noveboracensis*

STATUS AND ABUNDANCE: Very rare migrant.

HABITAT: Grassy meadows with some standing water.

RECORDS AND REMARKS: There are two records. A single individual was flushed once on 18 April and once on 19 April 1987 from an extensive field with vegetation seventeen to twenty-two centimeters tall in two to six centimeters of standing water near Paulton, Williamson Co. (WDR, TF). Another was found in similar habitat, also in Williamson Co., on 3–4 May 1994 (LS).

DOCUMENTATION: Written description—1987 record.

FIELD GUIDES: G=104; N=98; P=114.

Black Rail *Laterallus jamaicensis*

STATUS AND ABUNDANCE: Very rare migrant.

HABITAT: May occur in large, grassy fields. May also use alfalfa or winter wheat fields. In 1994 one was found along the periphery of a cattail marsh.

RECORDS AND REMARKS: One calling from a marsh just after midnight on 4 May 1994, near Harrisburg, Saline Co., was tape recorded (TF, KM, JD et al.). There are at least three undocumented fall records, all from Crab Orchard NWR: one on 7 October 1954, one on 15 October 1949, and two on 7 November 1952.

DOCUMENTATION: Voice recording—1, near Harrisburg, Saline Co., 1994 (SIU, uncatalogued).

FIELD GUIDES: G=104; N=98; P=114.

King Rail *Rallus elegans*
Mid-April–Late July

STATUS AND ABUNDANCE: Rare migrant. Very rare summer resident. Very rare winter visitor.

HABITAT: Cattail marshes and tall-sedge meadows.

RECORDS AND REMARKS: Formerly more numerous, but destruction of marshes and other wetlands has eliminated appropriate habitats. Use of recorded calls or lots of walking in marshy areas is required to see this species.
SPRING—First arrivals typically begin appearing about 15 April. Migration may continue until mid-May, but the thin breeding population obscures definite determination of departure dates.
1, Oakwood Bottoms, Jackson Co., 15 Mar 1994 (CS)
1, Oakwood Bottoms, Jackson Co., 14 Apr 1985 (JCR)
1, Lovett's Pond, Jackson Co., 18 Apr 1992 (TF, WDR)
2, Oakwood Bottoms, Jackson Co., 24 Apr 1976 (BP)
2, Mermet Lake CA, 7 May 1988 (WDR)
1, Union Co., 8 May 1976 (SBC)
SUMMER—No breeding records since the 1970s. Appropriate habitat still exists at Mermet Lake and on some reclaimed strip-mine ponds with extensive cattails. Could easily be overlooked.
2, Oakwood Bottoms, Jackson Co., 28 May 1976 (BP)
ad. and yg., e. of Vienna, Johnson Co., 7 June 1971 (VK)
ad. and yg., East Cape Girardeau, Alexander Co., 27 July 1974 (VK)
AUTUMN—Apparently migrates very early, because there are no

available records past July. Could reasonably occur into mid-September, however.

1, s. Alexander Co., 12–19 July 1986 (TF, WDR)

WINTER—male specimen, near Creal Springs, Williamson Co., 26 Feb 1957 (SIU)

DOCUMENTATION: Specimen—male, 2 miles n. of Creal Springs, Williamson Co., 26 Feb 1957 (SIU A-140).

FIELD GUIDES: G=106; N=96; P=112.

Virginia Rail *Rallus limicola*

Early April–Early May
Early September–Early November

STATUS AND ABUNDANCE: Uncommon migrant. Very rare summer visitor and winter visitor.

HABITAT: Cattail marshes, sedge meadows, and, especially in fall, hayfields.

RECORDS AND REMARKS: Inconspicuous, this rail is easily overlooked. Much walking and patience are required to see it, but it can be flushed with regularity from a good marshy habitat. I once was scanning a hayfield in spring for Bobolinks when a Virginia Rail fluttered up into view for about a second and then dropped back into the grass. They will also respond to playbacks of their calls during spring.

SPRING—First spring migrants appear near 1 April. Concentrations are rarely found. Most have departed by 10 May.

1, Oakwood Bottoms, Jackson Co., 29 Mar 1973 (MSw)

1, Grand Tower, Jackson Co., 13 Apr 1985 (JCR)

1, Crab Orchard NWR, 29 Apr 1986 (SO)

4, Jackson Co., 8 May 1976 (SBC)

SUMMER—Breeding has not been confirmed for the region but is possible in excellent habitat in some years. One midsummer record is suggestive of breeding:

4, Oakwood Bottoms, Jackson Co., 9 July 1973 (DH)

AUTUMN—Even more difficult to locate in fall, Virginias undoubtedly go undetected most of the time. There is a hunting season for Virginias (and the other rails) in the fall, but it does not seem to be a very popular sport.

1, Mt. Vernon, Jefferson Co., 3 Sep 1987 (TF)
male specimen, Bald Knob, Union Co., 12 Nov 1983 (SIU)
1, Oakwood Bottoms, Jackson Co., 14 Nov 1972 (MSw)
WINTER—1, near Unity, Alexander Co., 3 Jan 1976 (HDB, BP)
1, Oakwood Bottoms, Jackson Co., 17–18 Jan 1994 (CS)

DOCUMENTATION: Specimen—male, Bald Knob, Union Co., 12 Nov 1983 (SIU, uncatalogued).

FIELD GUIDES: G=104; N=98; P=112.

Sora *Porzana carolina*
Early April–Early May
Mid-August–Mid-October

STATUS AND ABUNDANCE: Fairly common migrant. Very rare winter visitor.

HABITAT: Marshes, wet grassy fields, sedge meadows, and hayfields.

RECORDS AND REMARKS: The most common of the rails, Soras sometimes congregate in good habitat. They readily flush when approached, first running, then taking flight. Pale greenish-yellow legs dangle behind as the bird flutters away.
SPRING—Migrants are often vocal and easy to flush. They will often call in response to an imitation of their whistle or a rock being tossed into the marsh.
1, Rend Lake, Jefferson Co., 27 Mar 1987 (TF)
1, Crab Orchard NWR, 28 Mar 1987 (WDR)
10, Oakwood Bottoms, Jackson Co., 18 Apr 1983 (TF)
1, Dutchman's Lake, Johnson Co., 27 May 1986 (WDR)
SUMMER—George (1968) said Soras were rare summer residents, but he provided no records to substantiate the idea. Fall migration can begin very early, however, so late-summer records could be misinterpreted as possible breeding.
AUTUMN—Soras tend to be found in drier fields more often during fall, which is probably just a reflection of habitat availability. They do not call as much during this season, so they must be flushed to be detected.
imm., Oakwood Bottoms, Jackson Co., 10 Aug 1973 (DH)
1, Rend Lake, Jefferson Co., 20 Aug 1988 (TF, WDR)
1, Crab Orchard NWR, 9 Oct 1984 (JCR)

1, West Frankfort, Franklin Co., 29 Nov 1993 (LS)
WINTER—The only winter record is a bird flushed from a marsh with standing vegetation and open water in the moist soil units at Crab Orchard NWR, 17 Dec 1988 (SO).

DOCUMENTATION: Specimen—female, Carbondale, Jackson Co., 9 Apr 1988 (SIU, uncatalogued).

FIELD GUIDES: G=104; N=98; P=114.

Purple Gallinule *Porphyrula martinica*

STATUS AND ABUNDANCE: Very rare migrant and summer resident.

HABITAT: Marshes and swamps with dense emergent vegetation, especially cattails and water lilies.

RECORDS AND REMARKS: Occurs irregularly, but has been noted often at Mermet Lake, the only site in Illinois where it has bred. Because it frequents dense marshy vegetation, it is difficult to detect and could conceivably be overlooked.
SPRING—1, Heron Pond, Johnson Co., 1 May 1987 (SO et al.)
1, Pine Hills, Union Co., 9 May 1974 (RM)
SUMMER—1 heard, Mermet Lake CA, 26 May 1985 (LH)
1, Oakwood Bottoms, Jackson Co., 2 June 1976 (BP)
nest with 8 eggs, Mermet Lake CA, 19 June 1973 (MH, MS)
1 heard repeatedly, Union Co. CA, 11–18 July 1987 (TF, WDR)
ad. and 2 yg., Mermet Lake CA, 20 July 1963 (Waldbauer and Hays 1964)
4, Horseshoe Lake CA, 5 Aug 1976 (BP)

DOCUMENTATION: Written description—Pine Hills, Union Co., 9 May 1974.

FIELD GUIDES: G=106; N=100; P=64.

Common Moorhen *Gallinula chloropus*
Mid-April–Mid-May
Mid-September–Mid-October

STATUS AND ABUNDANCE: Rare migrant. Very rare summer resident.

HABITAT: Cattail marshes and swamps.

RECORDS AND REMARKS: Moorhens stay in or at the edge of dense vegetation and can be difficult to see. They swim into the open infrequently and are not very vocal. They resemble coots but are smaller, have a white horizontal stripe on their sides, and a reddish bill.

SPRING—Migrants arrive during mid-April and have been detected into the third week of May. The majority of records involve single individuals.

1, Mermet Lake CA, 11 Apr 1986 (WDR)
1, Pine Hills, Union Co., 19 Apr 1975 (BP)
1, Oakwood Bottoms, Jackson Co., 27 Apr 1973 (VK, HDB)
1, Gallatin Co., 10 May 1980 (SBC)
2–4, Sparta, Randolph Co., 5–21 May 1986 (TF)
1–2, Union Co. CA, 7–19 May 1994 (VK, TF)
1, Crab Orchard NWR, 12–20 May 1954 (LB)

SUMMER—Known breeding and summering sites are primarily on reclaimed strip-mine ponds that have extensive emergent vegetation.

2 ad. and 5 yg., n. Randolph Co., 16 June 1985 (JCR)
9, Mermet Lake CA, late June 1990, but only 2 there in early July (TF et al.)
2, Rend Lake, Franklin Co., 10 July 1971 (VK et al.)
2 ads., Open Pond, Saline Co., July 1985 (RBu)
1 ad. and 2 juv., Willisville, Perry Co., 24 July 1990 (TF)
1, Union Co. CA, 30 July 1993 (TF)

AUTUMN—Very few autumn records are available, but this shy species may simply be overlooked.

1, s.w. Saline Co., 6 Sep 1990 (TF, JD)
1, Rend Lake, Jefferson Co., 30 Sep 1976 (BP)
6, Marion, Williamson Co., 1 Oct 1950 (RB)

DOCUMENTATION: Specimen—female, Alto Pass, Union Co., 2–3 May 1974 (SIU, uncatalogued).

FIELD GUIDES: G=106; N=100; P=64.

American Coot *Fulica americana*

Late September–Mid-December
Late February–Early May

STATUS AND ABUNDANCE: Common migrant. Uncommon winter resident. Rare summer resident.

HABITAT: Marshes, lakes, and flooded fields.

RECORDS AND REMARKS: Coots are highly gregarious birds. Flocks seem to be present in every cove of a lake during peak migration. Like diving ducks, they require a running start to become airborne. They usually forage in shallow water for submerged vegetable matter, invertebrates, and fish.

AUTUMN—Early migrants begin arriving during late summer, but migration is not in full swing until late September. Coots can at times be abundant on shallow lakes. They will linger late into winter as long as open water is available.

3, Randolph Co., 13 Aug 1983 (JCR)
1, Saline Co., 18 Aug 1987 (WDR)
1, Rend Lake, Franklin Co., 10 Sep 1988 (TF, WDR)
1,100, Carbondale, 23 Nov 1986 (WDR)

WINTER—Large numbers are sometimes recorded during mild winters. Even in severe winters, at least a few try to overwinter on warm-water lakes.

725, Crab Orchard NWR, 13 Jan 1989 (WDR)
85, Lake of Egypt, Williamson Co., 23 Jan 1985 (JCR)
600, Crab Orchard NWR, 31 Jan 1987 (WDR)

SPRING—Northward migration begins as soon as open water is available. Coots can seem even more common in spring than in fall.

25, Baldwin Lake, 17 Feb 1984 (TF)
2, Rend Lake, 4 Mar 1988 (TF)
1,203, Baldwin Lake, 31 Mar 1984 (TF)
1,185, Crab Orchard NWR, 11 Apr 1985 (JCR)
35, Massac Co., 10 May 1980 (SBC)

SUMMER—Coots are opportunistic breeders, taking advantage of flooded fields during very wet years for breeding. They also breed in cattail marshes along lake fringes. Surveys of strip-mine ponds with abundant emergent vegetation could produce more breeding records. Some late-summer records may represent very early fall migrants.

nest with eggs, Crab Orchard NWR, Apr 1950 (Bennett 1952)
39 young, Crab Orchard NWR, summers from 1949–1952 (Bennett 1957)

38 nests in a flooded wheat field, s.w. Jackson Co., summer 1973 (DH, VK)

10, Rend Lake, Franklin Co., 10 July 1971 (VK et al.)

ad., Union Co. CA, 18 July 1987 (WDR)

16, Mermet Lake CA, 22 July 1976 (BP)

1, Oakwood Bottoms, Jackson Co., 2 Aug 1975 (BP)

1, Crab Orchard NWR, 4 Aug 1972 (VK)

DOCUMENTATION: Specimen—Carbondale, Jackson Co., 2 Apr 1884 (SIU A-152).

FIELD GUIDES: G=106; N=100; P=64.

Family Gruidae: Cranes

Sandhill Crane *Grus canadensis*

Early October–Early April

STATUS AND ABUNDANCE: Rare migrant and winter resident.

HABITAT: Mudflats, marshes, plowed fields, and lake edges.

RECORDS AND REMARKS: The subspecies recorded in Illinois is *G. c. tabida* (Bohlen 1989), but there are skeletal records of *G. c. canadensis* from an archaeological excavation in Jackson Co. (Baker 1937). When in flight, cranes are distinguished from geese by their long trailing legs, but in very cold weather, they sometimes tuck in their legs (see photo in *IBB* 4:68). Southern Illinois is not in a migration path for cranes, so any encounters involve birds that are off course; they occur, therefore, only irregularly.

AUTUMN—More encounters are recorded for fall than during spring. Records seem to cluster from late October through November.

1, w. Jackson Co., 9 Sep 1993 (CS, BD)

1, Crab Orchard NWR, 7 Oct 1960 (LB)

1, Crab Orchard NWR, 24 Oct 1959 (LB)

1, near Shawneetown on the Ohio River, 6 Nov 1820 (Audubon 1929)

7, Crab Orchard NWR, 7 Nov 1952 (LB)

5, Cypress Creek NWR, 17 Nov 1992 (TF)

ad., Rend Lake, Jefferson Co., 25 Nov 1988 (TF, WDR)

WINTER—All winter records come from waterfowl refuges, where the cranes presumably feed on waste corn.

3, Rend Lake, Jefferson Co., 29 Nov 1987–mid-Jan 1988 (TF, WDR)

1, Union Co., 19 Dec 1985 (VK, MC)

imm., Crab Orchard NWR, 8 Jan–12 Mar 1985 (JCR)

imm., Baldwin Lake, 2 Feb–14 Mar 1984 (TF, m.ob.)

SPRING—Very few spring records. The occurrence of these birds may be related to strong wind patterns that blow them off course.

2, Union Co. CA, 27 Mar 1993 (KM)

1, Anna, Union Co., 5–6 Apr 1986 (RP, m.ob.)

1, s.w. Jackson Co., 14 Apr 1945 (JWH)

ad. with stained plumage, near Vienna, Johnson Co., 29 May 1993 (TF)

DOCUMENTATION: Photograph—3, Rend Lake, Jefferson Co., 5 Jan 1988 (*IBB* 4:68).

FIELD GUIDES: G=102; N=58; P=106.

Order Charadriiformes: Shorebirds, Gulls, and Terns

Family Charadriidae: Plovers

Black-bellied Plover *Pluvialis squatarola*

Early May–Late May
Early August–Mid-October

STATUS AND ABUNDANCE: Uncommon migrant.

HABITAT: Mudflats and the shallow water of flooded fields.

RECORDS AND REMARKS: Forages along the water's edge at extensive mudflats, sometimes wading into very shallow water. Often forages on drier parts of mudflats, too, where sedges and grasses are beginning to sprout. Black-bellies in winter plumage can be confused with golden-plovers, but the black axillaries, larger bill, larger overall size, and whiter overall appearance are characteristic of black-bellies.

SPRING—Arrives in late spring, with peak numbers passing through in mid-May. First arrivals are sometimes still in winter plumage, but by mid-May, almost all are in full breeding plumage.

2, Black Bottoms, Massac Co., 6 May 1989 (WDR, SO)
2, Randolph Co., 8 May 1976 (SBC)
3, Alexander Co., 10 May 1986 (JCR)
20, Rend Lake, Jefferson Co., 14 May, and 1 still there on 1 June 1987 (TF)
30, near Jacob, Jackson Co., 21 May 1993 (JD)

AUTUMN—Adults arrive before immatures and are often still in breeding plumage. By September the immatures begin arriving, and all are in winter plumage. Some birds linger quite late, until they are forced south by freezing weather.

1, Rend Lake, Jefferson Co., 2 Aug 1986 (TF)
6, Rend Lake, Jefferson Co., 13 Oct 1985 (LH, TF)
13, Crab Orchard NWR, 21 Oct 1989 (WDR)
1, Crab Orchard NWR, 30 Nov 1960 (LB)
1, Crab Orchard NWR, 1 Dec 1989 (WDR)

DOCUMENTATION: Photograph—Ward Branch, Rend Lake, Jefferson Co., 31 Aug 1988 (SIU AP-258).

FIELD GUIDES: G=112; N=108; P=118.

Lesser Golden-Plover *Pluvialis dominica*

Late March–Early May
Mid-August–Mid-October

STATUS AND ABUNDANCE: Common spring migrant in the Floodplains and the Till Plain. Uncommon spring migrant in the Shawnee Hills. Uncommon fall migrant throughout the region.

HABITAT: Large plowed fields and mudflats.

RECORDS AND REMARKS: During spring these shorebirds tend to frequent plowed agricultural fields, especially those with very finely tilled soil, whereas during fall most sightings are at mudflats. Many times, golden-plovers are more often detected as noisy flocks flying high overhead; indeed, they rarely stop in the Shawnee Hills, but they are regularly encountered as flybys during the peak of spring migration. The majority of golden-plovers migrate north through the Great Plains and the Mississippi River Valley, but they go to the East Coast then south to South America during the fall. The golden-plover that occurs in southern Illinois may soon be named the American Golden-Plover *(P. dominica)*; its close relative, the Pacific Golden-Plover *(P. fulva),* occurs in western North America and Asia. The British Ornithologists' Union has already split the two into distinct species, but the American Ornithologists' Union has not followed suit yet. Pacific Golden-Plovers could occur as vagrants; any golden-plover found at an odd season should be carefully scrutinized. Identification details are in Hayman et al. (1986).

SPRING—First spring arrivals are usually in winter plumage, but by April most are in molt and are quickly attaining breeding plumage. They can be especially numerous along the Mississippi River floodplains. The latest migrants usually occur at mudflats, because most agricultural crops have begun to grow by late May.

10, Alexander Co., 11 Mar 1993 (TF)
39, Alexander Co., 16 Mar 1985 (JCR)
580, Alexander Co., 31 Mar 1984 (JCR)
895, Union Co. CA, 10 Apr 1971 (VK)
6, Alexander Co., 26 May 1984 (TF, JCR)
1, Rend Lake, 27 May 1976 (BP)
1 (injured), Alexander Co., 3 June 1985 (TF, JCR)

AUTUMN—Southward migration begins with the arrival of adults by mid-August, but some early migrants have been seen during midsummer. Most golden-plovers are in winter plumage during fall migration through southern Illinois. Because most golden-plovers go to the East Coast before heading south to their wintering grounds, far fewer pass through southern Illinois in fall than during spring.

1, Alexander Co., 26 June 1978 (MMo)
2 in winter plumage, s. Alexander Co., 5–19 July 1986 (WDR, TF)
2, Rend Lake, Jefferson Co., 3 Aug 1986 (LH)
35, s. Alexander Co., 23 Aug 1973 (DH)
11, Rend Lake, Jefferson Co., 24 Sep 1985 (LH)
1, Carbondale, 1 Oct 1971 (VK)
1, Rend Lake, Jefferson Co., 11 Nov 1987 (TF)
2, Mermet Lake CA, 22 Nov 1986 (TF, WDR)

DOCUMENTATION: Specimen—ad. male, near Miller City, Alexander Co., 26 Apr 1969 (SIU A-1627).

FIELD GUIDES: G=112; N=108; P=118.

[Snowy Plover *Charadrius alexandrinus*]

STATUS AND ABUNDANCE: Hypothetical.

RECORDS AND REMARKS: One was seen by a single observer on a mudflat in a flooded field north of Gorham, Jackson Co., on 19 May 1993 (TF), and it remained for only a few hours. The record of that observation is the region's only report and represents the third Illinois record.

FIELD GUIDES: G=112; N=104; P=120.

Semipalmated Plover *Charadrius semipalmatus*

Late April–Late May
Late July–Early October

STATUS AND ABUNDANCE: Fairly common migrant.

HABITAT: Mudflats and shallowly flooded fields.

RECORDS AND REMARKS: Frequents the barren portions of mudflats that lack vegetation and standing water. Runs a short distance, stops and picks up a food item, pauses, and then repeats the process. Generally found in small, loosely formed flocks. Juvenile Killdeer can resemble these plovers at first glance.
SPRING—First arrival dates are somewhat dependent on weather and habitat availability. In wet springs when flooded fields are common, these plovers can seem very common. Migration peaks in mid-May, and some late migrants linger into June.
1, Union Co. CA, and 1, Cypress Creek NWR, 18 Apr 1992 (TF, WDR)
3, Alexander Co., 20 Apr 1985 (JCR)
9, Pope Co., 26 Apr 1986 (WDR)
68, Black Bottoms, Massac Co., 6 May 1989 (WDR, SO)
66, Union Co. CA, 9 May 1981 (VK)
60, Rend Lake, Jefferson Co., 12 May 1986 (TF, WDR)

28, Carbondale, 12 May 1986 (TF, WDR)
100+, Rend Lake, Jefferson Co., 13–26 May 1987 (TF, LH)
3, Rend Lake, Jefferson Co., 1 June 1987 (TF)
3, Rend Lake, Jefferson Co., 7 June 1986 (WDR)
AUTUMN—Fewer seem to be detected in fall, a time when the only shorebird habitat available is along the edges of reservoirs.
3, s.w. Jackson Co., 12 July 1986 (WDR)
2, Rend Lake, Jefferson Co., 20 July 1985 (TF, JCR)
4, Mermet Lake CA, 31 July 1984 (SO)
11, Rend Lake, Jefferson Co., 2 Aug 1986 (TF)
30, Rend Lake, Jefferson Co., 10 Sep 1988 (TF, WDR)
2, Rend Lake, Jefferson Co., 13 Oct 1986 (TF)
1, Crab Orchard NWR, 28 Oct 1989 (TF, WDR)

DOCUMENTATION: Specimen—ad. female, Jacob, Jackson Co., 11 May 1969 (SIU A-2078).

FIELD GUIDES: G=114; N=104; P=118.

Piping Plover *Charadrius melodus*
Late July–Mid-October

STATUS AND ABUNDANCE: Rare fall migrant.

HABITAT: Sandy mudflats.

RECORDS AND REMARKS: There is an unsubstantiated report of three birds from the Franklin Co. Spring Bird Count on 10 May 1980; otherwise there are no spring records. They should occur as rare migrants between late April and mid-May. Sometimes they associate with Semipalmated Plovers, but Piping Plovers prefer the portions of mudflats that are more sandy or pebbly. Currently listed on both the state and the federal endangered species lists.
AUTUMN—All recent records are from Rend Lake. Peak migration seems to be during early September.
1, Rend Lake, Jefferson Co., 18 July 1992 (TF)
1, Rend Lake, Franklin Co., 27–28 July 1986 (TF, LH, WDR)
1, Rend Lake, Jefferson Co., 17 Aug 1990 (TF, JD, WDR)
1, Rend Lake, 24 Aug, and another 1 there 3 Sep 1976 (BP)
1, Rend Lake, Jefferson Co., 26 Aug 1984 (LH)
1, Rend Lake, Jefferson Co., 2 Sep 1989 (TF, JH, WDR)

1, Bell Island, near Shawneetown, 7 Sep 1953 (RB, JWH)
1, Rend Lake, Jefferson Co., 8 Sep 1985 and 9 Sep 1986 (LH)
1, Carbondale, 14 Sep 1953 (RB, JWH)
1, Rend Lake, Jefferson Co., 13 Oct 1985 (LH)
1, Rend Lake, Jefferson Co., 24 Oct 1992 (TF)

DOCUMENTATION: Photograph—Rend Lake, Jefferson Co., 17 Aug 1990 (TF).

FIELD GUIDES: G=114; N=104; P=118.

Killdeer *Charadrius vociferus*
Mid-February–Early April
Early July–Mid-December

STATUS AND ABUNDANCE: Common migrant and summer resident. Uncommon winter resident.

HABITAT: Nearly any wetland area, golf course, agricultural field, mudflat, or large shopping mall.

RECORDS AND REMARKS: Killdeer are the ubiquitous shorebirds of town and country. In towns, they frequently can be seen foraging in parking lots and along mowed ditches; they nest on the ground as well as on gravel-roofed buildings.
SPRING—Migrants return soon after the first warm spell in February or even in late January in some years. Diurnal migrants, they can be seen moving north, calling and flying at low altitudes, especially on warm, clear days.
2, Union Co. CA, 4 Feb 1991 (TF)
30, Carbon Lake, Jackson Co., 19 Feb 1949 (RB)
SUMMER—Breeding begins in early April; two nests were found in Murphysboro on 6 April 1949 (RB). Nests are simple scrapes in patches of gravel where three or four eggs are laid. Downy young are seen from May through July. Some nest sites are seemingly poor choices, like those placed in the gravel piled up in the center or along the edge of rural roads.
43, Union Co., 5 May 1990 (VK et al.)
AUTUMN—Fall migration seems to have two phases. The first is the congregation of local breeders at the best mudflats, which happens during late June and throughout July. These birds seem to

move out during August. Presumably birds from farther north begin arriving by September. Their numbers can peak quite late, and many linger until freezing weather forces them south.

206, Rend Lake, Jefferson Co., 8 July 1986 (WDR)

280, Rend Lake, Jefferson Co., 1 Aug 1992 (TF)

200, Crab Orchard NWR, 5 Nov 1989 (WDR)

104, Alexander Co., 17 Nov 1984 (JCR)

WINTER—During mild winters, Killdeer may be present throughout December and January, but when mudflats and shorelines freeze, they depart the region.

100, Union Co. CBC, 22 Dec 1982

249, Horseshoe Lake CBC, 2 Jan 1987

DOCUMENTATION: Specimen—juv., 3 miles n.w. of Carbondale, Jackson Co., 10 July 1956 (SIU A-155).

FIELD GUIDES: G=114; N=106; P=118.

Family Recurvirostridae: Stilts and Avocets

Black-necked Stilt *Himantopus mexicanus*

STATUS AND ABUNDANCE: Very rare migrant and summer resident.

HABITAT: Mudflats and shallow-water areas.

RECORDS AND REMARKS: The first regional record of this striking black-and-white shorebird was established on 3 July 1992, when an adult female was found at Ward Branch, Rend Lake, in Jefferson Co. (JD, TF, DKa; DeNeal 1993). Surprisingly, a second female was discovered just a few days later near Ullin, Pulaski Co., on 4–9 July 1992 (JHe, TF). Then, in 1993, there was an onslaught of records, as the stilts responded to the abundant habitat available in the Jackson Co. floodplain as a result of the great Mississippi River flood. Three were found on 21 May in western Jackson Co. (BD), and a maximum of eleven different birds was present in the Grand Tower area and in extreme northwest Union Co. into July (SB). One pair even behaved as though it was attempting to breed; the female gave a broken-wing display, and the male displayed agitated flight on 24 June 1993 in southwest Jackson Co. (Fink 1994). The last 1993 sighting was of four birds near Jacob, Jackson Co., on 21

Black-necked Stilt nest, southwest Jackson Co., 11 June 1994

August (CS, BD). Then, in 1994, a spring arrival returned to Jackson Co. on 19 April 1994 (TF). Fewer birds were present in the summer than during 1993, but a nest with four eggs was found in southwest Jackson Co. on 11 June 1994 (TF, CW).

DOCUMENTATION: Photograph—ad. female, near Ullin, Pulaski Co., 7 July 1992 (SIU, uncatalogued).

FIELD GUIDES: G=108; N=102; P=116.

American Avocet *Recurvirostra americana*

Mid-July–Early November

STATUS AND ABUNDANCE: Very rare spring migrant. Rare fall migrant.

HABITAT: Mudflats and shallow-water areas.

RECORDS AND REMARKS: These handsome shorebirds forage by

American Avocets, Rend Lake, Jefferson Co., 27 August 1988

sweeping their bills from side to side in shallow water as they walk. Todd Fink and I watched a group of three foraging at Rend Lake; strangely, they would not defecate in the water where they were foraging but would sprint up onto the mudflat instead and then wade back into the water to resume foraging.

SPRING—There are only two spring records. Avocets could be recorded more often during spring, because they pass through other sections of Illinois in late April and early May.

1, Carbondale, 17 Apr 1982 (SO, MMl)

1, Crab Orchard NWR, 20–21 Apr 1991 (BD, TF)

AUTUMN—Generally encountered as single individuals until late autumn, when small groups have been recorded. Birds in winter plumage have gray heads instead of the striking rust of breeding plumage.

1, Crab Orchard NWR, 10 July 1987 (WDR, TF)

1, Rend Lake, Jefferson Co., 2 Aug 1989 (BD)

1, w. Jackson Co., 26 Aug 1993 (TF, CS)

3, Rend Lake, Jefferson Co., 27 Aug 1988 (TF, WDR)

1, Rend Lake, Jefferson Co., 22 and 28 Sep 1985 (TF)

1, Crab Orchard NWR, 1 Oct 1952 (LB)

1, Union Co. CA, 17 Oct 1976 (HDB et al.)

8, Crab Orchard NWR, 21–22 Oct 1993 (KP, TF)

4–7, Crab Orchard NWR, 3–12 Nov 1982 (BG, JCR et al.)
5, Rend Lake, 8 Nov 1975 (BP)

DOCUMENTATION: Photograph—Nason, Rend Lake, Jefferson Co.,
27 Aug 1988 (SIU AP-250).

FIELD GUIDES: G=108; N=102; P=116.

Family Scolopacidae: Shorebirds

Greater Yellowlegs *Tringa melanoleuca*
Late March–Mid-May
Mid-July–Early November

STATUS AND ABUNDANCE: Fairly common migrant.

HABITAT: Mudflats, wet grassy fields, and shallow flooded fields.

RECORDS AND REMARKS: Tends to wade in water when foraging.
Associates with, and is usually less numerous than, its congener,
the Lesser Yellowlegs. Yellowlegs migrate diurnally, and their loud
calls draw attention to them as they fly by.
SPRING—Migration peaks in late April and early May. Yellowlegs
do not need extensive mudflats as do some shorebird species; they
will often use small pools of water in agricultural fields, sewage pond
edges, and roadside ditches.
1, Pope Co., 14 Mar 1985 (JP)
1, Union Co., 25 Mar 1984 (TF, JCR)
33, Massac Co., 7 May 1977 (SBC)
1, Rend Lake, 25 May 1986 (TF)
AUTUMN—Usually not encountered in large numbers, but there
always seems to be a few at any appropriate habitat. Migration peaks
in September. Some birds linger quite late into November.
2, Rend Lake, Jefferson Co., 8 July 1986 (WDR)
1, s. Alexander Co., 12 July 1986 (TF, WDR)
15, Rend Lake, Jefferson Co., 28 July 1986 (KM)
3, s.w. Jackson Co., 17 Nov 1984 (JCR)
1, Crab Orchard NWR, 18 Nov 1989 (BD, WDR)
1, Carbondale, 24 Nov 1984 (JCR)

DOCUMENTATION: Photograph—Union Co. CA, Union Co., 29 Mar 1986 (SIU AP-38).

FIELD GUIDES: G=120; N=114; P=128.

Lesser Yellowlegs *Tringa flavipes*

Late March–Late May
Early July–Early November

STATUS AND ABUNDANCE: Common migrant. Very rare summer visitor.

HABITAT: Mudflats, pond and lake edges, and wet grassy fields.

RECORDS AND REMARKS: Forages in the very shallow water of mudflats and in pools of water in fields. This common shorebird can occur at nearly any wet area during the peak of migration, even in roadside ditches and along stream edges. Forms noisy flocks when flushed. Bobs its head up and down when alarmed. One specimen was obtained from a bird that collided with and killed itself on a chain-link fence (TF).

SPRING—First migrants arrive during the second half of March. Migration peaks in late April and early May. Most have departed by 20 May.

1, Pope Co., 14 Mar 1985 (JP)
4, Crab Orchard NWR, 14 Mar 1986 (WDR)
150, Pulaski Co., 18 Apr 1992 (TF, WDR)
130, Alexander Co., 5 May 1984 (TF)
75, s.w. Union Co., 2 May 1985 (VK)
49, Pope Co., 5 May 1977 (SBC)
1, Alexander Co., 26 May 1984 (TF, JCR)

SUMMER—One midsummer record could either be a very late spring migrant or a very early fall migrant:

1, Rend Lake, Jefferson Co., 14 June 1988 (TF).

AUTUMN—Adults return early. Migration peaks in September and early October. Large concentrations can occur in good habitat. Some birds linger late as long as the weather is mild.

1, s.w. Jackson Co., 29 June 1985 (JCR)
10, s.w. Jackson Co., 3 July 1973 (DH)
101, Rend Lake, Jefferson Co., 22 July 1994 (TF)

104, Rend Lake, Jefferson Co., 5 Sep 1994 (TF)
85, Crab Orchard NWR, 5 Oct 1983 (JCR)
1, Carbondale, 17 Nov 1984 (TF)
1, Crab Orchard NWR, 28 Nov 1989 (WDR)

DOCUMENTATION: Specimen—ad. male, Carbondale, Jackson Co., 5 May 1971 (SIU A-1740).

FIELD GUIDES: G=120; N=114; P=128.

Solitary Sandpiper *Tringa solitaria*
Late March–Mid-May
Mid-July–Mid-September

STATUS AND ABUNDANCE: Fairly common migrant.

HABITAT: Wet grassy fields, pond and lake borders, mudflats, and even along creeks.

RECORDS AND REMARKS: Forages in shallow water and at the mud/water interface on mudflats. Occur as single individuals in nearly any wetland habitat, even along the shores of small ponds in otherwise forested habitat. Sometimes congregate in a good habitat, but are never found in big groups. They are one of the few shorebirds that does not require very open habitats, often foraging alongside brushy vegetation or a woodland edge.
SPRING—First arrivals appear during the last week of March. Migration peaks during late April and early May.
1, Jackson Co., 23 Mar 1985 (JCR)
1, Giant City SP, 28 Mar 1989 (WDR)
30, Pulaski Co., 4 May 1994 (TF)
16, Williamson Co., 6 May 1985 (JCR)
14, Massac Co., 6 May 1989 (WDR, SO)
1, Union Co. CA, 21 May 1971 (VK et al.)
1, Crab Orchard NWR, 26 May 1987 (WDR)
AUTUMN—Migration begins and ends early. Late July and August bring peak numbers. Most Solitaries have migrated south by September.
1, Alexander Co., 29 June 1985 (JCR)
1, s.w. Jackson Co., 30 June 1989 (WDR)
2, Crab Orchard NWR, 5 July 1987 (WDR)

25, s.w. Jackson Co., 24 July 1986 (WDR)

2, Rend Lake, Jefferson Co., 10 Sep 1988 (TF, WDR)

1, Crab Orchard NWR, 17 Oct 1984 (JCR)

Documentation: Specimen—ad. male, Alexander Co., 3 May 1969 (SIU A-2124).

Field Guides: G=120; N=116; P=128.

Willet *Catoptrophorus semipalmatus*

Late April–Early May
Early July–Mid-September

Status and abundance: Rare migrant.

Habitat: Wet grassy fields, mudflats, and beaches.

Records and remarks: Willets are more numerous in spring than in fall, but they are nevertheless rare at both seasons. They forage in wet grassy fields during spring; sometimes they go unnoticed because they frequent fairly tall grass. If they did not have such loud calls and flashy wing patterns, they might be overlooked even more. Willets are famous for not staying at one place for more than a few hours.

SPRING—Tend to form flocks in spring. Most of them pass through in a two-week period centered at 1 May.

25, Pulaski Co., 6 Apr 1974 (*AB* 28:808)

4, Crab Orchard NWR, 23 Apr 1952 (LB)

1, Harrisburg, Saline Co., 27 Apr 1992 (JD)

44, Union Co., 29 Apr 1990 (BD)

10, Rend Lake, Jefferson Co., 30 Apr 1987 (LH)

7, Big Bay, Massac Co., 9 May 1981 (GW, HW, WDR)

13, Union Co., 9 May 1981 (SBC)

AUTUMN—Southward migration is of longer duration, but fewer birds have been recorded.

1, Union Co. CA, 3 July 1987 (RP)

4, Rend Lake, Jefferson Co., 3 July 1992 (TF, JD, DKa)

1, Rend Lake, Jefferson Co., 8 July 1986 (WDR)

10, Crab Orchard NWR, 14 Aug 1966 (George 1968)

1, Rend Lake, Jefferson Co., 17 Aug 1991 (TF)

2, w. Jackson Co., 24–26 Aug 1993 (CS, TF)

1, Rend Lake, 25 Aug 1976 (BP)
1, near Grand Tower, Jackson Co., 26 Aug 1990 (BD, WDR)
1, s.w. Jackson Co., 1 and 3 Sep 1973 (DH et al.)
1 juv. molting into first basic plumage, Rend Lake, Jefferson Co., 5 Sep 1994 (TF)

DOCUMENTATION: Photograph—1, Rend Lake, Jefferson Co., 5 Sep 1994 (SIU AP, uncatalogued). A male specimen labeled as collected in "southern Illinois" on 6 May 1875 (NMNH 94719) may have been obtained from outside the coverage area of this book, in Mt. Carmel, Wabash Co.

FIELD GUIDES: G=122; N=114; P=128.

Spotted Sandpiper *Actitis macularia*
Mid-April–Late May
Early July–Early October

STATUS AND ABUNDANCE: Fairly common migrant.

HABITAT: Rocky shores of lakes and rivers; beaches and mudflats.

RECORDS AND REMARKS: Usually forages at water's edge from rocky shores, such as those along dams and spillways, but also at the mud/water interface when on mudflats. Distinctive bobbing motion of the body and shallow, stiff wing beats are diagnostic fieldmarks. SPRING—A few arrive early in spring, but peak migration occurs in late April and the first half of May. Some present in early June could be breeders, but there are no mid-June records for the region, and breeding has never been confirmed.
1, Crab Orchard NWR, 28 Mar 1987 (WDR)
1, Carbondale, 6–7 Apr 1986 (WDR)
1, Rend Lake, Jefferson Co., 12 Apr 1988 (TF)
16, Massac Co., 5 May 1984 (SBC)
2, Little Grassy Lake, Williamson Co., 1 June 1985 (WDR)
1, Crab Orchard NWR, 2 June 1984 (EC)
AUTUMN—Earliest fall arrivals may be birds that bred just north of the region in Illinois; most early arrivals are adults. Migration peaks in July and August, and the majority have passed through the region by mid-September.

1, Union Co. CA, 28 June 1990 (WDR)
1, Crab Orchard NWR, 8 July 1987 (WDR)
11, Rend Lake, Jefferson Co., 14 July 1988 (WDR)
8, Mermet Lake CA, 6 Aug 1986 (WDR)
1, Rend Lake, Jefferson Co., 17 Oct 1985 (TF)

DOCUMENTATION: Specimen—ad. male, Alexander Co., 3 May 1969 (SIU A-1762).

FIELD GUIDES: G=124; N=116; P=132.

Upland Sandpiper *Bartramia longicauda*
Mid-April–Mid-May
Mid-July–Early September

STATUS AND ABUNDANCE: Locally uncommon migrant and summer visitor in the Till Plain. Rare migrant in the Floodplains and the Shawnee Hills.

HABITAT: Large grassy fields, pastures, airports, prairie, and hayfields.

RECORDS AND REMARKS: Sometimes difficult to see because they forage in tall-grass fields, Uplands frequently perch on posts and have a loud call like a wolf whistle that makes them more conspicuous. Because of the destruction of prairie habitat, they have opportunistically begun to use airports as foraging and, potentially, breeding habitat.

SPRING—In most years, the first arrivals appear early in the second week of April. Small groups can be found well into May in areas with a good habitat. Some records from later in May could be birds attempting to breed.

3, Union Co. CA, 5 Apr 1986 (KM)
1, Williamson Co. Airport, 10 Apr 1986 (TF)
7, Murphysboro, 10 Apr 1949 (JWH, RB)
5, Williamson Co. Airport, 12 Apr 1984 (JCR)
1, Mt. Vernon Airport, 14 Apr 1988 (TF)
2, Pulaski Co., 17 Apr 1992 (TF)
1, Rend Lake, 26 Apr 1983 (RZ)

SUMMER—No confirmation of breeding has been obtained, but

Upland Sandpiper, Williamson County Airport, Williamson Co., 31 August 1987

there are several summer records from appropriate habitat. Breeding may occur on the grasslands of some reclaimed strip mines in the Till Plain.

1, 2.5 miles n. of Jamestown, Perry Co., 11 June 1989 (WDR)

1, Ewing, Franklin Co., 19 June 1981 (JJ)

1, w. Perry Co., 19 June 1984 (VK)

AUTUMN—Some early-fall records probably represent local birds moving to good habitat before migrating south. They leave early, most having departed by early September.

1, Rend Lake, Jefferson Co., 13 July 1986 (LH)

13, Williamson Co. Airport, 18 July 1972 (VK, DH)
3, Rend Lake, Jefferson Co., 3 Aug 1986 (LH)
1, Rend Lake, Jefferson Co., 25 Aug 1985 (LH)
1, w. Jackson Co., 26 Aug 1993 (CS)
1, Rend Lake, Jefferson Co., 4 Sep 1986 (TF)

DOCUMENTATION: Specimen—male, 3 miles n.e. of Thebes, Alexander Co., 6 May 1961 (NIU 123).

FIELD GUIDES: G=122; N=134; P=130.

Whimbrel *Numenius phaeopus*

STATUS AND ABUNDANCE: Very rare fall visitor.

HABITAT: Extensive mudflats.

RECORDS AND REMARKS: There are only three records. This shorebird has an east–west migration route that takes it through the Great Lakes region, so it rarely passes through southern Illinois. It is possible, however, that some may be recorded during spring (probably in mid- to late May). Whimbrels forage on mudflats and in grassy fields flooded with shallow water.

AUTUMN—2, Rend Lake, Jefferson Co., 3 Sep 1988 (BD)
1, w. Jackson Co., 8 Sep 1993 (CS, BD)
1, Rend Lake, Jefferson Co., 21 Sep 1986 (TF)

DOCUMENTATION: Written description—Rend Lake, Jefferson Co., 21 Sep 1986.

FIELD GUIDES: G=118; N=112; P=126.

Hudsonian Godwit *Limosa haemastica*

Early May–Late May
Early September–Mid-October

STATUS AND ABUNDANCE: Rare migrant.

HABITAT: Mudflats and shallow-water areas of ponds and lakes.

RECORDS AND REMARKS: Forages by probing rapidly in water up to belly deep. Occurs in small flocks or singly, generally not remaining at one site for more than a day or so. Irregular, this species may not be recorded every year.

SPRING—Most are in bright breeding plumage during their May passage through the region. Fewer have been detected during spring than in fall.

3, Big Bay, Massac Co., 9 May 1981 (GW, HW, WDR)
4, Rend Lake, Jefferson Co., 15 May 1992 (TF, JD)
1, Rend Lake, Jefferson Co., 19 May 1987 (LH)
1, Prairie du Rocher, Randolph Co., 27 May 1984 (RG)
1, Rend Lake, Jefferson Co., 30 May 1987 (TF)

AUTUMN—Most are in gray winter plumage, but some may still be molting and have patches of rust on their underparts.

1, Rend Lake, Jefferson Co., 7 Sep 1986 (DJ)
1, Rend Lake, Jefferson Co., 23 Sep 1989 (BD)
6, Rend Lake, Jefferson Co., 6 Oct, and 2 there 13 Oct, but only 1 on 20 Oct 1985 (LH)
1, Carbondale, 17 Oct 1970 (VK, DH)
1, Rend Lake, Jefferson Co., 19–24 Oct 1992 (TF, JD, DKa)
1, Rend Lake, Jefferson Co., 23 Oct 1987 (TF)
1, Mermet Lake CA, 5 Nov 1991 (TF, JD)

DOCUMENTATION: Written description—3, Big Bay, Massac Co., 9 May 1981.

FIELD GUIDES: G=116; N=110; P=126.

Marbled Godwit *Limosa fedoa*

Late July–Early September

STATUS AND ABUNDANCE: Very rare fall migrant.

HABITAT: Mudflats and shallow-water areas of lakes and flooded fields.

RECORDS AND REMARKS: Could also occur during spring, probably from mid-April to mid-May. All records involve single birds. Forages by probing in shallow water, sometimes up to belly deep.

AUTUMN—1, Rend Lake, Jefferson Co., 9 July 1994 (TF)
1, Rend Lake, Jefferson Co., 20–21 July 1985 (JCR, SS, LH)
1, Rend Lake, Jefferson Co., 2 Aug 1986 (TF)
1, Rend Lake, Jefferson Co., 11 Aug 1991 (TF, JD)
1, s. Alexander Co., 16 Aug 1973 (DH)
1, Crab Orchard NWR, 22 Aug 1951 (LB)
1, Rend Lake, Jefferson Co., 18 Aug–5 Sep 1985 (LH, RP)

DOCUMENTATION: Written description—1, Rend Lake, Jefferson Co., 20–21 July 1985.

FIELD GUIDES: G=116; N=110; P=126.

Ruddy Turnstone *Arenaria interpres*
Mid-May–Early June
Early August–Late September

STATUS AND ABUNDANCE: Uncommon migrant.

HABITAT: Beaches and mudflats strewn with pebbles and small rocks.

RECORDS AND REMARKS: Forage by walking along and flipping over small pebbles and rocks. In a flooded field in Jackson Co., some flipped over pieces of corn stalks that had piled up because of the flood waters in September 1993 (CS). Flock sizes tend to be larger during spring than in fall.
SPRING—Form small flocks of brightly plumaged birds. Peak numbers appear during mid-May.
4, Rend Lake, 12 May 1987 (LH)
25, Rend Lake, 19 May 1987 (LH)
6, Rend Lake, Jefferson Co., 25 May 1986 (TF)
1, Rend Lake, Jefferson Co., 7 June 1986 (WDR)
AUTUMN—Fall migrants apparently move toward the East Coast via the Great Lakes, so fewer turnstones pass through southern Illinois. Most are in winter plumage by the end of August at least.
1, Rend Lake, 24 July 1976 (BP)
1, Crab Orchard NWR, 3 Aug 1972 (VK)
3, Rend Lake, Jefferson Co., 13 Aug 1988 (TF, WDR)
1, along Ohio River, near Mound City, Pulaski Co., 30 Aug 1875 (Nelson 1877)
13, w. Jackson Co., 6 Sep 1993 (CS)
1, Rend Lake, Jefferson Co., 19 Sep 1987 (TF)
3, Rend Lake, Jefferson Co., 22 Sep 1985 (LH)

DOCUMENTATION: Photograph—Ward Branch, Rend Lake, Jefferson Co., 19 Sep 1987 (SIU AP-42).

FIELD GUIDES: G=128; N=126; P=118.

Red Knot *Calidris canutus*

Late July–Early November

STATUS AND ABUNDANCE: Very rare spring migrant. Rare fall migrant.

HABITAT: Mudflats and beaches.

RECORDS AND REMARKS: Knots forage in shallow water and at the water's edge by short probing and picking motions. They are plump, robin-sized birds that sometimes associate with dowitchers.

SPRING—There is only one spring record: a bird in full breeding plumage was at Rend Lake, Jefferson Co., on 2 May 1987 (TF, LA, WDR).

AUTUMN—Early fall migrants are usually still in breeding plumage, but later ones are in their grayer winter plumage. All fall records are from Rend Lake, Jefferson Co.:

1, 22 July 1989 (BD)
1, 20–23 Aug 1986 (TF, LH, WDR)
1, 24 Aug 1976 (BP)
4 imm., 5 Sep 1992 (TF, JD, DKa)
1, 7 and 28–30 Sep (LH, DJ), but 2 there 20 Sep 1986 (WDR)
1, 22–23 Sep 1985 (TF et al.)
1 imm., 4 Nov 1991 (TF et al.)

DOCUMENTATION: Photograph—Rend Lake, Jefferson Co., 22–23 Sep 1985 (SIU AP-43).

FIELD GUIDES: G=130; N=128; P=124.

Sanderling *Calidris alba*

Early May–Late May
Early August–Mid-October

STATUS AND ABUNDANCE: Uncommon migrant.

HABITAT: Sandy beaches and mudflats.

RECORDS AND REMARKS: These hyperactive shorebirds seem always to be running. They sprint after food items washed up on shore by retreating waves and then quickly withdraw ahead of the next oncoming crest. They also are found away from shorelines on mudflats, but they still employ their active foraging method. Surprisingly few shorebird species make use of the extensive sandbars in the Mississippi and Ohio Rivers, but Sanderlings routinely use these sites during migration.

SPRING—The first migrants arrive at about the time of the Spring Bird Count, but the majority do not pass through until mid- or late May. They do not stay at one place very long, so they can be difficult to detect. Most birds are in full breeding plumage during spring.

1, Union Co., 7 May 1977 (VK)
1, Big Bay, Massac Co., 7 May 1988 (WDR)
36, Rend Lake, Jefferson Co., 18 May 1987 (TF)

AUTUMN—There are more records for fall than for spring. Fall migration seems to be more leisurely, so birds remaining at sites where there is favorable habitat for a few days or longer are more likely to be encountered by birders. The earliest arrivals sometimes still have some of their breeding plumage left, but most are in molt and soon obtain their black-and-white winter plumage.

2, Rend Lake, Franklin Co., 27 July 1986 (LH)
12, Rend Lake, 3 Aug 1986 (LH)
2, Crab Orchard NWR, 3 and 5 Aug 1972 (VK)
1, New Shawneetown, Gallatin Co., 10 Aug 1974 (DH)
1, near Chester, Randolph Co., 11 Aug 1987 (WDR)
13, Rend Lake, Jefferson Co., 13 Aug 1987 (TF)
5, Baldwin Lake, 31 Aug 1980 (RK)
1, Santa Fe Chute, Alexander Co., 3 Sep 1988 (WDR)
17, Rend Lake, 22 Sep 1976 (BP)
27, Rend Lake, Jefferson Co., 19 Oct 1992 (TF, JD)
1, Crab Orchard NWR, 26 Oct 1989 (WDR)
1, Rend Lake, Jefferson Co., 30 Oct 1987 (TF)

DOCUMENTATION: Photograph—Rend Lake, Franklin Co., 10 Sep 1988 (SIU AP-240).

FIELD GUIDES: G=130; N=128; P=130.

Semipalmated Sandpiper *Calidris pusilla*

Early May–Early June
Mid-July–Mid-October

STATUS AND ABUNDANCE: Common migrant.

HABITAT: Mudflats.

RECORDS AND REMARKS: Semipalms usually forage on the bare, open stretches of mudflats. They walk along rather slowly, picking rapidly at the surface of the ground. Sometimes they form large flocks that, when flushed, bunch together and maneuver erratically before settling back down some distance away. They are often seen together with other species of shorebirds, especially other peeps. Identification can be difficult, particularly in fall, when birds of many different ages and plumages are present together; Hayman et al. (1986) give identification criteria for all the peeps.
SPRING—First spring arrivals sometimes appear in late April, but in most years they are not found until early May. Peak numbers are present in mid- and late May, and a few linger well into June each summer.
1, Rend Lake, Jefferson Co., 21 Apr 1987 (TF)
2, Vienna, Johnson Co., 24 Apr 1982 (SO)
600, Rend Lake, Jefferson Co., 13 May 1987 (TF)
451, Rend Lake, Jefferson Co., 16 May 1986 (WDR)
200, Alexander Co., 26 May 1984 (TF)
115, Rend Lake, Jefferson Co., 1 June 1987 (TF)
2, Crab Orchard NWR, 2 June 1987 (WDR)
4, Saline Co., 3 June 1984 (JCR)
6, Rend Lake, Jefferson Co., 7 June 1986 (WDR)
AUTUMN—Only three or four weeks after the last spring migrants have departed, the first fall migrants arrive. Numbers are not quite as large in fall as during spring.
2, Rend Lake, Jefferson Co., 8 July 1986 (WDR)
1, Crab Orchard NWR, 10 July 1987 (WDR)
25, East Cape Girardeau, 19 July 1990 (WDR et al.)
200, Rend Lake, Jefferson Co., 4–16 Aug 1986 (TF, WDR)
200, Rend Lake, Jefferson Co., 13 Sep 1989 (WDR)
1, Rend Lake, Jefferson Co., 13 Oct 1986 (TF)
1, Rend Lake, Jefferson Co., 11 Nov 1989 (TF, WDR, JH)

DOCUMENTATION: Specimen—male, Neunert, Jackson Co., 10 May 1969 (SIU A-1991).

FIELD GUIDES: G=132; N=130; P=134.

Western Sandpiper *Calidris mauri*
Early May–Late May
Late July–Late October

STATUS AND ABUNDANCE: Rare spring migrant. Uncommon fall migrant.

HABITAT: Mudflats.

RECORDS AND REMARKS: Westerns are ecologically and physically similar to Semipalmated Sandpipers but are much less numerous. Sometimes they will wade and forage in shallow water, unlike most other peeps. They can be very difficult to separate from Semipalms, but they typically have longer bills that droop at the tip; a higher-pitched, sharper call note; and, in breeding plumage, more prominent flank streaking and chestnut scapulars. In winter plumage, identification is exceptionally difficult; not all Westerns have distinctly longer bills, so some must simply go unidentified (See Hayman et al. 1986 and Kaufman 1990). Although westerns do associate with other peeps, they commonly form their own small flocks.
SPRING—Most migrate north through the Great Plains, thus passing west of southern Illinois.
1, Union Co., 28 Apr 1988 (VK, LH)
1, Crab Orchard NWR, 8 May 1982 (SO)
10, Jackson Co., 10 May 1986 (SBC)
3, Rend Lake, 4 June 1977 (MMo)
AUTUMN—Southward migration begins early, as birds from Alaskan breeding grounds migrate southeastwardly toward the Atlantic Coast. Fall migration is longer than spring migration, spanning five months.
3, Rend Lake, Jefferson Co., 8 July 1988 (WDR)
ad., s.w. Jackson Co., 19 July 1975 (BP)
3, East Cape Girardeau, 19 July 1990 (WDR et al.)
1, Carbondale, 20 July 1985 (TF, JCR)
20, Rend Lake, Jefferson Co., 28 July 1985 (LH)
1, Mermet Lake CA, 6 Aug 1986 (WDR)
23, Rend Lake, Jefferson Co., 14 Sep 1989 (BD)
1, Rend Lake, Jefferson Co., 30 Oct 1987 (TF)
7, Crab Orchard NWR, 28 Nov, but only 2 there 1 Dec 1989 (WDR)

6, Rend Lake, 5 Dec 1975 (BP, MMo)

DOCUMENTATION: Photograph—Ward Branch, Rend Lake, Jefferson Co., 16 Sep 1987 (SIU AP-46).

FIELD GUIDES: G=132; N=130; P=134.

Least Sandpiper *Calidris minutilla*

Mid-April–Late May
Early July–Mid-November

STATUS AND ABUNDANCE: Common migrant. Very rare winter visitor.

HABITAT: Mudflats, pools of water in wet fields, and lake edges.

RECORDS AND REMARKS: These peeps with hunched posture move slowly along barren mudflats and through grassy wet fields, picking rapidly at food items. They form small flocks and readily intermingle with other peep species.

SPRING—Leasts arrive well ahead of most other peep species. Spring concentrations are much higher than those during fall.

1, Crab Orchard NWR, 29 Mar 1985 (JCR)
1, Rend Lake, Jefferson Co., 8 Apr 1988 (TF)
4, Saline Co., 9 Apr 1988 (WDR)
93, Pope Co., 5 May 1979 (SBC)
140, Carbondale, 8 May 1986 (WDR)
200, Rend Lake, Jefferson Co., 8 May 1987 (TF)
1, Rend Lake, Jefferson Co., 25 May 1987 (TF)

AUTUMN—Leasts arrive very early and linger very late during fall. Some birds linger very late, even into winter, until freezing weather forces them south. In mild winters, it is possible that a few might overwinter, because they routinely do so in the Memphis, Tennessee, area (J. C. Robinson 1990). Typically found in groups of less than thirty individuals.

1, s.w. Jackson Co., 29 June 1985 (JCR)
1, s.w. Jackson Co., 30 June 1989 (WDR)
26, s. Alexander Co., 5 July 1986 (WDR)
30, Rend Lake, Franklin Co., 30 Sep 1989 (WDR)
30, Rend Lake, Jefferson Co., 11 Nov 1989 (TF, JH, WDR)
1, Rend Lake, Jefferson Co., 27 Nov 1986 (JCR)

1, Crab Orchard NWR, 4 Dec 1960 (LHo)
15, Rend Lake, 13 Dec 1975 (BP)
3, Rend Lake, Franklin Co., 16 Dec 1987 (TF)
3–7, Rend Lake, Jefferson Co., 23 Nov–22 Dec 1990 (TF, WDR, JD)
WINTER—1, on a Mississippi River sandbar, Alexander Co., 29 Dec 1976 (MMo, DK)

DOCUMENTATION: Photograph—Ward Branch, Rend Lake, Jefferson Co., 16 Sep 1987 (SIU AP-47).

FIELD GUIDES: G=132; N=130; P=134.

White-rumped Sandpiper *Calidris fuscicollis*

Early May–Early June
Mid-August–Late October

STATUS AND ABUNDANCE: Uncommon spring migrant. Rare fall migrant.

HABITAT: Mudflats.

RECORDS AND REMARKS: White-rumps intermingle with other peeps on mudflats but are fairly readily identified by their somewhat larger size, white rump, and high, thin, "mousy" call note.
SPRING—The northward migration route for this species is through the Great Plains, so they are much more numerous here in spring than in fall. Numbers vary dramatically from year to year, however; in some years, very few are seen in our region.
2, Ullin, Pulaski Co., 26 Apr 1987 (SO)
3, Alexander Co., 4 May 1985 (SBC)
3, Rend Lake, Jefferson Co., 8 May 1987 (TF)
1, Mermet Lake CA, 9 May 1987 (WDR)
27, Alexander Co., 10 May 1986 (SBC)
50, Rend Lake, Jefferson Co., 19 May 1987 (LH)
15, s.w. Jackson Co., 26 May 1985 (RP)
28, Rend Lake, Jefferson Co., 7 June 1986 (WDR)
7, Rend Lake, Jefferson Co., 14 June 1988 (WDR)
AUTUMN—Most White-rumps migrate along the East Coast in fall, so they rarely pass through southern Illinois.
2, Rend Lake, Jefferson Co., 3 July 1992 (TF, JD, DKa)

2, Rend Lake, Franklin Co., 24 July 1976 (BP)
1, s.w. Jackson Co., 2 Aug 1975 (BP)
1, Rend Lake, Jefferson Co., 31 Aug 1986 (RC, SB)
4, Rend Lake, Franklin Co., 1 Sep 1975 (BP)
1, Crab Orchard NWR, 24–30 Oct 1982 (JCR)
1, Crab Orchard NWR, 26 Oct 1989 (WDR)

DOCUMENTATION: Written description—Rend Lake, Jefferson Co., 31 Aug 1986.

FIELD GUIDES: G=132; N=130; P=134.

Baird's Sandpiper *Calidris bairdii*

Late April–Mid-May
Mid-August–Mid-October

STATUS AND ABUNDANCE: Rare spring migrant. Uncommon fall migrant.

HABITAT: Mudflats and shorelines.

RECORDS AND REMARKS: Baird's typically forage on the drier portions of mudflats, where sparse, short vegetation is growing. Most birds move northward during spring, in a narrow path through the Great Plains; they are not encountered here every spring. In the fall, however, the birds move down along the oceanic coasts, so the front is wider, and more birds pass through southern Illinois.
SPRING—The few spring records come mostly from May, but some birds may arrive during the last few days of April.
3, Crab Orchard NWR, 6 May 1986 (SO)
4, Union Co., 9 May 1981 (SBC)
1, Union Co., 10 May 1986 (SBC)
11, Rend Lake, 14 May 1976 (BP)
2, Rend Lake, Jefferson Co., 7 June 1986 (WDR)
AUTUMN—Early arrivals are adults, which can be difficult to identify. Juveniles arrive later and are distinctly buffier, with scaly backs. Typically only small groups or single birds are encountered in the region. They seem to require wide-open habitats, without much brush or vegetation nearby.
1, Rend Lake, Jefferson Co., 20 July 1989 (BD)
2, Alexander Co., 26 July 1986 (WDR)

1, Mermet Lake CA, 6 Aug 1986 (WDR)
2, Crab Orchard NWR, 21 Aug 1987 (WDR)
7, Sparta, Randolph Co., 23 Aug–6 Sep 1971 (MMo)
21, Rend Lake, Jefferson Co., 16 Sep 1986 (LH)
1, Crab Orchard NWR, 1 Nov 1993 (TF)
1, Rend Lake, Jefferson Co., 3 Nov 1986 (TF)

DOCUMENTATION: Photograph—Ward Branch, Rend Lake, Jefferson Co., 14 Sep 1985 (SIU AP-48).

FIELD GUIDES: G=132; N=130; P=134.

Pectoral Sandpiper *Calidris melanotos*

Late March–Mid-May
Mid-July–Early November

STATUS AND ABUNDANCE: Common migrant.

HABITAT: Mudflats, plowed fields, pond and lake edges, and grassy pools of water.

RECORDS AND REMARKS: One of the region's most numerous shorebirds. Forages in a wide variety of habitats. Forms large flocks at times, often intermixing with other shorebird species, especially peeps.

SPRING—Timing of first arrivals is very dependent on weather patterns; in some years, none will be detected until very late March; in other years, it is possible that a few may even arrive in very late February. Peak numbers occur during April and early May, and then the birds are suddenly gone by about 20 May.

1, Jackson Co., 8 Mar 1951 (RB)
51, Union Co. CA, 8 Mar 1992 (TF, JD, DK)
7, Rend Lake, Jefferson Co., 20 Mar 1976 (BP)
360, Jackson Co., 31 Mar 1985 (JCR)
325, Union Co., 8 May 1976 (SBC)
2, Union Co. CA, 21 May 1971 (VK)
1, Crab Orchard NWR, 21 May 1985 (JCR)

AUTUMN—A few adults return very early each fall, but the majority of Pectorals do not pass through southern Illinois until late July and August. Some immatures may linger late.

1, s.w. Jackson Co., 27 June 1989 (WDR)

1, Crab Orchard NWR, 5 July 1985 (JCR)
400, Union Co., 26 July 1986 (WDR)
400, Rend Lake, Jefferson Co., 8 Aug 1986 (WDR)
1, Carbondale, 17–25 Nov 1984 (JCR)
1, Crab Orchard NWR, 5 Dec 1960 (LHo)

DOCUMENTATION: Specimen—ad. female, 6.5 miles w. of Murphysboro, Jackson Co., 11 Apr 1957 (SIU A-160).

FIELD GUIDES: G=130; N=134; P=130.

Dunlin *Calidris alpina*

Early May–Late May
Early October–Mid-November

STATUS AND ABUNDANCE: Uncommon migrant. Very rare winter visitor.

HABITAT: Mudflats.

RECORDS AND REMARKS: This shorebird forms tight flocks, which forage rather rapidly by probing and picking at food in shallow water and on mudflats. They sometimes will forage in grassy fields or pools of water on plowed agricultural fields, too. Uncommon, they can easily be missed in a day's birding, but when found, they are often in fairly large groups.

SPRING—Most birds do not arrive until May, and by then they are in their strikingly beautiful breeding plumage. Very early arrivals are still in gray winter plumage or are molting into breeding plumage.
1, Rend Lake, Jefferson Co., 4 Apr 1987 (TF)
2, Cypress Creek NWR, 17–18 Apr 1992 (TF, WDR)
47, Rend Lake, Jefferson Co., 16 May 1986 (WDR)
279, Rend Lake, Jefferson Co., 18 May 1987 (TF)
AUTUMN—Arrives late in fall, and sometimes lingers into December. May gather in large flocks at good habitat. All are in winter plumage by the time they arrive.
1, w. Jackson Co., 24 Aug 1993 (CS)
1, Crab Orchard NWR, 26 Sep 1989 (BD)
2, Rend Lake, Jefferson Co., 28 Sep 1987 (TF)
260, Crab Orchard NWR, 21 Oct 1989 (WDR)

225, Rend Lake, Jefferson Co., 23 Oct 1987 (TF)
200, Rend Lake, Jefferson Co., 27 Oct 1985 (LH)
7, Baldwin Lake, 20 Nov 1983 (BR)
2, Mermet Lake CA, 22 Nov 1986 (TF, WDR)
40, Crab Orchard NWR, 28 Nov 1989 (WDR)
15, Rend Lake, 5 Dec 1975 (BP, MMo)
WINTER—There is one midwinter record of a bird that stayed at
a sewage pond in Carbondale on 27–28 January 1988 (WDR, BM
et al.).

DOCUMENTATION: Photograph—Carbondale, Jackson Co., 18 Nov
1984 (SIU AP-51).

FIELD GUIDES: G=130; N=128; P=132.

Curlew Sandpiper *Calidris ferruginea*

STATUS AND ABUNDANCE: Very rare visitor.

RECORDS AND REMARKS: There is one record of this vagrant from
Asia. One in breeding plumage was found on a mudflat with other
shorebirds at Wayne-Fitzgerrell SP, Rend Lake, Franklin Co., on 23
July 1976 (Peterjohn and Morrison 1977). It was observed well, at
close range, near dusk; but it could not be relocated the next day.
This bird was the first record for Illinois; since then there have been
at least seven additional records (Bohlen 1989).

DOCUMENTATION: Written description—1976 record.

FIELD GUIDES: G=130; N=128; P=132.

Stilt Sandpiper *Calidris himantopus*

Early May–Late May
Mid-July–Mid-October

STATUS AND ABUNDANCE: Uncommon spring migrant. Fairly common fall migrant.

HABITAT: Mudflats and shallow-water areas of flooded fields.

RECORDS AND REMARKS: Stilts in breeding plumage are easily
identified by their barred bellies, but those in winter plumage look
superficially like Lesser Yellowlegs and can be passed over if not

carefully scrutinized. Winter plumage stilts have both a thicker bill with drooped tip and greener legs than yellowlegs have. Forages with quick, jerky probing motions in water up to belly deep. Often associates with dowitchers and yellowlegs.

SPRING—Arrival dates are highly variable; in some years, none arrive until after 10 May. Migration peaks in mid-May, and most birds have departed by 25 May.

2, Cypress Creek NWR, 18 Apr 1992 (TF, WDR)
2, Pope Co., 26 Apr 1986 (WDR)
1, Rend Lake, Jefferson Co., 30 Apr 1976 (BP)
6, Alexander Co., 7 May 1983 (SBC)
15, Rend Lake, Jefferson Co., 14 May 1987 (TF)
7, Baldwin Lake, 23 May 1982 (RK)

AUTUMN—During fall, birds congregate with other shorebirds at good habitat. Peak numbers are present during September, and most are gone by early October; some immatures may linger later.

2, s. Alexander Co., 5 July 1986 (WDR)
1, Crab Orchard NWR, 15 July 1987 (WDR)
45, Rend Lake, Jefferson Co., 2 Aug 1986 (TF)
51, w. Jackson Co., 11 Sep 1993 (CS)
70, Crab Orchard NWR, 12 Sep 1987 (WDR)
55, Crab Orchard NWR, 5 Oct 1983 (JCR)
2, Crab Orchard NWR, 5 Nov 1989 (WDR)

DOCUMENTATION: Photograph—Rend Lake, Jefferson Co., 12 Aug 1989 (SIU, uncatalogued).

FIELD GUIDES: G=122; N=124; P=132.

Buff-breasted Sandpiper *Tryngites subruficollis*
Mid-August–Early October

STATUS AND ABUNDANCE: Very rare spring migrant. Rare fall migrant, except at Rend Lake, where it is uncommon.

HABITAT: Extensive mudflats and short-grass fields.

RECORDS AND REMARKS: Forages on the drier portions of mudflats with short vegetation. Forms small groups and forages together, snatching insects off of vegetation and those flushed into the air.

Also forages in plowed fields, particularly those adjacent to large mudflats.

SPRING—There is only one record. Five were observed foraging with Pectoral Sandpipers on an unplowed bean-stubble field south of Willard, Alexander Co., on 5 April 1991 (TF, JD). If Buff-breasts frequent agricultural fields during spring, they may be routinely overlooked. Because their principal northward migration route is in the Great Plains, well west of southern Illinois, however, and because observers actually do check farm fields in spring (for golden-plovers), it seems likely that they are simply not present. Spring records are rare from other sites in Illinois and are typically much later, from late April through late May (Bohlen 1989).

AUTUMN—Occurs regularly at Rend Lake, especially at Ward Branch. Peak numbers are found during September. Away from Rend Lake, buff-breasts are found in expansive, open short-grass fields.

3, Rend Lake, Jefferson Co., 1 Aug 1992 (TF)
5, Rend Lake, Jefferson Co., 20 Aug 1988 (TF, WDR)
3, Union Co. CA, 1 Sep 1980 (HD)
19, s.w. Jackson Co., 3 Sep 1973 (DH et al.)
3, Miller City, Alexander Co., 6 Sep 1975 (BP)
26, Rend Lake, Jefferson Co., 8 Sep 1985 (LH)
15, Rend Lake, 22 Sep 1976 (BP)
1, Rend Lake, Jefferson Co., 13 Oct 1985 (TF)

DOCUMENTATION: Photograph—Ward Branch, Rend Lake, Jefferson Co., 8 Sep 1987 (SIU AP-53).

FIELD GUIDES: G=122; N=134; P=130.

Ruff *Philomachus pugnax*

STATUS AND ABUNDANCE: Very rare visitor.

HABITAT: Mudflats and shallow-water areas.

RECORDS AND REMARKS: There is one record of this Eurasian species. A male was present at Rend Lake, Jefferson Co., for one day, 20 Aug 1994 (TF, MSe). This species occurs almost annually in Illinois, thus it is somewhat surprising that it had not yet been reported from southern Illinois. Nearly all Illinois records are from fall migration.

DOCUMENTATION: Written description—1994 record.

FIELD GUIDES: G=122; N=134; P=130.

Short-billed Dowitcher *Limnodromus griseus*

Early May–Late May
Mid-July–Mid-September

STATUS AND ABUNDANCE: Uncommon spring migrant. Fairly common fall migrant.

HABITAT: Mudflats and shallow-water areas.

RECORDS AND REMARKS: Dowitchers forage in shallow water, probing vertically up and down into mud. Identification is difficult because Short-bills and Long-bills closely resemble each other. The best way to separate them is by voice: Short-bills give a *tu tu tu* call, whereas Long-bills utter a high-pitched *keek*. Wilds and Newlon (1983) and Hayman et al. (1986) give identification criteria. The Short-billed Dowitcher subspecies occurring in southern Illinois is *L. g. hendersoni* (Bohlen 1989).

SPRING—Peak numbers occur during the first half of May. Short-bills are in breeding plumage by the time they arrive in southern Illinois.

1, Rend Lake, Jefferson Co., 27 Apr 1987 (TF)
52, s. Alexander Co., 1 May 1971 (VK, DH)
1, Crab Orchard NWR, 2 May 1984 (JCR)
32, Alexander Co., 7 May 1983 (PK)
30, Gallatin Co., 10 May 1980 (SBC)
66, Rend Lake, 14 May 1976 (BP)
1, Alexander Co., 8 June 1985 (JCR)

AUTUMN—Adults still in breeding plumage arrive by early July. Immatures in juvenile plumage arrive in mid-August; they nearly always tend to have some rusty color to their underparts, which helps separate them from immature Long-bills, but voice is always the best identification cue.

2, Rend Lake, Jefferson Co., 8 July 1986 (WDR)
1, Crab Orchard NWR, 10 July 1971 (VK)

40, Rend Lake, Jefferson Co., 26 Aug 1984 (LH)
3, Union Co. CA, 3 Sep 1988 (WDR)
50, Rend Lake, Jefferson Co., 5 Sep 1985 (LH)
1, Rend Lake, Jefferson Co., 13 Oct 1985 (TF)

DOCUMENTATION: Photograph—Carbondale, Jackson Co., 6 Sep 1970 (VK).

FIELD GUIDES: G=124; N=122; P=124.

Long-billed Dowitcher *Limnodromus scolopaceus*
Mid-April–Early May
Early September–Late October

STATUS AND ABUNDANCE: Rare spring migrant. Uncommon fall migrant.

HABITAT: Shallow-water areas and mudflats.

RECORDS AND REMARKS: The less numerous of the two dowitcher species, Long-bills can be best separated from the similar Short-bills by voice. Their bills are not always conspicuously longer than those of Short-bills. Dowitchers forage by quickly probing up and down, rather sewing machine–like, into mud. They typically wade in shallow water while foraging, often up to belly deep.
SPRING—Long-bills arrive and depart much earlier than Short-bills. Only single individuals have been reported. The earliest arrivals are still in winter plumage, so identification should be verified by voice.
1, Union Co. CA, 6 Apr 1986 (WDR)
1, s. Alexander Co., 12 Apr 1986 (TF, WDR)
1, Cypress Creek NWR, 18 Apr 1992 (TF, WDR)
1, Rend Lake, Jefferson Co., 1 May 1987 (TF)
1, Willard, Alexander Co., 4 May 1984 (TF)
AUTUMN—The first Long-bills arrive much later than the first Short-bills. Adults arrive first, peak in September, and are mostly gone by about early October. Immatures arrive during late September and sometimes linger rather late.
1 ad., Rend Lake, Jefferson Co., 4 Aug 1988 (TF)
6, Union Co. CA, 3 Sep 1988 (WDR)
20, Rend Lake, Jefferson Co., 20 Oct 1985 (LH)

34, Crab Orchard NWR, 21 Oct 1993 (TF)
1, Rend Lake, Jefferson Co., 11 Nov 1987 (TF)
1, Crab Orchard NWR, 23 Nov 1982 (JCR)

DOCUMENTATION: Photograph—Willard, Alexander Co., 4 May 1984 (SIU AP-55).

FIELD GUIDES: G=124; N=122; P=124.

Common Snipe *Gallinago gallinago*

Late August–Mid-December
Late February–Early May

STATUS AND ABUNDANCE: Common migrant. Uncommon winter resident. Very rare summer visitor.

HABITAT: Marshes, wet grassy fields, grassy ditches, and mudflats.

RECORDS AND REMARKS: Forms loose flocks in moist, open habitats. Generally prefers areas where vegetation is dense, but will occasionally forage on open mudflats, especially during migration. Forages by quick, jerky, probing motions. Very well camouflaged, snipes often elude detection until they are flushed from appropriate habitat.

AUTUMN—First arrivals are often single birds found on open mudflats. Migration peaks in late fall, from late October to mid-November. Many linger late into winter, until freezing conditions force them south. The winter population makes determination of latest departure dates difficult.

1, s.w. Jackson Co., 17 Aug 1973 (DH)
1, Rend Lake, Jefferson Co., 20 Aug 1987 (TF)
20, w. Jackson Co., 25 Aug 1993 (CS)
50, Union Co. CA, 17 Oct 1976 (HDB et al.)

WINTER—As long as unfrozen soil is available, at least a few snipes will stay the entire winter, but numbers often diminish during January and early February. As during migration, good habitat will often harbor fairly large concentrations of birds.

65, Mermet Lake CA CBC, 21 Dec 1965
32, Union Co. CBC, 22 Dec 1982
44, Horseshoe Lake CBC, 2 Jan 1987
12, Union Co. CA, 20 Jan 1992 (TF, JD, DKa, CW)

SPRING—The presence of a winter population obscures the arrival of the first spring migrants, but birds begin moving northward soon after the first warm period in late February. Peak numbers pass through in late March and early April.

1, Cypress Creek NWR, 15 Feb 1991 (TF)
3, Crab Orchard NWR, 6 Mar 1986 (WDR)
45, Alexander and Union Cos., 29 Mar 1986 (TF, WDR)
1, Joppa, Massac Co., 10 May 1986 (WDR)

SUMMER—No confirmation of breeding has been obtained. Two midsummer records, however, are suggestive of possible breeding:

3 winnowing, Oakwood Bottoms, 6–9 June 1973 (DH, VK)
1, n. Randolph Co., 3 July 1985 (TF, JCR)

Snipes breed early (late April and May), so searches in appropriate habitat at these times may reveal that some individuals breed within the region.

DOCUMENTATION: Specimen—2 miles n. of Brownsfield, Pope Co., 23 Mar 1957 (SIU A-165).

FIELD GUIDES: G=126; N=124; P=124.

American Woodcock *Scolopax minor*
Early February–Late November

STATUS AND ABUNDANCE: Fairly common spring migrant. Uncommon summer resident and fall migrant. Rare winter resident.

HABITAT: Feeds and roosts in low, wet areas in woods and thickets during the day and in open grassy or brushy fields at night.

RECORDS AND REMARKS: Woodcocks are best known for the unusual aerial display they perform at dawn and, primarily, at dusk during early spring. Otherwise woodcocks are extremely inconspicuous and usually overlooked. They forage mostly at night, for earthworms. They are hunted during the fall. Because they are so difficult to detect, little is known about the population or its movements within the region.

SPRING—First spring arrivals are easily detected because they begin displaying immediately. Some arrive very early, following the first warm spell in late January or February; they may cease display-

ing for a while if freezing temperatures return. The presence of a
breeding population obscures the departure of the latest migrants.
1 displaying, Ozark, Johnson Co., 22 Jan 1990 (TF)
1 displaying, Makanda, 25 Jan 1989 (CPa)
9, Mt. Vernon, 5 Mar 1987 (TF)
8, Jackson Co., 9 May 1987 (SBC)
SUMMER—Breeding begins very early; eggs are often present by
early March.
downy young, Pulaski Co., 9 Apr 1990 (TG)
3, Heron Pond NP, 24 May 1989 (TF, WDR)
AUTUMN—Usually seen as single individuals flying across roads
at dusk or flushed from wet thickets. The beginning of southward
migration is obscured by the presence of the summer population.
Most fall observations occur during October and November.
1, Johnson Co., 22 Nov 1989 (TF)
1, Crab Orchard NWR, 4 Dec 1982 (JCR)
1, Carbondale, 5 Dec 1985 (TF)
WINTER—A few may linger late into winter, but most depart the
region ahead of freezing temperatures. In very mild winters, a small
winter population may be present, but in most years, few remain.
Probably overwintered in the Shawnee Hills during the 1992–1993
winter, because there were records from late December and mid-
and late January (TF).
1, Union Co. CBC, 19 Dec 1985
1, Union Co. CBC, 29 Dec 1974
1, Crab Orchard NWR, 6 Jan 1985 (ABa)

DOCUMENTATION: Photograph—Rudement, Saline Co., Feb 1986
(SIU).

FIELD GUIDES: G=126; N=124; P=124.

Wilson's Phalarope *Phalaropus tricolor*

Late April–Mid-May
Mid-August–Mid-September

STATUS AND ABUNDANCE: Rare migrant.

HABITAT: Shallow-water areas and wet grassy mudflats.

RECORDS AND REMARKS: More numerous in fall than in spring,

these active shorebirds often forage by spinning toplike while swim-ming in shallow water. They also sprint rapidly and erratically around mudflats, snatching insects off of mud and vegetation. Usu-ally only one or a few are seen at a time, but concentrations some-times occur during spring, especially on rainy days.

SPRING—Sexual dimorphism is reversed in phalaropes: the fe-males are the more colorful gender. This is the most likely phala-rope species to be seen in southern Illinois, but, nevertheless, it is not recorded every spring.

2, Alexander Co., 24 Apr 1993 (TF)
17, Alexander Co., 5 May 1984 (TF)
39, Crab Orchard NWR, 6 May 1978 (BG)
1, Rend Lake, Jefferson Co., 8–12 May 1987 (TF, LH)
1, Big Bay, Massac Co., 9 May 1981 (GW, HW, WDR)
1, Crab Orchard NWR, 26 May 1953 (LHo)

AUTUMN—A few are reported from the region every fall, but concentrations are small. Adults return first, but juveniles follow close behind, with first arrivals present by mid-August. Phalaropes tend to stay at a site only for a day or so.

1, Crab Orchard NWR, 5 and 19 Aug 1972 (VK)
juv., Rend Lake, Jefferson Co., 12 Aug 1989 (WDR, TF, BD)
4, Rend Lake, 14 Aug 1976 (BP)
4, Rend Lake, Jefferson Co., 27 Aug 1987 (TF)
2, Union Co. CA, 3 Sep 1988 (WDR)
1, Carbondale, 6 Sep 1970 (VK, DH)
5, Rend Lake, Jefferson Co., 8 Sep 1985 (LH)
1, Rend Lake, Jefferson Co., 16 Sep 1989 (BD)

DOCUMENTATION: Photograph—Willard, Alexander Co., 5 May 1984 (SIU AP-56).

FIELD GUIDES: G=126; N=120; P=136.

Red-necked Phalarope *Phalaropus lobatus*

Mid-August–Mid-September

STATUS AND ABUNDANCE: Rare fall migrant.

HABITAT: Shallow-water areas and wet grassy pools.

RECORDS AND REMARKS: Prefers to forage in shallow water, where it spins while swimming and also wades. Identification can be difficult, because the Red Phalarope is very similar. Red-necks have very thin bills, however, and usually occur earlier in fall than do Red Phalaropes. To make matters worse, most individuals are molting during fall, so a wide range of confusing plumages is possible. See Hayman et al. (1986) for identification criteria. There are no spring records, but they could occur during late May.

AUTUMN—1, Crab Orchard NWR, 19 Aug 1972 (VK)
4, Rend Lake, Jefferson Co., 21 Aug 1994 (BD, CS)
1, near Unity, Alexander Co., 30 Aug 1993 (HDB, RP)
1, Rend Lake, Jefferson Co., 9 Sep 1984 (LH)
1, Baldwin Lake, 12 Sep 1981 (RK)
1, Rend Lake, Jefferson Co., 13 Sep 1989 (WDR)
1, Rend Lake, Jefferson Co., 16 Sep 1987 (TF)
1, Crab Orchard NWR, 20 Sep 1952 (George 1968)

DOCUMENTATION: Photograph—Ward Branch, Rend Lake, Jefferson Co., 16 Sep 1987 (SIU AP-57).

FIELD GUIDES: G=126; N=120; P=136.

Red Phalarope *Phalaropus fulicaria*

Late September–Early November

STATUS AND ABUNDANCE: Very rare fall migrant.

HABITAT: Shallow-water areas, mudflats, and lakes.

RECORDS AND REMARKS: The rarest of the three phalarope species in the region. All records are of swimming birds that were in molt or entirely in winter plumage. This species sometimes stops during stormy weather and rests in the middle of large reservoirs. One late fall record of two whitish shorebirds with white wing stripes flying just over the water's surface at Rend Lake on 16 December 1991, seen from a great distance (SB), was probably this species. Another seen from a distance at Rend Lake, Jefferson Co., on 23 October 1987 was probably this species (TF). The thicker bill helps separate Red from Red-necked Phalaropes at close range, but identification requires experience with both species.

AUTUMN—Most encounters are from late fall; October through early November should be the best time to find this species.

1, Rend Lake, Jefferson Co., 31 Aug 1991 (TF)
juv., Baldwin Lake, 21 Sep 1980 (RK)
1, Crab Orchard NWR, 1 Oct 1992 (TF, JD)
1, Crab Orchard NWR, 2 Nov 1986 (BD)
1, Crab Orchard NWR, 3 Nov 1975 (BP)

DOCUMENTATION: Photograph—Rend Lake, Jefferson Co., 31 Aug 1991 (SIU, uncatalogued).

FIELD GUIDES: G=126; N=120; P=136.

Family Laridae: Jaegers, Gulls, and Terns

Pomarine Jaeger *Stercorarius pomarinus*

STATUS AND ABUNDANCE: Very rare migrant.

HABITAT: Large reservoirs.

RECORDS AND REMARKS: An immature was seen by several observers at Crab Orchard NWR, on 18 December 1982 (MMl et al.) and was thought to have been the same individual that was present at Carlyle Lake, Clinton Co., a few days earlier. A dark-phase immature was viewed at Rend Lake, Franklin Co., from 28 November to 8 December 1991 (TF, BD, JD). These are the only records identified to species level for the region. A light-phase adult jaeger (not a Long-tailed) was observed at Crab Orchard NWR on 29 Aug 1987, but the bird never came closer than three-quarters of a mile (WDR). The distance, combined with the difficulties of jaeger identification, prevented positive identification.

DOCUMENTATION: Written description—1991 record.

FIELD GUIDES: G=138; N=142; P=82.

[Long-tailed Jaeger *Stercorarius longicaudus*]

STATUS AND ABUNDANCE: Hypothetical.

HABITAT: Should occur along large rivers or reservoirs.

RECORDS AND REMARKS: W. H. Ballow examined a decayed bird found near Cairo, Alexander Co., in November 1876, but he did not save the specimen (Ridgway 1889). Other inland midwestern records of this species have occurred mainly in July and August. The only Long-tailed Jaeger specimen for Illinois was found slightly north of our region, in Nashville, Washington Co., on 21 October 1893 (SIU A-161).

FIELD GUIDES: G=138; N=142; P=82.

Laughing Gull *Larus atricilla*

Late April–Late May
Early August–Early October

STATUS AND ABUNDANCE: Rare migrant.

HABITAT: Large reservoirs and rivers.

RECORDS AND REMARKS: Associates with other gulls and terns on sandbars and mudflats. Similar to Franklin's Gull, but adults lack the white bar between the black on the tips of the primaries and the gray of the rest of the wing. Goetz (1983) and Kaufman (1990) provide identification information. Becoming regular; has occurred in each year since 1985.
SPRING—Much less numerous in spring than in fall. The destination of spring birds is unclear, because there is no breeding area directly north of the region.
1, Baldwin Lake, 18 Apr 1978 (KA)
ad. and 2 imm., Rend Lake, Franklin Co., 16–17 May 1986 (WDR, TF)
2nd-year bird, Rend Lake, 23 May 1992 (TF, JD)
ad., Mermet Lake CA, 24 May 1986 (KR, TF, LA, WDR)
AUTUMN—Birds occurring in fall may be postbreeding wanderers that move north up the Mississippi River Valley. They may not stay long at any one site, which may explain why most records are from Rend Lake, which is checked very frequently during fall for shorebirds and other water birds. Some could linger very late in fall; there are midwest records even for December.
1, Rend Lake, Jefferson Co., 2 July 1994 (TF)
imm., Grand Tower, Jackson Co., 10 July 1988 (WDR)
1, Rend Lake, 2–3 Aug 1986 (TF, LH)
1, Rend Lake, Jefferson Co., 13 Aug 1988 (TF, WDR)
ad., Rend Lake, Jefferson Co., 18–24 Aug 1985 (LH)

juv., Rend Lake, Jefferson Co., 2 Sep 1989 (TF, JH)
juv., Rend Lake, Jefferson Co., 5 Sep 1985 (LH)
2nd-winter, Rend Lake, Jefferson Co., 14–22 Sep 1985 (TF)
3, Rend Lake, Jefferson Co., 30 Sep 1989 (BD, WDR)
1st-winter, Crab Orchard NWR, 1 Oct 1989 (BD, WDR)

DOCUMENTATION: Written description—ad., Mermet Lake CA, Massac Co., 24 May 1986.

FIELD GUIDES: G=148; N=144; P=88.

Franklin's Gull *Larus pipixcan*
Mid-March–Late May
Late August–Early December

STATUS AND ABUNDANCE: Rare spring migrant. Uncommon fall migrant.

HABITAT: Large lakes and major rivers. May also occur in plowed fields.

RECORDS AND REMARKS: Usually occurs on mudflats and sandbars with other gulls, terns, and shorebirds, but may sometimes follow the plow and forage in agricultural fields. Franklin's is more common than the Laughing Gull.

SPRING—Does not occur in early spring every year; the arrival dates apparently depend on weather (especially wind) conditions, since most Franklin's Gulls migrate through the Great Plains. In most springs, the majority of Franklin's pass through the region in late May.
1, Crab Orchard NWR, 12–14 Mar 1987 (GW, WDR)
1, Crab Orchard NWR, 16–17 Apr 1936 (LB)
8, Crab Orchard NWR, 14 May 1986 (WDR)
2, Rend Lake, Franklin Co., 25 May 1986 (TF, WDR)
ad., w. Alexander Co., 7 June 1975 (HDB, RS)
AUTUMN—More numerous at this season. Individuals occur in a wide variety of plumages because of age and molt-stage differences, so identification should be made with care. Occasionally occurs in fairly large flocks during fall.
1, Rend Lake, Jefferson Co., 16 July 1988 (TF)
6, Rend Lake, Jefferson Co., 20 Aug 1986 (WDR)

imm., Carbondale, 23 Sep 1973 (VK)
75, Crab Orchard NWR, early Oct 1952 (LB)
14, Rend Lake, Jefferson Co., 9 Oct 1989 (TF, WDR)
50, Rend Lake, 27 Oct 1985 (LH)
1, Union Co. CA, 7 Nov 1970 (VK et al.)
40, Crab Orchard NWR, 12 Nov 1949 (RB)
1, Rend Lake, 30 Nov 1975 (BP)
1, Crab Orchard NWR, 7 Dec 1985 (TF)

DOCUMENTATION: Photograph—subad., Nason, Rend Lake, Jefferson Co., 16 July 1988 (SIU AP-271).

FIELD GUIDES: G=148; N=144; P=88.

Little Gull *Larus minutus*

STATUS AND ABUNDANCE: Very rare visitor.

HABITAT: Large lakes.

RECORDS AND REMARKS: One at Crab Orchard NWR on 9 April 1976 (BP, MH) was fully documented. Another report from Rend Lake, Franklin Co., on 25 November 1975 was not satisfactorily documented but may have been correct. Typically associates with Bonaparte's Gulls, which it superficially resembles.

DOCUMENTATION: Written description—1976 record.

FIELD GUIDES: G=148; N=146; P=88.

Common Black-headed Gull *Larus ridibundus*

STATUS AND ABUNDANCE: Very rare visitor.

HABITAT: Large reservoirs.

RECORDS AND REMARKS: A winter-plumaged adult at Crab Orchard NWR was originally discovered on 13 December 1987 (BD, WDR) and was viewed sporadically, often at very close range, throughout the next two weeks. It associated with Bonaparte's Gulls and sometimes came to bread thrown into the lake to attract it and other gulls.

DOCUMENTATION: Written description—1987 record.

FIELD GUIDES: G=148; N=146; P=88.

Bonaparte's Gull *Larus philadelphia*

Mid-October–Mid-December
Mid-March–Early May

STATUS AND ABUNDANCE: Fairly common migrant; common at the larger reservoirs. Rare winter resident.

HABITAT: Lakes and major rivers.

RECORDS AND REMARKS: Associates with other water birds on mudflats, but is most frequently encountered while foraging actively over water. Forms loose flocks when resting on the water. Because they forage by hunting from the air, they are constantly flying and can be difficult to accurately count.

AUTUMN—A few individuals appear early in fall, but the bulk of birds do not arrive until October. All are in winter (or juvenile) plumage. Some concentrations get very large, especially in December, and counts reported here are probably conservative. As long as open water is available, they will linger into winter.

juv., Rend Lake, Jefferson Co., 9–12 Aug 1989 (TF, BD, WDR)
1, Rend Lake, Jefferson Co., 23 Sep 1989 (TF)
4, Rend Lake, 13 Oct 1985 (LH)
50, Rend Lake, Franklin Co., 18 Nov 1989 (BD, WDR)
500, Crab Orchard NWR, 13 Dec 1987 (BD, WDR)
616, Rend Lake CBC, 15 Dec 1991
500, Crab Orchard NWR CBC, 20 Dec 1986
1,000, Rend Lake, 1 Jan 1992 (TF, JD)
140, Baldwin Lake, 3 Jan 1988 (RG)

WINTER—Although some linger until freezing conditions force them south, few Bonaparte's actually spend the entire winter. They tend to stay longer at the warm-water lakes.

9, Baldwin Lake, 23 Jan 1983 (RG, SRu)

SPRING—Occasionally a few will return with the first warm spell of the year, but most do not arrive until March. Concentrations are not as large in spring as they are during autumn. Those that arrive late in spring (mostly after late March) are in breeding plumage.

5, Crab Orchard NWR, 15 Jan 1990 (BD)
1, Crab Orchard NWR, 12 Feb 1949 (RB)
4, Union Co. CA, 8 Mar 1992 (TF)
3, Golconda, Pope Co., 3 Apr 1973 (VK)
270, Crab Orchard NWR, 11 Apr 1984 (JCR)

34, Crab Orchard NWR, 11 May 1985 (JCR)

DOCUMENTATION: Photograph—juv., Rend Lake, Jefferson Co., 12 Aug 1989 (SIU).

FIELD GUIDES: G=148; N=146; P=88.

Mew Gull *Larus canus*

STATUS AND ABUNDANCE: Very rare visitor.

HABITAT: Large reservoirs.

RECORDS AND REMARKS: A juvenile seen at Rend Lake, Franklin Co., on 7 October 1984 (LH, DJ, GB) represents the only acceptably documented record for this West Coast gull. Extremely similar in appearance to the Ring-billed Gull, the Mew can easily be overlooked; see Grant (1986) for identification details.

DOCUMENTATION: Written description—1984 record.

FIELD GUIDES: G=146; N=148; P=290.

Ring-billed Gull *Larus delawarensis*
Mid-August–Late December
Mid-February–Mid-May

STATUS AND ABUNDANCE: Common migrant and winter resident. Uncommon summer visitor at Rend Lake; rare summer visitor elsewhere.

HABITAT: Lakes and large rivers, plowed fields, dumps, and larger towns.

RECORDS AND REMARKS: This gull could sometimes be referred to as abundant. Any visit to a reservoir or lake in the region during the appropriate season is sure to turn up this species. Recently, they have been occurring more regularly around shopping mall parking lots, where they scavenge for scraps. The numerical dominance of this gull makes it seem like every other gull and tern on a mudflat or sandbar "associates" with it.

AUTUMN—A few birds routinely trickle in beginning in July, but most of the migration does not begin until September. Large concentrations occur at the larger lakes, especially in November and December.

2 1st-summers, Rend Lake, Jefferson Co., 14 July 1988 (WDR)
1st-summer, Jackson Co., 22 July 1972 (VK)
ad., Crab Orchard NWR, 31 July 1987 (WDR)
1,100, Rend Lake, Jefferson Co., 24 Sep 1989 (WDR)
5,000, Rend Lake, Jefferson Co., 18 Nov 1989 (BD, WDR)
5,500, Crab Orchard NWR, 18 Dec 1983 (JCR)
2,804, Rend Lake CBC, 22 Dec 1990

WINTER—Numbers vary widely from year to year. As long as open water is available, however, they are present. There is much winter movement throughout the region and state (Robinson 1988), so populations are constantly changing.

1,000, Crab Orchard NWR, 31 Jan 1987 (WDR)

SPRING—The start of northward movement is difficult to discern, because of the substantial winter population. They seem to follow the southern edge of the thaw line northward as lakes open up. Sometimes very large concentrations occur when this happens:

22,500, Crab Orchard NWR, 13–15 Feb 1988 (WDR, SO).

SUMMER—Some nonbreeding subadult birds spend the summer at Rend Lake every year, and some are sometimes encountered at Crab Orchard Lake or along the Mississippi or Ohio Rivers. At Rend Lake, numbers begin increasing in July, as the first adult and other subadult migrants arrive.

17, Rend Lake, Jefferson Co., summer 1986 (WDR)

DOCUMENTATION: Specimen—male, Carbondale, Jackson Co., 21 Dec 1962 (SIU A-1637).

FIELD GUIDES: G=146; N=148; P=86.

California Gull *Larus californicus*

STATUS AND ABUNDANCE: Very rare visitor.

HABITAT: Large reservoirs.

RECORDS AND REMARKS: An adult occurred at Rend Lake, Franklin Co., on 24 Feb 1985 (LH, GB, DJ). There are more fall than spring records for Illinois, so observers should be on the look out for this species (from mid-July to late October). Very similar to the

Ring-billed Gull, but adults have a darker mantle, a red spot on the bill, and dark eyes. Subadults are more difficult to identify; Grant (1986) gives complete details.

DOCUMENTATION: Written description—1985 record.

FIELD GUIDES: G=144; N=150; P=86.

Herring Gull *Larus argentatus*
Mid-September–Early April

STATUS AND ABUNDANCE: Fairly common migrant and winter resident. Very rare summer visitor.

HABITAT: Large lakes and rivers.

RECORDS AND REMARKS: The larger "version" of the Ring-billed Gull, Herring Gulls are distinctly larger, lack the ringed bill, and have pink legs as adults. Subadult age classes parallel those of the Ring-billed Gull, but Herrings require four years to mature instead of three. Most birds seen in the region are adults, but first-winter birds are the most likely age to occur at odd seasons, like summer, or as migrants at extreme dates.

AUTUMN—A few arrive early, but most do not appear until cold weather arrives. There are no large counts available for fall.

imm., Rend Lake, 16 Aug 1986 (RP)

ad., Rend Lake, Jefferson Co., 20 Sep 1986 (WDR)

WINTER—Numbers vary widely from year to year; in mild years, very few are seen.

120, Crab Orchard NWR, 16 Jan 1985 (JCR)

SPRING—The start of spring migration can be noticed by a distinct drop in the numbers of Herring Gulls in the region, because few winter south of our region. Significant increases during spring occur only in severe winters when the midwestern population is pushed further south than usual. They return as soon as the ice begins to thaw.

3,000, Crab Orchard NWR, 7 Feb 1976 (BP)

2,500, Crab Orchard NWR, 13–15 Feb 1988 (WDR, SO)

1, Alexander Co., 26 May 1984 (TF, JCR)

1, Rend Lake, Jefferson Co., 30 May 1987 (TF)

SUMMER—1–2, Rend Lake, all summer 1976 (BP)
DOCUMENTATION: Photograph—Baldwin Lake, St. Clair Co., 1 Mar 1985 (SIU AP-60).
FIELD GUIDES: G=144; N=150; P=86.

Thayer's Gull *Larus thayeri*
Late December–Mid-February
STATUS AND ABUNDANCE: Rare winter visitor.

HABITAT: Occurs at large lakes with other gulls.

RECORDS AND REMARKS: Closely resembles the Herring Gull; identification can be very difficult and should be made with caution. All regional reports involve adults or, primarily, first-winter birds. Lehman (1983) and Grant (1986) give identification details. Occurs with Herring Gulls during very cold weather. There are more records than shown here, but many have apparently not been published and are not available.
WINTER—1, Union Co. CA, 30 Dec 1977 (HDB)
1st-winter, Rend Lake, Franklin Co., 30 Dec 1986 (WDR)
1st-winter, Crab Orchard NWR, 31 Dec 1987 (WDR)
2, Crab Orchard NWR, 5 Jan 1986 (SO)
1, Crab Orchard NWR, 25 Jan 1987 (SO)
1st-winter, Crab Orchard NWR, 13 Feb 1987 (WDR)
ad., Rend Lake, 14 Feb 1987 (DJ)

DOCUMENTATION: Provisional acceptance. Several single-observer written descriptions are available.

FIELD GUIDES: G=not pictured; N=152; P=86.

Iceland Gull *Larus glaucoides*
STATUS AND ABUNDANCE: Very rare winter visitor.

RECORDS AND REMARKS: There are only two records. A first-winter bird was observed at Rend Lake, Franklin Co., on 16 January 1993 (TF, BD). Another first-winter bird was observed at Crab Orchard NWR on 5 February 1995 (BD). This species resembles Thayer's

Gull, but it is usually conspicuously paler overall. Could occur more often, but is likely to appear primarily in severely cold winters.

DOCUMENTATION: Written description—1993 record.

FIELD GUIDES: G=132; N=152; P=84.

[Lesser Black-backed Gull *Larus fuscus*]

STATUS AND ABUNDANCE: Hypothetical.

RECORDS AND REMARKS: A first- or second-winter bird was observed by a single observer at Rend Lake, Franklin Co., on 20 February 1993 but could not be relocated later (BD). This gull may appear during very cold winters, when it should associate with Herring and Ring-billed Gulls at the larger reservoirs.

FIELD GUIDES: G=not pictured; N=154; P=86.

Glaucous Gull *Larus hyperboreus*

Late December–Mid-February

STATUS AND ABUNDANCE: Rare winter visitor.

HABITAT: Large reservoirs.

RECORDS AND REMARKS: The appearance of this species usually accompanies a severe cold spell. They almost always are found with concentrations of Herring Gulls, which they often harass to attempt to steal food. All records thus far involve adults or first-winter birds.
WINTER—1, Crab Orchard NWR, 21 Dec 1981 (MMl)
1st-winter, Crab Orchard NWR, 5 Jan 1988 (BD, SO)
1st-winter, Jefferson Co., 12 Jan 1993 (TF)
1, Baldwin Lake, 18 Jan 1986 (RCo)
ad., Rend Lake, Franklin Co., 29 Jan 1988 (TF)
1, Crab Orchard NWR, 1 Feb 1982 (MMl)
2 ad., Crab Orchard NWR, 4–7 Feb 1976 (BP)
1, Crab Orchard NWR, 16–17 Feb 1980 (MMl)
1st-winter, Crab Orchard NWR, 17 Feb 1986 (SO)
1st-winter, Crab Orchard NWR, 21 Feb 1985 (TF)

DOCUMENTATION: Photograph—ad., Rend Lake, Franklin Co., 29 Jan 1988 (SIU AP-62).

FIELD GUIDES: G=140; N=152; P=84.

Great Black-backed Gull *Larus marinus*

STATUS AND ABUNDANCE: Very rare winter visitor.

HABITAT: Large reservoirs.

RECORDS AND REMARKS: As with the other large, rare gulls, this species is usually associated with Herring Gulls and occurs only in severely cold weather. It is a truly large bird, which makes it easier to identify than some of the other rare gull species; nevertheless, the multitude of plumages can make identification problematical, so caution should be used.

WINTER—ad., Crab Orchard NWR, 5–8 Feb 1976 (BP, DK)
1st-winter, Crab Orchard NWR, 17 Feb 1986 (SO)
1, Crab Orchard NWR, 24 Feb 1980 (MMl)

DOCUMENTATION: Photograph—ad., Crab Orchard NWR, Williamson Co., 5–8 Feb 1976 (ISM).

FIELD GUIDES: G=142; N=154; P=86.

Black-legged Kittiwake *Rissa tridactyla*

STATUS AND ABUNDANCE: Very rare migrant.

HABITAT: Large reservoirs.

RECORDS AND REMARKS: Only immature birds have been reported; their plumage has a distinctive black W pattern on the back and wings when in flight and a black collar on the nape. Two of the region's three records are from spring. In the rest of the state, however, they are encountered much more frequently during fall.

SPRING—imm., Rend Lake, Franklin Co., 17 Mar 1989 (BD)
imm., Rend Lake, Jefferson Co., 5 Apr 1987 (RP)
AUTUMN—imm., Crab Orchard NWR, 17–19 Nov 1990 (BD, m.ob.)

DOCUMENTATION: Photograph—imm., Crab Orchard NWR, Williamson Co., 19 Nov 1990 (SIU, uncatalogued).

FIELD GUIDES: G=146; N=158; P=86.

Sabine's Gull *Xema sabini*

STATUS AND ABUNDANCE: Very rare fall migrant.

HABITAT: Large lakes.

RECORDS AND REMARKS: Immatures of this pelagic gull have a striking black-and-white dorsal pattern in flight. No adults have been recorded so far.
AUTUMN—imm., Crab Orchard NWR, 24 Sep 1992 (BD)
imm., Rend Lake, Franklin Co., 26–28 Sep 1975 (BP, PB)
2 imm., Crab Orchard NWR, 1 Oct 1988 (BD)

DOCUMENTATION: Written description—imm., Rend Lake, Franklin Co., 26–28 Sep 1975.

FIELD GUIDES: G=148; N=158; P=88.

Caspian Tern *Sterna caspia*

Mid-April–Early June
Early July–Mid-October

STATUS AND ABUNDANCE: Uncommon migrant.

HABITAT: Large reservoirs and rivers.

RECORDS AND REMARKS: Rests on sandbars and mudflats along edges of rivers and lakes, often associating with other terns and gulls. This tern is about the size of a Ring-billed Gull, dwarfing other tern species found in the region.
SPRING—Less numerous than in fall. Regularly encountered as singles or in small groups, which typically arrive during the second week of April. Migration regularly extends into the first week of June.
9, Rend Lake, Jefferson Co., 10 Apr 1987 (TF)
2, Crab Orchard NWR, 22 Apr 1985 (JCR)
2, Fort Massac SP, Massac Co., 8 May 1988 (WDR)
1, Baldwin Lake, 4 June 1983 (RK)
6, Crab Orchard NWR, 7 June 1984 (EC)
AUTUMN—More numerous than in spring, the first arrivals begin appearing by midsummer, and in some cases it may be difficult to tell if one is a late spring migrant or an early fall migrant. A few may linger quite late.

1, w. Alexander Co., 22 June 1987 (TF)
1, Rend Lake, Jefferson Co., 8 July 1986 and 8 July 1988 (WDR)
8, Union Co. CA, 30 July 1983 (JCR)
1, Mermet Lake CA, 31 July 1984 (SO)
17, Rend Lake, Jefferson Co., 20 Aug 1986 (TF)
12, East Cape Girardeau, Alexander Co., 3 Sep 1988 (WDR)
25, Crab Orchard NWR, 18 Sep 1949 (RB)
17, Rend Lake, 26 Sep 1975 (BP)
1, Rend Lake, Jefferson Co., 2 Nov 1985 (LH, TF)

DOCUMENTATION: Photograph—Rend Lake, Jefferson Co., 13 Sep 1987 (SIU AP-111).

FIELD GUIDES: G=154; N=168; P=94.

[Royal Tern *Sterna maxima*]

STATUS AND ABUNDANCE: Hypothetical.

HABITAT: Large lakes.

RECORDS AND REMARKS: One reported from Crab Orchard NWR on 5 September 1962 was not documented. This species is similar to the Caspian Tern, so any report needs detailed evidence to substantiate it.

FIELD GUIDES: G=154; N=168; P=94.

Common Tern *Sterna hirundo*

Early May–Early June
Late July–Late September

STATUS AND ABUNDANCE: Uncommon migrant. Very rare summer visitor.

HABITAT: Large lakes and rivers.

RECORDS AND REMARKS: Common Terns are not common. They closely resemble, and are often confused with, the more numerous Forster's Tern. But Commons have darker primaries, a reddish bill, and comparatively shorter legs. When the two species are standing together on a mudflat or sandbar, these differences are quite apparent; also, Commons tend to have a more horizontal, short-necked

profile than Forster's. These terns are graceful fliers and feed by
plunge diving.

SPRING—Migration peaks in mid-May. Some may be overlooked
because of their similarity with Forster's Tern.

1, Crab Orchard NWR, 29 Apr 1985 (TF, KR)
2, Crab Orchard NWR, 2 May 1986 (WDR)
5, Rend Lake, Franklin Co., 6 May 1989 (BD)
5, Union Co., 7 May 1983 (VK)
2, Crab Orchard NWR, 25 May 1987 (WDR)
1, Pope Co., 31 May 1982 (VK et al.)

SUMMER—Summer records may represent very late spring migrants or nonbreeding birds.

6, Crab Orchard NWR, 12 June 1975 (BP)
1, Rend Lake, Jefferson Co., 17 June 1988 (TF)

AUTUMN—Migration begins in midsummer and ends fairly early;
very few are seen after September.

3, Rend Lake, 21 July 1985 (LH)
1, Baldwin Lake, 11 Aug 1987 (WDR)
1, Rend Lake, Jefferson Co., 13 Aug 1988 (TF, WDR)
20, Rend Lake, Jefferson Co., 5 Sep 1992 (TF)
1, Little Grassy Lake, Williamson Co., 11 Sep 1985 (JCR)
97, Rend Lake, Franklin Co., 19 Sep 1993 (TF)
1, Rend Lake, Franklin Co., 19 Nov 1993 (TF)
1, Baldwin Lake, 23 Nov 1984 (LA)

DOCUMENTATION: Photograph—Rend Lake, Jefferson Co., 13 Sep
1987 (SIU AP-111).

FIELD GUIDES: G=152; N=162; P=96.

Forster's Tern *Sterna forsteri*

Mid-April–Mid-May
Late July–Late October

STATUS AND ABUNDANCE: Fairly common migrant. Very rare summer visitor.

HABITAT: Lakes and rivers.

RECORDS AND REMARKS: Often associates with other terns, gulls,
and shorebirds on mudflats and sandbars. Much more numerous

than the Common Tern. Differs from the Common by having paler primaries, an oranger bill, longer legs, and a longer tail. Forages for small fish by plunge diving. Uses smaller ponds and lakes more regularly than the Common Tern, and can be seen sitting on buoys, docks, and even tree snags.

SPRING—Arrives earlier in spring than the Common Tern, and sometimes forms rather large flocks. Migration peaks during the first half of May.

1, Baldwin Lake, 16 Apr 1983 (RG)

1, Crab Orchard NWR, 16 Apr 1985 (JCR)

2, Perry Co., 21 Apr 1986 (TF)

7, Wolf Lake, Union Co., 2 May 1985 (VK)

32, Crab Orchard NWR, 5 May 1985 (TF, KR)

31, Rend Lake, 13 May 1988 (TF)

28, Crab Orchard NWR, 15 May 1986 (WDR)

1st-summer, Rend Lake, Franklin Co., 7 June 1986 (WDR)

SUMMER—1st-summer, Rend Lake, Jefferson Co., 22 May–9 July 1994 (TF et al.)

AUTUMN—Concentrations seem to be smaller in fall, but migration is spread out over three months. Small groups of up to five or six individuals are regularly encountered at the larger lakes and rivers.

ad., Rend Lake, Jefferson Co., 3 July 1992 (TF et al.)

1, Union Co., 20 July 1973 (DH)

1, Baldwin Lake, 11 Aug 1987 (WDR)

55, Crab Orchard NWR, 23 Sep 1989 (WDR)

12, Rend Lake, Jefferson Co., 4 Oct 1986 (TF, WDR)

2, Rend Lake, 27 Oct 1985 (LH)

DOCUMENTATION: Photograph—Streamline mine, Perry Co., 21 Apr 1986 (SIU AP-64).

FIELD GUIDES: G=152; N=164; P=96.

[Roseate Tern *Sterna dougallii*]

STATUS AND ABUNDANCE: Hypothetical.

HABITAT: Lakes and rivers.

RECORDS AND REMARKS: One reported from Crab Orchard NWR

on 7 May 1961 was not accompanied by documentary details. A specimen will probably be required before acceptance on the regional list, because of identification difficulties.

FIELD GUIDES: G=152; N=164; P=96.

Least Tern *Sterna antillarum*

Mid-May–Mid-June
Mid-July–Early September

STATUS AND ABUNDANCE: Fairly common migrant and summer resident along the Mississippi River in Alexander Co. Uncommon migrant and summer resident along the Ohio and Wabash Rivers and along the Mississippi River north of Alexander Co. Rare fall migrant at large inland reservoirs.

HABITAT: Major rivers and large reservoirs.

RECORDS AND REMARKS: This smallest of the region's terns nests on sandbars in major rivers and forages in the rivers and floodplain sloughs. They forage actively by plunge diving for small fish. Breeding is often evidenced by terns carrying fish for long distances from the floodplain sloughs back to breeding colonies on river sandbars. It is not unusual to see this species resting on small mudflats with shorebirds.

Least Terns have been reported in southern Illinois since at least the late 1800s (Widmann 1898), but they have probably never been very numerous; they require isolated sandbars to breed successfully. In 1990, however, high water levels in the Ohio and Mississippi Rivers flooded all the traditional breeding colonies, so the terns nested on land. Three colonies (four to twenty-seven nests) were placed in the middle of large tracts of plowed agricultural fields within a mile of the Mississippi River in southern Alexander Co. (WDR). Unfortunately, either the colonies were plowed under or the nests were depredated before any young were fledged. Apparently, the first breeding record for the region came from the discovery of a colony on Bell Island in the Ohio River (actually property of Kentucky) near Shawneetown in 1952; Brewer found three nests there on 5 July 1952 (Brewer 1954). Terns returned there on 25 May the next year and made thirty nests (Hardy 1957); the last terns left the island on 27 July. Currently-known colonies are moni-

Least Tern on nest, south Alexander Co., June 1990

tored each year by the Illinois and Missouri Departments of Conservation.

SPRING—Few terns are seen before mid-May. Migration continues into June, but some sightings in mid- or late June may be nonbreeding wandering birds. Terns wander long distances in search of foraging sites, and most late spring records are from areas that are near major rivers and, possibly, breeding sites.

1, Pope Co., 10 May 1980 (SBC)

1, s.w. Jackson Co., 15 May 1972 (VK)

2, near Thebes, Alexander Co., 21 May 1988 (WDR)

2, Mermet Lake CA, 4 June 1973 (DH)

1, Crab Orchard NWR, 21 June 1956 (SIU)

1, Baldwin Lake, 21 June 1980 (RK)

SUMMER—Terns begin nesting soon after arrival. Currently, active colonies are on Brown's Bar and Bumgard Island in Alexander Co. There are also periodically active colonies at the mouth of the Tennessee River across from Black Bottoms, Massac Co.; Grand Tower, Jackson Co.; and Bell Island, Pope Co.

60 nests, s. Alexander Co., summer 1989 (AW et al.)

1, near New Liberty, Pope Co., 16 June 1972 (VK)

2, Tower Rock, Hardin Co., 19 June 1977 (MMo)
3, Shawneetown, Gallatin Co., 24 June 1972 (VK, DH)
12, s.w. Jackson Co., 27 June 1989 (WDR)
4, Horseshoe Lake CA, 8 July 1976 (BP)
AUTUMN—Many birds wander north and inland away from the
rivers after breeding. These records usually involve only single birds,
but sometimes two or three will be seen together. Most of the flocks
occur along the major rivers.
ad., Carbondale, 20 July 1989 (BD)
1, Crab Orchard NWR, 28 July 1970 (VK)
50, Cairo, Alexander Co., 1 Aug 1907 (Bartsch 1922:101)
1–2, Rend Lake, Jefferson Co., 2–26 Aug 1986 (TF et al.)
11 ad. and 9 imm., Cairo, Alexander Co., 11 Aug 1974 (DH)
2 imm., Rend Lake, Jefferson Co., 12 Aug 1989 (TF, BD, WDR)
3, Baldwin Lake, 31 Aug 1980 (RK)
imm., Rend Lake, Jefferson Co., 17 Sep 1994 (BD)

DOCUMENTATION: Specimen—ad. female, Crab Orchard NWR,
Williamson Co., 21 June 1956 (SIU A-245).

FIELD GUIDES: G=152; N=166; P=96.

Black Tern *Chlidonias niger*
Early May–Early June
Mid-July–Mid-September

STATUS AND ABUNDANCE: Uncommon spring migrant. Fairly common fall migrant.

HABITAT: Lakes and rivers.

RECORDS AND REMARKS: Black Terns are graceful, buoyant fliers;
they forage by skimming food off the surface of the water. Although
there is no definite evidence available, they may have once been
breeding residents, because Audubon (1835) recorded them nesting
nearby in Kentucky.
SPRING—First arrivals appear in May; migration peaks in mid- to
late May, but concentrations are not as large as during fall. Many
apparently fly over the region without stopping, because most
groups of birds are seen during sudden thunderstorms, when the
birds come down to wait for better weather. Some migrants are still

present in June. Sightings in mid-June may be late migrants or non-breeding wandering birds.

1, Crab Orchard NWR, 3 May 1986 (WDR)
1, Rend Lake, Jefferson Co., 3 May 1988 (TF)
7, Rend Lake, Jefferson Co., 13 May 1987 (TF)
9, Carbondale, 22 May 1989 (WDR)
5, Miller City, Alexander Co., 1 June 1983 (VK)
1, Crab Orchard NWR, 8 June 1984 (EC)
3, Mt. Vernon, Jefferson Co., 14 June 1989 (TF)
AUTUMN—Southward movement begins very early. Most Black Terns pass through the region in August. Sometimes a single flock can have birds in many different plumages, ranging from all dark to patchy black-and-white birds. They migrate actively during the day, slowly moving southward down rivers as they forage.
ad., Shawneetown, Gallatin Co., 24 June 1972 (VK, DH)
1, Alexander Co., 28 June 1983 (MS)
1, Baldwin Lake, 3 July 1985 (TF)
1, s. Alexander Co., 12 July 1986 (TF, WDR)
29, McClure, Alexander Co., 17 July 1990 (SA, WDR, SKR)
38, s. Alexander Co., 16 Aug 1986 (WDR)
100, Baldwin Lake, 17 Aug 1977 (CM)
63, Rend Lake, 5 Sep 1992 (TF, DKa)
1, Crab Orchard NWR, 18 Oct 1985 (SO)

DOCUMENTATION: Photograph—Nason, Rend Lake, Jefferson Co., 31 Aug 1988 (SIU AP-236).

FIELD GUIDES: G=156; N=166; P=98.

Order Columbiformes: Pigeons and Doves

Family Columbidae: Pigeons and Doves

Rock Dove *Columba livia*

STATUS AND ABUNDANCE: Common year-round resident.

HABITAT: Residential areas, farms, bridges, and sometimes bluffs in wooded areas and along rivers.

RECORDS AND REMARKS: Rock Doves, or pigeons, were introduced into North America from Europe about 1621 (Long 1981). Plumages are highly variable; some birds are nearly fully white, cinnamon-colored, or normally plumaged. Large flocks often occur around towns and around farms where waste grain is available. Some birds breed in small groups on wooded bluffs, such as those at Giant City SP, Ferne Clyffe SP, and LaRue Pine Hills. Nesting can occur at almost any time of year but is most regular from February to September. Observers tend to neglect censusing this species, except during organized counts like Christmas and Spring Bird Counts.
306, Union Co. CBC, 3 Jan 1981
304, Rend Lake CBC, 15 Dec 1991

DOCUMENTATION: Photograph—Carbondale, Jackson Co., 30 Aug 1988 (SIU AP-230).

FIELD GUIDES: G=166; N=224; P=180.

Mourning Dove *Zenaida macroura*

Late February–Late April
Mid-August–Mid-November

STATUS AND ABUNDANCE: Common year-round resident.

HABITAT: Woodland edge, residential areas, and agricultural lands; especially fond of sunflower fields in fall and winter.

RECORDS AND REMARKS: Though present all year, significant migration occurs. Usually found in pairs or small groups, except during migration, when large flocks may congregate in fields where waste grain is available. As is the case with most common species, few counts by field observers have been published.
SPRING—Northward movements probably begin as early as late February and sometimes continue until about 1 May (Hanson and Kossack 1963), but systematic censuses have apparently not been done.
SUMMER—Breeding begins very early; eggs have been discovered at least as early as 24 February. Nesting continues well into September for some birds. Most early-season nests are placed in conifers, whereas later nests are placed in deciduous trees also.
AUTUMN—Southward migration begins by early August in some

years but normally peaks during early to mid-September. Fall departure dates are difficult to determine, because of the significant winter population. The high count is six hundred at Rend Lake on 16 Aug 1988 (TF).

WINTER—The population is higher in winter than during summer, because of the influx of northern birds.

1,014, Union Co. CBC, 31 Dec 1987

840, Horseshoe Lake CA CBC, 2 Jan 1987

DOCUMENTATION: Specimen—imm. male, 5 miles s. of Carbondale, Jackson Co., 4 May 1971 (SIU A-1739).

FIELD GUIDES: G=166; N=226; P=180.

Passenger Pigeon *Ectopistes migratorius*

STATUS AND ABUNDANCE: Extinct.

RECORDS AND REMARKS: Skeletal evidence from Native American midden deposits (800–1,000 A.D.) at the Pettit Site in northern Alexander Co. indicate that this once impressively abundant pigeon occurred in southern Illinois (Breitburg 1990). From descriptions of movements in other areas of Illinois and the Midwest, it is apparent that birds began their spring migration as early as February and continued until April. Migration was the time when the famous flocks of millions of birds darkened the daytime sky. They reportedly bred in forested areas, often in great colonies, where they foraged on beechnuts and acorns. In light of the extensive forests of southern Illinois, it is probably reasonable to assume that they bred here, but there is no solid evidence to support that assumption. Fall migration was as spectacular, if not more, than spring migration. Sightings of Passenger Pigeons were reported from Cairo on 16 October 1700 and 24 October 1807 (Schorger 1955). The fall movements may have continued into December, because a large flight was noted at the mouth of the Wabash River in Gallatin Co. on 2 December 1792 (Wright 1911). They apparently sometimes wintered in southern Illinois, however, because they were observed in Indiana across the Wabash River from White Co. all winter in 1832 (Thwaites 1906). Schorger (1955, 1973) describes the demise of the Passenger Pigeon; the last bird died in captivity in 1914.

DOCUMENTATION: Specimen—skeletal material, near Thebes, Alexander Co. (Breitburg 1990).

FIELD GUIDES: Not depicted.

Common Ground-Dove *Columbina passerina*

STATUS AND ABUNDANCE: Very rare visitor.

HABITAT: Hedgerows and weedy fields.

RECORDS AND REMARKS: The five records of this small species of the southeastern United States are all from fall and early winter. Ground-Doves have a fall dispersal flight that may take some of them as far north as Ontario. It is conceivable that Common Ground-Doves could occur annually in southern Illinois, but numbers are undoubtedly very small, and the brushy habitat they frequent is very extensive. The subspecies recorded in the region is *C. p. passerina* (Robinson 1991a).

AUTUMN—1, Crab Orchard NWR, 23 Oct 1964 (Ri, Ro)
male, Lake Chautauqua, Jackson Co., 10 Nov 1974 (SIU A-1869)
1 killed by a cat, Carbondale, 26 Nov 1977 (MJM, PB; specimen at ISM)
1, Union Co. CA, 23–28 Dec 1981 (MHa, VK, MMl, WDR)
1 photographed, n.e. Union Co., 4–5 Jan 1988 (DF)

DOCUMENTATION: Specimen—male, Lake Chautauqua, Jackson Co., 10 Nov 1974 (SIU A-1869).

FIELD GUIDES: G=168; N=228; P=180.

Order Psittaciformes: Parrots and Allies

Family Psittacidae: Parrots

Carolina Parakeet *Conuropsis carolinensis*

STATUS AND ABUNDANCE: Extinct.

RECORDS AND REMARKS: As with the Passenger Pigeon, information on the occurrence of Carolina Parakeets in southern Illinois is often scanty. In contrast, however, definite evidence has been preserved in the form of one (probably two) specimens. An adult male was collected by J. K. Townsend at Cairo, Alexander Co., in 1834 (possibly 29 April; USNM). A specimen in the CAS collection was taken by R. Kennicot in 1857 (or 1855), probably in Union Co.; however, there is suspicion that it might be from Union in northern Illinois, McHenry Co. (Bohlen 1989). Carolina Parakeets were apparently most numerous along river-bottom forests, where they roosted in cavities in sycamore trees and fed on cockleburs. Of particular mention in the literature is their regular occurrence in the forests along the Ohio River, from the Wabash River to Cairo, Alexander Co. Heckenwelder found some at the mouth of the Wabash River, Gallatin Co., in December 1792 (Wright 1912). Audubon (1929) also found some there on 5 November 1820. Edwin Janes saw "many" at Shawneetown, Gallatin Co., on 27 May 1819 (Wright 1912). They probably wintered in southern Illinois, because Thwaites (1906) mentions a wintering flock in Indiana across the Wabash River from White Co. in 1832. Additionally, in December 1810, Audubon (1942) reported "thousands" at the mouth of the Cache River, Alexander and Pulaski Cos. It is not clear if Carolina Parakeets bred in southern Illinois or if they were even migratory.

DOCUMENTATION: Specimen—ad. male, Cairo, Alexander Co., 1834 (USNM).

FIELD GUIDES: G and N=not depicted; P=178.

Order Cuculiformes: Cuckoos and Anis

Family Cuculidae: Cuckoos and Anis

Black-billed Cuckoo Coccyzus erythropthalmus
Early May–Early June
Early September–Mid-October

STATUS AND ABUNDANCE: Uncommon migrant. Very rare summer resident.

HABITAT: Deciduous woodland and mature hedgerows.

RECORDS AND REMARKS: This cuckoo is quiet and frequents dense understory and canopy vegetation, so it is often overlooked. Unlike the Eurasian cuckoos, both the Black-billed and Yellow-billed Cuckoos build their own nests; they do, however, sometimes lay their eggs in each other's nests. One Yellow-billed Cuckoo nest found at Pine Hills had two Yellow-billed Cuckoo eggs and one Black-billed Cuckoo egg. Black-bills have a distinctive rhythmic *cu-cucu* call, which they utter repeatedly; it is somewhat similar to some calls given by Yellow-billed Cuckoos, so observers should use care when identifying this species by voice.

SPRING—Migrants usually arrive in early May, but there is significant annual variation in the timing and magnitude of migration.

1, Pomona, 27 Apr 1987 (SO)
1, Ozark, Johnson Co., 27 Apr 1989 (TF)
3, Jackson Co., 7 May 1988 (SBC)
2, Giant City SP, 16 May 1989 (WDR)
male, Denny, Perry Co., 2 June 1989 (WDR)

SUMMER—Some mid-June sightings could be very late spring migrants, while July sightings may be early fall migrants. There are only two nest records, both from Union Co. One nest with three young was discovered on 8 May 1989 (KB, TC); it fledged a few days later. Backdating this nest indicates that nest building had to have begun in mid-April, well before most cuckoos even arrive in southern Illinois. The second nest was found one meter up in a dense blackberry bush at the Pine Hills Campground in May 1991 (CT); both eggs hatched, but the nest was depredated before fledging.

male, Bremen, Randolph Co., 11 June 1989 (WDR)
2, Johnson Co., 8 July 1984 (TF)
1 carrying food, Rend Lake, 16 July 1976 (BP)

AUTUMN—Fall migrants normally arrive in late August or early September and depart by mid-October. As in spring, sightings of more than one per day are unusual.

1, Ozark, 8–9 Aug 1989 (TF)

1, West Frankfort, Franklin Co., 14 Aug 1993 (LS)
1, Grimsby, Jackson Co., 29 Aug 1972 (VK)
1, Rend Lake, 14 Sep 1988 (TF)
1, Carbondale, 30 Sep 1971 (VK)
1, Carbondale, 31 Oct 1982 (KM)

DOCUMENTATION: Specimen—Carbondale, Jackson Co., fall 1981 (SIU A-2162).

FIELD GUIDES: G=172; N=236; P=182.

Yellow-billed Cuckoo *Coccyzus americanus*
Early May–Early June
Late August–Mid-October

STATUS AND ABUNDANCE: Common migrant and summer resident.

HABITAT: Deciduous woods and brushy or woodland thickets.

RECORDS AND REMARKS: This shy species is often vocal, but because it stays in the understory and canopy, it can be difficult to see. It has a slow song that in type can be mistaken for that of a Black-billed Cuckoo, but the Black-bill has a faster, more often repeated song. Both cuckoo species may sing at night, especially on clear, calm evenings.

SPRING—Latest departures are difficult to distinguish, because of the substantial summer population. In some years cuckoos may not arrive until mid-May. There is often still much migration occurring during June.
1, Oakwood Bottoms, Jackson Co., 22 Apr 1972 (DH, VK)
1, Heron Pond, Johnson Co., 24 Apr 1973 (HDB, VK)
91, Union Co., 4 May 1991 (SBC)
SUMMER—Populations vary widely each year, perhaps in response to variations in caterpillar populations. Cuckoos are numerous during cicada outbreaks, too. Most nests are placed two to twelve meters up in dense foliage, especially in vine tangles. Although cuckoos may lay their eggs in other cuckoos' nests, they do not parasitize other passerine species. One egg was laid in an artificial nest in Union Co., June 1991 (INHS).
32, Pulaski and Alexander Cos., 20 June 1973 (VK)
AUTUMN—Fall arrival dates are difficult to determine, because of

local breeders. Most encounters involve only one or two birds per day.

1 banded, Carbondale, 30 Oct 1970 (VK)

1, Crab Orchard NWR, 30 Oct 1985 (TF)

1 in a multiflora rose hedgerow, Crab Orchard NWR, 16 Nov 1982 (JCR)

DOCUMENTATION: Specimen—Crab Orchard NWR, Aug 1968 (SIU A-1706).

FIELD GUIDES: G=172; N=236; P=182.

[Groove-billed Ani *Crotophaga sulcirostris*]

STATUS AND ABUNDANCE: Hypothetical.

RECORDS AND REMARKS: An ani reported from Carbondale on 12 November 1978 was originally identified as a Smooth-billed Ani (*C. ani; AB* 33:184). However, Smooth-bills do not have a fall dispersal flight like Groove-bills do. Details are not sufficient to specifically identify the bird, though it was undoubtedly a Groove-bill. Groove-billed Anis normally occur in southern Texas, southwest Louisiana, and Mexico during fall and winter.

FIELD GUIDES: G=158; N=234; P=182.

Order Strigiformes: Owls

Family *Tytonidae: Barn Owls*

Barn Owl *Tyto alba*

STATUS AND ABUNDANCE: Rare year-round resident.

HABITAT: Extensive grassland areas, farms, and cypress swamps.

RECORDS AND REMARKS: Formerly more numerous, this owl has probably declined in the region in the last twenty or thirty years. Its quiet habits make it very difficult to detect, however, so many undoubtedly go unnoticed. There is some migration, but very few

Barn Owls are encountered outside the breeding season. There are probably more present than currently thought, especially in the Till Plain, where abandoned silos and barns provide nesting sites, and along the Cache River, where large cavities in cypress trees are available.

SUMMER—Like most owls, Barn Owls nest very early in spring. The breeding population may be much larger than currently thought. Recent fieldwork has shown a sizable population in Pulaski and Union Cos. Some pairs apparently breed nearly all year, raising as many as three broods in a single year.

1, Cambria, Williamson Co., 26 Mar 1974 (MH)
nest, Dahlgren, Hamilton Co., spring 1973 (VK)
nest, Mt. Vernon, Jefferson Co., 27 Apr 1974 (VK)
1, Ozark, Johnson Co., 10 May 1993 (TF)
nest with 2 yg. in cypress tree, Pulaski Co., 11 June 1983 (JW)
nest with 5 yg., Norris City, White Co., Apr–Aug 1984 (GF)
ad. male on diurnal roost in cypress, Buttonland Swamp, Pulaski Co., 4 May–8 June 1986 (TF)
nest with 6 yg. in silo, n. Randolph Co., Apr–June 1988 (TF et al.)
nest, Anna, Union Co., summer 1990 (AW et al.)
nest, Pulaski Co., 8 May–June 1992 (BL, TF)
nest fledged 3 yg., Union Co., 18 July 1993 (BL, TF)
nest fledged 3 yg., Pulaski Co., 24 Aug 1993 (BL, TF)
WINTER—1, Murphysboro, Jackson Co., 26 Jan 1977 (MT, MMo)
2 pairs wintered at nest site, Perks, Pulaski Co., 1992–1993 (TF)

DOCUMENTATION: Specimen—male, s.e. of Marion, Williamson Co., 19 June 1958 (SIU A-766).

FIELD GUIDES: G=176; N=238; P=174.

Family Strigidae: True Owls

Eastern Screech-Owl *Otus asio*

STATUS AND ABUNDANCE: Locally uncommon year-round resident.

HABITAT: Deciduous woodlots and, sometimes, residential areas.

RECORDS AND REMARKS: Few observers have conducted systematic censuses of this species. They are most often detected by their "screeching" whinny call or their alternate tooting call. "Screechies" show two basic color phases, red (appearing rufous) and gray, with many intermediate brownish forms, too. Most birds in southern Illinois are red phase. Little, if any, migration occurs, but there seems to be a postbreeding movement during July and August. Screech-Owls seem to be most numerous in the Till Plain and the Shawnee Hills, and they respond well to whistled imitations or playbacks of their calls.

SUMMER—Nesting begins in March, and the peak of fledging is in May. Nests are placed in tree cavities; sometimes boxes intended for Wood Ducks are used.

17, Union Co., 4 May 1991 (SBC)

nest with 5 yg., Wildcat Bluff, Johnson Co., 10 May 1985 (JW)

WINTER—8, Crab Orchard NWR, 1 Jan 1983 (JCR)

17, Union Co. CBC, 3 Jan 1987

DOCUMENTATION: Specimen—ad. female, 2 miles w. of Cobden, Union Co., 3 Jan 1956 (SIU A-182).

FIELD GUIDES: G=174; N=242; P=172.

Great Horned Owl *Bubo virginianus*

STATUS AND ABUNDANCE: Common year-round resident.

HABITAT: Woodlots and woodland edge, especially near fields.

RECORDS AND REMARKS: Southern Illinois's largest owl, Great Horns can often be seen perched in solitary trees, on telephone poles, or flying across fields at dusk. The familiar hoot can be heard throughout the year. Little, if any, migration occurs. Few organized censuses of this species have been conducted.

SUMMER—Nesting begins very early (some have eggs in January); Spring Bird Counts census the breeding population.

14, Alexander Co., 7 May 1977 (SBC)

WINTER—21, Crab Orchard NWR CBC, 15 Dec 1984

17, Union Co. CBC, 3 Jan 1987

10, Horseshoe Lake CA CBC, 21 Dec 1982

DOCUMENTATION: Specimen—juv. female, 2 miles s.w. of Carbondale, Jackson Co., 27 Mar 1959 (SIU A-860).

FIELD GUIDES: G=174; N=238; P=172.

Snowy Owl *Nyctea scandiaca*

STATUS AND ABUNDANCE: Very rare visitor.

HABITAT: Large crop and pasture lands and residential areas.

RECORDS AND REMARKS: This Arctic owl occurs in southern Illinois only during major irruption years. When in residential areas, it feeds on Rock Doves. Because it commonly forages diurnally, it can be very conspicuous when perched low or on the ground in open fields.

AUTUMN—1, Union Co. CA, 19 Nov 1980 (MC)

WINTER—1, Rend Lake, Franklin Co., 31 Dec 1975–3 Jan 1976 (BP)

1, Rend Lake, Franklin Co., 8 Feb 1992 (AB 46:273)

SPRING—1, Red Bud, Randolph Co., 10 Mar 1976 (OK)

Additionally, Bennett (1952) refers to two birds that were collected near Carbondale in 1933, but disposition of the specimens is now unknown. Further, there is an unsubstantiated report of one near Cobden, Union Co., in 1951 (GBi).

DOCUMENTATION: Photograph—Red Bud, Randolph Co., 10 Mar 1976 (cover of *IAB* 176).

FIELD GUIDES: G=176; N=240; P=174.

Barred Owl *Strix varia*

STATUS AND ABUNDANCE: Common year-round resident.

HABITAT: Bottomland woods and swamps; mature upland forest.

RECORDS AND REMARKS: The distinctive loud call of this owl is easily recognized. Barred Owls call during the day (especially on calm, cool days) as well as at night, and they will readily respond to imitations of their call. Like most nocturnal species, little census work has been done on this owl. It also nests very early in spring, with eggs present in nests by late February. There may be some migration, but the extent and timing of it is unknown.

SUMMER—Spring Bird Counts probably census breeding populations.

30, Alexander Co., 4 May 1985 (SBC)

WINTER—The winter population seems to be supplemented to some extent by an influx of birds that bred farther north.

35, Horseshoe Lake CA CBC, 30 Dec 1987
16, Union Co. CBC, 3 Jan 1987

DOCUMENTATION: Specimen—female, Cobden, Union Co., 17 Aug 1959 (SIU A-861).

FIELD GUIDES: G=176; N=240; P=174.

Long-eared Owl *Asio otus*
Early December–Late March

STATUS AND ABUNDANCE: Locally uncommon winter resident. Rare migrant. Very rare summer visitor.

HABITAT: Roosts communally in dense conifer stands and brushy woodland thickets near large grasslands and agricultural fields.

RECORDS AND REMARKS: These owls are strictly nocturnal and roost during the day. Their presence can sometimes be detected by searching for pellets or whitewash under groves of dense conifers. They usually flush readily but sometimes can be approached and observed closely. They are usually silent, so they are not likely to be encountered without a special search of appropriate roosting habitats.
AUTUMN—Fall and winter populations are difficult to separate, because these owls arrive so late in the year.
1, Carbondale, 25 Nov 1991 (JH)
WINTER—Those detected during winter may include some migrants, but few Long-ears winter south of Illinois.
1, Belle Rive, Jefferson Co., 5 Dec 1989 (TF)
1, Horseshoe Lake CA CBC, 20 Dec 1983
specimen, Libertyville, Saline Co., late Dec 1988 (TF)
10–15, near Carbondale, 29 Dec 1956–8 Apr 1957 (Birkenholz 1958)
2, Belle Rive, Jefferson Co., 11 Jan 1988, and 5 there on 15 Jan 1990 (TF, JD, WDR)
1, Little Black Slough, Johnson Co., 11 Jan 1990 (TF)
specimen, 2 miles s. of Makanda, in Union Co., 12 Jan 1974 (SIU)
SPRING—Migration is usually inconspicuous, but departures usually occur from mid-March to early April.
1, Little Black Slough, Johnson Co., 8 Mar 1992 (TF)

1, Rend Lake, Franklin Co., 20 Mar 1976 (BP)
SUMMER—One summer record—roadkill, Carbondale, 11 June 1977 (MMo, DK)—is suggestive of breeding, but the gonads of the specimen were not checked to determine breeding status. Additionally, there are sketchy reports in the Crab Orchard NWR staff files of one on the refuge in August 1968 and of a nesting pair there in March 1969.

DOCUMENTATION: Specimen—male, 2 miles s. of Makanda, in Union Co., 12 Jan 1974 (SIU A-1933).

FIELD GUIDES: G=174; N=238; P=172.

Short-eared Owl *Asio flammeus*

Early November–Early April

STATUS AND ABUNDANCE: Uncommon migrant and winter resident. Very rare summer visitor.

HABITAT: Roosts communally in large grassy fields, especially those with tall vegetation.

RECORDS AND REMARKS: Most active at dawn and dusk, this crepuscular owl can be seen flying low over grasslands, like a big moth. They roost on the ground, sometimes associating with Northern Harriers.

AUTUMN—A few appear in late fall, but most arrive with very cold weather in December.
1, Rend Lake, Franklin Co., 2 Nov 1985 (TF, SO)
1, w. Jackson Co., 14 Nov 1993 (CS)
1, n.w. Pope Co., 13 Dec 1988 (TF)
WINTER—Southward migration may still be in progress even in late December. Short-ears were recorded on twelve Christmas Bird Counts (from 1973–1992).
5, Union Co. CBC, 30 Dec 1988
1, Horseshoe Lake CBC, 18 Dec 1985
1, Rend Lake CBC, 31 Dec 1988
2, Alexander Co., 21 Dec 1983 (JEW)
2, Carbondale, 15 Jan 1984 (JCR, SS)
7, n.w. Union Co., Jan 1973 (DH)
4, Rend Lake, Franklin Co., 21 Feb 1976 (BP, MMo)

6, Will Scarlet Mine, Saline Co., 7 Mar 1992 (TF, JD)
SPRING—Northward movement begins at least by early March, and most birds are usually gone by the first week in April.
1, Stoneface, Saline Co., 19 Mar 1989 (TF, JD)
1, Rend Lake, Franklin Co., 2 Apr 1976 (BP, MMo)
SUMMER—It is possible that some may breed in the large grassy fields of reclaimed strip mines in the Till Plain. Two records are suggestive of this possibility:
2, near Logan, Franklin Co., all summer 1993 (LS, BD)
1, Pinckneyville, Perry Co., 19 June 1977 (MMo, MT)

DOCUMENTATION: Specimen—ad., Wayne-Fitzgerrell SP, Franklin Co., 2 Apr 1976 (SIU).

FIELD GUIDES: G=174; N=238; P=172.

Northern Saw-whet Owl *Aegolius acadicus*

STATUS AND ABUNDANCE: Very rare migrant and winter resident.

HABITAT: Deciduous woods, conifer plantations, and dense hedgerows.

RECORDS AND REMARKS: This tiny owl is very tame. It roosts in dense vegetation, usually conifer stands, during the day, and it hunts for mice and birds at night. It is typically very easy to approach and observe once discovered. Its tameness may mislead inexperienced observers, who may think it has been injured. These birds should *never* be detained longer than is necessary to obtain a few documentary photos. The stress and loss of hunting time these birds experience when captured can cause them great harm. Despite their approachability, Saw-whets are extremely inconspicuous and readily go unnoticed. Though there are currently only five records, they certainly must occur more often, because they have a fairly large wintering range south of Illinois.
AUTUMN—1 photographed, Carbondale, 13 Oct 1988 (SIU AP-300).
WINTER—1, Little Black Slough, Johnson Co., 8–9 Jan 1993 (TF)
2, Ozark, Johnson Co., 2 Feb–1 Mar 1986 (TF et al.)

Northern Saw-whet Owl, Ozark, Johnson Co., 1 March 1986

1, Ozark, Johnson Co., 5 Feb–29 Mar 1994 (TF)
1 alive and remains of a second found, Johnson Co., 17 Feb 1992
(TF, JD)
One of the two 1986 Ozark birds was captured and banded on 1
March. The birds were initially discovered when TF heard one giving its distinctive monotonous toot call. One or both birds called
during the entire month they were present. As an illustration of
the tameness of this species, after the Ozark owl was banded, it was
placed on a tree limb and photographed; it remained motionless,
except for blinking its eyes, for nearly an hour.

DOCUMENTATION: Photograph—ad., Ozark, Johnson Co., 1 Mar 1986 (SIU AP-301).

FIELD GUIDES: G=178; N=246; P=176.

Order Caprimulgiformes: Goatsuckers

Family Caprimulgidae: Goatsuckers

Common Nighthawk *Chordeiles minor*
Late April–Late May
Mid-August–Mid-October

STATUS AND ABUNDANCE: Common migrant and summer resident.

HABITAT: Residential areas with large flat-roofed buildings; extensive grassland areas. During migration they can be seen foraging over lakes and rivers in early morning.

RECORDS AND REMARKS: Three subspecies have been recorded in southern Illinois, all of which are generally separable only in-hand: *C. m. minor*, *C. m. chapmani*, and *C. m. sennetti* (Bohlen 1989). Nighthawks can often be seen migrating in flocks ahead of approaching weather systems. They sometimes roost on horizontal tree branches during the day.
SPRING—The first nighthawks to arrive are quite predictable: 25 April seems to be the most regular arrival date. Flocks of diurnally migrating birds are seen throughout May.
1, Carbondale, 21 Apr 1986 (KM)
70, Jackson Co., 8 May 1976 (SBC)
12, Mermet Lake CA, 24 May 1986 (WDR)
SUMMER—Nighthawks breed regularly in Carbondale, Marion, Mt. Vernon, and other towns throughout southern Illinois, but no nesting data have been gathered. Breeding may also occur on reclaimed strip mines where extensive grasslands with patches of sandy soil occur.
AUTUMN—Fall movements begin fairly early; groups of migrating birds are sometimes seen as early as late July, but these may be local

birds instead of groups from northern areas. Most migrants are de-tected in August. It is common to see groups flying south, some-times very high, just ahead of approaching storm fronts.

80, Ozark, Johnson Co., 20 Aug 1989 (TF)
373, Ozark, Johnson Co., 27 Aug 1989 (TF)
108, Carbondale, 21 Sep 1985 (TF)
1, Mt. Vernon, Jefferson Co., 20 Oct 1986 (TF)
2, Carbondale, 21 Oct 1985 (TF)

DOCUMENTATION: Specimen—*C. m. sennetti*, Blairsville, William-son Co., 15 Oct 1961 (SIU A-1204).

FIELD GUIDES: G=182; N=250; P=184.

Chuck-will's-widow *Caprimulgus carolinensis*

Late April–Mid-September

STATUS AND ABUNDANCE: Fairly common migrant and summer resident in the Shawnee Hills and the Floodplains. Uncommon mi-grant and summer resident in the Till Plain.

HABITAT: Deciduous woods, principally upland, scrubby edge areas. Forages over fields and sometimes around streetlights. Also inhabits bottomland forests and pine woods.

RECORDS AND REMARKS: Were it not for their loud nightly song, Chucks would rarely be detected. Indeed, after singing ceases in late July or early August, they are rarely encountered. It is some-times possible to see them by driving backroads on clear nights and spotting them with car headlights; their voice and large size distin-guishes them from Whip-poor-wills.

SPRING—Chucks arrive later than Whip-poor-wills. George (1968) gave 30 March as an early spring arrival, but that is prob-ably an error; they usually do not arrive before late April.

1 singing, s.e. Saline Co., 8 Apr 1993 (JD)
1 singing, s.e. Jackson Co., 15 Apr 1988 (WDR)
24, Alexander Co., 7 May 1977 (SBC)
21, Pope Co., 7 May 1988 (SBC)
2, Jefferson Co., 7 May 1988 (SBC)

SUMMER—The two cryptic eggs are placed on the ground among the leaf litter. Incubating birds are very difficult to see.

nest with 2 eggs, Rudement, Saline Co., mid-June 1988 (KP)
nest with one egg (infertile), Ozark, Johnson Co., 27 May–19 June
1990 (TF)
AUTUMN—Vocalization decreases during fall, so Chucks are hard
to find. They may sing once or twice at dusk and dawn during fall
migration. One was singing in southeast Saline Co. on 10 August
1994 (JD). There are few records past mid-August, but one Chuck
was at Murphysboro on 16 September 1947 (JWH).

DOCUMENTATION: Specimen—Carbondale, Jackson Co., 7 June
1965 (INHS CA-c-1).

FIELD GUIDES: G=182; N=248; P=184.

Whip-poor-will *Caprimulgus vociferus*
Late March–Early October

STATUS AND ABUNDANCE: Common migrant and summer resident.

HABITAT: Nearly any deciduous woods. Seems to prefer more mature woodlands than Chuck-will's-widow.

RECORDS AND REMARKS: Like Chucks, Whips are very vocal during spring and early summer. Their loud song is given most frequently during dawn and dusk but can be heard all night; they even
occasionally sing during the day. Whip-poor-wills can be seen fairly
readily by driving backroads and spotting them with car headlights.
SPRING—First arrivals are usually heard during the last few days
of March or just past the first of April. Singing may be brief and
restricted to a few minutes around dawn and dusk just after arrival.
By mid-April, however, singing may continue throughout the night.
1, Pope Co., 23 Mar 1975 (RGr)
2, Saline Co. (KP), and 1, Pope Co. (TF), 30 Mar 1986
92, Alexander Co., 7 May 1977 (SBC)
SUMMER—Whips are common nesters, but few data are available.
Nests are usually discovered accidentally by flushing incubating birds
from their ground nests. Nesting phenology may be highly variable.
1 juv. near fledging, Williamson Co., 28 May 1992 (BL)
nest with 2 freshly laid eggs, Ozark, Johnson Co., 10 June 1992 (TF)
AUTUMN—Singing is generally restricted to a few minutes at
dawn and dusk, so detection of fall birds is difficult. Beginning of

southward movements is unclear, but most Whip-poor-wills have left southern Illinois by late September.

1 singing, Giant City SP, 24 Sep 1983 (JCR)

specimen, near Cobden, Union Co., 6 Oct 1967 (SIU)

1 banded, Carbondale, 7 Oct 1971 (VK)

DOCUMENTATION: Specimen—ad. female, 2 miles n. of Cobden, Union Co., 6 Oct 1967 (SIU A-1572).

FIELD GUIDES: G=182; N=248; P=184.

Order Apodiformes: Swifts and Hummingbirds

Family Apodidae: Swifts

Chimney Swift *Chaetura pelagica*

Early April–Mid-October

STATUS AND ABUNDANCE: Common migrant and summer resident.

HABITAT: This nearly ubiquitous species can be found foraging high in the air anywhere. It breeds in chimneys in residential areas and in hollow trees in swamps.

RECORDS AND REMARKS: Swifts are gregarious and are commonly seen foraging in flocks during migration and the breeding season. They seem to fly low to the ground or over the surface of lakes early in the morning or late in the day, but much higher during midday.

SPRING—Swifts arrive early, about the same time the first whip-poor-wills appear. Apparently no large flocks have been seen in spring. Groups of up to fifty or so, however, are commonplace. Because of the summer population, it is unclear when the last migrants leave.

2, Rend Lake, Jefferson Co., 28 Mar 1988 (TF)

1, s.e. Jackson Co., 30 Mar 1986 (WDR)

SUMMER—Swifts probably breed in every township in southern Illinois, but no data are available on their summer populations. The largest breeding populations are in towns; some also breed in swamps, where they place their nests in hollow cypress trees.

AUTUMN—Wandering groups of birds begin appearing during late July, but these are probably flocks of local birds; hence, the start of southward migration is difficult to identify. Most swifts are gone by mid-October, so any seen afterward should be closely scrutinized to explore the possibility of western species occurring as vagrants.

250, Rend Lake, 28 July 1986 (WDR)
720, Carbondale, 12 Sep 1985 (TF)
500, Carbondale, 9 Oct 1971 (VK)
1, Carbondale, 27 Oct 1985 (SO)
1, Carbondale, 23 Nov 1974 (DK)

DOCUMENTATION: Specimen—juv. male, Carbondale, Jackson Co., 24 June 1959 (SIU A-886).

FIELD GUIDES: G=184; N=252; P=204.

Family Trochilidae: Hummingbirds

Ruby-throated Hummingbird *Archilochus colubris*
Late April–Early October

STATUS AND ABUNDANCE: Fairly common migrant and summer resident.

HABITAT: Deciduous woods, woodland edge, hedgerows, and residential areas near flowers and sugar-water feeders.

RECORDS AND REMARKS: Hummingbird numbers fluctuate greatly from year to year. They can be seen and studied at close range at feeders and around patches of such flowers as trumpet creepers and jewelweed.

SPRING—The first spring migrants usually arrive in late April, but peak numbers do not arrive until early May. Typical daily high counts do not exceed ten to twelve birds, but this varies considerably.

1, s.e. Saline Co., 10 Apr 1993 (JD)
1, Carbondale, 12 Apr 1985 (KM)
1, Murphysboro, Jackson Co., 15 Apr 1972 (VK)
28, Union Co., 4 May 1991 (SBC)

17, Massac Co., 7 May 1977 (SBC)
26 at buckeye blossoms, Alexander Co., 8 May 1982 (PK; mistakenly dated 1987 in Bohlen [1989])
SUMMER—Nests have been discovered as early as 4 May (Union Co., 1989 [TC]) and eggs by 9 May (Alexander Co., 1987 [ID]). Nests are usually placed on downsloping branches three to fifteen meters above ground. They can be found by following females that are gathering spider webs, who usually fly directly back to the nest. AUTUMN—Because of the breeding population, the start of fall migration is difficult to detect. Males seem to migrate first (Johnsgard 1983); and all late-fall records are of birds in female/immature plumage. Most hummers have departed by the first of October.
30, Giant City SP, 8 Sep 1990 (BD)
1, Carbondale, 21 Oct 1970 (AW)
1, Carbondale, 26 Oct 1989 (BD)

DOCUMENTATION: Specimen—ad. male, Carbondale, Jackson Co., 12 May 1960 (SIU A-1130).

FIELD GUIDES: G=186; N=258; P=186.

Rufous Hummingbird *Selasphorus rufus*

STATUS AND ABUNDANCE: Very rare visitor.

RECORDS AND REMARKS: One confirmed record and one hypothetical record exist for the region. One immature female present from 27 October 1993 through 15 January 1994 was captured, measured, photographed, and released in Murphysboro, Jackson Co. (BD). Two tail feathers were also taken to confirm the identification to species (Danley 1994). Another immature female was observed at close range in Carbondale from 23 to 28 October 1989 (BD, WDR), but it evaded capture. Both birds came to sugarwater feeders in residential areas. Rufous Hummingbirds breed in the western United States, sometimes occurring as vagrants in the eastern United States. Contrary to popular belief, it is not detrimental to hummingbirds to leave feeders out late in autumn. If Bob Danley had not maintained his feeders past the normal departure time of Ruby-throats, these birds would never have been identified. Feeders should, however, be cleaned regularly to prevent excessive fermentation or spoiling of the sugar water.

Hummingbird identification is notoriously difficult. Confirming identification of vagrant hummingbirds requires excellent diagnostic photographs, voice recordings, and/or specimens; in most cases, the birds themselves need not be sacrificed. If the suspected vagrant can be captured, tail feathers one, two, and five should be removed, secured by taping the shafts to an index card, carefully labeled, and deposited at an approved depository (see introduction). The measurements and color patterns of these tail feathers are usually sufficient to identify the birds to species level. Any late-fall hummingbird sighting, particularly during November, should be photographed and closely examined; moreover, experts should be contacted immediately.

FIELD GUIDES: G=172; N=260; P=not pictured.

[Anna's Hummingbird *Calypte anna*]

STATUS AND ABUNDANCE: Hypothetical.

RECORDS AND REMARKS: An immature female was carefully scrutinized and photographed at Carbondale from 17 to 29 September 1990 (BD, WDR et al.), but because of the difficulty of identification, the record is still in dispute. Observers who suspect they have a vagrant species of hummingbird visiting their feeder are encouraged to contact experts immediately; the experts can oversee efforts to capture the bird, to make in-hand measurements, and to obtain photographs. Voice recordings can also be helpful for identification.

FIELD GUIDES: G=172; N=258; P=not pictured.

Order Coraciiformes: Kingfishers

Family Alcedinidae: Kingfishers

Belted Kingfisher *Ceryle alcyon*

STATUS AND ABUNDANCE: Common migrant. Fairly common summer resident in the Shawnee Hills and the Floodplains. Uncommon summer resident in the Till Plain. Uncommon winter resident.

HABITAT: Creeks, ponds, lakes, and rivers. Requires dirt banks for nesting and trees as hunting perches.

RECORDS AND REMARKS: Kingfishers do migrate but apparently not on strict schedules as do many other birds. They will remain in northern breeding areas as long as open water is available, but when freeze-up begins, they move south. Kingfishers can be found in southern Illinois throughout the year, except during the most severe winters.

SPRING—Northward movements start when water areas begin thawing (in late January to early February in some years). Usually less than ten are seen per day.

SUMMER—Because kingfishers breed fairly early, data from Spring Bird Counts probably census breeding populations. Adults were entering a nest in Saline Co. on 9 April 1988 (WDR); most breeding occurs in May and June.

AUTUMN—Southward migration is difficult to detect, because of the presence of both breeding and wintering kingfishers. Systematic censuses could reveal when peak numbers pass through the region.

WINTER—As long as open water is available, kingfishers stay for the winter.

18, Union Co. CBC, 22 Dec 1982
26, Horseshoe Lake CA CBC, 2 Jan 1987
19, Crab Orchard NWR CBC, 4 Jan 1976

DOCUMENTATION: Specimen—female, Anna, Union Co., 28 Dec 1935 (SIU A-1764).

FIELD GUIDES: G=192; N=262; P=186.

Order Piciformes: Woodpeckers

Family Picidae: Woodpeckers

Red-headed Woodpecker *Melanerpes erythrocephalus*

Late February–Early May
Early September–Late October

STATUS AND ABUNDANCE: Common year-round resident in the

Floodplains. Uncommon year-round resident in the Shawnee Hills. Common migrant and summer resident, but uncommon winter resident in the Till Plain.

HABITAT: Deciduous woods, especially bottomlands and open, parklike situations.

RECORDS AND REMARKS: Populations vary considerably from year to year, especially in winter. These aggressive birds fight almost constantly with each other and with other species, especially with Red-bellied Woodpeckers. Immatures have duller plumage overall, a grayer head, and spots on the tips of the secondaries.

SPRING—Because a winter population exists in the region, it is often difficult to detect the start of spring migration. Northward movements probably begin as early as mid-February in some years; I have seen new arrivals about 20 February in areas I censused daily throughout the winter. Migration may continue until early May, but the summer population obscures detection of latest departures.

SUMMER—Red-heads compete with Starlings for nest sites and often lose. After breeding, they often form loose flocks and can be seen flycatching above the treetops.

49 flycatching, s.w. Jackson Co., 30 June 1989 (WDR)

AUTUMN—Fall migration is more obvious than spring migration, yet it is still inconspicuous. Small groups of traveling birds fly just above the treetops along the major river valleys, especially along the Mississippi River. Fourteen birds per hour were seen along the Ohio River one fall (Graber et al. 1977). Migration probably extends from early September through late October, but systematic censuses have not been done.

WINTER—There is pronounced annual fluctuation in the wintering population. In good mast years, many Red-heads stay the winter; in poor years, numbers of Red-heads are lower, but there are always at least a few around (usually in bottomland woods).

267, Horseshoe Lake CA CBC, 20 Dec 1983

331, Union Co. CBC, 29 Dec 1979

71, Crab Orchard NWR CBC, 28 Dec 1970

90, Oakwood Bottoms, Jackson Co., 16 Feb 1975 (BP)

DOCUMENTATION: Specimen—female, Campbell Lake, Franklin Co., 3 Dec 1960 (SIU A-1189).

FIELD GUIDES: G=198; N=266; P=188.

Red-bellied Woodpecker *Melanerpes carolinus*

STATUS AND ABUNDANCE: Common year-round resident.

HABITAT: Woods, both deciduous and coniferous, and parklike residential areas.

RECORDS AND REMARKS: Red-bellies probably do not migrate to any large extent, but Graber et al. (1977) reported a few migrating along the Mississippi and Ohio Rivers during fall (late September to late October). There are no data that show spring migration. One female banded in southeast Jackson Co. was present at the same locality for seven years (WDR).

SUMMER—Red-bellies undoubtedly breed in every township in southern Illinois. Nesting begins as early as late March and continues through early July. Nests are most conspicuous in mid- and late May, when most have old, loudly begging juveniles.

200, Union Co., 4 May 1991 (SBC)

WINTER—Red-bellies will come to feeders for sunflower seeds, corn, and suet. Most published winter counts come from Christmas Bird Counts:

331, Union Co. CBC, 22 Dec 1982

346, Horseshoe Lake CA CBC, 30 Dec 1987

96, Crab Orchard NWR CBC, 31 Dec 1976

DOCUMENTATION: Specimen—male, 3 miles e. of Texico, Jefferson Co., 19 Oct 1958 (SIU A-631).

FIELD GUIDES: G=196; N=264; P=190.

Yellow-bellied Sapsucker *Sphyrapicus varius*

Late September–Early November
Late March–Early May

STATUS AND ABUNDANCE: Fairly common migrant. Fairly common winter resident in the Floodplains and the Shawnee Hills. Uncommon winter resident in the Till Plain.

HABITAT: Deciduous and coniferous woods.

RECORDS AND REMARKS: Sapsuckers are less vocal than other woodpecker species, so they are often overlooked, but their presence is often revealed by the distinctive rows of holes they drill in trees. Graber et al. (1977) found a preference for drilling in overcup oaks, slash pines, tulip trees, pecan trees, red cedars, and maples. The red-naped form of the Yellow-bellied Sapsucker was recently raised to full species status (*S. nuchalis*; American Ornithologists' Union 1985); it has not been recorded in southern Illinois. Some Yellow-bellied Sapsuckers can show red on the nape, so identifications should be made with caution. See Kaufmann (1990) for field-marks to note.

AUTUMN—Peak numbers of sapsuckers pass through the region in October (Graber et al. 1977). The end of fall migration is obscured by the winter population.

1, Crab Orchard NWR, 19 Sep 1982 (JCR)

WINTER—During winter, Sapsuckers are most common in bottomland woods and pine stands. Numbers vary widely from year to year.

42, Horseshoe Lake CA CBC, 30 Dec 1987

77, Union Co. CBC, 2 Jan 1976

8, Crab Orchard NWR CBC, 4 Jan 1976

SPRING—Northward migration begins by late March but has been reported as early as late February (Graber et al. 1977). The influx of spring migrants is usually recognizable despite the presence of the wintering population. Most sapsuckers are gone by the end of April, but a few linger into early May each year.

15, Heron Pond, Johnson Co., 9 Apr 1972 (VK)

2, Jackson Co., 10 May 1986 (SBC)

SUMMER—There is one questionable report of a sapsucker at Horseshoe Lake CA on 13 August 1932 (Gower 1933). If correct, the bird may have been a very early fall migrant or possibly a local breeder.

DOCUMENTATION: Specimen—female, Carbondale, Jackson Co., 10 Dec 1960 (SIU A-1133).

FIELD GUIDES: G=198; N=268; P=190.

Downy Woodpecker *Picoides pubescens*

STATUS AND ABUNDANCE: Common year-round resident.

HABITAT: Woods, residential areas, and parks; even forages in old fields—on saplings, bushes, tall weeds, and cornstalks.

RECORDS AND REMARKS: Downies outnumber their larger look-alike, the Hairy Woodpecker, by four to five times. They readily visit feeders for suet, sunflower seeds, and peanut butter. No migration is known. They become rather inconspicuous in August and September, when they are molting (George 1972). As with most common species, surveys have only been conducted during Christmas and Spring Bird Counts.

SUMMER—Downies nest quite early; egg dates range from late March to mid-June. Hence, Spring Bird Counts census the breeding population.

40, Union Co., 4 May 1991 (SBC)

WINTER—Downies can often be found with other small birds—such as chickadees, nuthatches, and titmice—in winter foraging flocks that roam the forest and forest edges looking for food.

138, Crab Orchard NWR CBC, 15 Dec 1984

374, Union Co. CBC, 22 Dec 1982

273, Horseshoe Lake CA CBC, 30 Dec 1987

DOCUMENTATION: Specimen—ad. male, Belknap, Johnson Co., 19 Feb 1961 (SIU A-1184).

FIELD GUIDES: G=200; N=270; P=192.

Hairy Woodpecker *Picoides villosus*

STATUS AND ABUNDANCE: Fairly common year-round resident.

HABITAT: Woods. Although they occur in woodlots and wooded residential areas, they are most numerous in heavily forested regions.

RECORDS AND REMARKS: Compared to Downy Woodpeckers, the Hairy population seems low. Like Downies, Hairies probably do not migrate much. Usually less than a dozen Hairies are seen per day in the field. Few serious surveys have been done on this species.

SUMMER—Spring Bird Counts survey nesting birds, because Hairies nest early in spring, from mid-April to mid-July.

32, Union Co., 4 May 1991 (SBC)

WINTER—Hairies are more solitary than Downies and do not associate with winter foraging flocks as often.

87, Union Co. CBC, 22 Dec 1982

60, Horseshoe Lake CA CBC, 30 Dec 1987

26, Crab Orchard NWR CBC, 28 Dec 1974

DOCUMENTATION: Specimen—male, 3 miles e. of Carbondale, in Williamson Co., 19 Feb 1959 (SIU A-664).

FIELD GUIDES: G=200; N=270; P=192.

Northern Flicker *Colaptes auratus*
Late February–Mid-April
Mid-September–Early November

STATUS AND ABUNDANCE: Common migrant and winter resident. Fairly common summer resident.

HABITAT: Open deciduous woods, woodland edge, and hedgerows; flickers often forage on the ground in fields far from trees.

RECORDS AND REMARKS: Two subspecies of flicker have been reported from the region: the common form is the Yellow-shafted Flicker (*C. a. auratus*), and there is one record of a Red-shafted Flicker (*C. a. cafer*)—which breeds in western North America—in Alexander Co. on 2 January 1987 (RP, MD). Flickers are quite migratory. Migrating birds often follow the major river valleys, like those of the Mississippi and Ohio/Wabash Rivers, and travel in small groups in a fashion similar to Red-headed Woodpeckers and Blue Jays. It is not unusual during migration to see several groups of two to twenty flickers foraging in grassy areas along roadsides.
SPRING—Northward movements may begin in early or mid-February in some years but normally start in late February. Groups of twenty to forty are seen per day. Migration is usually over by about mid-April.
SUMMER—Flicker populations are relatively low during summer; they seem to be a little more numerous in the Till Plain than the Shawnee Hills and the Floodplains. Flickers nest from mid-April through early July. Spring Bird Counts most likely survey breeding populations.
71, Union Co., 4 May 1991 (SBC)
AUTUMN—Southward migration begins by mid-September and continues at least until early November, but the winter population obscures departure of the last migrants. Numbers per day counted in autumn are similar to those counted during spring.

WINTER—Flickers sometimes visit bird feeders for corn, suet, and sunflower seeds. They are numerous around agricultural fields, where they feed on waste grain.

115, Crab Orchard NWR CBC, 15 Dec 1984

271, Horseshoe Lake CA CBC, 30 Dec 1987

259, Union Co. CBC, 3 Jan 1981

Documentation: Specimen—ad. male, Carterville, Williamson Co., 3 Apr 1966 (SIU A-1594).

Field Guides: G=194; N=264; P=190.

Pileated Woodpecker *Dryocopus pileatus*

Status and abundance: Fairly common year-round resident in the Floodplains and the Shawnee Hills. Uncommon year-round resident in the Till Plain.

Habitat: Mature deciduous woodland, especially bottomland.

Records and remarks: Our region's largest extant woodpecker, the Pileated looks very similar to a crow in shape and color but has a red crest and white wing patches. It leaves distinctive oval or rectangular holes in dead trees where it has been searching for wood-boring beetles and ants. Pileateds are usually shy and tend to be difficult to approach closely. There is probably no migration.

SUMMER—Nests are in large trees; the large size of the entrance hole is a sure sign that Pileateds constructed it. Peak nesting time is in late April and May. Spring Bird Counts survey nesting birds.

70, Union Co., 4 May 1991 (SBC).

WINTER—Pileateds usually occur as singles or in pairs. Their loud calls sound something like a shortened version of a flicker. The number of Pileateds counted during the Union Co. Christmas Bird Counts is sometimes the highest of all Christmas Bird Counts in the country.

57, Horseshoe Lake CA CBC, 21 Dec 1982

21, Crab Orchard NWR CBC, 28 Dec 1974

133, Union Co. CBC, 3 Jan 1987

Documentation: Specimen—ad. male, 4 miles n. of Cobden, Union Co., 17 Aug 1955 (SIU A-205).

Field Guides: G=194; N=274; P=188.

Ivory-billed Woodpecker *Campephilus principalis*

STATUS AND ABUNDANCE: Extirpated; perhaps extinct.

RECORDS AND REMARKS: Apparently inhabited the extensive cypress swamps and riparian forests of the Floodplains. Unfortunately, no convincing evidence of its former presence has been preserved. Three references to it can be found in the literature. Audubon (1831) reported it from somewhere near Cairo: "Descending the Ohio, we meet with this splendid bird for the first time near the confluence of that beautiful river and the Mississippi." Ridgway (1889) suggested, "The writer has a distinct recollection of what he believes to have been this species in White County." Finally, Gault (1922) said, "the present writer feels quite certain of hearing its call note in a swamp near Ullin, Pulaski County in the fall of 1900." No further descriptions were given of what any of these three very skilled ornithologists saw or heard. Because skeletal evidence has been obtained from north of our region, in the St. Louis area (in Cahokia, Illinois [Parmalee 1967]), and because a specimen was collected in St. Louis in 1886 (Hahn 1963), the reports by Audubon, Ridgway, and Gault are probably correct.

DOCUMENTATION: Provisional acceptance.

FIELD GUIDES: G=194; N=274; P=188.

Order Passeriformes: Passerine Birds

Family *Tyrannidae*: *Tyrant Flycatchers*

Olive-sided Flycatcher *Contopus borealis*

Early May–Late May
Mid-August–Mid-September

STATUS AND ABUNDANCE: Rare to uncommon migrant.

HABITAT: Usually perches high on dead snags in deciduous woods; seems especially to prefer upland forests.

RECORDS AND REMARKS: This species sings a very distinctive song, which is often phoneticized as *Quick three beers!* It also gives a call note *(pip, pip)* that is quite similar to one of the calls of Great Crested Flycatchers. Daily counts rarely exceed one bird. Numbers seem to vary from year to year; very few are encountered in some years, and they can even be missed during a season.

SPRING—Most spring records are from Spring Bird Counts, but migration does not peak until after those counts. Migration should extend into the first week of June.

1, Union Co., 5 May 1973 (SBC)
2, Union Co., 7 May 1977 (SBC)
1, Kinkaid Lake, Jackson Co., 29 May 1983 (JCR)
1, Trail of Tears SF, 1 June 1990 (Robinson and Robinson 1992)
1, Ozark, Johnson Co., 10 June 1994 (TF)

AUTUMN—Southward movements may begin as early as the first week of August and probably peak between 20 August and 7 September. Singing usually does not occur in fall, but birds do sometimes call then.

1, near Woodlawn, Jefferson Co., 13 Aug 1988 (TF, WDR)
1, Ozark, Johnson Co., 13 Aug 1994 (TF)
1, Murphysboro, 23 Aug 1993 (CS)
1, Oakwood Bottoms, Jackson Co., 20 Sep 1975 (BP)
1, Giant City SP, in Union Co., 21 Sep 1986 (WDR)

DOCUMENTATION: Specimen—imm., 2 miles n. of Cobden, Union Co., 13 Sep 1968 (SIU).

FIELD GUIDES: G=216; N=284; P=196.

Eastern Wood-Pewee *Contopus virens*

Late April–Early October

STATUS AND ABUNDANCE: Common migrant and summer resident.

HABITAT: Deciduous woods; found in extensive forests and in some heavily wooded residential areas.

RECORDS AND REMARKS: Pewees usually are found high in trees, just below the canopy. They often perch on snags at the edge of clearings. Their song, which takes two forms, is most frequently given in early morning but can be heard all day.

SPRING—Pewees are usually first detected about the last two or three days of April. Migration peaks in the second week of May. The end of northward movements is unclear, because of the large breeding population. Observers should always identify early-spring pewees visually; Starlings are good mimics of the pewee's song and can easily be misleading (Bohlen 1989).

1, Carbondale, 20 Apr 1971 (PB)
1, Ozark, Johnson Co., 24 Apr 1989 (TF)
152, Union Co., 4 May 1991 (SBC)
55, Jackson Co., 7 May 1977 (SBC)
33, Giant City SP, 12 May 1984 (WDR)

SUMMER—Pewees build nests that resemble knots on tree branches. The nests are placed five to twenty meters up from the ground, on horizontal branches that hang out over gaps in the forest. Pewees probably breed in every township in southern Illinois. Of fourteen nests found in the Shawnee National Forest, 36 percent were parasitized by cowbirds. An average of 1.3 cowbird eggs per parasitized nest was found (INHS). Many pewees vigorously defend their nests from cowbirds, chasing and dive-bombing females until they depart the vicinity of the nest. Juveniles have a distinctive, burry call, which can be heard from late June through September as they beg from adults.

AUTUMN—Southward movements may begin in mid-August, but because breeding birds are present, it is difficult to be sure. Most pewees are gone by early October.

24, Jefferson Co., 13 Aug 1988 (TF, WDR)
2, Crab Orchard NWR, 15 Oct 1983 (JCR)
1, Carbondale, 17 Oct 1971 (DH)

DOCUMENTATION: Specimen—Massac Co., 8 May 1973 (INHS TY-w-5).

FIELD GUIDES: G=216; N=284; P=196.

Yellow-bellied Flycatcher *Empidonax flavescens*
Mid-May–Early June
Mid-August–Late September

STATUS AND ABUNDANCE: Rare to uncommon migrant.

HABITAT: Deciduous woods and woodland edge.

RECORDS AND REMARKS: Silent flycatchers in the genus *Empidonax* pose particularly difficult identification problems. Fortunately, with experience, most Yellow-bellied Flycatchers can be identified in the field. The underparts of this species are especially dark, often appearing greenish-gray on the sides and breast and yellowish on the belly (Kaufman 1990). It is always critical, however, that confirmation of identifications be made by vocal cues; especially in cases of very early or late records. Some individuals must simply be identified as *Empidonax* species. The numbers of migrant Yellow-bellied Flycatchers seem to vary substantially from year to year; in some years they are numerous, whereas in others they can be completely missed.

SPRING—Yellow-bellied Flycatchers are late migrants; most are not detected until mid-May. Migration probably extends into early June, but because they spend much of their time in thick cover, nonvocal birds often go unnoticed.

2, Massac Co., 4 May 1985 (SBC)
3, Giant City SP, 18 May 1989 (WDR)
1 windowkill, Ozark, Johnson Co., 28 May 1989 (TF)
1, Mermet Lake CA, 30 May 1982 (LH)
1, Pine Hills, 3 June 1991 (Robinson and Robinson 1992)
AUTUMN—Fall movements may begin very early (in early August), but few birds have been reported before late August. Most birds are not vocal during fall, and many undoubtedly are overlooked because of their secretive habits.

1 injured, Giant City SP, 12 Aug 1954 (RB)
1, Crab Orchard NWR, 21–22 Aug 1987 (WDR)
1 banded, Carbondale, 22 Aug 1970 (VK)
1, Woodlawn, Jefferson Co., 2 Sep 1988 (TF)
1, Ozark, Johnson Co., 5 Sep 1988 (TF)
1, s.e. Gallatin Co., 6 Sep 1986 (WDR)
1 banded, Carbondale, 26 Sep 1970 (VK)
1 vocal, Rend Lake, Franklin Co., 30 Sep 1989 (WDR)

DOCUMENTATION: Specimen—ad. male, 2 miles n. of Cobden, Union Co., 23 May 1968 (SIU).

FIELD GUIDES: G=212; N=292; P=198.

Acadian Flycatcher *Empidonax virescens*
Late April–Late September

STATUS AND ABUNDANCE: Common migrant and summer resident.

HABITAT: Moist deciduous woodlands with well-developed understories.

RECORDS AND REMARKS: One of the most common breeding passerines in the forests of southern Illinois. Acadians seem to require large tracts of forest, but a few pairs will occupy larger woodlots. They are less numerous in the Till Plain than they are in the Floodplains and the Shawnee Hills. Like other *Empidonax* flycatchers, nonvocal Acadians can be exceptionally difficult to identify, particularly in fall. Consequently, many birds must merely be identified to genus. Acadians are usually vocal, though, throughout the fall. Their single-syllable call note—if learned during the breeding season, when it is also commonly uttered—is characteristic and can be used during fall. Juveniles have buffy wing bars, whereas adults have whitish wing bars.
SPRING—First spring arrivals are usually encountered about 1 May, but sometimes earlier. Migration probably peaks during the second week of May, and northbound birds may still be passing through in early June while local breeders are beginning to nest.
1, Giant City SP, 24 Apr 1989 (WDR)
123, Union Co., 4 May 1991 (SBC)
47, Jackson Co., 10 May 1975 (SBC)
SUMMER—Acadian nests are very distinctive; a frail-looking structure of strong grasses is woven in a fork of a branch, well out from the trunk of a tree. The floor of the nest is sometimes so thin that the eggs can be seen from below. Thirty-six percent of 354 nests found in the Shawnee National Forest were parasitized by cowbirds. Most Acadians have clutches of three eggs, but those that are parasitized receive an average of 1.3 cowbird eggs per nest (INHS).
21, Union Co. CA, 14 June 1982 (PK)
65, Little Black Slough, Johnson Co., 7–8 June 1989 (TF, WDR)
AUTUMN—Fall migration probably peaks in mid- or late August, but few counts have been made during that time. Most Acadians have

departed by mid-September; however, George (1968) lists 2 October as a departure date, but no recent reports have been that late. 1, Union Co., 21 Sep 1986 (WDR)

DOCUMENTATION: Specimen—ad. male, 3 miles s.e. of Makanda, Jackson Co., 15 May 1976 (SIU A-1797).

FIELD GUIDES: G=212; N=290; P=198.

Alder Flycatcher *Empidonax alnorum*
Mid-May–Early June
Early September–Late September

STATUS AND ABUNDANCE: Rare to uncommon migrant.

HABITAT: Woodland edge, hedgerows, and willow swamps.

RECORDS AND REMARKS: Alder and Willow Flycatchers are, for all intents and purposes, inseparable in the field unless they are vocal. These two species together form the superspecies Traill's Flycatcher. Some authors suggest that habitat may be useful for identifying some birds, but in southern Illinois this identification is risky. Alders occur only in migration, and they use both upland edge habitats and wet willow thickets. The songs of the two flycatcher species are similar but distinctively different, and it may take practice to be able to confidently separate them.
SPRING—Alders are very late spring migrants. They peak in abundance during the last week of May; and migration may continue well into mid-June (or possibly later).
1, Giant City SP, 15 May 1989 (WDR)
1, Rend Lake, Jefferson Co., 16 May 1986 (WDR)
1, Little Grassy Lake, 22–23 May 1976 (BP)
1, Mermet Lake CA, 26 May 1986 (TF, WDR)
3, Cairo, Alexander Co., 26 May 1988 (WDR)
1, Pope Co., 1 June 1992 (TF)
1, Randolph Co., 14 June 1988 (WDR)
AUTUMN—Virtually nothing is known about fall movements, because of the difficulty of identifying nonvocal birds. Correct identification must be made by in-hand examination (as in band-

ing); or, with practice, by the call notes of the two Traill's species. Alders give a *pip*, whereas Willows give a *whip* (Bohlen 1989).

1, near Ozark, Pope Co., 29 Aug 1994 (TF)

1, s.e. Jackson Co., 7 Sep 1985 (WDR)

DOCUMENTATION: Provisional acceptance. A specimen or voice recording is needed.

FIELD GUIDES: G=212; N= 290; P=198.

Willow Flycatcher *Empidonax trailli*

Early May–Mid-September

STATUS AND ABUNDANCE: Uncommon migrant. Locally uncommon summer resident.

HABITAT: Willow thickets, hedgerows, and upland areas with scattered bushes and small trees.

RECORDS AND REMARKS: See the account for the Alder Flycatcher for a discussion of identification problems.

SPRING—Willows migrate slightly earlier than Alders but still are not usually found until the first week of May. Migration probably continues into early June, but the breeding population obscures migrant departures.

6, Jackson Co., 5 May 1984 (SBC)

15, Oakwood Bottoms, Jackson Co., 28 May 1975 (BP)

SUMMER—Willows are probably more numerous in southern Illinois than previously thought. There is extensive suitable habitat on reclaimed strip mines, which they readily use. Breeding populations have been found on mines in Williamson, Randolph, Perry, and Jackson Cos. They also regularly breed in willows along streams, probably in every county. Nonetheless, they are very local and can be difficult to detect at times.

6 pairs, Williamson Co. strip mines, June 1987 (WDR)

4 on territory, Rend Lake, Jefferson Co., 20 July 1985 (JCR)

AUTUMN—As with the Alder Flycatcher, little is known about the Willows' fall migration, because most birds are silent during fall. Indeed, even sight records of Traill's Flycatchers are few at this season. Migration probably starts in late July (most territorial birds are gone by then) and ends by late September.

1, Jackson Co., 2 Aug 1975 (BP)

DOCUMENTATION: Provisional acceptance. A specimen or voice recording is needed.

FIELD GUIDES: G=212; N=290; P=198.

Least Flycatcher *Empidonax minimus*
Late April–Late May
Late August–Early October

STATUS AND ABUNDANCE: Fairly common migrant. Very rare summer visitor.

HABITAT: Deciduous woodland edge and hedgerows.

RECORDS AND REMARKS: The smallest of the *Empidonax* species, Leasts can be identified by sight fairly easily with experience, but vocal cues should be used to confirm identifications. Leasts forage by hover-gleaning insects from the surface of leaves in the understory and shrub layer and, less commonly, by sallying out to snatch insects from midair.

SPRING—Migrants are very vocal upon arrival. First arrivals are normally encountered during the last few days of April, numbers peak about 10–14 May, and migration is largely over by 25 May.
1, Giant City SP, 18 Apr 1989 (WDR)
1, Perks, Pulaski Co., 23 Apr 1973 (HDB, VK)
25, Alexander Co., 4 May 1985 (SBC)
18, Alexander Co., 7 May 1977 (MMo)
1, Union Co. CA, 26 May 1984 (TF, KR)
SUMMER—There is one record of a territorial singing male present during summer, but no breeding activity was noted.
1, Trail of Tears SF, 3–26 June 1981 (MMl)
AUTUMN—Like many of the *Empidonax* species, Leasts are often not vocal during fall migration, and identification can be difficult. With experience, though, most can be correctly named; see Kaufman (1990) for pertinent fieldmarks. Southward movements go mostly unnoticed. Some adults, which have white wing bars, leave the breeding grounds exceptionally early (Hussel 1980) and are represented by the following midsummer records:

2 singing males, Trail of Tears SF, 24–25 June 1991, and 1 singing, Pine Hills, 7 July 1991 (Robinson and Robinson 1992)
ad. female, near Little Grassy Lake, in Jackson Co., 23 July 1971 (DH)
ad. female, Carbondale, 4 Aug 1971 (VK)
Most birds, including immatures, begin arriving much later, during August, and some should be present into early October.
ad., Crab Orchard NWR, 21 Aug 1987 (WDR)
2 banded, Carbondale, 27 Sep 1970 (VK)

DOCUMENTATION: Specimen—ad. female, Carbondale, Jackson Co., 4 Aug 1971 (SIU A-1748).

FIELD GUIDES: G=212; N=290; P=198.

Eastern Phoebe *Sayornis phoebe*

Early March–Early November

STATUS AND ABUNDANCE: Common migrant and fairly common summer resident in the Shawnee Hills. Fairly common migrant and summer resident in the Floodplains and the Till Plain. Rare winter resident.

HABITAT: Deciduous woods near water and bluffs or artificial structures; farmyards.

RECORDS AND REMARKS: Phoebes are the familiar, tail-pumping flycatcher of farms and creek borders. They commonly place their nests under bridges that span even the smallest creeks. They are very vocal on arrival in spring, but after April they become much more quiet and inconspicuous.
SPRING—First spring migrants are regularly encountered in the first week of March, but some arrive during February. Migration peaks in late March and early April and is mostly over by late April.
1, Crab Orchard NWR, 16 Feb 1950 (LB)
1, Golconda, Pope Co., 25 Feb 1987 (TF)
1 migrating diurnally, s.e. Jackson Co., 25 Feb 1988 (WDR)
15, Giant City SP, 19 Mar 1983 (JCR)
SUMMER—Breeding begins very early; eggs have been found as early as 1 April (Jackson Co., 1985). Phoebes use buildings, bridges, bluffs, and overhanging creekbanks for nest sites. Parasitism rates by Brown-headed Cowbirds vary considerably from site to site.

At Giant City SP, 50 percent ($N = 8$) of nests placed on bluffs received cowbird eggs, whereas none ($N = 24$) of those under bridges were parasitized. In the Dutch Creek area of Union Co. phoebe nests are hardly parasitized at all, including nests placed under overhanging creekbanks. Data from Spring Bird Counts are mostly of breeding birds; a very few migrants may still be passing through in early May.

74, Union Co., 4 May 1991 (SBC)

AUTUMN—Inception of southward movements is difficult to detect, because of the presence of local breeding populations. However, movements are probably in progress in early September, peaking in early October, and mostly ceasing by early November. Most December and early-January records are probably of straggling late migrants. There are 7 records from Christmas Bird Counts (from 1975–1988).

1, Ozark, Johnson Co., 11 Nov 1989 (TF)

3, near Tamms, Alexander Co., 18 Dec 1985 (WDR, SVa)

2, Pine Hills, Union Co., 29 Dec 1988 (WDR)

1, Union Co. CBC, 3 Jan 1980

WINTER—It is doubtful that phoebes attempt to winter in the region every year. Some years, though, a few are found during midwinter. These may be very late fall migrants; it has yet to be proved that they can successfully overwinter. If they can successfully overwinter and occasionally do, these same birds may account for the late-February "spring" records.

1, Jackson Co., 11 Jan 1976 (BP)

1, Johnson Co., 18 Jan 1976 (BP)

1, Ozark, Johnson Co., 21 Jan 1991 (JD, TF)

1, s.e. Saline Co., 2 Feb 1986 (SO)

DOCUMENTATION: Specimen—ad. male, 1.5 miles n. of Cobden, Union Co., 22 Mar 1978 (SIU).

FIELD GUIDES: G=210; N=286; P=196.

Say's Phoebe *Sayornis saya*

STATUS AND ABUNDANCE: Very rare visitor.

RECORDS AND REMARKS: An individual of this western species was observed during the Christmas Bird Count at Mermet Lake in

Joppa, Massac Co., on 30 Dec 1966 (RMo, LHo). While in view, it flew across the Ohio River into Kentucky and became that state's first record (Monroe et al. 1988). Vagrants in Illinois have been found around buildings, water, or open fields (Bohlen 1989).

DOCUMENTATION: Written description—1966 record.

FIELD GUIDES: G=210; N=286; P=196.

[Vermilion Flycatcher *Pyrocephalus rubinus*]

STATUS AND ABUNDANCE: Hypothetical.

RECORDS AND REMARKS: There is an undocumented record of a male of this brightly colored flycatcher at Crab Orchard NWR in April or May 1978. No further details are known.

FIELD GUIDES: G=190; N=286; P=196.

Great Crested Flycatcher *Myiarchus crinitus*

Late April–Mid-September

STATUS AND ABUNDANCE: Common migrant and summer resident.

HABITAT: Deciduous woods and woodland edge.

RECORDS AND REMARKS: Usually found in the canopy of a mature forest and in larger woodlots.

SPRING—The first spring arrivals are quite conspicuous because of the loud *threeep* call they give. Migration may continue into late May, but because the summer population is large, the last departure dates are difficult to detect.

1, w. Jackson Co., 15 Apr 1984 (JCR)
6, Crab Orchard NWR, 17 Apr 1972 (VK)
45, Alexander Co., 4 May 1985 (SBC)
127, Union Co., 4 May 1991 (SBC)

SUMMER—Nests are placed in both natural cavities of trees and those made by woodpeckers. Few data are available on the nesting cycle in the region, but birds have been seen feeding young from late May through late June. There are no records of this species being parasitized by cowbirds in southern Illinois.

26, Union Co. CA, 3 June 1982 (PK)

AUTUMN—The fall migration is inconspicuous. Crested flycatchers just seem to disappear at the end of the summer. They are not particularly vocal after about mid-July, which contributes to the lack of reports from fall migration. Migration probably begins by late July and peaks in August. Any *Myiarchus* flycatcher seen from October through March should be carefully identified; the Ash-throated Flycatcher *(M. cinerascens)* is more likely to be present at that season than is the Great Crested.

1, Williamson Co., 16 Sep 1983 (JCR)

1, Crab Orchard NWR, 17 Sep 1989 (WDR)

DOCUMENTATION: Specimen—ad. male, 2 miles n. of Cobden, Union Co., 28 Apr 1966 (SIU A-1581).

FIELD GUIDES: G=208; N=282; P=194.

[Western Kingbird *Tyrannus verticalis*]

STATUS AND ABUNDANCE: Hypothetical.

RECORDS AND REMARKS: These western U.S. vagrants occur in open habitats, especially around grassy and agricultural fields. They often sit on barbed-wire fences or electrical wires. Three definite records exist for the region; there is also one spring record for Crab Orchard NWR listed in Graber et al. (1974), but no additional information is given. Unfortunately, none of the records are supported by more than single-observer written descriptions.

1, Herrin, Williamson Co., 25 May 1965 (George 1968)

1, White Co., 1 June 1988 (AB 42:1296)

1, Union Co. CA, 10 June 1982 (PK)

FIELD GUIDES: G=206; N=278; P=194.

Eastern Kingbird *Tyrannus tyrannus*

Late April–Mid-September

STATUS AND ABUNDANCE: Common migrant and summer resident.

HABITAT: Woodland edge, hedgerows, and open parklike areas, often near water.

RECORDS AND REMARKS: This black-and-white flycatcher is commonly seen sitting on fences and electrical wires along roadsides in open habitats. It has a characteristically shallow wing beat and can be quite noisy.

SPRING—During peak migration (from early to mid-May), small flocks of kingbirds often occur in fields, where they sit on the ground or on short vegetation and sally for insects. They seem to migrate diurnally, so these flocks do not often stay at any one place for very long. Because of the presence of the breeding population, the departure of the latest migrants is obscured.

1, Crab Orchard NWR, 8 Apr 1972 (VK, GC)
1, Ozark, 10–11 Apr 1992 (TF)
1, Crab Orchard NWR, 11 Apr 1953 (LB)
1, Rend Lake, Jefferson Co., 21 Apr 1987 (TF)
99, Alexander Co., 4 May 1985 (SBC)
120, Union Co., 4 May 1991 (SBC)

SUMMER—Kingbirds place their bulky, grass nests from three to twelve meters high, usually near the tip of a long horizontal branch on an isolated tree along a hedgerow or creek. They vigorously defend their nests against crows, hawks, and predatory mammals by dive-bombing and chasing them from the vicinity of the nest site. Nesting begins by mid-May and continues into July.

AUTUMN—The beginning of southward migration is obscured by the breeding population, but it may start in late July. Small flocks (usually less than ten birds) are commonly encountered during August and early September.

167, Rend Lake, Jefferson Co., 30 Aug 1994 (BD)
5, Crab Orchard NWR, 21 Sep 1983 (JCR)
2, Jackson Co., 27 Sep 1984 (TF)

DOCUMENTATION: Specimen—Elkville, Jackson Co., 23 Aug 1941 (SIU A-1799).

FIELD GUIDES: G=206; N=276; P=194.

Scissor-tailed Flycatcher *Tyrannus forficatus*

STATUS AND ABUNDANCE: Very rare visitor.

RECORDS AND REMARKS: This long-tailed flycatcher of the Great Plains has been reported at least ten times in the region. Besides

the seven records listed in this account, there is an unverified report
from Crab Orchard NWR in the late 1970s; a report from Dixon
Springs Agricultural Center, Pope Co., in 1972; and two reports
from Randolph Co. in 1969 and 1972 (Graber et al. 1974). Given
the distinctiveness of the species, these records are undoubtedly
correct.

SPRING—1, near DeSoto, Jackson Co., late Apr 1987 (RMW)
1, Makanda, Jackson Co., 12 May 1987 (RZ)
1, n. of Murphysboro, Jackson Co., 20 May 1949 (RB)
1, Crab Orchard NWR, late May 1988 (GSma)
SUMMER—1, near Cobden, Union Co., 25 July 1970 (WGG,
SV)
1, Cypress Creek NWR, 10 July 1993 (McKee and McKee 1994)
WINTER—One bird viewed at close range flying across the Union
Co. floodplain represents the only winter record for the region and
the state. Interestingly, there were two phoebes present the same
day within 2 miles of this sighting; this instance may be the only
time two flycatcher species have been recorded on the same winter
day in Illinois.
1, 3 miles n.w. of Wolf Lake, Union Co., 29 Dec 1988 (WDR)

DOCUMENTATION: Photograph—Crab Orchard NWR, Williamson
Co., late May 1988 (Crab Orchard NWR).

FIELD GUIDES: G=204; N=280; P=194.

Family Alaudidae: Larks

Horned Lark *Eremophila alpestris*

STATUS AND ABUNDANCE: Common year-round resident in the
Floodplains and the Till Plain. Uncommon year-round resident in
the Shawnee Hills.

HABITAT: Expansive short-grass fields (such as airports) and agricultural areas.

RECORDS AND REMARKS: Larks are present throughout the region
all year, but the regional population varies considerably from season
to season. They are most numerous during the winter, and there is
considerable migration. Not much is known, however, about the

extent or timing of their movements. Weather is probably an important factor influencing the magnitude of migration. During heavy snows, many are forced to forage along roadsides and are killed by passing cars. They seem to be least numerous during the summer. The breeding subspecies is reportedly *E. a. praticola* (Bohlen 1989), and other subspecies occur during migration and winter.

SPRING—The initiation of northward migration is obscured by the presence of a large winter population, but the large flocks that characterize the Floodplains during winter have either migrated or disbanded into breeding pairs by mid-March.

SUMMER—Little is known about the breeding habits. Young have been seen at least as soon as early April, and breeding may continue into August. Horned Larks are rarely parasitized by cowbirds.

AUTUMN—Birds may begin arriving by late September, but no data are available to confirm this. The large flocks that can be found during late fall and winter begin to appear during mid-November.

WINTER—Sometimes large flocks form in areas of extensive agriculture, where they feed on waste grain and weed seeds. Lapland Longspurs can sometimes be found mixed in with flocks of Horned Larks.

1,068, Horseshoe Lake CBC, 18 Dec 1984
4,000, Union Co. CBC, 29 Dec 1988
125, Crab Orchard NWR CBC, 15 Dec 1984

DOCUMENTATION: Specimen—ad. male, Crab Orchard NWR, Williamson Co., 5 Mar 1956 (SIU A-220).

FIELD GUIDES: G=218; N=294; P=200.

Family Hirundinidae: Swallows

Purple Martin *Progne subis*
Mid-March–Mid-September

STATUS AND ABUNDANCE: Common migrant and summer resident.

HABITAT: Breeding birds frequent human habitations where martin houses are available. Can be found foraging over water, fields, and high in the air.

RECORDS AND REMARKS: Familiar around towns and farms where artificial nest boxes are placed. They forage over water, open fields, and high in the air. They are quite social at all times of the day and year; often, groups can be heard calling from high overhead before dawn, especially during spring and summer.
SPRING—The earliest arrivals typically appear around 12–15 March, rarely earlier; some February records may be of misidentified Starlings. Large flocks are uncommonly seen. The end of spring migration is difficult to detect, because of the presence of the breeding population, but some northward movement may extend into mid- or late May (Graber et al. 1972).
1, Metropolis, Massac Co., 24 Feb 1923 (Conley 1926)
1, Murphysboro, 28 Feb 1951 (RB)
14, Rend Lake, 3 Mar 1986 (KPi)
160, Perry Co., 7 May 1988 (SBC)
SUMMER—Nest building has been recorded at least as early as 24 March (Johnston and Hardy 1962), but eggs are apparently not laid before mid-April. The first fledglings are usually seen in late June.
AUTUMN—Flocks begin forming as soon as breeding ends. Post-breeding aggregations are especially common in the Floodplains. Migratory flocks are most commonly seen during August, and few are present after the first few days of September.
850, Union Co. CA, 26 July 1974 (VK)
1,500, Carbondale, 15 Aug 1976 (BP)
4,000 in roost, Carbondale, Aug and early Sep 1949 (RB)
6, Crab Orchard NWR, 12 Sep 1986 (WDR)

DOCUMENTATION: Specimen—imm. male, Crab Orchard NWR, Williamson Co., 26 June 1956 (SIU A-227).
FIELD GUIDES: G=220; N=296; P=202.

Tree Swallow *Tachycineta bicolor*
Mid-March–Early November

STATUS AND ABUNDANCE: Common migrant. Locally uncommon summer resident. Very rare winter visitor.

HABITAT: Migrants are usually seen foraging near rivers, lakes, or large open fields; they often rest on utility wires. Summer residents use bottomland sloughs and lakes where standing snags provide nesting sites.

RECORDS AND REMARKS: These hardy swallows arrive before the last cold snap in early spring and leave after the first cold snap of fall. During migration they can be seen in long lines on telephone wires or crowded onto the branches of shrubs or trees along the edges of lakes and rivers. They often intermix with other swallow species during migration.

SPRING—A few arrive each spring behind the first strong warm front in late February or early March, but generally earliest arrivals are not detected until after 10 March. Flocks of several hundred birds are regularly seen, usually over water. Because a breeding population is present, it is difficult to detect the last spring migrants, but most migrants have probably departed by mid-May.

2, Saline Co., 23 Feb 1991 (TF, JD)
5, Union Co., 23 Feb 1994 (TF)
1, Rend Lake, 6 Mar 1976 (BP)
2, Crab Orchard NWR, 6 Mar 1986 (WDR)
2,500, Union Co., 16 Apr 1993 (KM)
1,320, Massac Co., 6 May 1989 (SO, WDR)

SUMMER—Formerly a rare summer resident, the population is steadily increasing. Most breeders occur around lakes and rivers and nest in natural cavities in trees standing in water. Recently, however, some have been nesting in bluebird nest boxes in upland fields at Crab Orchard NWR (DDR).

38, Mermet Lake CA, 4 July 1986 (WDR)

AUTUMN—Postbreeding aggregations begin to form soon after breeding. Large flocks are common in the western Floodplains but less so in other regions. These flocks may linger in one area for several days or weeks before moving south; most birds are gone by early November, but some have lingered into early winter.

3,000, s. Alexander Co., 13 Sep 1986 (WDR)
3,000, Crab Orchard NWR, 14 Oct 1986 (WDR)
525, Crab Orchard NWR, 2 Nov 1989 (EW, WDR)
4, Union Co. CA, 19 Nov 1983 (JCR)
1, Crab Orchard NWR, 8 Dec 1983 (TF)

1, Rend Lake, Franklin Co., 16 Dec 1992 (TF, JD)
WINTER—4, Union Co., 26 Jan 1995 (TF)

DOCUMENTATION: Specimen—male, Horseshoe Lake CA, Alexander Co., 6 May 1961 (NIU 371).

FIELD GUIDES: G=220; N=296; P=204.

Northern Rough-winged Swallow
Stelgidopteryx serripennis
Early April–Mid-October

STATUS AND ABUNDANCE: Common migrant. Locally fairly common summer resident in the Floodplains. Locally uncommon summer resident in the Shawnee Hills and the Till Plain.

HABITAT: Forages over fields and water. Breeders nest in dirt embankments, crevices in bluffs, and small drainage pipes under bridges.

RECORDS AND REMARKS: Generally encountered in small groups of one to ten birds, except during migration, when large flocks are sometimes seen foraging over weedy fields, lakes, and rivers.
SPRING—Most years, the first arrivals are detected around 1 April, with peak numbers passing through in late April and early May. Breeding has begun by mid-May, so migration is probably largely over by then, but little is known about movements during late spring.
1, Saline Co., 21 Mar 1991 (TF)
2, Carbondale, 24 Mar 1990 (JH)
1, Rend Lake, 2 Apr 1988 (TF)
1,125, Massac Co., 6 May 1989 (SO, WDR)
SUMMER—Nests singly or in small, dispersed colonies of a few pairs; sometimes a few will nest on the periphery of Bank Swallow colonies. In mid- to late summer, family groups flock together before beginning fall migration. At that time, flocks of 20 to 150 birds are common, especially in the Floodplains.
100, s.w. Jackson Co., 27 June 1989 (WDR)
AUTUMN—Large numbers gather in the Floodplains, often in mixed-species flocks with other swallows, beginning in mid- to late July. By mid- to late October, only a few stragglers are left. Very late

reports of Rough-wings could be of misidentified immature Tree Swallows, which tend to linger regularly into November and early December.

1,000, s. Alexander Co., 26 July 1986 (WDR)

2,500, Williamson and Alexander Cos., 8 Oct 1984 (JCR)

21, Horseshoe Lake CA, 31 Oct 1982 (JCR)

DOCUMENTATION: Provisional acceptance.

FIELD GUIDES: G=220; N=298; P=204.

Bank Swallow *Riparia riparia*
Late April–Mid-September

STATUS AND ABUNDANCE: Common migrant in the western Floodplains. Uncommon spring migrant and fairly common fall migrant in the eastern Floodplains, the Shawnee Hills, and the Till Plain. Locally common summer resident.

HABITAT: Forages over fields and water. Nests colonially in dirt embankments, primarily near rivers and lakes.

RECORDS AND REMARKS: In the western Floodplains, large flocks can be seen sitting on telephone wires and foraging over open areas with other swallow species, especially during late summer.

SPRING—Most Bank Swallows arrive in late April, but a few may appear in early April or possibly even in very late March. Large concentrations occur most often in the western Floodplains, but even there it is unusual to see more than a few hundred in one flock. They often form mixed-species groups with Rough-winged and Tree Swallows. Spring migration is probably largely over by 20 May.

1, Union Co. CA, 5 Apr 1986 (KM)

4, Crab Orchard NWR, 24 Apr 1949 (RB, JWH)

1,260, Massac Co., 6 May 1989 (SO, WDR)

SUMMER—All known breeding colonies are in embankments along rivers or lakes. The overwhelming majority of the region's colonies are along the Ohio and Mississippi Rivers. Breeding begins with nest construction as early as late April, and the last young fledge by mid-August.

Colony of 510 burrows, 5 miles s. of Shawneetown, Gallatin Co., 24 June 1972 (VK, DH)
Colony of 100 to 200 burrows, near Thebes, Alexander Co., 1986–1990 (TF, WDR)
AUTUMN—Some local movements away from breeding sites apparently begin during late June, and large flocks gather by early July. Many hundreds can be seen foraging over agricultural fields and waterways with other swallow species throughout late summer. Most Bank Swallows have departed by early September.
400, Alexander Co., 1 July 1988 (WDR)
1,500, Wolf Lake, Union Co., 31 July 1971 (VK, FR)
400, Smithland Lock and Dam, Pope Co., 13 Aug 1987 (WDR)
1, s.w. Jackson Co., 6 Sep 1975 (BP)

DOCUMENTATION: Specimen—male, near Roots, Randolph Co., 26 July 1971 (ISM 604828).

FIELD GUIDES: G=220; N=298; P=204.

Cliff Swallow *Hirundo pyrrhonota*
Mid-April–Late September

STATUS AND ABUNDANCE: Fairly common migrant. Locally common summer resident.

HABITAT: Migrants generally forage over lakes and rivers but sometimes can be found with other swallows over fields. Summer residents breed under bridges or bluffs near lakes and rivers.

RECORDS AND REMARKS: Cliff Swallows were apparently common summer residents in the late 1800s (Ridgway 1887), but they declined precipitously by the early 1900s (Ridgway 1915). In 1944, the only nesting record known in the region was a single nest on the side of a barn near Murphysboro (JWH). The discovery of a small colony nesting with Barn Swallows at Crab Orchard NWR on 7 May 1952 (LB) signaled the return of the region's breeding population; they continue to increase today (Robinson 1989).
SPRING—Like other swallows, Cliffs are highly gregarious at all seasons; their migrant flocks are generally smaller, however, than those of the other species. Most migrants have probably departed for northern breeding sites by mid- to late May.

10, Crab Orchard NWR, 6 Apr 1986 (WDR)

308, Massac Co., 6 May 1989 (SO, WDR)

SUMMER—Colonies are built under bridges; nest building begins by late April, and some pairs are still building during June. The young fledge from mid-June through mid-August.

2,384 nests in 15 colonies throughout the region, June 1988 (WDR)

AUTUMN—The beginning of fall migration is somewhat obscured by the presence of the large colonies in the region, because few flocks are seen away from the vicinity of the colonies. There are typically, however, a few Cliffs mixed in with most large flocks of migrant Rough-winged, Tree, and Bank Swallows. There are no reports of flocks of more than 150 birds for the fall. Peak migration occurs in August.

6, Johnson Co., 4 Aug 1992 (TF)

75, Rend Lake, Jefferson Co., 27 Aug 1987 (TF)

1, Crab Orchard NWR, 14 Oct 1986 (WDR)

DOCUMENTATION: Photograph—ad., Smithland Lock and Dam, Pope Co., 19 June 1988 (SIU AP-117).

FIELD GUIDES: G=218; N=298; P=202.

Barn Swallow *Hirundo rustica*

Late March–Mid-October

STATUS AND ABUNDANCE: Common migrant and summer resident. Very rare winter visitor.

HABITAT: Nearly ubiquitous. Occurs in all habitats except forest. Especially common around towns, farms, and lakes or rivers. Commonly forages over fields and water.

RECORDS AND REMARKS: Although Barn Swallows are common now, they have apparently not always been so numerous. Ridgway (1915) reported that they had become uncommon summer residents by the early 1900s, but by the mid-1950s they were common again (Graber and Graber 1963). The reasons for their decline and subsequent recovery are unknown.

SPRING—Migration spans several weeks, with birds arriving in small flocks through mid-May. Few large concentrations have been reported.

1, Saline Co., 5 Mar 1986 (TF)
4, Crab Orchard NWR, 16 Mar 1976 (BP)
283, Massac Co., 6 May 1989 (SO, WDR)
689, Pope Co., 5 May 1979 (SBC)

SUMMER—Breeding begins by mid-April; eggs have been found as early as 15 April. Some young may still be in the nest during late August. Nests are commonly placed under bridges and eaves of buildings and inside barns. Apparently no large counts have been published for the summer, but it is commonplace to see fifty to seventy-five birds in a day.

AUTUMN—Apparently Barn Swallows simply drift southward over the course of several weeks during the fall, because very few large counts have been made. Barn Swallows commonly associate with flocks of Tree Swallows that gather in the Floodplains during August and September, but there are usually never more than a few hundred Barn Swallows even in the largest mixed-species flocks. Most Barn Swallows are gone by mid-October, but a few regularly linger into November.

1, Union Co. CA, 12 Nov 1983 (JCR)

WINTER—There is one record: 2, Carbondale, 29 Dec 1954 (RB et al.; AFN 9:172).

DOCUMENTATION: Specimen—ad., 1 mile w. of Carbondale, Jackson Co., 8 May 1971 (SIU A-1730).

FIELD GUIDES: G=218; N=298; P=202.

Family Corvidae: Jays and Crows

Blue Jay Cyanocitta cristata

STATUS AND ABUNDANCE: Common year-round resident.

HABITAT: Woodlands, including deciduous, coniferous, and residential areas.

RECORDS AND REMARKS: Extensive migration occurs, but the year-round presence of jays obscures the arrival and departure dates and even the peak movements. Most, if not all, migration is diurnal;

small flocks usually fly at treetop level along river valleys. During the spring and summer, jays are important predators on songbird eggs and young. Some researchers have speculated that the impact of this predation on songbird populations may continue to increase, because overwinter survival of jays is enhanced by the ready availability of seeds and suet at winter feeding stations (Terborgh 1989).
SPRING—Because jays are present all year long, the spring migration is usually difficult to detect. Northward movements probably begin by mid-March and extend at least through 10 May, possibly later, with peak numbers in late April and early May. Migrating birds generally occur in smaller flocks in spring than they do during fall, but larger counts are made occasionally. Spring Bird Counts census breeders and migrants.
150, Oakwood Bottoms, Jackson Co., 27 Apr 1975 (BP)
185, Union Co, 4 May 1991 (SBC)
10 migrating, Mermet Lake, Massac Co., 10 May 1986 (WDR)
SUMMER—Jays begin nesting in April (e.g., 2 Apr 1990 in Carbondale). In towns, nests are often placed four to ten meters above the ground, but in forest, nests are usually placed higher than ten meters. The height, in combination with the secretive behavior of nesting jays, makes forest nests difficult to locate. Jays are not successfully parasitized by cowbirds.
AUTUMN—Fall migration is obscured by the presence of the large breeding population, but it is sometimes conspicuous as small flocks of birds move south, usually along the Mississippi and Ohio Rivers (Graber et al. 1987). First fall arrivals are generally present by mid-September, and migration continues until early November.
60 in 2 hours, s.e. Saline Co., 28 Sep 1986 (SO)
WINTER—The region's winter population is supplemented by migrants from the north. Jays are common feeder visitors, consuming large amounts of sunflower seeds, corn, and other grains. Most large counts come from Christmas Bird Counts.
593, Horseshoe Lake CBC, 30 Dec 1987
488, Crab Orchard NWR CBC, 28 Dec 1970
460, Union Co. CBC, 31 Dec 1987

DOCUMENTATION: Specimen—ad. male, near Carbondale, Jackson Co., 12 Mar 1961 (SIU A-1165).

FIELD GUIDES: G=222; N=302; P=208.

American Crow *Corvus brachyrhynchos*

STATUS AND ABUNDANCE: Common year-round resident.

HABITAT: Very widespread, but usually associated with agricultural lands.

RECORDS AND REMARKS: There is some migration, but the movements are difficult to detect, because of the daily wanderings of flocks of crows at all seasons. The spring migration probably begins in late February and continues throughout March, whereas the fall migration seems most noticeable in October and November. Apparently crows were formerly more numerous, because none of the huge roosts reported from the early 1900s are still extant. The decline might have occurred because of improved grain harvesting efficiency, which has significantly decreased the amount of waste grain left in agricultural fields. Nevertheless, crows are still so common that few observers bother reporting their observations; most records are therefore old or from organized surveys like Christmas Bird Counts.

WINTER—100,000 in roost, near Rockwood, Randolph Co., winters of 1918–1938 (Black 1941)

40,000 in roost, near Cairo, Alexander Co., winters of 1935–1938 (Black 1941)

700, Horseshoe Lake CBC, 29 Dec 1977

218, Crab Orchard NWR CBC, 15 Dec 1984

207, Union Co. CBC, 19 Dec 1984

400, Hardin Co., 9 Feb 1988 (WDR)

DOCUMENTATION: Specimen—Carbondale, Jackson Co., 1935 (SIU, uncatalogued).

FIELD GUIDES: G=226; N=306; P=206.

Fish Crow *Corvus ossifragus*

Early March–Late October

STATUS AND ABUNDANCE: Common migrant and summer resident in the Mississippi River floodplain. Progressively decreases in abundance as you move eastward up the Ohio River floodplain (common at Cairo, rare at Shawneetown). Rare spring migrant inland at the larger reservoirs.

HABITAT: Along major rivers and in agricultural areas and wood-lands near these rivers.

RECORDS AND REMARKS: Increasing. Fish Crows invaded the region from the southern United States via the Mississippi River floodplain in the early 1960s. They may have been present histori-cally, because bone fragments have been found in Randolph Co. archaeological deposits dated at ten thousand years before the pre-sent (Parmalee 1967); but there is some speculation that these bones may have been traded with Native Americans of the South. SPRING—First spring migrants typically arrive by March, but they continue to appear earlier and earlier each year, perhaps as the win-tering range extends northward along the Mississippi River toward Illinois. Migrational movements continue into mid- or late May.
3, Union Co. CA, 4 Feb 1991 (TF)
11, Union Co., 18 Feb 1990 (BD)
13, Alexander and Union Cos., 5 Mar 1974 (VK, HDB)
61, Alexander Co., 19 Mar 1993 (TF)
3, Crab Orchard NWR, 11 Apr 1985 (JCR)
2, Pomona, 19 Apr 1970 (VK)
9, Mermet Lake CA, 7 May 1988 (WDR)
1, Giant City SP, 10 May 1989 (WDR)
5, Crab Orchard NWR, 15 May 1984 (TF, JCR)
1, Rend Lake, Franklin Co., 19 May 1988 (WDR)
SUMMER—Has probably bred in the region for years, but no confirmed evidence was obtained until the late 1980s; the first nest was found in 1992.
ad. nest building, Union Co. CA, 26 Apr 1992 (WDR)
ad. repeatedly carrying food in same direction, Pine Hills, Union Co., 28 May 1988 (WDR)
ad. with fledglings, Union Co. CA, 15 June 1988 (WDR)
15, Fort Kaskaskia SP, Randolph Co., 20 June 1981 (RK)
18, Union Co., 29 July 1988 (WDR)
unsuccessful nest, Fort Massac SP, Massac Co., June 1992 (Kleen and Schwegman 1993)
AUTUMN—Postbreeding aggregations form in July, but it is un-clear when southward migration begins. Presently, most Fish Crows leave the region by late October, but some birds continue to linger into winter.

112, Black Bottoms, Massac Co., 30 Aug 1989 (TF)
100, Union Co. CA, 15 Sep 1991 (TF, JD, DKa, CW)
30, s.w. Jackson Co., 10 Oct 1984 (JCR)
WINTER—The first winter records were obtained in 1991–1992, but more are expected. Graber et al. (1987) speculated that Fish Crows could be overlooked during winter if they ceased calling, because of their similarities with American Crows. Extensive observations throughout southern Illinois, however, suggest that Fish Crows have not been present during winter, because Fish Crows are visually separable from American Crows if careful, close observations can be made. Furthermore, there is no evidence to support the idea that they become silent here during winter; they do not do so in other parts of their winter range.
3, Horseshoe Lake CA, 17 Dec 1991 (SB, VK, TF), and 1 there, 20 Jan 1992 (TF)

DOCUMENTATION: Specimen—ad. female, levee road s. of Mound City, Pulaski Co., 20 Apr 1968 (SIU A-1643).
FIELD GUIDES: G=226; N=306; P=206.

Family Paridae: Titmice

[Black-capped Chickadee *Parus atricapillus*]
STATUS AND ABUNDANCE: Hypothetical.

RECORDS AND REMARKS: A banded bird captured and measured on three occasions between 31 December 1985 and 28 February 1986 in southeast Jackson Co. was identified as this species by wing and tail measurements. Without the specimen, however, there is not sufficient information to rule out the possibility of a Carolina and Black-capped hybrid. Sight records of this species are unacceptable because it is difficult to distinguish from the Carolina Chickadee. A specimen is essential to verify occurrence of Black-capped Chickadees in the region. Visual separation of the two chickadee species is complicated by much individual variation in bib size, tail length, and amount of white in the wings (but see Kaufman 1990 for discussion of useful fieldmarks). Additionally, Carolina Chickadees frequently sing atypical songs that sound like Black-capped

Chickadees (Lunk 1952). The ranges of the two species meet at a line that extends through central Illinois from Madison Co. northeastward to about Vermilion Co. (Brewer 1963). In some winters Black-capped wander south of their summer range, but they very rarely, if ever, come this far south. There is a possibly correct sight record for Rend Lake, Jefferson Co., on 15 Nov 1975 (BP).

FIELD GUIDES: G=228; N=310; P=210.

Carolina Chickadee *Parus carolinensis*

STATUS AND ABUNDANCE: Common year-round resident.

HABITAT: Found in nearly any habitat that has woody vegetation, but most numerous in bottomland woods and along forest edges. Can also be found in weedy fields, especially during winter.

RECORDS AND REMARKS: Commonly attracted to feeders that offer sunflower seed or suet. During fall and winter, form mixed-species flocks with Tufted Titmice, White-breasted Nuthatches, Downy Woodpeckers, and Golden-crowned Kinglets. As is the case with most common residents, few counts have been published, except for those from organized Christmas and Spring Bird Counts. No evidence of migration has been reported.

SUMMER—Albano (1992) reported on nest-site selection and breeding behavior of chickadees in Jackson and Union Cos. Nest-site excavation began in early March, the peak period of incubation was in mid-April, and most nests fledged in mid-May. Of fifty-six nests, twenty-six were situated along the edges of clearings. Average clutch size was 5.7 eggs, and average number of chicks fledged was 3.9. Most chickadees excavated their own nests, but a few were able to use holes excavated previously. Chickadees may also nest in Bluebird boxes.

WINTER—676, Union Co. CBC, 22 Dec 1982
614, Horseshoe Lake CBC, 21 Dec 1982
361, Crab Orchard NWR CBC, 15 Dec 1984

DOCUMENTATION: Specimen—ad. male, Crab Orchard NWR, Williamson Co., 18 Feb 1956 (SIU A-232).

FIELD GUIDES: G=228; N=310; P=210.

Tufted Titmouse *Parus bicolor*

STATUS AND ABUNDANCE: Common year-round resident.

HABITAT: Found in nearly any woodland, but most common in mature deciduous woods.

RECORDS AND REMARKS: Titmice are one of the most abundant forest bird species at all seasons. No evidence of migration has been reported. During fall and winter, titmice forage in mixed-species flocks with chickadees, nuthatches, Downy Woodpeckers, and kinglets. They readily come to feeders for sunflower seeds and suet. Because they are present year-round and common, few counts have been published.

SUMMER—Titmice prefer to breed in natural cavities, especially those formed in tree trunks by scars left after a large branch breaks; they will also nest in bluebird boxes. Nest activity begins in early spring; courtship feeding has been witnessed in early February. Nest building (titmice line their cavities with moss, hair, and fine grasses) begins by late March and early April. Spring Bird Counts census breeding populations.

247, Union Co., 4 May 1991 (SBC)

WINTER—470, Horseshoe Lake CBC, 21 Dec 1982

462, Union Co. CBC, 22 Dec 1982

136, Crab Orchard NWR CBC, 28 Dec 1974

DOCUMENTATION: Specimen—ad. male, Carbondale, Jackson Co., 7 Nov 1956 (SIU A-239).

FIELD GUIDES: G=230; N=308; P=210.

Family Sittidae: Nuthatches

Red-breasted Nuthatch *Sitta canadensis*

Mid-September–Early May

STATUS AND ABUNDANCE: Uncommon migrant and winter resident.

HABITAT: Coniferous trees. Sometimes found in deciduous woods during migration.

RECORDS AND REMARKS: An irruptive species, Red-breasted Nuthatches are very common in some years and very uncommon in others. Nevertheless, at least a few can always be found wintering in the region each year. They tend to prefer larger tracts of conifers with lots of cones. Given the rarity of native pines in the region, they may have been historically rare migrants and winter residents. They often join mixed-species flocks with kinglets, chickadees, creepers, and Yellow-rumped Warblers, and they will sometimes visit feeders for sunflower seeds.

AUTUMN—Most first arrivals appear in September, but occasionally some arrive in late August. Many fall migrants pass through the region for destinations south of the region, but departure dates are not known because of the presence of the wintering population.

1, near Cobden, Union Co., 31 Aug 1965 (WGG)

15, Crab Orchard NWR, 8 Nov 1986 (WDR)

WINTER—Large numbers are reported on Christmas Bird Counts in some years, but most often only a few (two to twenty) are observed.

67, Horseshoe Lake CBC, 3 Jan 1975

33, Union Co. CBC, 2 Jan 1975

188, Crab Orchard NWR CBC, 4 Jan 1976

SPRING—The beginning of spring migration is obscured by the presence of the wintering population, but some have been seen in deciduous woods during mid-April, which is probably indicative of active migration. Most Red-breasted Nuthatches have departed by the first week of May.

6, Crab Orchard NWR, 5 May 1984 (JCR)

SUMMER—There is one hypothetical breeding record. A pair were possibly feeding young at Old Dillinger Cemetery near Desoto, Jackson Co., on 14 July 1989. Unfortunately, satisfactory documentation was not obtained for this potential first breeding record for southern Illinois.

DOCUMENTATION: Specimen—imm., 2 miles n. of Cobden, Union Co., 21 Sep 1965 (SIU A-1347).

FIELD GUIDES: G=234; N=314; P=212.

White-breasted Nuthatch *Sitta carolinensis*

STATUS AND ABUNDANCE: Common year-round resident.

HABITAT: Deciduous woodlands; seems to be more numerous in upland than in bottomland woods.

RECORDS AND REMARKS: During fall and winter, nuthatches forage in mixed-species flocks with chickadees, titmice, woodpeckers, kinglets, and creepers. They are usually found in pairs, even in winter. They readily visit feeders for sunflower seeds, corn, or suet. The highest population densities are in forests, but they also occur in towns where large trees are common. They are often very tame; I once walked up to one and plucked it off the side of a tree! An adult female banded near Carbondale in 1982 was last seen in 1988. There is no evidence of migration.

SUMMER—Most nests are placed in cavities formed by knotholes, although they sometimes build in nestboxes. Breeding begins early in spring; courtship feeding has been seen from mid-February through April. Nuthatches are often secretive during the breeding season. Fledglings appear by late May, and family groups are common during June.

56, Union Co., 4 May 1991 (SBC)

WINTER—Nuthatches are conspicuous components of forest bird communities during winter, being much more vocal at this season than during summer.

200, Union Co. CBC, 3 Jan 1986

170, Horseshoe Lake CBC, 21 Dec 1982

25, Rend Lake CBC, 19 Dec 1992

DOCUMENTATION: Specimen—ad. male, Bald Knob, Union Co., 9 Apr 1966 (SIU A-1338).

FIELD GUIDES: G=234; N=314; P=212.

Family Certhiidae: Creepers

Brown Creeper *Certhia americana*

Early October–Mid-April

STATUS AND ABUNDANCE: Fairly common migrant and winter resident in the Shawnee Hills and the Floodplains. Uncommon migrant and winter resident in the Till Plain. Occasional summer visitor; very rare summer resident.

HABITAT: Mature deciduous and coniferous woodlands. Summer visitors are typically found in mature bottomland forests. Migrants sometimes occur in hedgerows and in towns with large trees.

RECORDS AND REMARKS: Creepers glean prey from small crevices in bark that they find as they spiral up tree trunks. They often associate with mixed-species flocks of forest birds, especially during winter. They are inconspicuous and can easily be overlooked.

AUTUMN—In most years, the first fall arrivals come in with the first cold front in October, but some may arrive considerably earlier. August records could possibly be of birds that summered. It is usually difficult to separate fall migrants from wintering birds, so fall departure dates are unclear.

female, Union Co., 20 Aug 1968 (WGG)

1, Horseshoe Lake CA, 31 Aug 1967 (JHa)

WINTER—Most published counts during winter come from Christmas Bird Counts.

86, Horseshoe Lake CBC, 21 Dec 1982

61, Union Co. CBC, 22 Dec 1982

SPRING—The beginning of northward migration is obscured by the winter population, but there is a more noticeable influx of birds at this season than during fall. This increase is usually most noticeable in mid- to late March. Most migrants are gone by mid-April, but a few linger later, and some may be breed.

1, Giant City SP, 9 May 1989 (WDR)

SUMMER—At present, there is only one confirmed breeding record, but the numerous summer records strongly suggest that there is a small breeding population. An adult was seen carrying food to a nest behind a piece of elm bark four meters above the ground at Union Co. CA on 4 June 1982 (PK). Creepers are encountered in appropriate breeding habitat nearly annually now.

1, Crab Orchard NWR, 1 June 1986 and 18–20 June 1985 (JCR)

pair caught in mist net (female with brood patch), Crab Orchard NWR, 4 June 1970 (VK)

2, Union Co. CA, 4–10 June 1982 (PK)

4, Horseshoe Lake CA, 9 June 1969 (JHa)

pair, Crab Orchard NWR, 13 June 1976 (BP)

2, Bell Pond, Johnson Co., 25 June 1989 (TF)

2, Heron Pond, Johnson Co., 30 June 1985 (JCR)

1, Horseshoe Lake CA, 3 July 1968 (JHa)

1, Heron Pond, Johnson Co., 18 July 1973 (MH), and 15 and 28 July 1984 (SO)

4, Little Black Slough, Johnson Co., 24 July 1992 (TF)

DOCUMENTATION: Specimen—ad. female, Bald Knob, Union Co., 21 Mar 1966 (SIU A-1339).

FIELD GUIDES: G=234; N=314; P=212.

Family Troglodytidae: Wrens

Rock Wren *Salpinctes obsoletus*

STATUS AND ABUNDANCE: Very rare vagrant.

RECORDS AND REMARKS: There are two documented records of this wren of western North America. One was found in an area with burned tree stumps near Olive Branch, Alexander Co., from 30 December 1974 through 28 January 1975 (VK, m.ob.). The second was seen along the rocky riprap on the dam at Crab Orchard Lake, Williamson Co., from 14 January through 6 March 1993 (BD, m.ob.).

DOCUMENTATION: Photograph—1, Crab Orchard NWR, Williamson Co., 25 Jan 1993 (SIU, uncatalogued).

FIELD GUIDES: G=224; N=318; P=214.

Rock Wren, Crab Orchard NWR, 25 January 1993

Carolina Wren *Thryothorus ludovicianus*

STATUS AND ABUNDANCE: Common year-round resident.

HABITAT: Most numerous in bottomland woods, but also common in upland forests and residential areas, especially where the shrub layer is dense and where brush piles or treefalls are present.

RECORDS AND REMARKS: These wrens are vocal at all times of the year, which greatly increases their conspicuousness. They are annoyed easily, so they respond well to spishing noises. There is no evidence of migration. During years with severe winters when snow or ice cover their food sources, wren populations are decimated. During the winter of 1992–1993, the upland population declined much more than the bottomland populations (SKR). It may take a decade for their numbers to recover after a severe winter. Wrens will occasionally visit feeders for seed scraps, suet, or peanut butter. SUMMER—Nest building begins by mid-March (e.g., on 11 March 1990 in Carbondale), and the first eggs are laid in late March and early April. Wrens may be triple-brooded in the region, because nests with young about to fledge have been seen as late as 7 August (Crab Orchard NWR, 1953, [LB]). Nests are placed in a wide variety of cavities: under streambanks, on the ground among the root buttresses of trees, in old woodpecker holes, and in artificial structures. Breeding populations are especially dense in forests where slash piles are numerous, like the selectively logged plots at Trail of Tears SF. Spring Bird Counts census the breeding population.
203, Union Co., 4 May 1991 (SBC)
58, Jackson Co., 10 May 1975 (SBC).
WINTER—Wrens are usually a conspicuous component of the winter bird community.
132, Crab Orchard NWR CBC, 28 Dec 1974
175, Horseshoe Lake CBC, 30 Dec 1987
209, Union Co. CBC, 2 Jan 1975

DOCUMENTATION: Specimen—ad. female, Carbondale, Jackson Co., 9 Apr 1956 (SIU A-237).

FIELD GUIDES: G=236; N=316; P=214.

Bewick's Wren *Thryomanes bewickii*
Mid-April–Late October

STATUS AND ABUNDANCE: Rare migrant and summer resident. Very rare winter resident.

HABITAT: Brushy areas near clearings and streams.

RECORDS AND REMARKS: Declining. Apparently formerly common in towns and around farms from the late 1800s (Ridgway 1889) into the early 1900s; by the 1940s and 1950s, they had noticeably decreased. Some reports are of misidentified Carolina Wrens; records of up to seven individuals in Jefferson Co. during the 1980s fall into this category. Bewick's Wrens have much longer tails with white outer corners (not light, buffy corners like some Carolinas), which they switch back and forth more often than do Carolina Wrens; they are also much paler below (no buffiness) and have a whitish tip to their tails. Their calls and songs are also distinctly different. The speculation that Bewick's Wrens declined because of competition with House Wrens is not supported by convincing evidence.

SPRING—Most arrivals are detected during April, but a few appear during March; these early records may represent birds that wintered nearby. Spring birds rarely stay at one place more than a day or so. I observed one on 21 May 1989 that flew in ahead of a midday storm, sang and foraged from a hedgerow for one minute, flew about one hundred meters north, sang again, and then disappeared out of sight to the north.

1, near Carbondale, 23 Mar 1972 (DH)
1, Little Grand Canyon, Jackson Co., 9 Apr 1949 (RB)
1, Crab Orchard NWR, 10 Apr 1984 (TF)
1, Lake of Egypt, Johnson Co., 21 Apr 1991 (TF, JD)
1, near Crab Orchard NWR, 28 Apr 1983 (MSw)
1, Ozark, Johnson Co., 29 Apr 1990 (TF)
1, s.e. Jackson Co., 21 May 1989 (WDR)

SUMMER—Surprisingly quiet on the nesting grounds; they sing during territory establishment but are typically silent thereafter. A nesting pair was present in a cemetery at Murphysboro from 1949–1953 (RB).

nest, Ferne Clyffe SP, Johnson Co., 15 May 1973 (VK)

pair nested twice, Marion, Williamson Co., May–June 1987 (VB, m.ob.)

pair nested in bow of upturned canoe, near Jonesboro, Union Co., May–June 1991 (Ma)

1, Cambria, Williamson Co., early June 1980 (LB)

family of 7 banded, Pope Co., 21 June 1973 (VK, DH)

nest, Wildcat Bluff NP, Johnson Co., June 1981 (JW)

1, Carbondale, 10 July 1982 (SO)

pair with 4 yg., Robbs, Pope Co., June–July 1990 (TF et al.)

AUTUMN—These wrens seem to just disappear after they breed; there are few fall records. Fall sightings from central Illinois and Kentucky suggest that the latest departure dates should occur during late October.

1, Pope Co., 10 Sep 1991 (TF)

WINTER—Apparently a few formerly overwintered, but there is only one recent winter record.

1, Murphysboro CBC, 27 Dec 1948

2, Murphysboro CBC, 27 Dec 1955

1 at feeder, near Carbondale, 27 Nov 1984–31 Jan 1985 (SS)

DOCUMENTATION: Photograph—1, Carbondale, Jackson Co., 12 Jan 1985 (SIU A-90).

FIELD GUIDES: G=236; N=316; P=214.

House Wren *Troglodytes aedon*

Mid-April–Mid-October

STATUS AND ABUNDANCE: Common migrant. Common summer resident in all counties except Union, Alexander, Pulaski, Massac, Pope, and Hardin, where it is uncommon but increasing. Rare winter visitor. Very rare winter resident.

HABITAT: Thickets and woodland edge during migration. Most summer residents occur in residential areas, but there is an exceptional summer population in riparian woods (especially willows and cottonwoods) along the Mississippi and Ohio Rivers.

RECORDS AND REMARKS: These feisty wrens are highly aggressive and territorial. They commonly occur in towns and riparian woods, where they will sneak into nests of other bird species and puncture the eggs. They are vigorous singers; their gurgling song can be heard throughout the entire day during spring migration and the breeding season.

SPRING—First arrivals appear in early to mid-April; departure dates are obscured by the presence of the breeding population, but most migrants have probably departed by mid-May.

male, Carterville, Williamson Co., 6 Apr 1986 (WDR)
1, Mt. Vernon, Jefferson Co., 15 Apr 1988 (TF)
31, Randolph Co., 7 May 1977 (SBC)

SUMMER—Breeding activities begin soon after arrival. Eggs have been found from early May to early August. Wrens nest in natural cavities and in artificial structures, such as clothesline poles and nest boxes.

AUTUMN—Southward migration begins by late August and is quite protracted, extending into late October, with stragglers lingering into November.

18, Harrisburg, Saline Co., 7 Sep 1986 (WDR)
1 banded, Carbondale, 23 Nov 1985 (SS, TF)

WINTER—A few sometimes linger into early winter; and some have apparently even attempted to overwinter, because there are records from every month of winter. Winter birds are usually found in dense hedgerows or brush piles, often near open water.

1, Carbondale, 14 Dec 1985 (TF)
4, Horseshoe Lake CBC, 18 Dec 1984, and 1 there, 22 Dec 1992
1, Crab Orchard NWR, 30 Dec 1972 (DH)
1, Horseshoe Lake CBC, 3 Jan 1975
1, Energy, Williamson Co., 4 Feb 1983 (JCR)
1, Oakwood Bottoms, Jackson Co., 8 Mar 1975 (BP)

There are three records of single birds from Union Co. Christmas Bird Counts: 2 Jan 1976, 19 Dec 1984, and 3 Jan 1987.

DOCUMENTATION: Specimen—ad., Crab Orchard NWR, Williamson Co., 25 Apr 1961 (SIU A-1201).

FIELD GUIDES: G=236; N=316; P=214.

Winter Wren *Trogolodytes troglodytes*
Early October–Late April

STATUS AND ABUNDANCE: Fairly common migrant. Uncommon winter resident.

HABITAT: Brushy, wet areas of bottomland woods; coniferous woods; and along streams of upland forest.

RECORDS AND REMARKS: This tiny wren frequents the cavities of overhanging creekbanks and the crevices of moss-covered logs and bluffs. Its distinctive double-noted call reveals its presence.

AUTUMN—Although some occasionally arrive during September, the first fall arrivals are usually associated with the first cold front in October. Fall migration peaks in late October and early November; departure dates are obscured by the winter population.

1, Rend Lake, 20 Sep 1985 (KM)

1 banded, Carbondale, 7 Oct 1971 (VK)

WINTER—Most winter high counts are from Christmas Bird Counts; typically, three to six birds can be found in a day by a single observer.

15, Crab Orchard NWR CBC, 15 Dec 1984

30, Horseshoe Lake CBC, 18 Dec 1984

38, Union Co. CBC, 3 Jan 1987

SPRING—The beginning of spring migration is sometimes difficult to detect because of the winter population, but an influx of birds seems to occur around mid-March, when a dozen or more birds can be counted in a day. Their incredible song can occasionally be heard during late March and April. Most have departed by mid-April, but a few linger later.

4, Crab Orchard NWR, 24 Apr 1984 (JCR)

DOCUMENTATION: Specimen—ad. male, Pine Hills, Union Co., 2 Apr 1966 (SIU A-1340).

FIELD GUIDES: G=236; N=316; P=214.

Sedge Wren *Cistothorus platensis*

Late April–Mid-May
Mid-July–Late October

STATUS AND ABUNDANCE: Occasional spring migrant. Uncommon fall migrant. Locally uncommon summer visitor; rare summer resident. Rare winter visitor.

HABITAT: Dense sedge meadows and wet weedy fields.

RECORDS AND REMARKS: The phenology of this wren is confusing.

Some arrive in April and May but apparently depart without breeding. They are then virtually absent until mid-July, when they show up at about the time that stands of grasses become tall and dense. Apparently they set up territories in these grassy areas and begin breeding, but there is only one instance of confirmed breeding for the region.

SPRING—1, Crab Orchard NWR, 23 Apr 1989 (TF, SO)
1, Union Co., 4 May 1985 (KM)
male, Dutchman Lake, Johnson Co., 24 May 1986 (TF et al.)
SUMMER—The presence of both migrants and breeders during summer is quite possible, but more systematic surveys of appropriate breeding habitat, especially during June, are needed.
1, s.w. Jackson Co., 12 July 1986 (WDR)
1 migrant, near Ozark, Pope Co., 16 July 1994 (TF)
3, Crab Orchard NWR, 18 July 1987 (WDR)
9 males, s.w. Jackson Co., 1 Aug 1976 (BP), and a fledgling there, 12 Aug 1976 (BP)
AUTUMN—The beginning of fall migration is unclear; it may begin in mid-July, if the sudden increase of birds at that time is mostly or partially indicative of transients; otherwise, there is little evidence available to suggest a different set of arrival dates. Most Sedge Wrens have departed by late October, and a few regularly linger into early winter.
3–7, Rend Lake, Jefferson Co., 24 July–26 Sep 1993 (TF)
5, Crab Orchard NWR, 14 Oct 1984 (JCR)
1, Crab Orchard NWR, 22 Nov 1982 (JCR)
WINTER—Late fall migrants have been encountered regularly during early winter in the last few years. There is no evidence yet for attempted overwintering.
1, Rudement, Saline Co., 11 Dec 1992 (JD)
1, near Ewing, Franklin Co., 15 Dec 1991 (WDR)
1, near Sandusky, Pulaski Co., 18 Dec 1990 (SB, WDR)
2, Crab Orchard NWR, 19 Dec 1987 (JCR)
1, Pulaski Co., 21 Dec 1982 (LMc)
2, Oakwood Bottoms, Jackson Co., 10–11 Jan 1976 (BP)

Documentation: Photograph—Ward Branch, Rend Lake, Jefferson Co., 27 Aug 1987 (SIU AP-88).

Field Guides: G=238; N=318; P=214.

Marsh Wren *Cistothorus palustris*

Mid-April–Mid-May
Mid-September–Late October

STATUS AND ABUNDANCE: Uncommon migrant. Very rare winter visitor.

HABITAT: Cattail marshes, wet grassy meadows, and, occasionally, *Phragmites* marshes.

RECORDS AND REMARKS: Secretive habits and dense vegetation make observation of this wren difficult, but it responds well to spishing noises. Its trill-like song is rather inconspicuous, but it gives a distinctive two-note call.

SPRING—There are few published records for spring, but they regularly pass through the region. Most encounters are of only one to three birds per day.

male, n. Randolph Co., 15 Apr 1988 (WDR)
3, Lovett's Pond, Jackson Co., 25 Apr 1992 (TF, JD)
1, Giant City SP, 11 May 1984 (WDR)

AUTUMN—A few fall migrants may arrive as early as late August, but apparently little fieldwork has been done in the appropriate habitats during that time. They seem to be more numerous in fall than in spring. Last departures occur during late October, but some linger into early winter.

1, Carbondale, 27 Sep 1970 (VK, DH)
1, Oakwood Bottoms, Jackson Co., 27 Sep 1975 (BP)
9, Crab Orchard NWR, 14 Oct 1984 (JCR)
1 singing, Carbondale, 29 Oct 1989 (BD)

WINTER—Winter records are probably of late migrants; there is no evidence that any wrens attempt to overwinter, but the possibility exists, because they regularly winter just south of the region, in Arkansas and Tennessee.

2, Crab Orchard NWR, 19 Dec 1987 (JCR)
1, Rend Lake, Jefferson Co., 16–19 Dec 1992 (TF, m.ob.)
2, Alexander Co., 21 Dec 1982 (HDB et al.)
1, Rend Lake, Jefferson Co., 31 Dec 1988 (BD)

DOCUMENTATION: Provisional acceptance.

FIELD GUIDES: G=238; N=318; P=214.

Family Muscicapidae: Muscicapids

Subfamily Sylviinae: Kinglets and Gnatcatchers

Golden-crowned Kinglet *Regulus satrapa*

Early October–Mid-April

STATUS AND ABUNDANCE: Common migrant and winter resident.

HABITAT: Most common in coniferous woods, but also frequents deciduous forests, especially during migration.

RECORDS AND REMARKS: Kinglets join mixed-species flocks with creepers, chickadees, titmice, and warblers. Can be quite tame, and they sometimes allow close approach. Kinglets forage by hover-gleaning foliage and bark at all levels of the forest, from nearly on the ground to the top of the canopy.

AUTUMN—A few kinglets may appear in September, but most arrive following the first cold front in October. Peak numbers pass through the region in late October and early November, but the pulse is not particularly distinguishable from the winter population, although at times it is possible to count thirty to forty birds in a day. The end of fall migration is unclear, but Graber et al. (1979) suspected it is largely over by mid-December.

2, Saline Co., 23 Sep 1987 (KP)

WINTER—Kinglets are quite susceptible to severe weather. They may be fairly common in an area before a severe storm and then rare or entirely absent afterward; whether the decrease is because of mortality or migration is unclear.

125, Horseshoe Lake CBC, 21 Dec 1982

152, Union Co. CBC, 22 Dec 1982

189, Crab Orchard NWR CBC, 28 Dec 1974

SPRING—The beginning of spring migration is difficult to detect because of the wintering population, but there seems to be a definite pulse of migrants in late March, when daily counts of forty birds are not unusual. Most kinglets are gone by 20 April, but a few stragglers have been seen later.

1, Pomona, 28 Apr 1989 (WDR)

1, Massac Co., 7 May 1977 (SBC)

DOCUMENTATION: Specimen—female, Carbondale, Jackson Co., 24 Oct 1975 (SIU A-1896).

FIELD GUIDES: G=252; N=322; P=216.

Ruby-crowned Kinglet *Regulus calendula*
Late September–Mid-November
Late March–Early May

STATUS AND ABUNDANCE: Common migrant. Fairly common winter resident in the Shawnee Hills and the Floodplains. Uncommon winter resident in the Till Plain.

HABITAT: Woodland edge and coniferous and deciduous woods.

RECORDS AND REMARKS: Sometimes join mixed-species flocks, but are also encountered singly and in small monospecific groups. They hover-glean insects from branch tips and leaves. They are hyperactive foragers that have a distinctive wing-flicking behavior as they move from branch to branch.
AUTUMN—Small numbers begin arriving during September, but peak numbers do not pass through until mid- to late October. Departure dates are obscured by the winter population, but numbers seem to stabilize after mid-November.
1, Ferne Clyffe SP, Johnson Co., 4 Sep 1988 (WDR)
1, Rend Lake, Jefferson Co., 23 Sep 1987 (TF)
14, Crab Orchard NWR, 15 Oct 1983 (JCR)
WINTER—Numbers are higher in early winter than later (e.g., in February), which suggests that many of the birds found in December may be late migrants. Prefers conifers or dense brushy vegetation near open water during winter.
49, Horseshoe Lake CBC, 18 Dec 1984
7, Rend Lake CBC, 19 Dec 1992
30, Union Co. CBC, 2 Jan 1975
53, Crab Orchard NWR CBC, 4 Jan 1976
SPRING—The first spring arrivals are not usually detected until the last few days of March; earlier sightings may be very early migrants or birds that wintered nearby. On some days in mid-April, kinglets can be exceptionally common; counts of twenty to thirty

birds are not unusual. Most kinglets have departed by 10 May, some rarely lingering into late May.

1, Union Co., 1 Mar 1975 (BP)
1, Crab Orchard NWR, 15 Mar 1990 (BD)
57, LaRue Pine Hills, Union Co., 14 Apr 1990 (WDR)
1, Williamson Co., 17 May 1983 (JCR)
1, Giant City SP, 22 May 1975 (BP)

DOCUMENTATION: Specimen—ad. male, Carbondale, Jackson Co., 5 May 1961 (SIU A-1113).

FIELD GUIDES: G=252; N=322; P=216.

Blue-gray Gnatcatcher *Polioptila caerulea*

Late March–Mid-September

STATUS AND ABUNDANCE: Common spring migrant and summer resident. Uncommon fall migrant. Very rare winter visitor.

HABITAT: Deciduous woodlands and woodland edge, usually near water; particularly common in bottomland forests.

RECORDS AND REMARKS: Actively forages by flushing insects with a flash of its tail and vigorously pursuing the startled prey. These frenetic birds spend most of their time in the mid- to upper levels of the canopy, but they will also search for food near the ground. They often come near the ground when searching for spider webs to use in their nests.

SPRING—First arrivals are detected during the last few days of March, but the migrational peak does not occur until late April and early May. They can be exceptionally common at times; daily counts of fifty to seventy-five birds are not unusual.

1, Pomona, 27 Mar 1984 (TF)
1, s.e. Saline Co., 31 Mar 1986 (SO)
111, Massac Co., 4 May 1985 (SBC)
404, Union Co., 4 May 1991 (SBC)

SUMMER—Nest building begins as early as mid-April, and fledglings are out by mid-May. Nestling and fledgling gnatcatchers are very noisy, but because most nests are placed high in the canopy, little is known about breeding success in the region. Often parasitized by cowbirds, but the impacts have not been quantified.

AUTUMN—Fall migration is hardly detectable; the breeding population seems to simply drift southward. Most gnatcatchers are gone by 10 September.
1, Giant City SP, 17 Sep 1983 (JCR)
1, Rend Lake, 24 Sep 1986 (KM)
WINTER—1 foraging in cedars in a cemetery, Rend Lake, Jefferson Co., 15–16 Dec 1990 (BD, WDR, TF, JD)

DOCUMENTATION: Specimen—ad. male, Crab Orchard NWR, Williamson Co., 4 Apr 1956 (SIU A-271).

FIELD GUIDES: G=252; N=322; P=216.

Subfamily *Turdinae: Thrushes*

Eastern Bluebird *Sialia sialis*

STATUS AND ABUNDANCE: Common year-round resident.

HABITAT: Woodland edge, old fields, and pastures.

RECORDS AND REMARKS: There is extensive migration, but it is often obscured by the presence of large breeding and wintering populations. Bluebirds form loose flocks during migration and winter and are commonly seen perched along roadsides on electrical wires and fences. They will sometimes visit feeders for peanut butter, suet, or fruit during severe winter weather. Ridgway (1915) suggested that bluebird populations were declining in and around towns because of competition with House Sparrows; bluebirds remain uncommon in residential areas today.
SPRING—An influx of spring migrants typically occurs during early to mid-February, and migration is probably largely over by late March. Peak numbers pass through the region during late February and early March, at which time daily counts of thirty to forty bluebirds are common.
SUMMER—Nesting begins early in spring; eggs are laid in mid-March, and the first fledglings are out by mid- to late April. Bluebirds may sometimes be triple-brooded in southern Illinois. Most nests are placed in bluebird nest boxes, but some still nest in natural cavities along woodland edge and in cavities in fence posts. Spring Bird Counts census the breeding population.
114, Union Co., 4 May 1991 (SBC)

38, Massac Co., 6 May 1989 (SBC).

AUTUMN—As with many species that breed in the region, the fall migration is not well documented. The migration period seems to extend, however, from early September through mid-November. During this time, it is common to see forty to sixty bluebirds in a day in appropriate habitat. Most of the migration is probably over by the beginning of December, but censuses of banded birds are needed to establish this date more precisely.

WINTER—Most large counts come from Christmas Bird Counts.
81, Crab Orchard NWR CBC, 18 Dec 1971
40 in one flock, Ozark, Johnson Co., 24 Dec 1992–14 Feb 1993 (TF)
159, Horseshoe Lake CBC, 20 Dec 1994
170, Cypress Creek NWR CBC, 21 Dec 1994
199, Union Co. CBC, 22 Dec 1994
94, s.e. Saline Co., 5 Jan 1994 (JD)

DOCUMENTATION: Specimen—ad. female, Little Grassy Lake, Williamson Co., 18 Feb 1956 (SIU A-235).

FIELD GUIDES: G=250; N=324; P=220.

[Mountain Bluebird *Sialia currocoides*]

STATUS AND ABUNDANCE: Hypothetical.

RECORDS AND REMARKS: One report of three adult males at Rudement, Saline Co., on 30 April 1987 was fully documented by written description (GCD), but it was not accepted by the IORC, "due to the combination of rather late spring date, extraordinary number, and the inexperience [with this species] of the observers." A photograph or specimen is needed to verify the species for the regional list.

FIELD GUIDES: G=234; N=324; P=220.

[Townsend's Solitaire *Myadestes townsendi*]

STATUS AND ABUNDANCE: Hypothetical.

RECORDS AND REMARKS: One foraging on hawthorn berries at Crab Orchard NWR on 25 January 1979 was seen by only a single observer (SH). A written description was made, but no photograph could be obtained.

FIELD GUIDES: G=230; N=324; P=218.

Veery *Catharus fuscescens*

Late April–Late May
Late August–Late September

STATUS AND ABUNDANCE: Fairly common spring migrant. Uncommon fall migrant.

HABITAT: Mature deciduous woodland.

RECORDS AND REMARKS: Much more numerous in spring than in fall, although the fact that Veeries sing in spring and not in fall certainly affects the perception of their abundance. They forage on or near the ground in deeply shaded woods.

SPRING—Most early arrivals appear during the last week of April, and peak numbers pass through during early and mid-May. A few stragglers linger into early June.

1, Heron Pond NP, Johnson Co., 24 Apr 1973 (VK, HDB)
76, Union Co., 4 May 1991 (SBC)
14, Massac Co., 6 May 1989 (WDR, SO)
1, Little Black Slough, Johnson Co., 24 May 1989 (TF, WDR)
1, Dutch Creek, near Jonesboro, Union Co., 8 June 1988 (SKR)

SUMMER—One midsummer record may be of a very late spring migrant: male mist-netted, Trail of Tears SF, 23 June 1992 (LJ). The nearest confirmed breeding is from Vermilion Co., Illinois.

AUTUMN—Like most other woodland thrushes, only a few Veeries are detected by an observer in a typical autumn. High counts for a day rarely exceed three or four birds. Because they are so retiring and inconspicuous, mist-netting might sample the fall populations better.

1, Saline Co. CA, 18 Aug 1987 (WDR)
1, Woodlawn, Jefferson Co., 2 Sep 1988 (TF)
2, Crab Orchard NWR, 19 Sep 1982 (JCR)
1 banded, Carbondale, 27 Sep 1972 (VK)

DOCUMENTATION: Specimen—ad. male, 2 miles n. of Cobden, Union Co., 9 May 1966 (SIU A-1345).

FIELD GUIDES: G=248; N=326; P=222.

Gray-cheeked Thrush *Catharus minimus*

Late April–Late May
Mid-September–Early October

STATUS AND ABUNDANCE: Fairly common spring migrant. Uncommon fall migrant.

HABITAT: Upland and lowland mature deciduous forest.

RECORDS AND REMARKS: Usually forages on the ground in shaded forest, but may also glean insects off of tree trunks or large branches up to about ten meters off the ground. Much more numerous in spring than in fall.

SPRING—The first arrivals are usually detected by their songs during the last week of April. Less than fifteen birds are usually detected in a single day, but sometimes there are large fallouts of migrating thrushes (see 4 May 1991 and 12 May 1984). Virtually all Gray-cheeks are gone by 20 May, but a few linger later.

1, Carbondale, 22 Apr 1985 (JCR)
1 banded, Pomona, 24 Apr 1972 (VK)
397, Union Co., 4 May 1991 (SBC)
52, Giant City SP, 12 May 1984 (WDR)
1, Cairo, Alexander Co., 26 May 1988 (WDR)
1, Trail of Tears SF, 30 May 1991 (Robinson and Robinson 1992)

AUTUMN—Very inconspicuous during fall migration; counts of more than two or three in a day are noteworthy.

5, Murphysboro, 5 Sep 1949 (RB)
1, Crab Orchard NWR, 19 Sep 1982 (JCR)
3, Rend Lake, Franklin Co., 30 Sep 1989 (WDR)
1 banded, Carbondale, 7 Oct 1972 (VK)

DOCUMENTATION: Specimen—ad. female, Bald Knob, Union Co., 30 Apr 1966 (SIU A-1344).

FIELD GUIDES: G=248; N=326; P=222.

Swainson's Thrush *Catharus ustulatus*

Late April–Late May
Early September–Mid-October

STATUS AND ABUNDANCE: Common spring migrant. Uncommon fall migrant.

HABITAT: Deciduous woods and woodland edge.

RECORDS AND REMARKS: The most numerous of the *Catharus* thrushes during migration, Swainson's commonly forage at mid-heights of trees, where they sally out to snatch insects off the bark of tree trunks and large branches; they also forage on the ground. On fallout days, large counts have been made of this common species. They sing much more than Gray-cheeks and Veeries, and the forest can seem to be alive with Swainson's songs and calls in early and mid-May.

SPRING—Migration peaks in early and mid-May, and a few late migrants routinely linger into late May and early June.

1, Saline Co., 17 Apr 1987 (KP) and 17 Apr 1991 (TF)
1, Giant City SP, 18 Apr 1989 (WDR)
564, Union Co., 4 May 1991 (SBC)
57, Massac Co., 5 May 1984 (SVa, WDR)
51, Giant City SP, 12 May 1984 (WDR)
1, Pope Co., 27 May 1989 (TF, LA)
male, Kinkaid Lake, Jackson Co., 29–30 May 1983 (JCR)
singing male, Dutch Creek Camp, near Jonesboro, Union Co., 5 June 1992 (CT, WDR, SKR)

AUTUMN—Far fewer are detected in fall than in spring. High counts of more than four or five birds are noteworthy. Graber et al. (1971) suggested that the migration of Swainson's is deflected eastward north of the region and that most Swainson's simply do not pass through southern Illinois. Nevertheless, some are encountered each fall.

1 banded, Grimsby, Jackson Co., 11 Sep 1972 (VK)
1, Crab Orchard NWR, 9 Oct 1982 (JCR)

DOCUMENTATION: Specimen—ad. male, Bald Knob, Union Co., 30 Apr 1966 (SIU A-1343).

FIELD GUIDES: G=248; N=326; P=222.

Hermit Thrush *Catharus guttatus*
Early October–Mid-April

STATUS AND ABUNDANCE: Uncommon migrant. Uncommon winter resident in the Shawnee Hills and the Floodplains. Occasional winter resident in the Till Plain.

HABITAT: Deciduous forest and forest edge, coniferous thickets, and hedgerows.

RECORDS AND REMARKS: Hermit Thrushes arrive after most of the other *Catharus* thrushes have left the region. They forage on berries and invertebrates in dense thickets. Their inconspicuous call note, *churk,* is easily overlooked. They often respond to spishing noises but do not come completely out into the open; they have the habit of quickly raising their tail and then slowly lowering it.

AUTUMN—The first fall migrants arrive behind the first cold front in October. During peak passage in late October and early November, up to ten birds can be seen in a day. Departure dates are obscured by the winter population, but numbers have stabilized by mid-November.

1 banded, Carbondale, 7 Oct 1972 (VK)

WINTER—Most of the winter population is in the Shawnee Hills; even in the Till Plain around Crab Orchard NWR, where coniferous thickets are common, Hermit Thrushes are quite uncommon. High counts come from Christmas Bird Counts.

4, Rend Lake CBC, 19 Dec 1992

32, Union Co. CBC, 20 Dec 1983

35, Horseshoe Lake CBC, 30 Dec 1987

5, Crab Orchard NWR CBC, 4 Jan 1976

SPRING—The winter population obscures the beginning of spring migration, but there are at least some local movements as early as mid-February; full migration seems to be underway in mid- to late March, with peak passage of migrants in early April. Generally, less than seven or eight birds are seen per day. Sometimes, on cool, clear mornings, Hermit Thrushes will sing, but it is uncommon. The last migrants are usually gone by 20 April, but a few may linger into the first week of May, especially during unusually cool springs.

2, Murphysboro, 19 Feb 1949 (RB)

1, Heron Pond NP, Johnson Co., 23 Apr 1973 (VK, HDB)

1, Union Co., 7 May 1983 (SBC)

1, Oakwood Bottoms, Jackson Co., 8 May 1976 (BP)

DOCUMENTATION: Specimen—ad. male, Pine Hills, Union Co., 2 Apr 1966 (SIU A-1342).

FIELD GUIDES: G=248; N=326; P=222.

Wood Thrush *Hylocichla mustelina*

Late April–Early October

STATUS AND ABUNDANCE: Common migrant and summer resident.

HABITAT: Mature deciduous woodland.

RECORDS AND REMARKS: Possibly declining; does not breed in some smaller woodlots that formerly would have had one or two pairs. Currently the focus of intensive study because of heavy parasitism by Brown-headed Cowbirds.

SPRING—First arrivals usually appear around 20 April, sometimes earlier. There is no obvious peak in numbers of migrants, because

Wood Thrush on nest, Pine Hills, Union Co., June 1992

of the large breeding population; it is also not clear when the last migrants have departed.

1, Carbondale, 29 Mar 1979 (DK)
1, Pomona, 14 Apr 1972 (VK)
2, LaRue Pine Hills, Union Co., 14 Apr 1990 (WDR)
179, Union Co., 4 May 1991 (SBC)

SUMMER—Nest building begins soon after arrival in early to mid-May. Eggs are laid from mid-May through mid-July; there are often two broods. Of 345 nests in Alexander and Union Cos., 89 percent were parasitized by cowbirds and received an average of 3 cowbird eggs per nest. This parasitization, in combination with high rates of nest predation, results in an average of less than one Wood Thrush young fledged per nest (INHS).

AUTUMN—As with many other breeding species, Wood Thrushes seem to just disappear after the breeding season; there are usually no detectable increases in the population during fall. If their loud scolding call was not heard once in while, they might go completely undetected after late August. Most have probably departed by late September, but apparently a few linger later.

1, Ozark, Johnson Co., 7 Sep 1992 (TF)
1 banded, Carbondale, 16 Oct 1971 (VK, DH)

DOCUMENTATION: Specimen—ad. male, Carbondale, Jackson Co., 25 May 1965 (SIU A-1341).

FIELD GUIDES: G=248; N=326; P=222.

American Robin *Turdus migratorius*

STATUS AND ABUNDANCE: Common year-round resident, though sometimes an uncommon winter resident in the Till Plain.

HABITAT: Residential areas, open woods, and woodland edge.

RECORDS AND REMARKS: A familiar species to all. Extensively migratory, and highly gregarious during migration and winter.

SPRING—Northward movements begin by mid- to late January in most years, with peak migration in late February and early March; counts of two hundred to three hundred birds are common. Because of the large breeding population, departure dates are difficult to determine.

SUMMER—Nests are placed from one to twenty meters above

ground, with most about six to eight meters high. Robins vigorously
defend their nests against just about anything that moves, so they
are very rarely parasitized by cowbirds. They often raise two broods.
Fledglings have been noted as late as late September.

AUTUMN—Fall migration may begin during August, when flocks
of forty to fifty birds begin to form, and it is well underway by mid-
September. Peak movements occur from mid-October to mid-November. Usually, flocks of two hundred to three hundred birds are
regularly seen, but it is not uncommon to see larger concentrations.
One massive movement has been noted in the region: 300,000 migrating south, Mt. Vernon, Jefferson Co., 19 Oct 1987 (TF). The
departure dates are difficult to identify, because of the substantial
winter population.

WINTER—Robins forage on fruit for most of the winter, so they
are usually found in small flocks. I have seen them eat whole kernels
of corn during severe weather when their food supply was ice- and
snow-covered. They are most common in the Shawnee Hills and
the Floodplains.

1,762, Union Co. CBC, 31 Dec 1987

DOCUMENTATION: Specimen—male, 5 miles w. of Carterville, Williamson Co., 31 Mar 1959 (SIU A-753).

FIELD GUIDES: G=244; N=330; P=220.

Family Mimidae: Mockingbirds and Thrashers

Gray Catbird *Dumetella carolinensis*

Late April–Late October

STATUS AND ABUNDANCE: Common migrant and summer resident.
Rare winter visitor.

HABITAT: Brushy areas along woodland edge, riparian brush, and,
especially in the Till Plain, residential areas.

RECORDS AND REMARKS: Catbirds seem to be more numerous in
the Floodplains and the Till Plain than in the Shawnee Hills, but
there are no quantitative data available. They are common in
swampy second growth.

SPRING—Song is usually the first indication that catbirds have
arrived in spring, but they often whisper their songs for the first

few days after spring arrival. The first arrivals appear in late April, peak numbers pass through in early and mid-May, and the last migrants have probably departed by late May, although the precise dates are obscured by the breeding population.

1, Oakwood Bottoms, Jackson Co., 17 Apr 1991 (KM)

1, Mermet Lake CA, 21 Apr 1979 (MMl)

1, Carbondale, 23 Apr 1984 (SO)

30, Massac Co., 5 May 1984 (SVa, WDR)

SUMMER—Catbirds usually place their robinlike nests less than four meters high in shrubs. The nesting season extends from late April through August. Brewer (1955) measured the territory size of catbirds at Pomona to be between 0.16 and 0.36 acres. Little is known about the impact of cowbirds on catbirds in the region; but Catbirds are apparently rarely parasitized.

AUTUMN—Fall migration is usually rather inconspicuous. Daily high counts are typically on the order of four or five birds. The last migrants are usually gone by late October, but some probably linger later almost every year; a few even linger into the period of the Christmas Bird Count in December.

5, Rend Lake, Franklin Co., 30 Sep 1989 (WDR)

1, Murphysboro, 29 Oct 1949 (RB)

1, Massac Co., 1 Nov 1989 (TF)

WINTER—Winter birds are usually found in hedgerows and dense thickets. Most records are from Christmas Bird Counts. There is no evidence of attempted overwintering. There are five records of single birds from Crab Orchard NWR Christmas Bird Counts: 28 Dec 1970, 28 Dec 1974, 31 Dec 1977, 15 Dec 1984, and 19 Dec 1987.

1, Diswood, Alexander Co., 16 Dec 1989 (SB, WDR)

1, Rend Lake, Franklin Co., 18 Dec 1993 (DKa)

1, Murphysboro, 22 Dec 1951 (JWH)

DOCUMENTATION: Specimen—ad. female, Jackson Co., 24 May 1975 (SIU A-1901).

FIELD GUIDES: G=240; N=334; P=218.

Northern Mockingbird *Mimus polyglottos*

STATUS AND ABUNDANCE: Common year-round resident.

HABITAT: Brushy hedgerows, woodland edge, and residential areas.

RECORDS AND REMARKS: During summer, "Mockers" are most numerous in the Till Plain, where there seems to be at least one pair in every hedgerow; they are also common in the Shawnee Hills and the Floodplain, but not to the same degree. There is some migration, but it is often difficult to detect; spring movements seem to begin in mid-March and extend through April, whereas fall migration is more protracted, extending from late August through early November. Observers should take care to count mockers (and other common year-round residents) and then should publish their data, so that we can better understand the timing of migrational movements.

SUMMER—Nests are placed in dense bushes. Egg laying begins in early April, and the last young are fledged during August. Mockingbirds may be double-brooded in the region. They are not successfully parasitized by cowbirds.

WINTER—The region's wintering population is supplemented by migrants from the north. Mockers are territorial even in winter, and they will vigorously defend berry-producing bushes against all other birds.

199, Crab Orchard NWR CBC, 18 Dec 1971
27, Rend Lake CBC, 19 Dec 1992
78, Horseshoe Lake CBC, 21 Dec 1982
50, Union Co. CBC, 31 Dec 1972

DOCUMENTATION: Specimen—ad. male, Crab Orchard NWR, Williamson Co., 15 May 1968 (SIU A-1712).

FIELD GUIDES: G=226; N=336; P=218.

Brown Thrasher *Toxostoma rufum*

Late March–Late October

STATUS AND ABUNDANCE: Common migrant and summer resident. Occasional winter resident in the Till Plain; uncommon winter resident in the Shawnee Hills and the Floodplains.

HABITAT: Brushy woodland edge, hedgerows, and old fields with briar patches and bushes.

RECORDS AND REMARKS: Thrashers are hedgerow specialists. They are common in nonforest habitats in which dense shrubbery and thickets predominate. Their song is similar to Mockingbirds' songs, but the phrases are uttered in pairs rather than in groups of three or more.

SPRING—There seems to be two migration episodes. A few arrive very early, often in late February and early March, but the largest pulse of arrivals does not develop until late March. The earliest group may be mostly the breeding population, and the latter may be mostly composed of migrants. Peak numbers of thrashers are present during April and early May.

2, Giant City SP, 2 Mar 1990 (WDR)

1, Mt. Vernon, Jefferson Co., 23 Mar 1988 (TF)

73, Massac Co., 10 May 1986 (SBC)

SUMMER—Thrashers begin nesting soon after their arrival in March; egg dates range from early April through July. They are occasionally parasitized by cowbirds, but they rarely raise cowbird young.

AUTUMN—The beginning of fall migration is obscured by the breeding population, but noticeable increases in numbers of thrashers occur in early September (daily counts of ten to fifteen birds are typical); most of the migrants have departed by mid-October, but a few are regularly encountered through late October. Lingering thrashers may be late migrants or winter residents.

WINTER—Thrashers successfully overwinter in most years, but they are decidedly scarce during severe winters. They are most numerous in the extreme southern tier of counties.

9, Union Co. CBC, 22 Dec 1982

18, Horseshoe Lake CBC, 30 Dec 1987

15, Crab Orchard NWR CBC, 4 Jan 1976

2, Giant City SP, 21 Feb 1983 (JCR)

DOCUMENTATION: Specimen—ad. male, Crab Orchard NWR, Williamson Co., 11 Apr 1956 (SIU A-243).

FIELD GUIDES: G=240; N=336; P=218.

Curve-billed Thrasher *Toxostoma curvirostre*

STATUS AND ABUNDANCE: Very rare winter visitor.

RECORDS AND REMARKS: There is one record of this thrasher, which is typically found in the southwestern United States and Mexico. An adult was found in a dense hedgerow at the Silo Access

Curve-billed Thrasher, Rend Lake, Jefferson Co., December 1992

Area at Rend Lake, Jefferson Co., on 16 December 1992 (TF, JD); it remained there at least through 24 January 1993 and was seen by dozens of birders. This record is the only one for the region and the state (Fink 1993a).

DOCUMENTATION: Photograph—above record (SIU, uncatalogued).

FIELD GUIDES: G=228; N=338; P=not pictured.

Family Motacillidae: Pipits

American Pipit *Anthus rubescens*
Mid-March–Mid-May
Late September–Mid-November

STATUS AND ABUNDANCE: Uncommon migrant. Rare winter visitor.

HABITAT: Mudflats, wet short-grass and legume fields, and plowed agricultural fields.

RECORDS AND REMARKS: Pipits often form loose flocks that forage on the ground in fields with short or sparse vegetation, so they can sometimes be confused with Horned Larks. But their voices are more forceful and squeakier, and they lack the black breast band and facial markings of larks.

SPRING—There are two periods of spring migration; the first begins in mid-March and extends into mid-April, and the second begins in late April and ends in mid-May. The early migration period usually involves the most birds.

2, Horseshoe Lake CA, 26 Feb 1991 (JCR, TF, JD)
1, Saline Co., 8 Mar 1992 (TF, JD)
45, Pope Co., 9 Mar 1984 (JP)
1, Rend Lake, 13 Mar 1987 (TF)
340, Perks, Pulaski Co., 13 Mar 1992 (TF)
28, Williamson Co., 14 Mar 1987 (WDR)
50, Horseshoe Lake CA, 3 Apr 1987 (TF)
80, Union Co. CA, 30 Apr 1971 (VK, DH)
3, Rend Lake, Jefferson Co., 12 May 1986 (TF, WDR)
2, Crab Orchard NWR, 14 May 1984 (JCR)

AUTUMN—Fall migration is less noticeable, and it is not divided into two periods as is spring migration. Most migrants arrive after 20 September.

1, Rend Lake, Jefferson Co., 10 Sep 1988 (TF, WDR)
72, Paulton, Williamson Co., 12 Sep 1987 (WDR)
5, Crab Orchard NWR, 28 Oct 1989 (WDR)
1, Rend Lake, Jefferson Co., 11 Nov 1987 (TF)

WINTER—Pipits regularly winter as close as Tennessee and Arkansas, so it is possible that a few could attempt to overwinter in mild years. However, as yet, there are very few winter records.

1, Lake of Egypt, Williamson Co., 18 Dec 1984 (JCR)
7, Rend Lake CBC, 18 Dec 1993
26, Horseshoe Lake CA, 19 Dec 1989 (SB, WDR)
1, Crab Orchard NWR, 21 Dec 1953 (RB)
3, Murphysboro CBC, 26 Dec 1953
1, Mermet, Massac Co., 28 Jan 1989 (WDR)

DOCUMENTATION: Photograph—Nason, Rend Lake, Jefferson Co., 10 Sep 1988 (SIU AP-247). There is a note in the Grabers' files (at INHS) that a specimen was collected near Cairo, Alexander Co., on 31 Oct 1906, but the disposition of the specimen is unknown.

FIELD GUIDES: G=256; N=340; P=200.

Sprague's Pipit *Anthus spragueii*

STATUS AND ABUNDANCE: Very rare migrant and winter visitor.

HABITAT: Large, open short-grass fields, especially where alfalfa is planted.

RECORDS AND REMARKS: Probably more numerous than the few records indicate, because few observers take the time to search the appropriate habitat. The distinctive call of this species, a high-pitched *squeet, squeet,* is uttered when the species is flushed from its grassy habitat. Sprague's Pipits can be confused with immature Horned Larks, so observers should use caution when identifying these pipits. There are no fall records, but they should be present in small numbers from early October through November, and they may be present later, since a few may winter in the region.
SPRING—There are not enough records to fully define the period of spring migration; based on records from nearby regions, the range of dates should extend from mid-March through the end of April.
6 or 7 in alfalfa, Omaha, Gallatin Co., 16 Mar 1957 (Graber 1957)
1 in alfalfa and a nearby heavily grazed pasture, near Perks, Pulaski Co., 18 Apr 1992 (Fink and Robinson 1992)
WINTER—Two records of birds in alfalfa fields are the only winter sightings:
4, Omaha, Gallatin Co., 13 Jan 1957 (Graber 1957)
imm. male collected, Cora, Jackson Co., 10 Jan 1957 (Graber 1957).

DOCUMENTATION: Specimen—imm. male, Cora, Jackson Co., 10 Jan 1957 (INHS).

FIELD GUIDES: G=256; N=340; P=200.

Family Bombycillidae: Waxwings

[Bohemian Waxwing *Bombycilla garrulus*]

STATUS AND ABUNDANCE: Hypothetical.

RECORDS AND REMARKS: Ridgway (1889) noted that one was collected at Villa Ridge, Pulaski Co., on 18 December 1879, but the disposition of the specimen is unknown.

FIELD GUIDES: G=258; N=344; P=224.

Cedar Waxwing *Bombycilla cedrorum*

STATUS AND ABUNDANCE: Common migrant. Uncommon, irregular summer resident and winter resident.

HABITAT: Flocks are often found in both lowland and upland forest, in hedgerows, and in residential areas near berry-producing plants.

RECORDS AND REMARKS: Waxwings form tight flocks that fly quickly overhead, twisting and turning, and then alight in the tops of trees, all the while uttering their high-pitched, hissing calls. They forage for fruit during migration and winter, and they also flycatch during warmer weather. They have an unusual split migration during spring; observers should keep careful records on their observations of waxwings to shed more light on the timing of migration.

SPRING—Migration is divided into two sections that are distinctly separate in most years but that are blended together in others. The first migrant flocks begin appearing as early as mid- or late January; numbers peak in February and March, and the end of the early migration period comes during early April. There is then a gap during mid-April, when only a few waxwings occur. The next pulse of migrants appears in late April or early May and extends into late May or even early June. Some birds that linger into June may stay to breed.

55, Energy, Williamson Co., 26 Feb 1984 (JCR)

324, Union Co., 10 May 1986 (SBC)

35, Alexander and Union Cos., 26 May 1984 (JCR)

4, Pope Co., 3 June 1984 (JCR)

SUMMER—Breeding populations are highly variable from year to year. In some years, no waxwings can be found during summer, but in others, they are relatively common. There are few nest data available from the region.

10, Alexander Co., 11 July 1988 (WDR)

Cedar Waxwing at nest, Pankeyville, Saline Co., July 1994

2, Johnson Co., 16 July 1983 (JCR)
AUTUMN—Fall migrational movements begin in late August and peak in late October and early November. Because of the winter population, departure dates are difficult to define.
173, Crab Orchard NWR, 11 Nov 1984 (TF)
WINTER—Winter populations are highly irregular, probably depending on the size of the fruit crops. They appear to be least numerous in the Till Plain. Most published counts are from Christmas Bird Counts.
194, Crab Orchard NWR, 17 Dec 1988 (WDR, KM)
45, Rend Lake CBC, 19 Dec 1992
397, Horseshoe Lake CBC, 20 Dec 1983
215, Union Co. CBC, 30 Dec 1976

DOCUMENTATION: Specimen—ad. male, Crab Orchard NWR, Williamson Co., 26 June 1956 (SIU A-258).

FIELD GUIDES: G=258; N=344; P=224.

Family Laniidae: Shrikes

Loggerhead Shrike *Lanius ludovicianus*

STATUS AND ABUNDANCE: Fairly common year-round resident.

HABITAT: Brushy fields and hedgerows. Often seen perched along roadsides on telephone wires and fences.

RECORDS AND REMARKS: Apparently declining. The clearing of hedgerows from agricultural lands and the application of insecticides have negatively affected shrike populations. There is extensive migration, but because there are both breeding and wintering populations in the region, it is not very conspicuous. Sometimes shrike caches can be found; dead insects, rodents, or small birds are impaled on thorns or barbed-wire fences.

SPRING—Migration probably begins in late February and extends into early April, with a peak during late March (Graber et al. 1973). To what extent the region's breeding population is supplemented by migrants from the south is unclear, but the summer population is definitely higher than the winter population.

SUMMER—Shrikes build a bulky stick nest in thorny bushes and trees, cedars, and vine tangles. They nest early; eggs are laid from late March through June, but most breeding takes place in April and early May. Average clutch size is 5.7 eggs (Graber et al. 1973). Shrikes are not successfully parasitized by cowbirds. Spring Bird Counts census the breeding population.

23, Massac Co., 5 May 1990 (SBC)

21, Pope Co., 10 May 1980 (SBC)

AUTUMN—Fall migration is difficult to detect, because it is obscured by the summer population, and because few shrikes breed north of southern Illinois. Most migrants have probably departed by early October, because numbers seem to stabilize for the duration of the winter after that time.

WINTER—During winter, shrikes are most numerous in the Shawnee Hills and the southern Floodplains and least numerous in the Till Plain. They sometimes attack small birds at feeders.

48, Horseshoe Lake CBC, 21 Dec 1982

35, Crab Orchard NWR CBC, 28 Dec 1974

26, Union Co. CBC, 31 Dec 1972
9, Rend Lake CBC, 31 Dec 1988

DOCUMENTATION: Specimen—ad., 2 miles s.e. of Murphysboro, Jackson Co., 4 Feb 1971 (SIU A-1728).

FIELD GUIDES: G=260; N=334; P=224.

Family Sturnidae: Starlings

European Starling *Sturnus vulgaris*

STATUS AND ABUNDANCE: Common year-round resident.

HABITAT: Nearly ubiquitous. Most common in residential areas and around farms. Generally not found within the largest forest tracts in the Shawnee Hills.

RECORDS AND REMARKS: Starlings were introduced to New York in the late 1800s and spread to Illinois by 1922 (Ford 1956, Bohlen 1978). Large flocks migrate through southern Illinois in fall and early spring. They often join flocks and roosts with other blackbird species. Very large roosts are common during winter, especially near strip mines. The spring migrations are most noticeable from late February through March, but fall migration is spread out over many weeks. The first autumnal migration is the formation of flocks of juveniles in their gray plumage during June and July. They are joined by adults in September and October, sometimes later. Migrant flocks are difficult to separate from the huge flocks that move daily over wide areas to and from their winter roosts. Starlings begin nesting in February and may raise as many as three broods during a summer. They compete for nest cavities with bluebirds and woodpeckers and will readily nest in nest boxes. Few observers pay them much attention, because of the stigma attached to Starlings as an introduced species.

DOCUMENTATION: Specimen—ad. male, near Old DuQuoin, Perry Co., 10 Oct 1967 (SIU A-1597).

FIELD GUIDES: G=260; N=346; P=256.

Family Vireonidae: Vireos

White-eyed Vireo *Vireo griseus*

Mid-April–Early October

STATUS AND ABUNDANCE: Common migrant and summer resident.

HABITAT: Old fields with scattered shrubs, hedgerows, woodland edge, and treefalls in forests.

RECORDS AND REMARKS: These loud songsters are the source of one of the most familiar sounds of southern Illinois spring and summer. They begin singing immediately on their spring arrival, and they sing all day, everyday, until late in the summer.

SPRING—In most years, the first spring migrants arrive in mid-April, but sometimes a few are detected during the first week of the month. Migration peaks in early May, when forty or more white-eyes can be easily counted by a single observer in a day. Most migrants have probably departed by 20 May.

1, Jackson Co., 5 Apr 1975 (PB)
1, Carbondale, 7 Apr 1986 (TF)
1, Saline Co., 9 Apr 1988 (WDR)
245, Union Co., 4 May 1991 (SBC)
135, Jackson Co., 7 May 1977 (SBC)
62, Giant City SP, 12 May 1984 (WDR)

SUMMER—Nest building begins by late April. Nests are hung from the fork of branches 0.3 to 3.0 meters above ground; they are usually placed in dense vegetation, but occasionally they are simply built in the open in a sapling—even then they are remarkably easily overlooked. These vireos are heavily parasitized by cowbirds; 39 percent of fifty-one nests in Union and Alexander Cos. were parasitized and received an average of 1.5 cowbird eggs per nest. Parasitism and high nest predation rates combine to severely reduce vireo reproductive success. Less than 15 percent of White-eyed Vireos banded at Trail of Tears SF during the late summers of 1990–1992 were juveniles.

27, Devil's Kitchen Lake, Williamson Co., 27 May 1985 (WDR)

AUTUMN—Fall migration is inconspicuous because of the large breeding population, but numbers begin to increase during late August. By early October, most white-eyes have departed.

White-eyed Vireo at nest, Ozark, Johnson Co., June 1994

14, n. Union Co., 21 Sep 1986 (WDR)

2, Crab Orchard NWR, 9 Oct 1982 (JCR)

DOCUMENTATION: Specimen—ad. male, 2 miles n. of Cobden, Union Co., 9 May 1966 (SIU A-1348).

FIELD GUIDES: G=264; N=348; P=228.

Bell's Vireo *Vireo bellii*

Early May–Early September

STATUS AND ABUNDANCE: Locally uncommon migrant and summer resident in the Till Plain. Rare migrant in the Floodplains and the Shawnee Hills.

HABITAT: Shrubby areas and hedgerows in prairielike fields. Regularly found on reclaimed strip mines with some scattered trees and shrubs.

RECORDS AND REMARKS: Males sing all summer, even during the hottest part of the day. The best places to find these vireos are in the Till Plain, especially around Rend Lake and the strip mines in Franklin and Williamson Cos.

SPRING—A very few arrive the last couple of days of April, but most do not arrive until the first week of May. Few are seen away from the breeding areas, so one seen in Pope Co. on 3 June 1984 must have been a late migrant.

1, Carbondale, 29 Apr 1972 (VK, PB)

1, Rend Lake, Jefferson Co., 30 Apr 1988 (TF)

2, Mermet Lake CA, 5 May 1984 (WDR)

1, Pulaski Co., 11 May 1991 (TF, JD)

1, Pope Co., 3 June 1984 (JCR)

SUMMER—This is probably one of the few species that has benefited to some extent from strip-mining. Reclaimed strip mines with extensive, savanna-like habitat are one of the best places to find Bell's Vireos. Whether they are productive there or not remains to be studied, because they are common victims of cowbird parasitism.

5, Williamson Co., 10 July 1983 (JCR)

7, Rend Lake, 19 July 1981 (MMl)

AUTUMN—Rarely detected during fall, Bell's Vireos seem to simply disappear until the following spring. Most migrants probably pass through (or over) the region in August, but few have been observed.

1, s.e. Saline Co., 18 Aug 1994 (JD)

1, Gallatin Co., 6 Sep 1986 (WDR)

1, Jackson Co., 20 Sep 1984 (TF)

1, n. Union Co., 21 Sep 1986 (WDR)

DOCUMENTATION: Specimen—imm. female, Carbondale, Jackson Co., 1 Sep 1966 (SIU A-1683).

FIELD GUIDES: G=264; N=350; P=228.

Solitary Vireo *Vireo solitarius*

Late April–Early May
Mid-September–Late October

STATUS AND ABUNDANCE: Uncommon migrant.

HABITAT: Deciduous woodland and woodland edge; sometimes coniferous woods.

RECORDS AND REMARKS: Although this vireo is uncommon, it may be overlooked because its song is similar to the more common Red-eyed Vireo. Solitaries have a higher-pitched, sweeter song, with longer pauses between the phrases. They usually forage in the canopy or upper levels of the understory, which adds to the difficulty of detecting them. They forage by scanning foliage and bark from a perched position, then fly up to glean prey. If they are even seen in a day, counts of one to three birds are the norm.

SPRING—Most arrival dates are in the last few days of April, but some return in mid-April. Their peak passage is during the first week of May, and most have departed by 10 May, but George (1968) lists 19 May as the latest departure date.

1, Carbondale, 14 Apr 1986 (TF)
1, Ozark, Johnson Co., 24 Apr 1992 (JD, TF)
7, Union Co., 4 May 1991 (SBC)

AUTUMN—Fall migration is even less conspicuous than spring, because these vireos do not sing in fall. They can sometimes be seen in mixed-species flocks of warblers wandering along a forest edge. Peak fall migration is during the last week of September and early October.

1, LaRue Pine Hills, 30 Aug 1990 (BD)
1, Carbondale, 12 Sep 1986 (WDR)
1, Giant City SP, 28 Oct 1984 (JCR)

DOCUMENTATION: Specimen—ad. male, 2 miles n. of Cobden, Union Co., 27 Apr 1966 (SIU A-1350).

FIELD GUIDES: G=262; N=350; P=228.

Yellow-throated Vireo *Vireo flavifrons*
Mid-April–Late September

STATUS AND ABUNDANCE: Fairly common migrant and summer resident.

HABITAT: Upland and bottomland deciduous woods.

RECORDS AND REMARKS: Forages by gleaning arthropod prey off the bark of large branches and foliage in the forest canopy. If not

Yellow-throated Vireo at nest with cowbird nestling, Teal Pond, Pope Co., 27 May 1991

for their distinctive, hoarse, slow vireo song, they could be easily overlooked. These vireos seem to occur at fairly low densities in extensive forest tracts, but their territories are large and evenly dispersed throughout the forest.

SPRING—The first arrivals usually appear early in the second week of April. Peak passage of migrants occurs in late April and early May. Because of the breeding population, the end of spring migration is difficult to determine.

1, Union Co. CA, 5 Apr 1991 (TF, JD)

1, s.e. Saline Co., 6 Apr 1986 (SO)

1, Crab Orchard NWR, 15 Apr 1970 (VK)
26, Cache River, Johnson Co., 24 Apr 1973 (VK, HDB)
87, Union Co., 4 May 1991 (SBC)
SUMMER—Nests are placed in the fork of a horizontal branch from five to twenty-five meters above ground; most nests are placed in the canopy, so there is not much data on nesting success from the region. The limited data available suggest that these vireos are heavily parasitized by cowbirds.
AUTUMN—Like many other species with substantial regional summer populations, the fall migration is not remarkable. They sometimes sing during fall, which enhances their detectability. Most are gone by the last days of September.
8, n. Union Co., 21 Sep 1986 (WDR)
1, Crab Orchard NWR, 9 Oct 1982 (JCR)

DOCUMENTATION: Specimen—ad. female, Bald Knob, Union Co., 30 Apr 1966 (SIU A-1349).

FIELD GUIDES: G=264; N=348; P=228.

Warbling Vireo *Vireo gilvus*

Mid-April–Late September

STATUS AND ABUNDANCE: Common migrant and summer resident.

HABITAT: Open, parklike woods near streams and lakes; occasionally residential areas; also riparian woods along rivers.

RECORDS AND REMARKS: Drably plumaged, these vireos forage by gleaning insects from foliage in the understory and canopy of trees, especially along the edges of lakes and rivers. Graber et al. (1985) suggest that they are more common in the western regions of southern Illinois than in the eastern regions.
SPRING—Most early arrivals have been found in willows along the edges of water courses. Migration peaks in early May, and most migrants have passed by mid-May.
1, Union Co. CA, 10 Apr 1992 (TF)
7, Union Co., 16 Apr 1986 (WDR)
77, Union Co., 9 May 1987 (SBC)
1 in upland forest, Trail of Tears SF, 18 May 1990 (WDR)
SUMMER—The breeding population seems to be highest in the

forest corridor along the Mississippi River. Few nest data are available, but what is available suggests that Warbling Vireos are common victims of cowbird parasitism, although the intensity seems to be less than in the forest vireos. Nests are placed from three to twenty-five meters above ground. Eggs are laid from late April through late June.

55, Randolph Co., 19 May 1988 (WDR)

AUTUMN—Few are seen after the breeding season, especially from late July through mid-August, because of the decrease in singing; there is some resurgence of song in late August, but it is infrequent. Generally, less than three birds are seen per day.

1, Ozark, Johnson Co., 12 Sep 1987 (TF)
1, Giant City SP, 24 Sep 1983 (JCR)
1, Crab Orchard NWR, 30 Sep 1972 (VK)

DOCUMENTATION: Specimen—ad. male, 2 miles n. of Cobden, Union Co., 27 Apr 1966 (SIU A-1350).

FIELD GUIDES: G=266; N=352; P=226.

Philadelphia Vireo *Vireo philadelphicus*

Early May–Late May
Early September–Early October

STATUS AND ABUNDANCE: Occasional migrant.

HABITAT: Upland and bottomland deciduous forest.

RECORDS AND REMARKS: Easily overlooked because its song is so similar to that of the Red-eyed Vireo; Philadelphias tend to repeat their phrases more often, and their songs are somewhat higher pitched, with longer pauses between them. They forage from midunderstory to high in the forest canopy.

SPRING—The first "Phillies" of the year are usually seen around the first of May; peak numbers pass through the region in mid-May, but daily counts are less than five birds. Most have departed by 20 May, but some may linger even into June.

1, Ozark, Johnson Co., 30 Apr 1989 (TF)
1, Crab Orchard NWR, 3 May 1984 (JCR)
5, Massac Co., 4 May 1985 (WDR)

1, near Jonesboro, Union Co., 25 May 1990 (Robinson and Robinson 1992)

male, s. Randolph Co., 11 June 1989 (WDR)

AUTUMN—Fall arrivals may appear as early as August, but most are not detected until September. Few are seen during fall, because they are usually silent and forage in the canopy.

1, Rend Lake, 16 Aug 1986 (RP)

1, Gallatin Co., 6 Sep 1986 (WDR)

2 banded, Carbondale, 17 Sep 1971 (VK)

1, near Carbondale, 8 Oct 1968 (PG)

1, s.e. Jackson Co., 8 Oct 1986 (WDR)

DOCUMENTATION: Specimen—ad. male, 2 miles n. of Cobden, Union Co., 19 May 1966 (SIU A-1393).

FIELD GUIDES: G=266; N=352; P=226.

Red-eyed Vireo *Vireo olivaceus*

Late April–Early October

STATUS AND ABUNDANCE: Common migrant and summer resident.

HABITAT: Upland and bottomland deciduous forests.

RECORDS AND REMARKS: One of our most common forest birds; its monotonous, persistent song is a familiar sound from April through August.

SPRING—The first migrants appear in mid-April in some years, but usually the first Red-eyes are detected after 20 April. Migration peaks in early May, and numbers substantially decrease after 20 May. Red-eyes seem to form small aggregations of singing males in large forest tracts during the breeding season.

1, Pomona, 13 Apr 1985 (JCR)

305, Union Co., 4 May 1991 (SBC)

70, Jackson Co., 8 May 1976 (SBC)

SUMMER—Heavily parasitized by cowbirds; eleven of twelve nests found in Union Co. were parasitized and contained an average of 2.4 cowbird eggs per nest (INHS). Few Red-eye fledglings are produced in this region. Nests are placed two to twenty-five meters high, with most between five and fifteen meters. Graber et al. (1985) discuss the nesting cycle.

AUTUMN—The breeding population obscures the arrival of the first migrants. Migration is not conspicuous, even during peak passage in September; daily counts of less than eight birds are normal. The last migrants are typically gone by 10 October, but few may linger until the last week of October.

4, s.e. Jackson Co., 8 Oct 1986 (WDR)
1, Crab Orchard NWR, 15 Oct 1984 (JCR)

DOCUMENTATION: Specimen—ad. male, Crab Orchard NWR, Williamson Co., 16 Apr 1961 (SIU A-1208).

FIELD GUIDES: G=266; N=352; P=226.

Family Emberizidae: Emberizids

Subfamily Parulinae: Wood-Warblers

[Bachman's Warbler *Vermivora bachmanii*]

STATUS AND ABUNDANCE: Hypothetical.

RECORDS AND REMARKS: There are two published reports of this probably extinct warbler. A male observed at Crab Orchard NWR on 25 April 1951 (LB) is probably a valid record, but unfortunately no documentary details were preserved (George 1968). Another male, viewed briefly and heard singing from a thicket near Cache, Alexander Co., on 20 July 1958, was discounted by the observers themselves based in part on the brevity of the sighting (Graber et al. 1983).

FIELD GUIDES: G=272; N=356; P=242.

Blue-winged Warbler *Vermivora pinus*

Mid-April–Mid-September

STATUS AND ABUNDANCE: Fairly common migrant and locally fairly common summer resident in the Shawnee Hills. Uncommon migrant and locally uncommon summer resident in the Floodplains and the Till Plain.

HABITAT: Bushy clearings and old fields.

RECORDS AND REMARKS: Very local. They can be quite common where extensive areas of second growth are present, but away from that habitat, they are rarely encountered. Most of the time, the familiar *Zeeee-bzzzz* song is heard, but male blue-wings also sing at least three other types of songs, which can even be quite confusing for experienced listeners (Graber et al. 1983). Blue-wings occasionally hybridize with Golden-winged Warblers; there is apparently only one record from southern Illinois of either of the two types: a Brewster's Warbler was seen at Crab Orchard NWR on 6 May 1953 (LB).

SPRING—The first arrivals are usually males singing their distinctive song; in most years, the first birds are detected after 15 April. Migration probably extends into mid-May, but the presence of the breeding population obscures the migration patterns.

1, Pomona, 10 Apr 1991 (KM)
1, Pomona, 14 Apr 1972 (VK)
1, Alexander Co., 17 Apr 1988 (TF, WDR)
17, Union Co., 4 May 1991 (SBC)

SUMMER—Blue-wings breed early in spring; nests with eggs have been found as early as late April. Nests are placed on the ground, under an overhanging tussock of grass or a fern, so they are difficult to find. They are parasitized by cowbirds, but not enough nests have been discovered to quantify the impacts that cowbirds may have on their reproductive success.

8, Pope Co., 28 May 1986 (WDR)
13, Giant City SP, all June 1986 (TF)
7, Kinkaid Lake, Jackson Co., 5 June 1983 (JCR)

AUTUMN—Very inconspicuous after breeding ceases, so the fall migration is hardly noticeable; rarely is more than one bird seen in a day. The first arrivals may appear in early or mid-August, and most birds are gone by 15 September.

1 banded, Carbondale, 8 Aug 1970 (VK)
male, Carbondale, 14 Aug 1988 (WDR)
1, Pomona, 18 Sep 1982 (TF)
1, Rend Lake, Franklin Co., 30 Sep 1989 (WDR)

DOCUMENTATION: Specimen—ad. male, Bald Knob, Union Co., 30 Apr 1966 (SIU A-1356).

FIELD GUIDES: G=272; N=354; P=238.

Golden-winged Warbler *Vermivora chrysoptera*
Late April–Mid-May
Late August–Late September

STATUS AND ABUNDANCE: Uncommon spring migrant. Occasional fall migrant.

HABITAT: Deciduous woods and woodland edge.

RECORDS AND REMARKS: Generally forage in the understory or lower canopy of forests, but are often overlooked because their song is not very loud. Although they are found in both bottomland and upland forest, they seem to be more numerous in uplands.

SPRING—Typically, less than five birds are seen in a day, even during peak passage in early May. The first arrivals are usually detected during the last few days of April, and most birds have departed by 15 May.

1, s.e. Jackson Co., 23 Apr 1989 (WDR)
1, Williamson Co., 27 Apr 1985 (JCR)
34, Union Co., 4 May 1991 (SBC)
1 female, Ft. Kaskaskia SP, Randolph Co., 23 May 1973 (VK)
1, Trail of Tears SF, 28 May 1992 (TRR)

AUTUMN—Very inconspicuous during fall migration; usually encountered in small mixed-species flocks of warblers foraging along forest edge. Peak numbers probably pass through the region in early September.

1, Saline Co. CA, 18 Aug 1987 (WDR)
1, Pinckneyville, Perry Co., 24 Aug 1987 (TF)
1, Giant City SP, 23 Sep 1989 (BD)
1 banded, Carbondale, 27 Sep 1971 (VK)

DOCUMENTATION: Specimen—ad. male, 2 miles n. of Cobden, Union Co., 3 May 1966 (SIU A-1355).

FIELD GUIDES: G=272; N=354; P=242.

Tennessee Warbler *Vermivora peregrina*
Late April–Late May
Late August–Mid-October

STATUS AND ABUNDANCE: Common migrant.

HABITAT: Found in nearly any place with trees, including forests, towns, and farmsteads. Most numerous in mature forests. During autumn, they also forage in weedy patches and hedgerows.

RECORDS AND REMARKS: An extremely vociferous and common migrant, Tennessees fill the spring air with their monotonous three-part trill. They apparently hold small territories for a few days at a time during migration, and they may actually mate before reaching their breeding grounds (Quay 1989). During fall they are nearly as common, but the lack of song gives the impression that they are not; they have a fairly distinctive call note, however, that can be learned with practice. They forage from near ground level well up into the canopy.

SPRING—First arrivals are typically detected by 20 April, numbers peak in early to mid-May, and the latest departures are usually gone by 30 May.

1, Pomona, 14 Apr 1979 (MMl)
20, Oakwood Bottoms, Jackson Co., 22 Apr 1972 (VK, DH)
408, Union Co., 4 May 1991 (SBC)
84, Massac Co., 9 May 1987 (SBC)
1, Mermet Lake CA, 4 June 1973 (DH)
1, Dutch Creek, Jonesboro, Union Co., 7 June 1990 (Robinson and Robinson 1992)

AUTUMN—Form small monospecific flocks or join mixed-species flocks of warblers along woodland edge. First arrivals appear during mid- to late August, but there are several July records for central Illinois, so a few may appear in the region even earlier than our records indicate. Peak numbers occur from mid-September through early October, and most have departed southward by 20 October.

1, Saline Co. CA, 18 Aug 1987 (WDR)
38, Jackson and Union Cos., 13 Sep 1975 (BP)
1, near Little Grassy Lake, Williamson Co., 25 Oct 1987 (WDR)
1, Jackson Co., 28 Oct 1984 (JCR)
1, Murphysboro, 29 Oct 1949 (RB)

DOCUMENTATION: Specimen—male, Pomona, Jackson Co., 29 Sep 1968 (SIU A-1664).

FIELD GUIDES: G=274; N=356; P=240.

Orange-crowned Warbler *Vermivora celata*
Mid-April–Early May
Late September–Late October

STATUS AND ABUNDANCE: Uncommon migrant. Very rare winter visitor.

HABITAT: Woodland edge, hedgerows, and forest understory.

RECORDS AND REMARKS: Inconspicuous; its song is a weak trill that is heard only infrequently. Usually found near dense cover along edges. Forages on trees and shrubs for insects and probably for nectar from flowers, and also forages for insects on leaf surfaces. Generally encountered as single individuals, but they sometimes associate with other warbler flocks, especially during fall.

SPRING—Some arrive in early April, but most often, the first arrivals are not detected until after 15 April. There is not really a conspicuous peak either, because it is unusual to count more than three birds in a day. Late departure dates are early compared to most other warbler species; nearly all Orange-crowns have departed by 10 May.

1, Giant City SP, 6 Apr 1986 (WDR)
1, Carbondale, 8 Apr 1986 (WDR)
7, Union Co., 4 May 1991 (SBC)
1, Giant City SP, 11 May 1989 (WDR)

AUTUMN—Rarely encountered before the last few days of September. Orange-crowns frequent shrubs and dense cover along woodland edge and respond well to spishing. They have a distinctive, forceful chip note that can be learned with practice. Most birds are gone by the end of October, but a few may linger into winter.

1, Rend Lake, Jefferson Co., 2 Sep 1988 (TF)
3, Ozark, Johnson Co., 8 Oct 1989 (TF)
1, Crab Orchard NWR, 29 Oct 1989 (WDR)
1 banded, Carbondale, 31 Oct 1970 (VK)

WINTER—The few winter records are of birds encountered in hedgerows, often where small flocks of sparrows were present.

1, Horseshoe Lake CBC, 18 Dec 1984
1, Cypress Creek NWR, 21 Dec 1994 (TF)

1, Crab Orchard NWR CBC, 4 Jan 1976
1, Crab Orchard NWR, 18 Jan 1983 (JCR)

DOCUMENTATION: Specimen—male, Carbondale, Jackson Co., 17 Oct 1960 (SIU A-1114).

FIELD GUIDES: G=274; N=356; P=240.

Nashville Warbler *Vermivora ruficapilla*

Late April–Mid-May
Late August–Mid-October

STATUS AND ABUNDANCE: Fairly common spring migrant. Uncommon fall migrant.

HABITAT: Woodland edge, hedgerows, and deciduous woods.

RECORDS AND REMARKS: Found from low in the understory to the lower and middle portions of forest canopy. Has a migration schedule very similar to that of the Tennessee Warbler, and the first spring arrivals of both warblers are often detected on the same day. Much less numerous than Tennessee Warblers, however.

SPRING—Nearly as vocal as Tennessee Warblers; their song is composed of a two-part (rather than three-part) trill. First arrivals appear around 20 April, migration peaks in late April and early May, and the last migrants are typically gone by 15 May.

1, Pomona, 14 Apr 1993 (KM)
1, Oakwood Bottoms, Jackson Co., 16 Apr 1986 (WDR)
60, Union Co., 4 May 1991 (SBC)
28, Massac Co., 5 May 1984 (SBC)
1, Giant City SP, 16 May 1989 (WDR)

AUTUMN—The first fall arrivals are generally not reported until after 1 September, but they certainly arrive before that each year. There are no high counts available, but daily counts of up to ten birds are not unexpected for late September and early October; Nashvilles are regular participants in mixed-species flocks of warblers. A few lingering birds are seen into the first few days of November—very rarely even later.

1, Saline Co. CA, 18 Aug 1987 (WDR)
1, Williamson Co., 19 Oct 1983 (JCR)
1, Crab Orchard NWR, 3 Nov 1990 (WDR)

1, Union Co. CA, 23 Dec 1993 (HDB)

DOCUMENTATION: Specimen—male, 2 miles n. of Cobden, Union Co., 25 Apr 1966 (SIU A-1360).

FIELD GUIDES: G=274; N=358; P=244.

Northern Parula *Parula americana*

Early April–Early October

STATUS AND ABUNDANCE: Common spring migrant and summer resident. Uncommon fall migrant. Very rare winter visitor.

HABITAT: Breeds in mature deciduous woods. More numerous in bottomland than upland woods during the breeding season, but migrants regularly use both habitats. Graber et al. (1983) reported American sycamore to be an important component of Parula habitat. Fall migrants are also regularly found in forest edge.

RECORDS AND REMARKS: Found from the upper understory to the very top of the forest canopy. Forages by gleaning arthropods from leaves, often hovering briefly at the terminal clusters of leaves on the outer edge of a tree's canopy. There are several different song types, but all are buzzy.

SPRING—One of the first warbler species to return in spring; most early arrivals are detected in the first few days of April. The peak of spring migration is somewhat obscured by the breeding population, but Parulas are especially common during late April and early May. The departure of northward bound migrants is unclear.

1, Fountain Bluff, Jackson Co., 29 Mar 1986 (SO)
1, s.e. Saline Co., 31 Mar 1986 (SO)
61, Cache River, Johnson Co., 24 Apr 1973 (HDB, VK)
105, Union Co., 4 May 1991 (SBC)

SUMMER—Few nests have been found, because they are often placed in vine tangles or dense clusters of leaves high in the canopy. Of two nests for which the contents could be determined, one was parasitized by cowbirds (INHS). The lowest nest found was six meters over a gravel road, in a pine tree at Pine Hills, Union Co. Parulas are frequently parasitized, however, because there have been many sightings of adults feeding fledgling cowbirds.

AUTUMN—Like many migrant species that breed in the region,

Parulas just seem to disappear after the breeding season. A few are found with flocks of other warbler species along forest edge, but it is unusual to find more than two in a day, especially after 10 September.

1, Rend Lake, Franklin Co., 4 Oct 1986 (TF, WDR)

1, Carbondale, 13 Oct 1983 (TF)

WINTER—One adult was found freshly dead in a pine plantation near Cypress Creek NWR on 20 December 1994 (TF, specimen at ISM).

DOCUMENTATION: Specimen—male, Crab Orchard NWR, Williamson Co., 11 Apr 1956 (SIU A-246).

FIELD GUIDES: G=276; N=358; P=230.

Yellow Warbler *Dendroica petechia*

Mid-April–Mid-September

STATUS AND ABUNDANCE: Common migrant. Fairly common summer resident.

HABITAT: Wet woodland edges, willow thickets, and hedgerows bordering streams.

RECORDS AND REMARKS: There is some suggestion that this warbler has experienced a substantial population decline in recent times, at least in part because of habitat destruction and perhaps also because of cowbird parasitism (Graber et al. 1983). Nevertheless, it remains one of the most common breeding species of riparian thickets and wet woodland edges. They are also numerous on surface-mined lands.

SPRING—Most first arrivals are not detected until after 15 April, although a few appear earlier, especially in unusually warm springs. Peak migration occurs during late April and early May. The breeding population obscures the departure of the latest migrants, but migration may extend into late May, because a singing male was encountered in upland forest habitat near Atwood Ridge, Union Co., on 25 May 1991 (WDR).

1, Union Co., 10 Apr 1992 (TF)

1, Mermet Lake CA, 11 Apr 1986 (WDR)

87, Massac Co., 5 May 1984 (WDR)

SUMMER—Nests are placed from one to twelve meters up in the crotch of a tree, usually along the banks of some body of water. They can be difficult to find, because they are often well hidden among a cluster of leaves. Cowbirds readily parasitize Yellow Warblers' nests, but there are no quantitative data available from southern Illinois to assess the impact of cowbirds on Yellow Warblers. One defensive strategy Yellow Warblers employ against parasitism is to build a layer of nesting material over the cowbird egg and the remainder of their own clutch and then lay a new clutch. Few birds use upland shrubby habitats for breeding in southern Illinois, which contrasts with their habits in central and northern Illinois, where they regularly use such habitat.

AUTUMN—As with many breeding species, Yellow Warblers seem to disappear after their breeding season, which is somewhat surprising because they have an extensive breeding population to the north of Illinois. Their peak passage through southern Illinois seems to occur during August.

male, Rend Lake, Jefferson Co., 7 Sep 1988 (TF, WDR)
1, Carbondale, 17 Sep 1971 (VK)

DOCUMENTATION: Specimen—male, Carbondale, Jackson Co., 5 May 1961 (SIU A-1111).

FIELD GUIDES: G=278; N=370; P=238.

Chestnut-sided Warbler *Dendroica pensylvanica*

Late April–Late May
Late August–Early October

STATUS AND ABUNDANCE: Fairly common migrant. Very rare summer resident.

HABITAT: Forest edge and deciduous woodland during migration. Summer visitors have been found in clearcuts with extremely dense patches of regenerating vegetation.

RECORDS AND REMARKS: Forages from midheights to midcanopy of forests and edges. The many different song types can make identification by voice somewhat problematic.

SPRING—Usually first detected during the last few days of April, becoming numerous during the first and second weeks of May, and

Chestnut-sided Warbler (female) at nest, northeast Johnson Co., July 1990

mostly absent after 25 May. A few regularly linger into the first few days of June.

1, Murphysboro, Jackson Co., 23 Apr 1970 (VK)
1, Crab Orchard NWR, 26 Apr 1985 (JCR)
90, Union Co., 4 May 1991 (SBC)
22, Alexander Co., 8 May 1976 (SBC)
1, Giant City SP, 2 June 1984 (EC)
male, Trail of Tears SF, 5 June 1992 (WDR)
male, s.e. Massac Co., 15 June 1989 (VK)

SUMMER—Southern Illinois is at least 250 miles south of the usual southern limit of the breeding range, but Chestnut-sideds have opportunistically extended their breeding range in response to the availability of appropriate habitat in some of the clearcuts in southeastern Illinois. Not all clearcuts have had summering Chestnut-sideds, however; none have been found in the clearcuts of southwestern Illinois, but summering birds have been detected in

at least three clearcuts in Johnson and Pope Cos. The one confirmed nesting record is of a pair that built a nest 1.2 meters up in a patch of blackberry brambles in a clearcut in northeast Johnson Co.; the nest had three warbler eggs, two of which were hatching, when it was discovered on 26 June 1990 (WDR, TF). The nest successfully fledged two young on 4 or 5 July. The third egg was apparently infertile; it was collected and deposited at ISM.
2 males, Williams Hill, Pope Co., 27 May–at least 22 June 1990 (SKR, TF, WDR)
AUTUMN—Most birds are in nonbreeding plumage upon arrival in August. This species is one of the most common participants in mixed-species flocks of warblers. Most migrants have departed by 10 October.
2, Saline Co. CA, 18 Aug 1987 (WDR)
14, Crab Orchard NWR, 13 Sep 1986 (WDR)
1, Carbondale, 11 Oct 1970 (VK)
1, Williamson Co., 15 Oct 1983 (JCR)

DOCUMENTATION: Specimen—male, 2 miles n. of Cobden, Union Co., 8 May 1966 (SIU A-1367).

FIELD GUIDES: G=284; N=362; P=236.

Magnolia Warbler *Dendroica magnolia*

Early May–Late May
Early September–Mid-October

STATUS AND ABUNDANCE: Fairly common migrant.

HABITAT: Understory of deciduous woods and forest edge. During fall migration, also found in hedgerows.

RECORDS AND REMARKS: Forage among dense foliage in the understory and lower canopy of forest and forest edge. Often associated with forest gaps where dense vegetation is common. Their song is distinctive but somewhat inconspicuous. In fall, most birds are in nonbreeding plumage.
SPRING—First arrivals usually appear around 1 May, but they may occur as early as 14 April (George 1968). They are most numerous from 5 to 15 May; some linger into very late May or early June.

Usually less than five or six are counted in a day, but during "fall-out" days they can be quite common.

1, Pomona, and 1, New Burnside, Johnson Co., 28 Apr 1989 (TF, WDR)

52, Union Co., 4 May 1991 (SBC)

18, Massac Co., 10 May 1986 (WDR)

1, Johnson Co., 30 May 1988 (TF)

1, Giant City SP, 2 June 1984 (EC)

AUTUMN—Some may arrive during August, but first fall arrivals are most often detected in early September. Less than five or six are usually seen per day during peak passage, but occasionally more are seen. Most have departed by about 15 October.

3, Rend Lake, Jefferson Co., 7 Sep 1988 (TF, WDR)

1 banded, Carbondale, 10 Sep 1971 (VK)

1, Williamson Co., 19 Oct 1983 (JCR)

DOCUMENTATION: Specimen—male, Crab Orchard NWR, Williamson Co., Apr 1961 (SIU A-1216).

FIELD GUIDES: G=278; N=362; P=234.

Cape May Warbler *Dendroica tigrina*

Early May–Mid-May
Early September–Mid-October

STATUS AND ABUNDANCE: Uncommon spring migrant. Occasional fall migrant. Very rare winter visitor.

HABITAT: Principally found in deciduous woodland, but also found in patches of large spruce trees (such as those at cemeteries) and even in willow thickets along the edges of bottomland forest.

RECORDS AND REMARKS: An easily overlooked species because of its very high-pitched, lisping song. Forages by gleaning insects from leaves and flowers, from midheights to the upper canopy. Conspicuously variable in numbers from year to year.

SPRING—Not usually encountered before 30 April. Even in years when populations are high, most daily high counts do not exceed three birds. Few are detected after 15 May.

16, Union Co., 4 May 1991 (SBC)

6, Massac Co., 9 May 1987 (WDR)

4, Rend Lake, 15 May 1992 (TF, JD)
1, Giant City SP, 16 May 1989 (WDR)
AUTUMN—Even less numerous in fall than in spring. Participates in mixed-species flocks of warblers that forage along forest edge. Most birds have departed by late October, but a few may linger later, even into winter on rare occasions.
1, Crab Orchard NWR, 2 Sep 1976 (BP)
2, Carbondale, 30 Sep 1989 (JH)
1, Carbondale, 22 Oct 1983 (TF)
1, Carterville, Williamson Co., 11–21 Nov 1973 (MH)
WINTER—1 visiting a feeder, Makanda, Jackson Co., 7 Dec 1983 (PHu)

DOCUMENTATION: Specimen—male, 2 miles n. of Cobden, Union Co., 14 May 1966 (SIU A-1398).

FIELD GUIDES: G=278; N=362; P=236.

Black-throated Blue Warbler *Dendroica caerulescens*

Late April–Mid-May
Mid-September–Mid-October

STATUS AND ABUNDANCE: Rare migrant.

HABITAT: Dense understory of deciduous woods; woodland edge.

RECORDS AND REMARKS: One of the region's rarest warblers. Its diagonal migration path takes the bulk of its population well north of the region in both spring and fall. Forages in the understory and lower levels of the forest canopy. Their lazy, buzzy song is distinctive.
SPRING—Most records are from the first half of May; but some have been detected as early as mid-April (e.g., 19 Apr 1927 [Cahn and Hyde 1929]).
2, Cave Creek Valley, Jackson Co., 29 Apr 1967 (WGG, PG)
male, LaRue Pine Hills, 4 May 1975 (BP)
male, s.e. Jackson Co., 6 May 1984 (WDR)
male, Union Co., 8 May 1993 (SKR)
1, Crab Orchard NWR, 11 May 1947 (JWH), and 1 there on 17 May 1951 (LB)
1, Giant City SP, 19 May 1989 (WDR)

AUTUMN—Males retain breeding plumage throughout the year. This species participates in mixed-species flocks with other warblers; the best way to encounter it is to spend as many hours in the field as possible.

male, near Woodlawn, Jefferson Co., 10 Sep 1988 (TF, WDR)

1, Sparta, Randolph Co., 11 Sep 1971 (MMo)

1 female, Rend Lake, and 1 female, Giant City SP, 30 Sep 1989 (WDR, BD)

2, Murphysboro, 4 Oct 1945 (JWH)

1, near Cobden, Union Co., 4 Oct 1967 (WGG)

1, Pomona, 4 Oct 1994 (TF)

male, Giant City SP, 6 Oct 1984 (JCR)

DOCUMENTATION: Specimen—imm. male, 2 miles n. of Pomona, Jackson Co., 21 Sep 1968 (WGG 2268).

FIELD GUIDES: G=282; N=360; P=232.

Yellow-rumped Warbler *Dendroica coronata*

Mid-September–Late November
Mid-March–Early May

STATUS AND ABUNDANCE: Common migrant. Fairly common winter resident in the Shawnee Hills and the Floodplains. Uncommon winter resident in the Till Plain.

HABITAT: Found in virtually any area with trees—woods, edge, hedgerows, and towns. Frequents coniferous woods also, especially during winter. During peak migration, also occurs in marshes and old fields.

RECORDS AND REMARKS: One of the most common warbler species. Its song is unremarkable, but it is fairly loud, and that factor in combination with the recognizable chip note and the abundance of the species makes Yellow-rumps quite conspicuous. They forage mostly in the understory and canopy of forests, but they also occur near or even on the ground along edges and in marshes. There are apparently no reports of the western subspecies, Audubon's Warbler, for the region.

AUTUMN—First arrivals are most often detected in the last few

days of September. During peak migration, large numbers can be found in dispersed flocks that may pass over an area in groups of two to ten birds as they fly from one tree to another. The end of migration is obscured by the overwintering population, especially in the Shawnee Hills, where the largest winter population occurs.
1 banded, Carbondale, 17 Sep 1971 (VK)
20, Rend Lake, Jefferson Co., 24 Sep 1989 (WDR)
180, Rend Lake, Jefferson Co., 10 Oct 1987 (TF, JCR)
71, Crab Orchard NWR, 15 Oct 1983 (JCR)
WINTER—Wintering populations are highest in early winter and slowly decrease until spring migration starts. Many overwintering birds are associated with habitats that offer good cover, such as conifer stands. They often forage on poison ivy fruits and on grapes.
399, Crab Orchard NWR CBC, 19 Dec 1962
177, Union Co. CBC, 19 Dec 1971
75, Union Co. CA, 2 Jan 1976 (BP)
63, Ferne Clyffe SP, 23 Jan 1992 (TF)
SPRING—Because of the overwintering population, the beginning of spring migration is obscured, but there is a definite increase in mid- to late March. Most birds are still in nonbreeding plumage in early spring, but by mid-April, many males are gaining bright breeding plumage. Peak abundances are found in late April and the first five days of May. After 10 May, most Yellow-rumps have departed.
184, Massac Co., 5 May 1984 (SBC)
123, Massac Co., 4 May 1985 (SBC)
1, Giant City SP, 16 May 1989 (WDR)
1, Trail of Tears SF, 24 May 1990 (WDR)

DOCUMENTATION: Specimen—male, Crab Orchard NWR, Williamson Co., 11 Apr 1956 (SIU A-268).

FIELD GUIDES: G=278; N=362; P=234.

Black-throated Green Warbler *Dendroica virens*
Mid-April–Late May
Early September–Late October

STATUS AND ABUNDANCE: Fairly common spring migrant. Common fall migrant.

HABITAT: Deciduous forest and forest edge.

RECORDS AND REMARKS: Feeds for insects by gleaning leaves, from midheights up into the canopy. Its song is distinctive and markedly increases the detectability of this species during spring; its call note can be learned with practice, which aids in detecting it during fall. SPRING—There seems to be a small number of males that arrive about one month ahead of the major population of migrants. Most of these early birds were discovered in cypress swamps.
1, Horseshoe Lake CA, 25 Mar 1986 (ID)
1, Horseshoe Lake CA, 31 Mar 1984 (JCR)
1, Heron Pond NP, Johnson Co., 3 Apr 1971 (PB)
1, Heron Pond NP, Johnson Co., 9 Apr 1972 (VK)
There are curiously few similar records for the rest of Illinois, and Black-throated Greens are generally not associated with cypress later in spring. Records of other early arrivals follow:
1, Ozark, Johnson Co., 29 Mar 1992 (TF)
1, Giant City SP, 31 Mar 1992 (TF)
1, Carbondale, 4 Apr 1984 (SO)
1, Etherton, Jackson Co., 16 Apr 1971 (VK)
Peak numbers pass through in early May, with high counts usually less than a dozen or so birds per observer in a day. Most birds have departed by 25 May, but a few have lingered into June.
37, Union Co., 4 May 1991 (SBC)
14, Pope Co., 10 May 1980 (SBC)
1, n.w. Pope Co., 27 May 1986 (WDR)
male, Trail of Tears SF, 8 June 1992 (SB)
male, near Jonesboro, Union Co., 12 June 1993 (LM)
male, Trail of Tears SF, 13 June 1981 (MMl)
AUTUMN—More numerous in fall than in spring. A frequent participant in mixed-species warbler flocks. Often forages along forest edge. Peak numbers occur from mid-September to mid-October.
2, Little Grassy Lake, Williamson Co., 31 Aug 1976 (BP)
1, Heron Pond NP, Johnson Co., 4 Sep 1988 (WDR)
25, Jackson & Perry Cos., 18 Sep 1982 (JCR)
30, Giant City SP, 6 Oct 1984 (JCR)

1, Carbondale, 26 Oct 1989 (WDR)

DOCUMENTATION: Specimen—male, Pomona, Jackson Co., 29 Sep 1968 (SIU A-1662).

FIELD GUIDES: G=280; N=364; P=230.

Blackburnian Warbler *Dendroica fusca*
Late April–Late May
Late August–Early October

STATUS AND ABUNDANCE: Uncommon migrant.

HABITAT: Deciduous woods and woodland edge.

RECORDS AND REMARKS: Often found only in the mid- to upper portions of forest canopy, especially during spring. In fall, comes lower to join flocks of warblers foraging in the understory and lower canopy along forest edge.

SPRING—Most first arrivals are detected during the last few days of April. Peak numbers (usually less than five are seen in a day) are present in the first half of May, and the last migrants have usually left by 25 May. A few birds routinely occur later, even into early June.

1, Simpson, Johnson Co., 17 Apr 1989 (TF)

1, Hamburg Hill, Union Co., 18 Apr 1992 (WDR, TF)

29, Union Co., 4 May 1991 (SBC)

7, Saline Co., 13 May 1988 (WDR)

male, Atwood Ridge, Union Co., 7 June 1990 (SKR)

male, Trail of Tears SF, 15 June 1992 (WDR)

AUTUMN—Usually not encountered until September. Less numerous than in spring, with typical daily high counts of less than three birds.

1, Crab Orchard NWR, 23 Aug 1987 (WDR)

1, near Woodlawn, Jefferson Co., 10 Sep 1988 (TF, WDR)

1, Union Co., 11 Oct 1975 (BP)

1, s.e. Saline Co., 11 Oct 1985 (SO)

DOCUMENTATION: Specimen—female, 20 miles n.w. of Carbondale, Jackson Co., 22 May 1968 (SIU A-1661).

FIELD GUIDES: G=284; N=360; P=236.

Yellow-throated Warbler *Dendroica dominica*
Early April–Late September

STATUS AND ABUNDANCE: Common migrant and summer resident.

HABITAT: Mature bottomland woods, cypress swamps, and pine woods. Also found in upland forest, especially when a large sycamore or pine is present.

RECORDS AND REMARKS: A treetop warbler that would be easily overlooked if not for its distinctive song, which has been phoneticized as *See see see look up at me*. Females are not often seen, because they do not sing, but they will sometimes come down into the understory to gather nesting material. They forage by gleaning prey from leaves and from the bark on branches.

SPRING—One of the first warblers to arrive in spring; Yellow-throateds appear as soon as the trees begin to leaf out, which is usually about 1 April. There does not seem to be any conspicuous peak of migrants, probably because the breeding range does not extend very far north of the region.
1, Heron Pond NP, Johnson Co., 27 Mar 1976 (BP)
1, Giant City SP, 29 Mar 1989 (WDR)
1, LaRue Pine Hills, 31 Mar 1985 (JCR)
32, Crab Orchard NWR, 18 Apr 1985 (JCR)
18, Cache River, Johnson Co., 24 Apr 1973 (VK, HDB)
SUMMER—Nests are small and placed high in the canopy, so few have been found; one nest found in a pine tree at Trail of Tears SF was 22 meters above the ground (INHS). Cowbird parasitism is probably common, because adults have frequently been seen feeding fledgling cowbirds. Breeding begins very early (nest building has been seen in mid-April), so Spring Bird Counts typically census nesting populations.
51, Union Co., 4 May 1991 (SBC)
15, Pope Co., 12 June 1986 (WDR)
AUTUMN—Not often observed during fall migration. Rarely are more than two or three seen in a day. Forages with other warblers along forest edge, readily coming down to the ground to bathe in puddles. Most have departed by the last week of September, but a few linger later.
1, Mt. Vernon, Jefferson Co., 22 Sep 1991 (TF)

1, Carbondale, 7 Oct 1972 (VK)
1, Giant City SP, 10 Oct 1982 (JCR)
DOCUMENTATION: Specimen—female, 2 miles n. of Cobden, Union Co., 17 Apr 1966 (SIU A-1366).
FIELD GUIDES: G=282; N=366; P=230.

Pine Warbler *Dendroica pinus*

Early March–Late October

STATUS AND ABUNDANCE: Fairly common migrant and summer resident in pine woods. Occasional migrant in deciduous forest. Rare winter resident.

HABITAT: Mature pine woods.

RECORDS AND REMARKS: A species that has taken distinct advantage of human alteration of natural habitats. Historically, Pine Warblers were probably uncommon migrants as they passed through the region on their way to and from coniferous forests in the northern United States and Canada and the southeastern United States. The native pines in the Ozark Hills of Alexander, Union, Jackson, and Randolph Cos. may have supported a breeding population, but it was almost certainly very small. Today, the extensive plantations of pine that are common in the Shawnee Hills provide abundant habitat for breeding, and probably wintering, populations. They forage by probing for insects in the terminal clusters of needles at the tips of branches and by gleaning prey from the bark of branches. There are two song types; the song typically heard in this region is very reminiscent of a junco's song. The other song type sounds more like a Chipping Sparrow or Worm-eating Warbler, but I have never heard it in this region. Reports of the latter song type from Pomona are probably of misidentified Chipping Sparrows, because "Chippies" also breed in the same pine stands.

SPRING—There seems to be two migration "pulses" into southern Illinois. The first occurs as early as late February and typically by mid-March, and it probably indicates the arrival of the local breeding population.

1 at feeder, Carbondale, mid-Feb 1971 (HC, VK)
male, Pope Co., 20 Feb 1990 (TF)

male, s.e. Jackson Co., 22 Feb 1990 (WDR)

male, Crab Orchard NWR, 26 Feb 1976 (BP)

1, Jackson Co., 5 Mar 1983 (JCR)

The second influx of migrants occurs in mid-April, with migrants continuing to occur until early May; these birds may be those that breed north of our region, perhaps in the Great Lakes states and southern Canada.

male, Mermet Lake CA, 6 May 1989 (WDR)

SUMMER—Few nests have been found, because they are placed high in pines (usually above 6 meters), among dense clusters of needles. Breeding begins early, however; nests have been found as early as 27 March, and fledglings have been seen by 24 April. They may be double-brooded, because many dependent juveniles were seen in Pope Co. in late May 1986. Although recorded in native pines during the summer, no confirmed evidence of breeding is available.

17, Pope Co., 10 May 1980 (SBC)

28, Pope Co., 27 May 1986 (WDR)

singing male in native pines, Pine Hills, Union Co., 6 June 1992 (WDR)

AUTUMN—The start of fall migration is unclear, but it probably initiates by early September, and it continues into late November. Local, postbreeding movements into areas where breeding did not take place may occur much earlier.

1 at Pine Hills Campground, 13 July 1992 (WDR)

2, Carbondale, 19 Nov 1983 (TF, JCR)

WINTER—Small numbers of Pine Warblers probably regularly overwinter, especially in areas with extensive pine woods, such as Crab Orchard NWR. Wintering birds often associate with flocks of kinglets, creepers, nuthatches, and chickadees. There are many more winter records than are reported here. Some records (all of single birds) from Crab Orchard NWR include 17 Dec 1983 (SS), 27 Dec 1954 (JWH), 28 Dec 1974 (HDB), 11 Jan 1986 (WDR), 18 Jan–16 Mar 1975 (BP), 9 Feb 1988 (WDR).

4 (2 ad. and 2 imm.), Ozark, Johnson Co., 2 Jan–14 Feb 1991 (TF)

1, Benton Lake, Franklin Co., 17 Dec 1994 (WDR)

DOCUMENTATION: Specimen—juv., Pomona, Jackson Co., 30 Apr 1976 (SIU A-1887).

FIELD GUIDES: G=286; N=368; P=238.

Prairie Warbler *Dendroica discolor*
Early April–Late September

STATUS AND ABUNDANCE: Common migrant and summer resident in the Shawnee Hills, especially in Johnson and Pope Cos. Occasional migrant in the Floodplains and the Till Plain.

HABITAT: Shrubby, upland, old fields.

RECORDS AND REMARKS: One of the most thoroughly studied North American songbirds (Nolan 1978). Easily detected in appropriate habitat by its characteristic song of evenly spaced, ascending, buzzy notes; but can be difficult to see because of the dense vegetation it favors. The song can be somewhat variable in speed and frequency; one recorded at Ferne Clyffe SP was singing a Field Sparrow song (WDR).

SPRING—First arrivals are most often detected after 10 April, though in "early" springs they may arrive earlier. There is not much of a breeding population north of the Shawnee Hills, so most birds encountered here are likely to be breeders.

1, Carbondale, 4 Apr 1991 (BD)
1, Giant City SP, 6 Apr 1986 (WDR)
1, Johnson Co., 8 Apr 1988 (TF)
87, Pope Co., 10 May 1980 (SBC)

SUMMER—Only a few nests have been found; most of them have been 0.5 to 4 meters up in a deciduous (often elm) sapling, but prairies will also nest in pine saplings. Eggs have been found in late April, but the peak of breeding probably occurs during May and June. Prairies are parasitized by cowbirds, but there is no quantitative information available. The bulk of the regional breeding population is in Pope, Johnson, eastern Union, southern Williamson, and southeastern Jackson Cos.

23 territorial males, Giant City SP, June 1986 (TF)

AUTUMN—Fall migration goes largely undetected. Most birds are gone by 15 September, but some regularly linger into the first few days of October.

1 banded, Carbondale, 9 Aug 1970 (VK)
1 singing, Ozark, Johnson Co., 17 Sep 1989 (TF)
1, Franklin Co., 23 Sep 1994 (TF)
1, New Burnside, Johnson Co., 2 Oct 1988 (TF)
1, s.e. Jackson Co., 4 Oct 1987 (WDR)

Prairie Warbler at nest, northeast Johnson Co., June 1990

1, Crab Orchard NWR, 23 Nov 1959 (LB)

DOCUMENTATION: Photograph—pair at nest, n.e. Johnson Co., June 1990 (TF).

FIELD GUIDES: G=286; N=366; P=238.

Palm Warbler *Dendroica palmarum*
Mid-April–Early May
Mid-September–Mid-October

STATUS AND ABUNDANCE: Common spring migrant. Uncommon fall migrant.

HABITAT: Woodlands, forest edge, shrubby old fields, hedgerows, marshes, and willow thickets. Uses a wide variety of habitats.

RECORDS AND REMARKS: They forage on or near the ground, though they also feed in the understory and canopy during spring

migration. They pump their tails as they hop from perch to perch. A rump patch is present, but it is often dull and inconspicuous. SPRING—The first arrivals are usually found about 20 April; peak numbers pass through in late April; and most have departed by 10 May. Although they will use forest habitats, they are most numerous in the thickets along stream courses and in savanna-like habitats.
1, Crab Orchard NWR, 13 Apr 1970 (VK)
1, Pomona, 14 Apr 1979 (MMl)
40, Perks, Pulaski Co., 23 Apr 1973 (VK, HDB)
51, Massac Co., 5 May 1984 (WDR)
1, South Ripple Hollow, Alexander Co., 13 May 1989 (SKR)
1, Little Grassy Lake, Williamson Co., 15 May 1976 (BP)
AUTUMN—Less numerous than in spring. Found along forest edges with other warbler species and in marshy habitat.
7, Carbondale, 13 Oct 1984 (TF)
1, Crab Orchard NWR, 2 Nov 1989 (EW, WDR)

DOCUMENTATION: Specimen—Bald Knob, Union Co., 30 Apr 1966 (SIU A-1659).

FIELD GUIDES: G=286; N=368; P=238.

Bay-breasted Warbler *Dendroica castanea*

Early May–Late May
Early September–Mid-October

STATUS AND ABUNDANCE: Fairly common spring migrant. Common fall migrant.

HABITAT: Mature bottomland and upland woods.

RECORDS AND REMARKS: Forage by gleaning leaves in the canopies of forests. Its high-pitched song does not carry far and can be confused with similar songs of other warbler species. Numbers seem to be highly variable from year to year, especially in spring. During fall, males are in nonbreeding plumage, which can be difficult to separate from the nonbreeding plumage of the Blackpoll Warbler. Bay-breasted Warblers are more common, often retain some wash of bay on the sides, and have dark feet and buffy undertail coverts. SPRING—Not often detected before 1 May. Numbers peak between 5 and 20 May. Most are gone by 25 May, but some may linger into early June.

3, Giant City SP, 27 Apr 1989 (WDR)
36, Massac Co., 10 May 1986 (WDR)
1, Giant City SP, 2 June 1984 (EC)

AUTUMN—First fall arrivals are usually found after 5 September. They often associate with mixed-species flocks of warblers and will forage at midheights along forest edges. Migration peaks in early October, and most birds have departed by 10 October.

1, Mermet Lake CA, 18 Aug 1988 (WDR)
12, Woodlawn, Jefferson Co., 10 Sep 1988 (TF, WDR)
18, Giant City SP, 6 Oct 1984 (JCR)
1, Atwood Ridge, Union Co., 14 Oct 1989 (WDR)
1 banded, Carbondale, 16 Oct 1971 (VK)

DOCUMENTATION: Specimen—male, 2 miles n. of Cobden, Union Co., 28 Apr 1966 (SIU A-1369).

FIELD GUIDES: G=284; N=368; P=236.

Blackpoll Warbler *Dendroica striata*

Late April–Late May
Mid-September–Mid-October

STATUS AND ABUNDANCE: Common spring migrant. Occasional fall migrant.

HABITAT: Mature deciduous woods.

RECORDS AND REMARKS: Forages in the forest canopy. Its high-pitched song is loud enough to make this species rather conspicuous during spring. In some springs, Blackpolls could be realistically categorized as abundant.

SPRING—Typically first detected during the last few days of April, but not common until the first week of May. Abundance begins to decline precipitously after 20 May, though some are usually present throughout May.

1, Carbondale, 17 Apr 1982 (SO, MMl)
1, Horseshoe Lake CA, 19 Apr 1991 (TF)
15, Oakwood Bottoms, Jackson Co., 29 Apr 1972 (VK, PB)
164, Union Co., 4 May 1991 (SBC)

125, Massac Co., 8 May 1982 (SBC)
1, Little Black Slough, Johnson Co., 25 May 1989 (WDR)
male, Trail of Tears SF, 10 June 1991 (WDR)
AUTUMN—The fall migration path takes Blackpolls east from their Canadian breeding range to the Atlantic Coast and then out over the ocean to the Bahamas, before turning due south to South America; therefore very few Blackpolls pass through this region during fall. The few that do are often in the region in late September or October.
1, Giant City SP, 12 Sep 1982 (JCR)
1, Little Grassy Lake, Williamson Co., 19 Oct 1975 (BP)
1, Carbondale, 28 Oct 1949 (JWH)
1, Murphysboro, 2 Nov 1947 (JWH)

DOCUMENTATION: Specimen—male, 2 miles n. of Cobden, Union Co., 25 Apr 1966 (SIU A-1389).

FIELD GUIDES: G=284; N=368; P=232.

Cerulean Warbler *Dendroica cerulea*

Mid-April–Early September

STATUS AND ABUNDANCE: Fairly common migrant and summer resident.

HABITAT: Forested areas with large trees; most numerous in mature bottomland forest along streams and rivers, but also found in mature upland forest. Also occurs in some disturbed forest areas where the canopy has opened up.

RECORDS AND REMARKS: A canopy species that can be difficult to see because it stays so high in mature forests. Its song is a distinctive series of buzzy notes; without its song, the species would undoubtedly be largely overlooked. Breeding Bird Survey data showed a 3.4 percent national decline per year in Cerulean populations—in large part caused by habitat destruction—which has elicited concern that the species may be in jeopardy (Sauer and Droege 1992).
SPRING—Most first arrivals are detected about 15 April, but birds are still arriving in late April. Some have been reported as early as 3 April (Graber et al. 1983), but some published early reports may be of birds that were only heard and that were actually misidentified

Northern Parulas, a species with similar song that characteristically arrives much earlier.

58, Cache River, Johnson Co., 24 Apr 1973 (VK, HDB)

17, Johnson Co., 5 May 1984 (SBC)

SUMMER—Relatively few nests have been found, although William G. George found sixteen nests in Jackson Co., all of which were in American elms (Graber et al. 1983). Most nests are placed between six and twenty-seven meters above the ground. Ceruleans are common victims of cowbird parasitism, but because their nests are difficult to find, few quantitative data are available. Nesting begins at least by 25 April and extends into June. An extensive survey of prime habitat in Cave Creek Valley, near Pomona, revealed 110 territorial males during the 1992 summer (GV).

AUTUMN—Fall migration is nearly undetected; when singing ceases after the breeding season, Ceruleans are difficult to find. Most have probably departed by late August, but some records extend into mid-September. One undocumented report for 6 November at Horseshoe Lake CA (Findley 1949) is questionable.

1 banded, Carbondale, 16 Sep 1970 (VK)

1, n. Union Co., 21 Sep 1986 (WDR)

DOCUMENTATION: Specimen—male, Pine Hills, Union Co., 7 May 1966 (SIU A-1363).

FIELD GUIDES: G=282; N=360; P=232.

Black-and-white Warbler *Mniotilta varia*

Mid-April–Mid-May
Late August–Early October

STATUS AND ABUNDANCE: Fairly common migrant. Occasional summer resident. Very rare winter visitor.

HABITAT: Deciduous woods and woodland edge, hedgerows, and residential areas where large trees are present.

RECORDS AND REMARKS: Forages by creeping along tree trunks and large branches like a nuthatch. Prefers open, dry deciduous forest, and thus appears to be more numerous in the eastern portion of the region, at least during the breeding season. Migrants use a wide variety of habitats.

SPRING—Most migrants are seen after 20 April; those that arrive in early April may be potential breeders. Migration peaks in early May, and most have departed northward by 15 May. Lingering birds may also be breeders.

1, Ozark, Johnson Co., 3 Apr 1991 (TF)

1, Pope Co., 6 Apr 1986 (RP)

1, LaRue Pine Hills, 12 Apr 1987 (TF)

18, Pope Co., 10 May 1980 (SBC)

1, Carbondale, 30 May 1984 (TF)

SUMMER—Two nests plus two additional family groups represent the only confirmed breeding evidence for the region, despite the known presence of a thin summer population for years, especially in Pope Co. Many summer records come from disturbed woodlands along the edges of clearcuts or from selectively logged forests. At least one of the four confirmed breeding attempts was parasitized by cowbirds. The two nests were placed on the ground under the edge of a fallen log. Confirmed breeding records follow:

male with fledgling, Williams Hill, Pope Co., 22 June 1989 (TF, WDR)

nest, Dutch Creek, near Jonesboro, Union Co., May 1990 (SA, LM)

empty nest with recently fledged young nearby, Trail of Tears SF, June 1990 (SB)

pair with 3 fledglings, Dutch Creek, late May 1992 (TRR, LM)

Other summer records are numerous:

male, Ozark, Johnson Co., all summer 1985 (TF)

2 males, Giant City SP, June 1986 (TF)

male, LaRue Pine Hills, 14 June 1986 (WDR)

1, Pomona, 15 June 1975 (BP)

male, Little Grand Canyon, 28 June 1986 (WDR)

1, Garden of the Gods, Saline Co., 5 July 1975 (BP)

1, Pope Co., 9 July and 9 Aug 1973 (DH)

1, Crab Orchard NWR, 16 and 19 July 1985 (JCR)

female, Pomona, 19 July 1988 (WDR)

AUTUMN—Southward migration may begin early in August or perhaps even in July, as local breeders wander from their breeding sites. The bulk of migrants from north of the region probably do not arrive until early September. Daily counts of four or five birds are typical during peak migration. Most birds have departed by 1 October, but some may linger later, even into winter.

1, Carbondale, 13 Aug 1971 (FR)
4, Saline Co. CA, 18 Aug 1987 (WDR)
1, Carbondale, 7 Oct 1972 (VK)
WINTER—The only documented record is of a female at Horseshoe Lake CA, on 30 Dec 1974 (RS, HDB). An undocumented
record from Rudement, Saline Co., in early December 1985 is also
unusual.

DOCUMENTATION: Specimen—male, 2 miles n. of Cobden, Union
Co., 21 Apr 1966 (SIU A-1352).

FIELD GUIDES: G=270; N=360; P=232.

American Redstart *Setophaga ruticilla*

Late April–Late May
Late August–Early October

STATUS AND ABUNDANCE: Common migrant. Locally common
summer resident.

HABITAT: Breeds in mature bottomland forest. Migrants also frequent upland forest and forest edge.

RECORDS AND REMARKS: Notoriously frenetic foragers, redstarts are
extremely active and adept at pursuing insects they flush by flicking
open their wings and tail. They usually forage in the upper understory and lower canopy of forest trees. One of the most common
warbler species during migration, they can occur in just about any
place that has trees. Their song is highly variable, loud, and lisping.
Males do not attain full adult plumage until their second breeding
season; theirs closely resembles female plumage until that point.
Adult males retain the black-and-orange plumage throughout the
year.

SPRING—The first arrivals of the season usually appear around
20 April but may arrive earlier in "early" springs. Large numbers
occur in both upland and bottomland forest from the last week of
April through mid-May, after which time most migrants have probably departed. A substantial breeding population obscures the detection of departure dates from bottomland forest, but few redstarts
breed in upland forest, so any occurring there in late May or early
June are likely to be late migrants.

1, near Carbondale, 5 Apr 1966 (WGG)
113, Union Co., 4 May 1991 (SBC)
12, Bumgard Island, Alexander Co., 24 May 1988 (WDR)
1, Pine Hills, 29 May 1989 (Robinson and Robinson 1992)
SUMMER—Surprisingly little is known about the nesting cycle. Nests are usually placed in the crotch of a small tree from one to seventeen meters above the ground, and eggs have been found as early as 4 May. Redstarts are sometimes parasitized by cowbirds, but no quantitative data are available. Cave Creek Valley near Pomona probably houses one of the largest regional breeding populations; a casual survey turned up twenty territorial males on 14 June 1975 (BP), but there are probably nearly two hundred territories along the entire drainage. Another population center is along the Kaskaskia River Bottoms.
AUTUMN—Fall arrivals begin appearing by late August, but the presence of the breeding population dampens any obvious influx un-til about mid-September, when there is a noticeable increase in the number of redstarts along forest edges. They regularly associate with mixed-species flocks of warblers. Peak counts of ten birds per day are typical and usually occur during late September. Most have de-parted by 10 October, but a few linger later.
1, Carbondale, 25 Oct 1989 (JH)

DOCUMENTATION: Specimen—female, 2 miles n. of Cobden, Un-ion Co., 4 May 1966 (SIU A-1376).

FIELD GUIDES: G=292; N=378; P=236.

Prothonotary Warbler *Protonotaria citrea*
Mid-April–Early September

STATUS AND ABUNDANCE: Common migrant and summer resident.

HABITAT: Swamps and flooded woodland along rivers and lakes.

RECORDS AND REMARKS: Often forages low in thickets and around brush piles on the borders of swamps, streams, and lakes. Its loud song is a conspicuous and characteristic component of riparian bird communities.
SPRING—Some may arrive as early as 1 April, but there are no recent records for such early dates. More typically, the first arrivals

appear about 15 April. Migration probably peaks in late April and the first week of May, but the large breeding population obscures any obvious pattern. Spring Bird Counts sometimes produce large counts, but they probably census both migrant and breeding populations.

1, Heron Pond NP, Johnson Co., 9 Apr 1972 (VK)
1, Black Bottoms, Massac Co., 11 Apr 1986 (WDR)
146, Union Co., 4 May 1991 (SBC)
58, Massac Co., 9 May 1987 (SBC)
1, Ozark, Johnson Co., 14 May 1988 (TF)

SUMMER—Nests are placed in tree cavities, usually over water, from one to eight meters above ground level. Eggs have been found at least as early as 24 April, and breeding continues well into July. Even though they nest in cavities, Prothonotaries are sometimes parasitized by cowbirds. Usually, the nests with the larger entrances are more likely to be parasitized. Kleen (1973a) gives details on the population dynamics from a site at Crab Orchard NWR.

28, Union Co. CA, 9 June 1982 (PK)
16, Crab Orchard NWR, 20 June 1984 (JCR)

AUTUMN—Fall migration is difficult to detect. After breeding, little singing is heard. The distinctive call note is the only auditory cue to this species' presence in late summer and early fall. A few can still be found foraging along the edges of swamps in thickets through August and into early September; only a few stragglers are seen later.

1, Carbondale, 20 Sep 1970 (VK)

DOCUMENTATION: Specimen—male, Carbondale, Jackson Co., 5 May 1961 (SIU A-1110).

FIELD GUIDES: G=270; N=354; P=230.

Worm-eating Warbler *Helmitheros vermivorus*
Late April–Mid-September

STATUS AND ABUNDANCE: Common migrant and summer resident in the Shawnee Hills. Rare migrant and summer resident in the Floodplains and the Till Plain.

HABITAT: Breeds on steep slopes of upland forest. Migrants may also use woodlots and bottomland forest.

RECORDS AND REMARKS: "Wormers" forage from ground to canopy levels within extensive tracts of forest. Contrary to their name, they do not consume many "worms," but they eat lots of caterpillars and spiders. Most of their foraging time is concentrated in the shrub and understory layer, where they specialize on gathering hidden prey from inside dead, curled leaves that are suspended above the ground (the "aerial leaf litter"). They do this either by pinching the outside of the curled leaves and madly pursuing any frightened insect that flushes out, or by peering into an opening and extracting any discovered prey. The Wormers' song is a flat, thin trill that is similar to, but less mechanical than, a Chipping Sparrow song.

SPRING—Singing males arrive soon after 20 April, occasionally earlier. Peak passage of migrants is difficult to discern, because there is a small breeding population north of southern Illinois and a large one in this region. Most migrants have probably departed, however, by mid-May. Daily counts of twenty or more birds are typical in the Shawnee Hills. Elsewhere, more than one or two is significant.

male, Giant City SP, 18 Apr 1989 (WDR)
1, LaRue Pine Hills, 20 Apr 1985 (JCR, KM)
3, Johnson Co., 23 Apr 1988 (TF)
105, Union Co., 4 May 1991 (SBC)

SUMMER—Nests are placed on the ground, under a drift of dead leaves that has accumulated on the upslope side of the base of a sapling or other plant. Contrary to the reports of Graber et al. (1983), north- and east-facing slopes are not preferentially chosen for nest sites; the distribution appears to be random (SA). Although nests are well hidden, nest predation rates are very high in the Shawnee Hills; only about 40 percent of nests produce fledglings (INHS). The high parasitism rate (44 percent of thirty-nine nests) is also surprising given the inconspicuous nature of the nests (INHS). Nest building begins soon after first arrival in late April, and egg laying is underway by early May. Nests with eggs have been found throughout May and June. Adults lead fledglings to nearby areas of dense cover, such as treefall gaps. Adults with fledglings exhibit a bold distraction display when their young are endangered; I once followed an adult feigning injury for a few meters and then turned and walked in exactly the opposite direction. Within a few steps, I found a Worm-eating Warbler fledgling that was fresh out of the nest; the adult flew by me to near the fledgling, landed on the ground and spread its wings, and then charged toward me; it actually made physical contact with me and began to climb up my leg before it finally flew off to continue scolding me from a nearby bush. AUTUMN—Fall migration is unremarkable. Some birds wander away from breeding areas even during midsummer, but most migration is probably not under way until late July or August. Few birds are encountered after 1 September.

1, Bumgard Island, Alexander Co., 1 July 1988 (WDR)
1 banded, Carbondale, 3 Aug 1970 (VK)
2, near Woodlawn, Jefferson Co., 10 Sep 1988 (TF, WDR)
1, Ozark, Johnson Co., 3 Oct 1993 (TF)

DOCUMENTATION: Specimen—ad. female, 2 miles n. of Pomona, Jackson Co., 7 July 1966 (SIU A-1397).

FIELD GUIDES: G=270; N=374; P=240.

Swainson's Warbler *Limnothlypis swainsonii*
Late April–Early September

STATUS AND ABUNDANCE: Locally uncommon summer resident at traditional breeding sites. Very rare migrant away from breeding grounds.

HABITAT: Mature bottomland forest with moist, heavily shaded, dense thickets. Breeders are usually, but not always, associated with patches of giant cane (*Arundinaria gigantea*). Eddleman et al. (1980) suggested that contiguous tracts of forest at least 350 hectares in size are required for breeding.

RECORDS AND REMARKS: One of the most highly sought birds in the region, this species draws numerous birders from all around the state to Pomona each spring. It was first reported in southern Illinois in 1907, when a singing male was observed four miles north of DuQuoin, Perry Co., by Howard Ray and Alfred O. Gross (Gross 1908). Howell (1910) reported two sightings of individual birds from Olive Branch, Alexander Co. (15–20 May 1909), and Reevesville, Pope Co. (21 June 1909). It was nearly thirty years before the next report, when Ammann (1939) collected one near Cairo on 1 September 1938. On 29 April 1951, Richard Brewer and J. W. Hardy discovered a singing male in Cave Creek Valley, north of Pomona (Hardy 1955); they discovered evidence of breeding on 1 July, when a bird carrying food exhibited a distraction display as if a fledgling was nearby. Singing birds were again found there each year from 1952 to 1957 (Brewer 1958). Little mention is made in the literature of searches for Swainson's Warblers during the 1960s, but they were undoubtedly present, because George (1969) found an adult feeding a fledgling on 8 August 1966. William G. George found and collected two nests (after they fledged young) in Cave Creek Valley in 1971; the nests are now in the SIU bird collection. Meanwhile, up to five birds were present at Heron Pond NP in the early 1970s (Kleen 1976); one bird banded there by Kleen in 1973 returned to the same territory in April 1974 (Graber et al. 1983). Eddleman (1978) censused approximately five hundred hectares of Cave Creek Valley in 1976 and found twenty-two singing males. Eddleman et al. (1980) reported that Swainson's Warblers required dense overstory (80 percent canopy cover) and dense cane thickets (up to twenty thousand stems per hectare); they also recommended that forests be thinned or cut to promote the growth of cane stands. Apparently in response to this recommendation, the Forest Service clearcut the area with the largest known population of warblers in the early 1980s. Since then, the warbler population has declined precipitously. The disappearance from the Pomona area may not be entirely linked to forestry activities, however, because the warblers disappeared from the Heron Pond sites, which were not logged, at about the same time.

Recent fieldwork in Cave Creek Valley has revealed one to three singing males nearly every spring, but the birds have been found farther and farther from the traditional sites. Unfortunately, information on the true abundance has been somewhat obscured by questionable reports from observers who are not completely familiar with the Swainson's song. Its song can easily be confused with that of a Hooded Warbler or with that of a Louisiana Waterthrush. Observers should, therefore, only report records of Swainson's Warbler for which good visual contact was made; reports of birds that were only heard should be regarded as suspicious unless the observer has extensive experience with this species.

SPRING—First arrivals are generally detected during the last week of April, and they are usually considered to be breeders, because southern Illinois is at the northern limit of the breeding range.

1, Pomona, 24 Apr 1983 (TF)

4, Cave Creek Valley, Jackson Co., 27 Apr 1972 (VK)

1, Pope Co., 4 May 1972 (PB)

4, Union Co., 5 May 1973 (VK)

pair, Fort Massac SP, Massac Co., 8 May 1982 (WDR, HW, GW)

1, Crab Orchard NWR, 10 May 1950 (LB)

SUMMER—Little is known about the nesting cycle. Both nests collected by George were placed in cane near the ground. Fledglings have been seen at least as early as 8–31 August but should probably occur earlier.

1, Murphysboro, 30 May 1946 (JWH, GP)

male, Iron Mountain, Union Co., 6 June 1988 (SB)

12, Cedar Creek, Jackson Co., June 1975 (MH, MSw)

1, Union Co. CA, 4 and 10 June 1982 (PK)

1, near Thebes, Alexander Co., 14 June 1984 (TF)

1, Pulaski Co., 24 June 1993 (TF, JHe)

pair, near Roots, Randolph Co., 8 July 1972 (RA)

pair with yg., Heron Pond NP, Johnson Co., 31 Aug 1973 (MH, VK)

AUTUMN—Not often detected away from breeding areas. Some may linger well into September, because fledglings were still being fed at Heron Pond on 31 August 1973.

1, Cairo, Alexander Co., 1 Sep 1939 (Ammann 1939)

DOCUMENTATION: Specimen—female, 2 miles n. of Pomona, Jackson Co., 8 Aug 1966 (SIU A-1394).

FIELD GUIDES: G=270; N=374; P=240.

Ovenbird *Seiurus aurocapillus*

Late April–Late May
Late August–Mid-October

STATUS AND ABUNDANCE: Fairly common migrant. Fairly common summer resident in the Shawnee Hills. Locally uncommon summer resident in the Floodplains and the Till Plain.

HABITAT: Mature deciduous woodland. Typically breeds on flat-

Ovenbird at nest, Trail of Tears SF, Union Co., June 1992

topped ridges of hills in rolling terrain, but may also use wide valleys and gently sloping hillsides. Does not necessarily require deciduous canopy; quite numerous in pine stands in the southeastern Shawnee National Forest in Pope and Johnson Cos.

RECORDS AND REMARKS: The loud explosive song uttered by this ground-foraging warbler advertises its presence. The song increases in volume as it progresses, which is distinctive. One male sang a song of the Common Yellowthroat throughout May 1989 at Giant City SP (WDR).
SPRING—Most begin arriving after 20 April. Migration peaks between the last few days of April and 15 May. Detection of departure dates is obscured by the presence of the breeding population.
1, Pope Co., 14 Apr 1992 (TF)
1, Giant City SP, 17 Apr 1989 (WDR)
1, Crab Orchard NWR, 22 Apr 1970 (VK)
92, Union Co., 4 May 1991 (SBC)
29, Jackson Co., 8 May 1976 (SBC)
SUMMER—The breeding distribution is spotty, and clusters of ter-

ritories move around from year to year; many sites that appear to be "good" Ovenbird habitat lack breeders. Although nests are well hidden under a dome of dead leaves on the ground, seven of nine nests in the Shawnee Hills were parasitized by cowbirds (INHS). Eggs have been found as soon as early May, and fledglings have been found in late July.

5 pairs, Giant City SP, throughout June 1986 (TF)

32 territorial males, n. Pope Co., throughout June 1986 (WDR)

AUTUMN—Found along forest edge in thickets, where they forage on and near the ground. Daily high counts usually do not exceed five or six birds. Migrants begin arriving at least by late August, and most Ovenbirds have departed by 15 October.

1 banded, Carbondale, 23 Aug 1970 (VK)

1, Carbondale, 20 Oct 1971 (VK)

DOCUMENTATION: Specimen—male, Carbondale, Jackson Co., 22 May 1958 (SIU A-744).

FIELD GUIDES: G=288; N=374; P=246.

Northern Waterthrush *Seiurus noveboracensis*

Mid-April–Mid-May

Late August–Early October

STATUS AND ABUNDANCE: Common spring migrant. Uncommon fall migrant.

HABITAT: Moist bottomland forest, often near standing water. Also, wooded thickets near streams, particularly in fall.

RECORDS AND REMARKS: This migrant species is easily confused with the breeding Louisiana Waterthrush, but Louisiana Waterthrushes have larger bills, cleaner white underparts with an unstreaked white throat, bright pink legs, and a distinctly different song. Northerns have a jumbled, loud song that lacks the clear introductory whistles of the Louisianas' song. Northerns are usually found more often at the edges of stagnant pools of water, whereas Louisianas prefer flowing water. I have, however, seen northerns foraging along flowing creeks in Louisiana Waterthrush territories.

SPRING—Migrants often begin arriving a few days after 15 April.

Peak numbers are present from the last few days of April through 10 May, after which time most birds have departed.
1, Crab Orchard NWR, 15 Apr 1985 (JCR)
3, Oakwood Bottoms, Jackson Co., 22 Apr 1972 (VK)
66, Union Co., 4 May 1991 (SBC)
49, Massac Co., 5 May 1984 (WDR)
50, Alexander Co., 7 May 1977 (SBC)
male, near Thebes, Alexander Co., 21 May 1988 (WDR)
AUTUMN—Migrants are much less noticeable in fall than during spring, because they do not sing in fall. The chip note is explosive and distinctive, and it can be learned with practice. Maximum daily counts are usually less than six birds.
1 banded, Carbondale, 23 Aug 1970 (VK)
3, Rend Lake, 24 Aug 1985 (RP)
1 banded, Carbondale, 11 Oct 1970 (VK)

DOCUMENTATION: Photograph—imm., Grimsby, Jackson Co., 28 Aug 1972 (SIU AP-uncatalogued).

FIELD GUIDES: G=288; N=374; P=246.

Louisiana Waterthrush *Seiurus motacilla*
Late March–Mid-September

STATUS AND ABUNDANCE: Common migrant and summer resident in the Shawnee Hills. Uncommon migrant and summer resident in the Floodplains and the Till Plain.

HABITAT: Most numerous along rocky creeks in upland deciduous forest, but also found along muddy streams in bottomland forest and in cypress swamps.

RECORDS AND REMARKS: The loud, ringing song of this warbler marks the arrival of spring. Waterthrushes forage for invertebrates by walking alongside streams and picking prey from shallow water, leaf surfaces, or the ground; they also tug submerged dead leaves out of the water and turn them over to reveal hidden prey. The body and tail teeter as the bird walks.
SPRING—Males regularly arrive during the last week of March. Often, territorial males all arrive on the same day. At Giant City

SP in 1989, the first females arrived four days after the first males (W. D. Robinson 1990).

1, Giant City SP, 22 Mar 1990 (WDR)

1, Pope Co., 23 Mar 1975 (RGr)

16 males, Giant City SP, 29 Mar 1989 (WDR)

SUMMER—Nest sites are selected by both members of a pair. Nests are built under upturned tree roots or in cavities of stream-banks. They are often extremely well hidden. Of seven pairs studied at Giant City SP, five were incubating between 27 April and 13 May; the earliest pair began incubation on 19 April, and the latest pair began on 8 May (W. D. Robinson 1990). The earliest fledging date was 12 May. Parasitism rates vary within the region; seven of nine nests (78 percent) were parasitized at Giant City SP, but only three of twenty-four (12.5 percent) were parasitized near Dutch Creek, Jonesboro (INHS). W. D. Robinson (1990) gives additional details on the reproductive behavior.

62, Union Co., 4 May 1991 (SBC)

21, Alexander Co., 8 May 1976 (SBC)

15, Little Black Slough, Johnson Co., 24 May 1989 (TF, WDR)

AUTUMN—Fall migration is very inconspicuous; most birds have departed breeding territories by late July, and few are encountered past August. George (1968) listed 18 October as a departure date, but that must be considered unusually late.

1, Carbondale, 9 Aug 1970 (VK)

1, Union Co. CA, 3 Sep 1988 (WDR)

DOCUMENTATION: Specimen—female, 3 miles w. of Alto Pass, Union Co., 16 Apr 1966 (SIU A-1374).

FIELD GUIDES: G=288; N=374; P=246.

Kentucky Warbler *Oporornis formosus*

Late April–Mid-September

STATUS AND ABUNDANCE: Common spring migrant and summer resident. Uncommon fall migrant.

HABITAT: Forest; in upland woods, generally found in valleys rather than on ridges. Sometimes numerous in areas that lack deep shade

Kentucky Warbler, Wildcat Bluff, Johnson Co., June 1993

but have dense ground cover, such as clearcut edges and treefalls in forests.

RECORDS AND REMARKS: "This bird always acts as if it is hiding something. It often lurks in the undergrowth, muttering to itself like an old woman" (JWH). Kentuckys forage on and near the ground, gleaning prey from the leaf litter and from leaf surfaces of herbaceous and shrubby plants. They can be difficult to see as they skulk around in the shade of dense cover.

SPRING—Most first arrivals are detected just before 20 April, but the first big influx does not occur until about a week later. The migrant population peaks during the first half of May, but the presence of the breeding population obscures accurate determination of departure dates.

1, Union Co. CA, 16 Apr 1986 (WDR)
18, Cache River, Johnson Co., 24 Apr 1973 (VK, HDB)
262, Union Co., 4 May 1991 (SBC)

SUMMER—One of the most common breeding forest birds of the Shawnee Hills. Nests are placed on the ground, at the base of an herbaceous plant or fern. Often parasitized by cowbirds; 37.3 per-

cent of 166 nests found in Union and Alexander Cos. contained
cowbird eggs or young (INHS). Egg dates range from late April
through 18 July. Family groups are conspicuous because of their
constant chipping; adults take the young into areas of dense cover,
such as treefall gaps, as soon as the fledglings leave the nest.

AUTUMN—As with many common breeding species, fall migration is unremarkable. After breeding, birds seem to just drift southward out of the region. Most birds are gone by 15 September, but
a few will linger later.

1 banded, Carbondale, 19 Sep 1971 (VK)

1, near Cobden, Union Co., 1–6 Oct 1967 (WGG)

DOCUMENTATION: Specimen—male, LaRue Pine Hills, Union Co.,
3 May 1956 (SIU A-261).

FIELD GUIDES: G=290; N=372; P=244.

Connecticut Warbler *Oporornis agilis*

Mid-May–Early June
Mid-September–Late September

STATUS AND ABUNDANCE: Rare spring migrant. Very rare fall migrant.

HABITAT: Dense, moist thickets near forest edge; areas of dense undergrowth within forests; and, during fall especially, weedy patches
near hedgerows.

RECORDS AND REMARKS: Numbers seem to vary widely from year
to year; in some years none are found, whereas in others an observer may record several different birds. Most are detected by their
song first, a slow *Chippy chuppy chippy chuppy*, before, and if, they
are seen. Their habit of skulking on the ground in dense, moist
thickets makes them exceptionally difficult to see. Connecticuts can
be separated from the Mourning Warbler (which is similar in appearance) by the presence of complete white eyerings, the lack of
any black on their breasts, and their habit of walking rather than
hopping.

SPRING—Very few have arrived in time for the annual Spring
Bird Count; most first arrivals are detected after 10 May. Daily
counts rarely exceed a single bird, even in good habitat. Migrant

populations probably peak between 16 and 25 May in most years. A few are still present during the first few days of June.

1, Massac Co., 5 May 1979 (SBC)
1, Jackson Co., 7 May 1983 (SBC)
4, South Ripple Hollow, Alexander Co., 25 May 1991 (WDR)
male, Winkle, Perry Co., 2 June 1989 (WDR)
1, near Jonesboro, Union Co., 4 June 1992 (WDR)
1, Belknap, Pulaski Co., 5 June 1984 (VK)

AUTUMN—The fall migration path takes most Connecticuts to the Atlantic Coast before they turn southward, so even fewer are detected in our region in fall than in spring. They tend to favor weedy habitats more at this season.

imm., Carbondale, 15 Sep 1984 (TF)
1, near Little Grassy Lake, Jackson Co., 28 Sep 1975 (BP)

DOCUMENTATION: Specimen—1.5 miles n. of Cobden, Union Co., 23 May 1971 (WGG 2384).

FIELD GUIDES: G=290; N=370; P=244.

Mourning Warbler *Oporornis philadelphia*

Mid-May–Early June
Late August–Early October

STATUS AND ABUNDANCE: Occasional spring migrant. Rare fall migrant.

HABITAT: Dense thickets and underbrush in forests and along forest edge.

RECORDS AND REMARKS: An inhabitant of dark, dense thickets that is easily overlooked unless it is singing. The song is often uttered very quietly, however, so it often has a ventriloquial quality; a singing bird may seem to be many meters away when it is actually very near. Mournings seem to have a fondness for *Rubus* thickets.

SPRING—Only rarely detected before 5 May. Migrant populations peak in mid-May, and some are regularly present into the first week of June.

1 found dead, Crab Orchard NWR, 29 Apr 1970 (VK et al.)
1, Jackson Co., 4 May 1974 (SBC)
7, Trail of Tears SF, 21 May 1991 (WDR)

1, Dutch Creek, Jonesboro, 7 June 1990 (Robinson and Robinson 1992)
male, LaRue Pine Hills, 14 June 1986 (WDR)
AUTUMN—Generally silent during fall, so easily overlooked. Frequents dense brush and weedy patches along hedgerows.
1, Rend Lake, Jefferson Co., 16 Aug 1989 (WDR)
1 banded, Carbondale, 23 Aug 1970 (VK)
1 banded, Grimsby, Jackson Co., 25 Aug 1972 (VK)
1 banded, Carbondale, 10 Oct 1970 (VK)

DOCUMENTATION: Specimen—ad., Creal Springs, Williamson Co., 1 Oct 1965 (INHS W-mo-2).

FIELD GUIDES: G=290; N=370; P=244.

Common Yellowthroat *Geothlypis trichas*
Mid-April–Late October

STATUS AND ABUNDANCE: Common migrant and summer resident. Rare winter resident.

HABITAT: Marshes, weedy fields, hedgerows, and forest edge.

RECORDS AND REMARKS: Ubiquitous away from forest interior. At times, could easily be categorized as "abundant."
SPRING—The first conspicuous appearance of migrants typically occurs just before 20 April, but some appear earlier, perhaps from nearby wintering areas. Spring Bird Counts probably census both breeding and migrant populations. The substantial breeding population makes detection of departure dates difficult.
1, Union Co. CA, 11 Apr 1992 (TF)
1, Carbondale, 15 Apr 1979 (HD)
278, Union Co., 4 May 1991 (SBC)
129, Jackson Co., 7 May 1977 (SBC)
SUMMER—Nesting begins by early May; eggs have been found as early as 15 May. The breeding season is long, though, because adults have been seen tending young during August. Yellowthroats are parasitized by cowbirds, but there is little quantitative data to assess any possible impact on their populations. Graber et al. (1983) reported that 27.3 percent of eleven nests for which they had data were parasitized.
AUTUMN—Fall migration is protracted, as some birds tend to lin-

ger very late into fall, but the bulk of the population has departed by the end of October.

23, Harrisburg, Saline Co., 7 Sep 1986 (WDR)

1, Crab Orchard NWR, 29 Nov 1982 (JCR)

WINTER—A few winter records probably involve fall migrants that have lingered very late, but there are records from throughout the winter months, indicating that at least in some years a few birds may overwinter. Winter habitats include hedgerows, marshes, and weedy fields. The distinctive call note, a dry *chet,* is often given. Yellowthroats will often respond well to spishing.

1, s.w. Union Co., 19 Dec 1985 (WDR, RP)

4, Union Co. CA, 3 Jan 1987 (TF, m.ob.)

3, Oakwood Bottoms, Jackson Co., 11 Jan 1976 (BP, MMo)

1, Crab Orchard NWR, 19 Jan 1980 (MMl)

male, Crab Orchard NWR, 12 Feb 1983 (JCR)

female, Crab Orchard NWR, 20 Feb 1983 (JCR)

1, Jackson Co., 8 Mar 1975 (BP)

DOCUMENTATION: Specimen—female, Alexander Co., 3 May 1969 (SIU A-1729).

FIELD GUIDES: G=288; N=376; P=246.

Hooded Warbler *Wilsonia citrina*

Late April–Mid-September

STATUS AND ABUNDANCE: Uncommon migrant. Locally uncommon to fairly common summer resident.

HABITAT: Woodland with dense shrub layer. Typically most numerous in upland and bottomland forest, near treefalls or other openings where brambles, saplings, and other vegetation is most dense. Also present in pine woods where the thin canopy allows proliferation of thick undergrowth.

RECORDS AND REMARKS: Hoodeds occur in both upland and bottomland forest. Within each, they prefer areas with high densities of shrubs and ground cover; such areas are often associated with treefall gaps. High population densities of Hoodeds are often found in selectively logged forests, such as that at Trail of Tears SF, because of the numerous patches of disturbed forest that mimic natural treefalls.

SPRING—The first Hoodeds usually arrive during the third week of April, but occasionally some appear earlier. Maximum daily counts are usually less than five birds. The breeding population makes detection of departure dates difficult, but some Hoodeds have been seen in sites where they did not subsequently breed during late May.

1, Crab Orchard NWR, 30 Mar 1950 (LB)
1, Union Co., 16 Apr 1992 (TF)
1, near Perks, Pulaski Co., 23 Apr 1973 (VK, HDB)
21, Union Co., 4 May 1991 (SBC)
male, Rend Lake, Franklin Co., 19 May 1988 (WDR)

SUMMER—Nests are placed within two meters of the ground, often in the crotch of a sapling or in a patch of dense briars. Frequent victims of cowbird parasitism (twelve of sixteen nests were parasitized in Union and Alexander Cos.), Hoodeds rarely raise any of their own young in our region. Nest predation rates are extremely high as well; only 12 percent of nests fledged any young (cowbird or warbler) from 1989–1991 (INHS).

male, Little Black Slough, Johnson Co., 24 May 1989 (TF, WDR)
17 territorial males, n. Pope Co., throughout June 1986 (WDR)
3, Giant City SP, throughout June 1986 (TF)
5, Lusk Creek, Pope Co., 5 July 1971 (RGr)

AUTUMN—Few are detected during fall. Migration probably begins during August, but it is largely unnoticed.

1, Rend Lake, Franklin Co., 3 Sep 1976 (BP)
1, Saline Co., 16 Sep 1994 (JD)

DOCUMENTATION: Specimen—ad. male, 2 miles n. of Pomona, Jackson Co., 29 Apr 1967 (WGG 2204).

FIELD GUIDES: G=292; N=372; P=242.

Wilson's Warbler *Wilsonia pusilla*

Early May–Late May
Early September–Mid-October

STATUS AND ABUNDANCE: Uncommon spring migrant. Occasional fall migrant. Very rare winter visitor.

HABITAT: Forest, forest edge, and willow thickets.

RECORDS AND REMARKS: Inconspicuous and easily overlooked.

The song is a short, sputtered trill that does not much increase the conspicuousness of the singing bird. Spring migrants often occur in both upland and bottomland forest and in willow thickets, whereas fall migrants tend to prefer forest edge and willows.

SPRING—First migrants appear near the first of May, and peak numbers are present by the middle of May. Daily high counts usually do not exceed five or six birds. Populations soon pass northward, and few are present after 25 May.

1, Union Co., 27 Apr 1984 (TF, KR)
4, Pope Co., 10 May 1980 (SBC)
9, Rend Lake, 15 May 1992 (TF, JD)
1, Alexander Co., 26 May 1984 (TF, JCR)
1, Cairo, Alexander Co., 26 May 1988 (WDR)
1, Trail of Tears SF, 27 May 1991 (Robinson and Robinson 1992)

AUTUMN—Fall migration is protracted, extending throughout September and October. Wilson's sometimes associate with mixed-species flocks of warblers along forest edges.

1, Crab Orchard NWR, 1 Sep 1976 (BP)
1, Ferne Clyffe SP, Johnson Co., 4 Sep 1988 (WDR)
1, Carbondale, 5 Oct 1986 (TF)
1, Carbondale, 24 Oct 1970 (VK)

WINTER—The sole winter record probably involves a very late fall migrant.

1, Union Co. CA, 22 Dec 1982 (HDB)

DOCUMENTATION: Specimen—male, 2 miles n. of Cobden, Union Co., 9 Oct 1967 (SIU A-1667).

FIELD GUIDES: G=292; N=372; P=242.

Canada Warbler *Wilsonia canadensis*

Early May–Late May
Late August–Mid-September

STATUS AND ABUNDANCE: Uncommon migrant. Very rare summer visitor.

HABITAT: Dense understory of forest and forest edge.

RECORDS AND REMARKS: Canadas are often associated with gaps in forests and along forest edges where the understory level is well developed. They tend to forage from the understory up to the lower extent of the forest canopy; sometimes they will also forage near the ground. Their song is distinctive because of its lack of rhythmic structure. Consequently, some observers have suggested that the best way to identify the song is by process of elimination; after eliminating every other possibility, all that is left is the Canada!

SPRING—Although a few migrants may appear in very late April, the first Canadas are usually not encountered until May. They are never very numerous, but populations peak between 5 and 20 May. A few birds regularly linger later.

1, Eldorado, Saline Co., 28 Apr 1993 (JD)

9, Massac Co., 10 May 1986 (WDR)

1, Pine Hills, Union Co., 29 May 1989 (Robinson and Robinson 1992)

1, Kinkaid Lake, Jackson Co., 5 June 1983 (JCR)

SUMMER—One male with a partial necklace was observed in selectively logged forest at Trail of Tears SF, Union Co., on 22 June 1991 (SKR); it should probably be considered a very late spring migrant.

AUTUMN—The fall migration route takes Canadas east to the Atlantic Coast from their Canadian breeding range, so most of them bypass southern Illinois. The majority of birds that do occur here probably pass through in the first two weeks of September. They often associate with mixed-species flocks of warblers.

imm. female collected, Mermet Lake, Massac Co., 9 Aug 1968 (INHS)

1, Carbondale, 23 Aug 1970 (VK)

1, Perry Co., 24 Aug 1987 (TF)

1, Carbondale, 4 Oct 1986 (WDR)

DOCUMENTATION: Specimen—imm. female, Mermet Lake, Massac Co., 9 Aug 1968 (INHS W-ca-2).

FIELD GUIDES: G=292; N=372; P=234.

Yellow-breasted Chat *Icteria virens*

Late April–Early September

STATUS AND ABUNDANCE: Common spring migrant and summer resident. Uncommon fall migrant.

HABITAT: Shrubby old fields, hedgerows, and forest edge.

RECORDS AND REMARKS: The largest of the warblers, chats have interesting behaviors that can be humorous at times. In their flight display, male chats sing a series of evenly spaced barking notes while fluttering up into the air like a butterfly, and then they drop back down to a perch. Chats often sing at night as well, especially when it is clear and calm.

SPRING—Some chats arrive early in April, but most are not detected until the last week of April. Peak numbers are present in the last few days of April and the first week of May. The presence of the breeding population obscures detection of departure dates, but most migrants have probably left by the end of May.

1, Giant City SP, 6 Apr 1986 (WDR)
1, Giant City SP, 18 Apr 1989 (WDR)
1, Johnson Co., 23 Apr 1988 (TF)
89, Union Co., 4 May 1991 (SBC)
75, Alexander Co., 7 May 1977 (SBC)

SUMMER—Nests are constructed of grasses and placed between 0.5 and 2 meters above the ground, in briar patches. They lay fairly large clutches (four to seven eggs) but are frequently parasitized by cowbirds. Egg dates range from early May to mid-July.

AUTUMN—Chats basically disappear after the breeding season; they are not often seen past mid-August. They still utilize shrubby habitats in fall, but they skulk around in dense cover and are reluctant to come out.

1, Mt. Vernon, Jefferson Co., 27 Aug 1987 (TF)
1, Pomona, 15 Sep 1991 (TF)
1, Saline Co., 16 Sep 1994 (JD)
1, Crab Orchard NWR, 21 Sep 1986 (WDR)

DOCUMENTATION: Specimen—male, LaRue Pine Hills, Union Co., 3 May 1956 (SIU A-251).

FIELD GUIDES: G=288; N=376; P=246.

Subfamily Thraupinae: Tanagers

Summer Tanager *Piranga rubra*
Late April–Early October

STATUS AND ABUNDANCE: Fairly common migrant. Fairly common

Summer Tanager on nest, Ozark, Johnson Co., June 1992

summer resident in the Shawnee Hills. Uncommon summer resident in the Floodplains and the Till Plain.

HABITAT: Deciduous woods, often near edges of openings in the canopy.

RECORDS AND REMARKS: Forages in the understory and canopy. Shy (1984) reported that they are interspecifically territorial with Scarlet Tanagers, but song playback experiments in the Shawnee Hills revealed that they are not (WDR). Summers catch fairly large insects for food, often consuming wasps and bees. They also exhibit delayed plumage maturation; males in their first breeding season are usually blotched with patches of yellow and green. After pair formation, singing rates decrease substantially, and the most commonly heard vocalization becomes the distinctive *tikukuk* call.

SPRING—The first spring arrivals usually appear just before 20 April. Migrant populations peak in early May. Because of the breeding population, the departure of migrants is not conspicuous.

2, Union Co., 16 Apr 1976 (BP)

1, Giant City SP, 18 Apr 1989 (WDR)

109, Union Co., 4 May 1991 (SBC)

SUMMER—Heavily parasitized by Brown-headed Cowbirds. Summer Tanagers probably raise more cowbirds than tanagers in southern Illinois. Eighty-five percent of thirteen nests were parasitized and received an average of 2.9 cowbird eggs per nest in Alexander and Union Cos. (INHS). The nest is a ragged cup of grasses placed three to twenty-five meters (an average of nine meters) above the ground, often at the tip of a long horizontal branch that hangs out into an opening in the canopy. A nesting female that was banded in Johnson Co. in 1992 returned in 1993 to nest in the same tree (TF).

AUTUMN—After breeding, the best clue to the continued presence of Summers is their call, which is still occasionally given. Otherwise, they can be difficult to detect; some may participate in mixed-species flocks of migrants, especially with Rose-breasted Grosbeaks. Most Summers have departed by 5 October.

11, Giant City SP, 18 Sep 1982 (JCR)
1, Carbondale, 11 Oct 1982 (MMl)
1, Mermet Lake CA, 18 Oct 1986 (WDR)

DOCUMENTATION: Specimen—ad. male, Carbondale, Jackson Co., 11 May 1959 (SIU A-882).

FIELD GUIDES: G=306; N=430; P=260.

Scarlet Tanager *Piranga olivacea*
Late April–Early October

STATUS AND ABUNDANCE: Common migrant. Common summer resident in the Shawnee Hills. Fairly common summer resident in the Floodplains and the Till Plain.

HABITAT: Mature deciduous woods.

RECORDS AND REMARKS: Scarlets generally prefer moister forest than do Summer Tanagers. Although Scarlets occur along forest edge, they are more of a forest interior species than are Summers. Contrary to the reports of Shy (1984), interspecific aggression between the two species is minimal, although some brief skirmishes do occur. Scarlets forage in the canopy, for caterpillars and other medium-sized insects. Males show delayed plumage maturation, but the differences between subadult and adult plumages are more subtle than those among Summer Tanagers.

SPRING—The first spring sightings are routinely made just before

20 April. Migrant populations reach their maxima in late April and early May and taper off by late May.

1, near Harrisburg, Saline Co., 12 Apr 1993 (JD)
1, Heron Pond NP, Johnson Co., 17 Apr 1982 (SO, MMl)
5, Giant City SP, 18 Apr 1989 (WDR)
119, Union Co., 4 May 1991 (SBC)

SUMMER—The frail, open, cuplike nests are placed in a cluster of leaves or vine tangle high above the ground (an average of eighteen meters). The contents of only a few nests have been checked because of the height at which they are placed, but four of five were parasitized and contained an average of 3.3 cowbird eggs per nest. Additionally, Scarlet adults are commonly seen feeding fledgling cowbirds throughout the summer. It would not be surprising to discover that Scarlets raise more cowbirds than tanagers in this region.

AUTUMN—Migration may begin as early as mid-August. Peak numbers are detected during mid-September, when they are frequent participants in mixed-species flocks. The males acquire femalelike plumage for the winter. Most Scarlets have departed by 5 October.

13, Giant City SP, 18 Sep 1982 (JCR)
1, Giant City SP, 10 Oct 1982 (JCR)

DOCUMENTATION: Specimen—ad. male, LaRue Pine Hills, Union Co., 3 May 1956 (SIU A-267).

FIELD GUIDES: G=306; N=430; P=260.

[Western Tanager *Piranga ludoviciana*]

STATUS AND ABUNDANCE: Hypothetical

RECORDS AND REMARKS: The only report is of a sighting by Lee Bush on 14 May 1948. Smith and Parmalee (1955) indicated that the bird was seen five miles northwest of Carbondale, whereas George (1968) referred to Williamson Co. as the locality; the bird was actually observed at Crab Orchard NWR in Williamson Co. Because of the distinctive fieldmarks of this species and the experience of the observer, the record is likely correct. No documentary details were preserved, however, so the presence of the Western Tanager in southern Illinois must remain hypothetical.

FIELD GUIDES: G=288; N=430; P=260.

Subfamily *Cardinalinae*: Cardinals, Grosbeaks, and Allies

Northern Cardinal *Cardinalis cardinalis*

STATUS AND ABUNDANCE: Common year-round resident.

HABITAT: Shrubby fields, forest edge, residential areas, and forests in which a dense shrub layer is present.

RECORDS AND REMARKS: Cardinals are not known to migrate, but they seem to increase in abundance during late fall and winter, probably because of their tendency to form flocks during these seasons. By the time breeding starts in late February or March, they have paired up and dispersed into individually defended territories. Singing begins early in the year, usually after the first warm spell in January. Nests are usually placed in dense bushes, a few meters above the ground, but they may also be built in vine tangles up to seventeen meters above the ground. Cardinals are parasitized by cowbirds, but apparently they can eject the parasite's egg. Of 150 nests found in Union and Alexander Cos., 40 percent were parasitized. Cowbird and Cardinal eggs are extremely similar in appearance, but Cardinal eggs are larger and tend to have larger brown spots and streaks. Eggs have been found as early as the first week of April, but nesting begins even earlier; one pair was building in Carbondale in mid-March, 1989. They may raise up to three broods in a summer.

During winter, Cardinals occupy hedgerows and shrubby old fields and form flocks with other finches, especially sparrows and juncos. They readily come to bird feeders for sunflower and safflower seeds, cracked corn, and millet. About the only published counts available are those from Spring and Christmas Bird Counts.
409, Union Co., 4 May 1991 (SBC)
1,529, Horseshoe Lake CBC, 20 Dec 1983
889, Crab Orchard NWR CBC, 4 Jan 1976
758, Union Co. CBC, 3 Jan 1986

DOCUMENTATION: Specimen—ad. male, 5 miles w. of Carterville, Williamson Co., 31 Mar 1959 (SIU A-755).

FIELD GUIDES: G=308; N=382; P=268.

Rose-breasted Grosbeak *Pheucticus ludovicianus*

Late April–Mid-May
Early September–Mid-October

STATUS AND ABUNDANCE: Common spring migrant. Rare summer resident. Fairly common fall migrant.

HABITAT: Deciduous forest and forest edge.

RECORDS AND REMARKS: Forages in the understory and the lower to middle canopy. Its rich, liquid, robinlike song is distinctive, as is its squeaky *Eek* call note.

SPRING—A few grosbeaks arrive around 20 April, but most are not detected until the last week of the month. Peak numbers are present from 1 to 15 May, and then the population declines abruptly. Some birds occasionally linger into the first few days of June; some of these lingerers may be potential breeders.

2, Crab Orchard NWR, 19 Apr 1972 (VK)
1, Jackson Co., 22 Apr 1984 (JCR)
45, LaRue Pine Hills, 26 Apr 1975 (BP)
138, Union Co., 4 May 1991 (SBC)
1, Trail of Tears SF, Union Co., 1 June 1990 (WDR)
1, Carbondale, 2 June 1976 (BP)

SUMMER—Only recently confirmed as a breeder in southern Illinois. Most summer records are from the western Floodplains and the Till Plain. Although cowbirds are known to parasitize grosbeaks, so few nests have been found in this region that it is difficult to predict the possible impact of parasitism on grosbeak populations.

pair with nest, near Cutler, Perry Co., 3 June 1989 (WDR)
pair with nest, Turkey Island, Randolph Co., 4 June 1989 (WDR)
pair with yg., Picayune Chute, Alexander Co., 29 June 1988 (WDR)

At least thirteen other records of singing males or pairs have occurred; these records are summarized in Robinson (1991b).

AUTUMN—Migrants begin appearing by early September in most years. Daily high counts are usually of eight to ten birds during peak passage, which is in mid- and late September. Most grosbeaks have moved southward by 10 October.

1, near Little Grassy Lake, Jackson Co., 29 Aug 1976 (BP)
1, Ozark, Johnson Co., 14 Oct 1989 (TF)

Rose-breasted Grosbeak, Ozark, Johnson Co., 10 May 1992

1, Carbondale, 26 Oct 1983 (BC)

DOCUMENTATION: Specimen—imm. male, Marion, Williamson Co., 3 Aug 1935 (SIU A-1903).

FIELD GUIDES: G=310; N=380; P=276.

Black-headed Grosbeak *Pheucticus melanocephalus*

STATUS AND ABUNDANCE: Very rare visitor.

RECORDS AND REMARKS: There is only one record. A male visited a Carbondale feeder from mid-February to 23 March 1972 (DB; Kleen 1972).

DOCUMENTATION: Photograph—Kleen (1972).

FIELD GUIDES: G=292; N=380; P=276.

Blue Grosbeak *Guiraca caerulea*
Late April–Mid-September

STATUS AND ABUNDANCE: Fairly common migrant and summer resident in the Shawnee Hills. Uncommon migrant and summer resident in the Floodplains and the Till Plain.

HABITAT: Hedgerows, shrubby fields, and forest edge.

RECORDS AND REMARKS: Often sings from telephone wires or fence posts, much the same as the similar, but smaller, Indigo Bunting. Its two buffy-orange wing bars and heavier bill separate it from buntings. Males retain the brown femalelike plumage in their first breeding season.

SPRING—The first spring arrivals are usually detected just after 20 April, but a few have been found earlier. Daily counts of five or six birds are not unusual from the Shawnee Hills; slightly smaller counts are expected from the Till Plain and the Floodplains.

1, Fort Massac SP, Massac Co., 13 Apr 1982 (RBr)
2, Crab Orchard NWR, 17 Apr 1972 (VK)
18, Massac Co., 6 May 1972 (SBC)
10, Saline Co., 9 May 1987 (SBC)

SUMMER—Nests are usually placed within three meters of the ground, in a dense shrub or sapling, often in a hedgerow. Snakeskins, plastic, and paper are readily used as nesting material. Few nest data have been gathered. Cowbirds parasitize this species, but the impact on the regional population is not known. Nests with eggs have been found from mid-May through early July.

AUTUMN—Fall migration is unremarkable. Sometimes two to four birds will be found with flocks of other finches in weedy patches or hedgerows during September. Southward migration probably begins in mid-August, but differentiating migrants from summer residents is difficult.

6, Randolph Co., 11 Aug 1987 (WDR)

4, Crab Orchard NWR, 24 Sep 1985 (TF)
1, Ozark, Johnson Co., 4 Oct 1987 (TF)
DOCUMENTATION: Specimen—male, 1 mile s.e. of Dongola, Union
Co., 22 May 1976 (ISU 1700).
FIELD GUIDES: G=310; N=382; P=274.

Indigo Bunting *Passerina cyanea*
Late April–Late October

STATUS AND ABUNDANCE: Common migrant and summer resident.
Rare winter visitor.

HABITAT: Woodland edge, roadsides, and shrubby old fields.

RECORDS AND REMARKS: One of the most abundant songbirds in
the region. Buntings can be found in almost any habitat except for
urbanized areas and deep forest. They may even occur in a forest
if there is an opening in the canopy caused by a road, stream, or
treefall. Males in their first breeding season have patchy blue-and-
brown plumage.
SPRING—First arrivals are not yet in full song; rather they seem
to skulk around in cover and whisper their songs for a few days
before they begin to sing fully. The bulk of first arrivals appear during the last week of April, but some may arrive as early as 10 April;
a published report from 3 April 1986 (AB 40:480) should be considered erroneous. Often the first arrivals are found at bird feeders,
where they feed on sunflower seeds.
2, Rudement, Saline Co., 10 Apr 1992 (JD)
1, Carbondale, 18 Apr 1985 (KM)
768, Union Co., 4 May 1991 (SBC)
258, Massac Co., 9 May 1987 (SBC)
SUMMER—Buntings place their nests near the ground (.3 to 8
meters above), in the crotch of a sapling or bush or woven into the
stalks of several weedy plants. They probably raise two broods when
possible, but high nest predation rates and cowbird parasitism may
impede their success. Of sixty-five nests, 37 percent were parasitized and received an average of 1.7 cowbird eggs per nest in Union
and Alexander Cos. (INHS).
AUTUMN—After breeding, buntings form loose flocks; males molt

into femalelike plumage. Southward migration seems to begin in late August, peaking in September. By the end of October, most buntings have left southern Illinois. A few linger later, even into winter.

migrant flock of 30, Jackson Co., 30 Aug 1975 (BP)

1, Mermet Lake CA, 22 Nov 1986 (TF, WDR)

WINTER—Most winter records are from December and early January, which suggests that these birds are late fall migrants. They usually associate with sparrow flocks in hedgerows and forest edges near patches of unharvested grain, such as sorghum.

1, Crab Orchard NWR, 17 Dec 1988 (KM, WDR)

1, Crab Orchard NWR, 18 Dec 1982 (WDR)

2, Alexander Co., 18 Dec 1984 (VK)

1, Horseshoe Lake CA, 18 Dec 1990 (WDR, SB)

1, Rend Lake, Jefferson Co., 18 Dec 1993 (KM, MSe)

1, Alexander Co., 28 Dec 1979 (HDB, VK)

1, Horseshoe Lake CA, 28 Dec 1988 (SB, WDR)

1, Union Co. CA, 31 Dec 1972–24 Jan 1973 (Kleen 1973b)

male, Carbondale, 4–5 Jan 1985 (MW)

5, Union Co. CA, 19 Dec 1985, with 4 still there on 7 Jan 1986 (VK, RP, WDR)

DOCUMENTATION: Specimen—ad. male, Little Grassy Creek, Williamson Co., 14 Apr 1956 (SIU A-296).

FIELD GUIDES: G=294; N=384; P=274.

Painted Bunting *Passerina ciris*

STATUS AND ABUNDANCE: Very rare visitor.

RECORDS AND REMARKS: An adult male visited a thistle feeder near Makanda, Jackson Co., from 20 to 22 April 1993 (BAM; Gelman 1993)—the region's only record.

DOCUMENTATION: Photograph—1993 record (SIU AP-uncatalogued).

FIELD GUIDES: G=294; N=384; P=274.

Dickcissel *Spiza americana*
Late April–Early October

STATUS AND ABUNDANCE: Common migrant and summer resident. Very rare winter visitor.

HABITAT: Large weedy fields, especially of alfalfa and clover; tends to avoid fescue. Also occurs along grassy ditches around agricultural lands.

RECORDS AND REMARKS: A common roadside bird of agricultural areas, often perches on telephone wires and fence posts. Males sing all day, helping little with nesting activities; females sneak around in cover and can be difficult to find. Numbers seem to vary widely from year to year.

SPRING—By 25 April, the first arrivals have typically been found. Often, the very first birds are detected by their distinctive flight call, a *zrrak*, rather than by song or sight. Dickcissels may not become numerous until well into May. Typical daily high counts range from ten to twenty or more birds. Migrants are difficult to separate from summer residents, so departure dates are unclear.

1, Horseshoe Lake CA, 19 Apr 1991 (TF)
1, Massac Co., 23 Apr 1973 (VK, HDB)
142, Union Co., 8 May 1993 (SBC)
63, Johnson Co., 10 May 1975 (SBC)

SUMMER—Few nests have been found, despite this species' commonness. Nests are placed on or near the ground. Fledged young are present as late as late August.

41, Union Co. CA, 2 June 1982 (PK)

AUTUMN—Form loose flocks after breeding. Rather inconspicuous, they skulk around in weedy patches and must be flushed or spished up to be found. Most are gone by late September, but a few regularly stay into October. Few counts have been made during fall.

WINTER—Overwintering has not been confirmed, but there are three records of birds that were probably very late fall migrants. Such birds sometimes associate with sparrows at feeders.

1, Horseshoe Lake CBC, 3 Jan 1976 (HDB, PW, WO)
1, Rend Lake, Franklin Co., 9 Jan 1994 (TF, JD)
1, Harrisburg, 18 Jan 1986 (KP)

DOCUMENTATION: Written description—Horseshoe Lake CA, Alexander Co., 3 Jan 1976.

FIELD GUIDES: G=322; N=416; P=262.

Subfamily Emberizinae: Emberizines

Green-tailed Towhee *Pipilo chlorurus*

STATUS AND ABUNDANCE: Very rare visitor.

RECORDS AND REMARKS: There are two records of this vagrant that comes from western North America. The 1987 bird frequented an abandoned pig lot that had become overgrown with ragweed; many other sparrows were also present there.

1, near Murphysboro, Jackson Co., 17 Apr 1953 (RB)
1, near Union Co. CA, 3–10 Jan 1987 (MD, RP, m.ob.)

DOCUMENTATION: Written description—1987 record.

FIELD GUIDES: G=324; N=386; P=276.

Rufous-sided Towhee *Pipilo erythrophthalmus*

Mid-February–Mid-April
Mid-September–Mid-November

STATUS AND ABUNDANCE: Common year-round resident.

HABITAT: Brushy areas in woods, hedgerows, shrubby fields, and forest edge.

RECORDS AND REMARKS: Migratory, but the presence of year-round populations makes the separation of migrants from summer residents and winter residents difficult. Migrant populations probably peak in March and October.

SPRING—Towhees begin moving northward early, soon after the first February warm spell. They begin singing at about the same time. Small groups may be encountered during spring, but they do not form the larger, loose flocks typical of fall migration. Typical daily counts range from six to fifteen birds.

SUMMER—Early season nests are often placed on the ground, whereas later nests are placed above the ground in bushes or vine tangles. Towhees are parasitized by cowbirds; 59 percent of forty-four nests were parasitized in Union and Alexander Cos. and received an average of 1.7 cowbird eggs per nest (INHS). Nests with eggs have been found from early May through July. Spring Bird Counts probably census mostly the breeding population.

150, Union Co., 4 May 1991 (SBC)

75, Johnson Co., 7 May 1988 (SBC)

AUTUMN—Because of the breeding population, detection of the first migrants is problematic. Numbers peak during October, when small groups of four to fifteen or more birds can be found associating with sparrows and cardinals in hedgerows and weedy fields.

18, Crab Orchard NWR, 30 Oct 1982 (JCR)

WINTER—Visit rural and suburban bird feeders for corn and millet. They congregate in preferred habitats with flocks of sparrows and can easily be attracted by spishing.

87, Horseshoe Lake CBC, 29 Dec 1976

77, Crab Orchard NWR CBC, 15 Dec 1984

37, Union Co. CBC, 30 Dec 1977

There are at least two records of the western form, the Spotted Towhee:

1, Crab Orchard NWR, 27 Dec 1954 (RB, JWH)

female, Crab Orchard NWR, 16 Dec 1989 (WDR)

DOCUMENTATION: Specimen—ad. male, Carbondale, Jackson Co., 21 Dec 1960 (SIU A-1138).

FIELD GUIDES: G=324; N=386; P=276.

Bachman's Sparrow *Aimophila aestivalis*

Late March–Early September

STATUS AND ABUNDANCE: Very rare (formerly locally uncommon) migrant and summer resident.

HABITAT: Hicks (in Brooks 1938) described the habitat: "The choicest locations are about 50 to 100 yards down from the ridgetops in old deserted fields. A typical territory is a circle 150 feet each way from an eroded gully which has healed and is now well-covered with miscellaneous trees, shrubs, and particularly blackberry brambles. The territory is more attractive after about 5% of the open grass land adjacent to the gullies is dotted with blackberry briars. Usually the center of the territory is close to the upper end of the gully, and the abundant plants are the dry soil goldenrods and asters, wild oat grass, and various other grasses, composites, and miscellaneous weeds typical of dry, eroded slopes." They may also use two somewhat different habitat types. On 17 July 1951, Mengel (1965) found a singing male in Kentucky, across the Ohio River from Joppa, Illinois, "in a flat, poorly tended orchard encroached upon by dense grassy ground cover, with no blackberries or erosion gullies." In northwest Tennessee, they inhabit clearcuts that have been planted with pine seedlings; apparently their abundance peaks when the pines are four to twelve years old (J. C. Robinson 1990). Most southern Illinois records are from habitats that approximate that described by Hicks.

RECORDS AND REMARKS: No records of this elusive sparrow have been obtained since 1975. With the advent of forest destruction for pasturing in the 1800s, the habitat of Bachman's Sparrow became quite available in the region. It is unclear whether there was a prehistorical population in southern Illinois. There is not much reference to this species until the 1940s, but some were probably present earlier, because there are records for central Illinois much earlier in the century. Brewer described them as fairly common summer residents around Murphysboro in 1948, being present from March through July. He did not detect any more, however, until 19 July 1952, when he and J. W. Hardy found a singing male at Cave Hill Ridge south of Harrisburg. A singing male was back near Murphysboro on 10 June 1953 (RB), in an old field adjacent to a pine plantation. In addition, several pairs were found around Crab Orchard NWR that same summer by Lee Bush, but they were rare there by 1954. No others were reported until the mid-1960s, when some apparently nested at Gum Springs on the Massac-Johnson county line (George 1971). In the early seventies, there was a run of records that may be indicative of the increase in observer effort during those years:
1, Crab Orchard NWR, 29 Apr 1972 (VK, PB)
1, Ferne Clyffe SP, Johnson Co., 29 Apr–3 June 1972 (RR, JGre)
1, Pope Co., all summer 1974 (RGr)
ad. and imm., near Little Grassy Lake, Jackson Co., 7 Sep 1975 (BP)

It is unclear why Bachman's Sparrows have disappeared from the region, but nationwide declines in their populations because of habitat destruction throughout their range may be an important part of the explanation.

DOCUMENTATION: Provisional acceptance.

FIELD GUIDES: G=336; N=396; P=282.

American Tree Sparrow *Spizella arborea*
Early November–Late March

STATUS AND ABUNDANCE: Common migrant and winter resident.

HABITAT: Weedy fields and hedgerows.

RECORDS AND REMARKS: Arrive much later than most migrants, sometimes not appearing in any numbers until December. Numbers vary from year to year, apparently depending on the severity of the winter; in mild years, most of the population may stay further north. Form flocks with juncos and with Field Sparrows, Song Sparrows, and other sparrows. Easily spished into view, they pop up to the tops of nearby bushes and trees almost immediately.

AUTUMN—Arrival of first migrants is not very obvious, partly because only a few arrive at first, and also because most observers have focused their efforts on waterbirds, which characteristically arrive much later than songbird migrants.

1, Rend Lake, 15 Nov 1975 (BP)

35, Carbondale, 27 Nov 1948 (RB)

WINTER—Most high counts come from Christmas Bird Counts. Tree Sparrows will occasionally visit bird feeders for millet or other small seeds and will especially come if the food is spread on the ground.

595, Crab Orchard NWR CBC, 28 Dec 1974

586, Union Co. CBC, 2 Jan 1976

398, Horseshoe Lake CBC, 3 Jan 1976

SPRING—Nearly all have departed by the last days of March. The departure is basically a northward withdrawal and is not very conspicuous.

2, Union Co., 5 Apr 1975 (BP)

DOCUMENTATION: Specimen—ad. female, Crab Orchard NWR, Williamson Co., 1 Feb 1961 (SIU A-668).

FIELD GUIDES: G=338; N=398; P=280.

Chipping Sparrow *Spizella passerina*
Late March–Early November

STATUS AND ABUNDANCE: Common migrant and summer resident. Very rare winter visitor.

HABITAT: Short-grass fields, such as golf courses, parks, and yards in towns, as well as open pine and deciduous woodland. During migration, can be found with other sparrows in weedy fields.

RECORDS AND REMARKS: A common bird of the suburban yard and park. Its song is a flat, mechanical trill that seems to be too long for such a small bird to utter. "Chippies" will often visit feeders for millet or other small seeds.

SPRING—During the last week of March, the first birds are reliably found. Sometimes a few will arrive much earlier. They seem to settle on territory right away, so discriminating between migrants and summer residents is difficult; small flocks of four to twenty-five birds encountered along roadsides, however, are likely to be migrants. Such flocks have been seen up through the first week of May, so migration may extend at least that late.

1, Carbondale, 17 Mar 1986 (SO)

1, Ozark, Johnson Co., 18 Mar 1992 (TF)

22, Jackson Co., 14 Apr 1993 (KM)

SUMMER—Despite the species' commonness as a breeder, few quantitative data on its nesting cycle are available. The small, open, cuplike nests are usually placed in evergreen bushes or trees, from one to eight meters above the ground. Nests are often lined with hair before the three or four bluish eggs are laid. Eggs have been found between late April and early July. Spring Bird Counts probably census the breeding population.

58, Jackson Co., 4 May 1974 (SBC)

74, Union Co., 4 May 1991 (SBC)

AUTUMN—After the nesting season, Chippies form small flocks and sometimes associate with other sparrows. They seem to prefer to flock with their own species, though. Peak numbers are present from mid-September to mid-October, and most birds are gone by the first few days of November. Occasionally some will linger into early winter.

70, near Ozark, Pope Co., 14–16 Sep 1993 (TF)

1, Carbondale, 16 Nov 1983 (TF)

1, Williamson Co., 5 Dec 1982 (JCR)

WINTER—Winter records pose an identification problem. Most Chipping Sparrows do not exhibit a rusty cap during winter; rather their crown becomes dull brown with diffuse black streaking. Some winter reports are likely erroneous, because observers report the presence of an unstreaked rusty cap, which is more likely to be present on American Tree Sparrows or Field Sparrows.

1, Union Co. CA, 22 Dec 1994 (HDB)

1, s.e. Jackson Co., 7 Jan 1983 (WDR)

1, Rudement, Saline Co., 9–11 Jan 1992 (JD)

Documentation: Specimen—imm., 3 miles e. of Texico, Jefferson Co., 19 Oct 1958 (SIU A-668).

Field Guides: G=338; N=400; P=280.

Clay-colored Sparrow *Spizella pallida*

Status and abundance: Very rare migrant.

Habitat: Weedy fields and hedgerows.

Records and remarks: Very similar to the Chipping Sparrow, especially during fall and winter, but with a brownish rump and a conspicuous, whitish whisker stripe. May associate with Field and Chipping Sparrows during migration. May be more likely to occur after extended periods of strong westerly winds, because the principal migration path is through the Great Plains.

SPRING—1, Crab Orchard NWR, 24 Apr 1951 (LB)

1 banded, Harrisburg, Saline Co., 29 Apr 1984 (WDR)

AUTUMN—1, Pomona, 21 Oct 1950 (RB, JWH)

Documentation: Provisional acceptance.

Field Guides: G=338; N=400; P=282.

Field Sparrow *Spizella pusilla*

Late February–Late April
Late September–Mid-November

STATUS AND ABUNDANCE: Common year-round resident.

HABITAT: Shrubby fields, roadside edges, and hedgerows.

RECORDS AND REMARKS: A small sparrow with a pink bill, white eyerings, and white wing bars. The song—a sweetly whistled trill that starts out slowly and speeds up toward the end—is a conspicuous part of any second-growth habitat community. Field Sparrows migrate extensively, but southern Illinois lies within both their breeding and their wintering ranges, so some are present all year.
SPRING—Migration is difficult to detect, because of the substantial wintering and breeding populations, but numbers tend to peak during late March and early April. Small flocks of six to fifteen birds are commonly seen, and daily counts of up to forty birds are not unusual.
SUMMER—Breeding begins early; eggs have been found as early as late April. Two broods are probably raised, because dependent fledglings have been seen throughout the summer into August. Nests are placed on or near the ground in fairly dense cover. They are moderately parasitized by cowbirds, but few quantitative data are available. Counts of twenty to forty or more birds per day are typical. Spring Bird Counts census mostly the breeding population.
82, Union Co., 4 May 1991 (SBC)
78, Johnson Co., 5 May 1984 (SBC)
AUTUMN—Migrants begin arriving by the last days of September, but their arrival is usually not conspicuous. They often associate with other sparrows in appropriate habitat.
60, Crab Orchard NWR, 24 Oct 1982 (JCR)
WINTER—Congregate in weedy fields and hedgerows with other sparrows and finches, sometimes in large dispersed flocks of up to eighty individuals. Will visit feeders for millet and other small seeds. During very severe winters, many either die or move south out of the region, because late winter populations are considerably lower than early winter numbers.
282, Horseshoe Lake CBC, 20 Dec 1983
249, Crab Orchard NWR CBC, 4 Jan 1976
171, Union Co. CBC, 3 Jan 1987

DOCUMENTATION: Specimen—female, Carbondale, Jackson Co., 7 Jan 1973 (ISM 605487).

FIELD GUIDES: G=338; N=398; P=280.

Vesper Sparrow *Pooecetes gramineus*
Late March–Late April
Mid-September–Early November

STATUS AND ABUNDANCE: Uncommon spring migrant. Occasional fall migrant. Rare winter visitor. Very rare summer resident.

HABITAT: Extensive open grassy fields.

RECORDS AND REMARKS: Most Vespers are found along the Mississippi River floodplain, especially along the levees and adjacent agricultural fields. They do not often sing on their passage through southern Illinois for some reason, which significantly reduces the rate at which they are detected by birders.

SPRING—Small groups of up to six birds are seen in short-grass fields, especially during late March and early April. Few birds linger past 25 April.

1, s.w. Jackson Co., 8 Mar 1992 (TF, JD)
1, Williamson Co., 15 Mar 1984 (JCR)
1, Carbondale, 17 Mar 1989 (BD)
10, Gorham, Jackson Co., 1 Apr 1972 (VK)
1, Unionville, Massac Co., 7 May 1988 (WDR)

SUMMER—There is one record of breeding. A nest with eggs was found among bean stubble in a field near Thompsonville, Saline Co., on 2 May 1994 (TF). The only other summer record is of a singing male at Todds Mill, Perry Co., on 2 June 1989 (WDR).

AUTUMN—Very inconspicuous during fall. Few are encountered; most records are of only a single individual. Most have departed by early November; those encountered later may linger into early winter.

1, Rend Lake, Jefferson Co., 4 Oct 1993 (TF)
1, Williamson Co., 24 Nov 1982 (JCR)

WINTER—There are several winter records, but overwintering has not been confirmed. Most records come from December and early January, which suggests that these birds are late fall migrants. They are typically found as singles or in groups of up to two or three,

often in weedy fields with other species of sparrows, especially when some unharvested grain is left standing nearby.
1, Rend Lake, Franklin Co., 31 Dec 1975 (BP)
1, Ware, Union Co., 3 Jan 1986 (TF)
1, n.w. Union Co., 6 Jan 1973 (VK, HDB et al.)
1, Union Co. CA, 7 Jan 1986 (WDR)
Some recent records from Christmas Bird Counts follow: Horseshoe Lake—1, 30 Dec 1974; 6, 2 Jan 1981; 1, 20 Dec 1983; 3, 29 Dec 1987; 4, 17 Dec 1991. Union Co.—1, 23 Dec 1981. Crab Orchard NWR—1, 30 Dec 1972.

Documentation: Written description—1, near Tamms, Alexander Co., 29 Dec 1987 (TF, WDR).

FIELD GUIDES: G=332; N=392; P=284.

Lark Sparrow *Chondestes grammacus*

Late April–Late September

STATUS AND ABUNDANCE: Occasional migrant. Locally uncommon summer resident in the Till Plain.

HABITAT: Weedy fields with scattered bare patches of sandy soil (e.g., strip mines).

RECORDS AND REMARKS: A species of open grasslands that has apparently undergone a recent population decline. Ridgway (1878) described them as common summer residents, but Graber and Graber (1963) noted a substantial population decline. The cause of the decline is unclear.
SPRING—Not often seen away from breeding areas, but some have been encountered in groups of two to six birds along weedy roadsides, especially along levees. They sometimes associate with other sparrow species. Most migrant flocks have been found during late April. The breeding population obscures the departure of migrants, but most migrants have probably departed by mid-May.
2, w. Williamson Co., 19 Apr 1986 (TF, WDR)
1, Union Co. CA, 3 May 1987 (TF et al.)
1, Saline Co., 9 May 1987 (SO)
SUMMER—Pairs are found in areas where sandy soil is prevalent. Few nests have been discovered, but several family groups have

been reported, especially during June and July. Nests are placed on the ground, at the base of a tuft of grasses.

pair with young, near Pinckneyville, Perry Co., 9 June 1956 (RB)

2 males, near Bremen, Randolph Co., 14 June 1988 (WDR)

4 ad. and 5 juv., w. Williamson Co., 16 June 1984 (TF)

2 ad. and 2 juv., Tamaroa, Perry Co., 17 June 1989 (WDR)

6, near DeSoto, Jackson Co., 1 July 1972 (VK, DH)

1 ad. and 1 juv., Carbondale, 24 July 1990 (WDR)

AUTUMN—Very few are detected after the breeding season. The largest population of migrants may pass through during August, a month when few observers survey habitats that this species prefers.

1, Herod, Saline Co., 15 Aug 1988 (JD)

DOCUMENTATION: Specimen—ad. male, 3 miles n. of Ava, Jackson Co., 22 May 1968 (SIU, uncatalogued).

FIELD GUIDES: G=332; N=394; P=282.

Savannah Sparrow *Passerculus sandwichensis*

Late September–Mid-November
Mid-March–Mid-May

STATUS AND ABUNDANCE: Common migrant. Uncommon winter resident. Very rare summer visitor.

HABITAT: Large weedy fields, fallow fields, and pastures.

RECORDS AND REMARKS: Often overlooked because it frequents expansive grassy fields and agricultural fields. Savannahs are most readily found by walking through such fields and flushing them; they tend to fly directly and rather far compared to other sparrows. They also tend to look grayer and have a somewhat triangular-shaped tail when viewed from behind; lighting and wind can make using these characteristics for identification difficult. They also tend to run on the ground once they land, so it can be frustrating to locate them when trying to flush them up again.

AUTUMN—The first fall migrants begin appearing during the last week of September. Numbers peak during October, but the wintering population obscures this peak and the departure dates of migrants.

2, Rend Lake, Jefferson Co., 30 Sep 1989 (BD, WDR)

60, Royalton, Franklin Co., 14 Oct 1993 (LS)

WINTER—Winter numbers seem to vary from year to year, probably depending on the availability of untilled agricultural fields. Savannahs seem to be especially common in foxtail fields. Most high counts come from Christmas Bird Counts.

67, Horseshoe Lake CBC, 18 Dec 1984
46, Cypress Creek NWR CBC, 21 Dec 1994
20, Union Co. CBC, 22 Dec 1994
29, Crab Orchard NWR, 1 Jan 1983 (JCR)
6, Baldwin Lake, Randolph Co., 2 Jan 1984 (TF)

SPRING—Because of the presence of the wintering population, the beginning of spring migration is unclear, but there appears to be an influx of birds during March. Populations peak in April, when large concentrations can sometimes be found in excellent habitat. Most birds have departed by 15 May, but a few may linger later.

129, near Perks, Pulaski Co., 18 Apr 1992 (TF, WDR)
1, Williamson Co., 14 May 1984 (JCR)
1, Ft. Defiance SP, Alexander Co., 26 May 1988 (WDR)

SUMMER—There is no confirmed evidence of breeding yet. There may be a very sparse summer population in the Till Plain.

1, Rudement, Saline Co., 11 June 1991 (TF, JD)
1, Jefferson Co., 21 June 1991 (TF)
1, s. of Murphysboro, 22 July 1951 (JWH)

DOCUMENTATION: Specimen—ad., near Mound City, Pulaski Co., 6 Apr 1968 (SIU, uncatalogued).

FIELD GUIDES: G=328; N=392; P=286.

Grasshopper Sparrow *Ammodramus savannarum*

Mid-April–Early November

STATUS AND ABUNDANCE: Uncommon migrant. Locally uncommon summer resident in the Till Plain. Rare summer resident in the Floodplains and the Shawnee Hills. Very rare winter visitor.

HABITAT: Weedy fields, especially of clover and alfalfa; tends to avoid fescue. Also uses pastures (even short-grass pastures) during migration.

RECORDS AND REMARKS: Its insectlike song is virtually the only clue that this species is present. It is rarely seen unless it is vocal, and even then it is surprisingly difficult to observe. Singing birds tend to perch atop tall weeds. When the bird is flushed, its back appears to be rather gray, and its flight is direct, with rapid bursts of wing beats. SPRING—The arrival dates of migrants may have changed in recent times; many early records from the 1940s and 1950s are from late March, whereas recent early dates are all from mid- to late April. Numbers peak in late April and early May. The presence of the breeding population obscures detection of late departure dates.

3, Carbondale, 24 Mar 1949 (RB)

1, Ozark, Johnson Co., 17 Apr 1991 (TF)

10, Paulton, Williamson Co., 18 Apr 1987 (WDR)

36, Pope Co., 10 May 1980 (SBC)

SUMMER—Very few nests have been discovered in the region, primarily because the small, ground nests are hidden in vast fields of grasses. Consequently, little is known about its breeding success or the timing of its breeding activities.

nest with 4 eggs, north of Murphysboro, 4 June 1949 (JWH)

AUTUMN—Not often detected, undoubtedly because the birds are silent during fall migration. Some may be flushed from extensive weedy fields, however, when a concerted search is made. The typical date of departure is unclear; some birds apparently linger late into winter.

1, Rend Lake, Jefferson Co., 13 Aug, and a different bird there, 31 Aug 1994 (CS, TF)

imm., Rend Lake, Jefferson Co., 7 Sep 1988 (TF, WDR)

1, near Murphysboro, 8 Nov 1947 (JWH)

WINTER—1 banded, Carbondale, 10 Jan 1972 (VK, DH)

DOCUMENTATION: Photograph—1, Carbondale, Jackson Co., 10 Jan 1972 (SIU AP-uncatalogued).

FIELD GUIDES: G=328; N=388; P=286.

Henslow's Sparrow *Ammodramus henslowii*

Late April–Late October

STATUS AND ABUNDANCE: Rare migrant and summer resident. Very rare winter visitor.

HABITAT: Tall-grass fields, primarily those that have not been mown or burned within the last three years.

RECORDS AND REMARKS: An inconspicuous species that may be

Henslow's Sparrow, near Delwood, Pope Co., June 1986

overlooked easily because of its elusive nature and insectlike *tsi-lik* song. Sometimes will perch on tall weeds when they sing, but they often sing from lower perches, too, which can make them very difficult to see. When not singing, they are remarkably difficult to locate. When flushed up, they fly low and seem to pull themselves forward in jerky spurts, often with their body diagonally out of alignment with the direction of flight. Formerly probably most numerous in the Till Plain, where patches of prairie were available, but because of intense land use practices and habitat destruction, most current records come from the Shawnee Hills, where hayfields are apparently allowed to remain unharvested longer than those in the Till Plain.

SPRING—First arrivals are usually detected by 20 April. Most spring records seem to be of breeders arriving on nesting territories rather than of true transients.

3 or 4, Rudement, Saline Co., 7 Apr 1993 (JD)

1 banded, Oakwood Bottoms, Jackson Co., 15 Apr 1972 (VK)

3, near Anna, Union Co., 18 Apr 1992 (TF)

1, Paulton, Williamson Co., 19 Apr 1987 (TF, WDR)

4, near Anna, Union Co., 4 May 1991 (SBC)

13, Saline Co., 8 May 1994 (BW)

SUMMER—No nests have been reported, but nest building and juveniles have been seen. Birds remain on their territory at least through July, perhaps even into August, but there are few reports after mid-July, possibly because territorial birds have been displaced because of mowing.

singing male, Pope Co., 31 May–5 June 1986 (TF, WDR)

2 pairs, Pope Co., early June–19 July 1988 (TF, WDR)

1, Pope Co., 1 June 1989 (TF)

3 or 4 territories, Rudement, Saline Co., with nest building on 8 June 1993 (JD)

2 ad. and 2 juv., Lake of Egypt, Johnson Co., 12–21 July 1981 (MMl)

singing male, Giant City SP, 30 July 1983 (JCR)

10, Pope Co., 31 July 1994 (BW)

5 singing, near Logan, Franklin Co., 1–14 Aug 1993 (LS, BD)

AUTUMN—The start of fall migration is unclear. Singing stops during late August, so very few are detected thereafter. Migration may extend into early November or later, and some may attempt to overwinter, but there are no recent winter records.

1, Rend Lake, 21 Oct 1984 (LH)

WINTER—Perhaps formerly a more regular winter resident; Cooke (1888) and Ridgway (1889) suggested they wintered in the region but did not provide any supporting details.

1, Murphysboro, 27 Dec 1950 (JWH, KS)

1, Jackson Co., 21 Jan 1950 (RB)

1, Carbondale, 26 Feb 1949 (RB)

DOCUMENTATION: Photograph—ad. male, Pope Co., 19 June 1988 (SIU AP-118).

FIELD GUIDES: G=328; N=388; P=286.

Le Conte's Sparrow *Ammodramus leconteii*

Mid-October–Mid-April

STATUS AND ABUNDANCE: Uncommon migrant and winter resident.

HABITAT: Grassy fields, usually dominated by foxtail. Generally prefers portions of the field where foxtail is still standing and dense and the ground is wet.

RECORDS AND REMARKS: An elusive species that rarely vocalizes in the region. To find LeConte's, one must walk through grassy foxtail fields and watch carefully for small, grayish, short-tailed sparrows that flush up at the last possible second, fly a short distance, and then drop straight back down into the grass. These birds usually run on the ground after being flushed, so they can be hard to find and flush again. Sometimes, after they have been flushed several times, they will "tire out" and perch in the open for a few minutes. Because of the difficulties involved in seeing and correctly identifying LeConte's Sparrow, little is known about the timing or magnitude of their migrant and winter populations. There appears to be a fall migration pulse in October and November and a spring migration pulse in March and early April.

AUTUMN—First fall arrivals appear during October. Good numbers are usually present throughout November and early December. By mid-December the population seems lower, but systematic surveys are needed to determine when fall migration ends and to determine the winter population sizes.

2, Crab Orchard NWR, 14 Oct 1984 (JCR)

WINTER—Winter populations fluctuate widely; numbers seem to depend directly on the amount of foxtail fields available. In good habitat, typical daily counts are of one to four birds.

12, Crab Orchard NWR CBC, 19 Dec 1987
23, Cypress Creek NWR CBC, 22 Dec 1994
9, Union Co. CBC, 22 Dec 1982
11, Crab Orchard NWR, 1 Jan 1983 (JCR)
1, Baldwin Lake, Randolph Co., 2 and 6 Jan 1984 (TF)
66, Rend Lake CBC, 2 Jan 1977

SPRING—Northward migration may begin as early as the last two weeks of February, but more observations are needed. Certainly, migration is underway by mid-March, and it extends into April, but rarely later.

1, Will Scarlet Mine, Saline Co., 7 Mar 1992 (TF, JD)
1, Crab Orchard NWR, 15 Mar 1986 (WDR)
1, near Carbondale, 22 Apr 1972 (VK, DH)
1, Rend Lake, Jefferson Co., 3 May 1988 (TF, JCR et al.)

DOCUMENTATION: Specimen—female, Bald Knob, Union Co., 2 Nov 1974 (SIU A-1922).

FIELD GUIDES: G=330; N=390; P=288.

Sharp-tailed Sparrow *Ammodramus caudacutus*

Late September–Late October

STATUS AND ABUNDANCE: Very rare migrant.

HABITAT: Dense grassy vegetation in large fields and marshes, usually near water.

RECORDS AND REMARKS: An easily overlooked sparrow that is probably more numerous than the few records indicate. Closely resembles LeConte's Sparrow, but has a gray central crown stripe and unstreaked nape. Not known to vocalize in the region (though it may give chip notes if alarmed), so discovery of this skulker requires flushing one.

SPRING—As yet, no records are known from spring. Should occur during mid- or late May.

AUTUMN—1, Rend Lake, Jefferson Co., 18 Sep 1994 (TF)
1 to 2, Baldwin Lake, Randolph Co., 21–27 Sep 1980 (RK)
1, Rend Lake, Jefferson Co., 10–12 Oct 1987 (TF, JCR)
1, Rend Lake, Jefferson Co., 13 Oct 1985 (LH)
1, Crab Orchard NWR, 22 Oct 1950 (JWH, RB)

DOCUMENTATION: Written description—1, Rend Lake, Jefferson Co., 10–12 Oct 1987.

FIELD GUIDES: G=330; N=390; P=288.

Fox Sparrow *Passerella iliaca*

Early October–Late November
Mid-February–Mid-April

STATUS AND ABUNDANCE: Fairly common migrant. Fairly common winter resident in the Shawnee Hills and the Floodplains. Uncommon winter resident in the Till Plain.

HABITAT: Woodland edge, weedy fields (especially those with giant ragweed), and multiflora hedgerows.

RECORDS AND REMARKS: A large sparrow that forages on the ground by scratching in the leaf litter; sometimes also takes seeds and berries from understory vegetation. The call note is a distinctive, loud, juncolike *tuk*. Sometimes forms small flocks, especially in favored habitat. Associates with other sparrow and finch species in weedy fields and hedgerows.

AUTUMN—First arrivals are detected in early October, but numbers do not peak until late October and November. The end of fall migration is obscured by the substantial winter population in the Shawnee Hills and the Floodplains, but numbers drop conspicuously after late November in the Till Plain.

1, near Little Grassy Lake, Jackson Co., 2 Oct 1976 (BP)
1, s.w. Williamson Co., 4 Oct 1987 (WDR)
21, West Frankfort, Franklin Co., 10 Nov 1993 (LS)

WINTER—Most of the winter population is in the Shawnee Hills and the southern Floodplains, where daily counts of three to ten birds are typical. Most high counts come from Christmas Bird Counts.

38, Crab Orchard NWR CBC, 17 Dec 1983
7, Rend Lake CBC, 17 Dec 1994
50, Cypress Creek NWR CBC, 21 Dec 1994
117, Horseshoe Lake CBC, 30 Dec 1987
45, Union Co. CBC, 31 Dec 1987

SPRING—The beginning of spring migration is obscured by the winter population. Some arrivals may occur as early as mid-February, probably depending on weather. In colder springs, the northward movement may be delayed until March. The rich, beautiful song is sometimes heard during March and April.

29, Pomona, 17 Mar 1972 (VK)
2, Giant City SP, 13 Apr 1989 (WDR)

DOCUMENTATION: Specimen—ad. female, 2 miles n. of Cobden, Union Co., 30 Mar 1966 (SIU A-1384).

FIELD GUIDES: G=342; N=406; P=284.

Song Sparrow *Melospiza melodia*

STATUS AND ABUNDANCE: Common year-round resident.

HABITAT: Weedy fields, marshes, residential areas, roadsides, and hedgerows.

RECORDS AND REMARKS: One of the most numerous sparrows. A frequent component of mixed-species flocks of sparrows and finches. Can be found in almost any weedy patch or hedgerow during late fall and winter. There is definite migration, but the large winter and breeding populations obscure the arrivals and departures of migrants. Spring migration seems to peak in March, whereas fall migration peaks in October and November.

SUMMER—A rare breeder in the late 1800s and early 1900s, but has increased dramatically and now breeds throughout the region, though it is not yet common during summer in some sections. Breeding populations appear to be highest in and near brushy marshes and willow thickets. Some breed in towns, especially where shrubs are present, but not in numbers comparable to central or northern regions of Illinois. Song Sparrows are parasitized by cowbirds in the region, but there are few data available. Nest dates range from early April into early August. Most Spring Bird Counts census the breeding population.

80, Union Co., 4 May 1991 (SBC)

WINTER—Sometimes congregates in large numbers in good habitat; most high counts are from Christmas Bird Counts. Typical daily counts by single observers are twenty-five to seventy-five birds, with the highest numbers occurring in the southern Floodplains.

721, Horseshoe Lake CBC, 30 Dec 1987
894, Union Co. CBC, 22 Dec 1994
438, Crab Orchard NWR, 4 Jan 1976

DOCUMENTATION: Specimen—male, Carbondale, Jackson Co., 15 Mar 1970 (SIU A-1568).

FIELD GUIDES: G=322; N=392; P=284.

Lincoln's Sparrow *Melospiza lincolnii*

Late April–Mid-May
Late September–Early November

STATUS AND ABUNDANCE: Uncommon migrant. Very rare winter resident.

HABITAT: Brushy marshes, weedy fields, hedgerows, and shrubby patches in swamps.

RECORDS AND REMARKS: A rather inconspicuous sparrow that skulks in dense cover. Its song has a distinctive sound, rather like House Wren's. Sometimes confused with immature Swamp Sparrows, especially during fall and winter, but note the chestnut in the greater wing coverts and the grayer breast of Swamp Sparrows.

SPRING—Usually not encountered until after 20 April, though sometimes arrives earlier. Maximum daily counts rarely exceed three individuals. Numbers peak in early May and then rapidly decline; the last birds have departed by about 20 May.

2, Oakwood Bottoms, Jackson Co., 15 Apr 1972 (VK)
1, Carbondale, 15 Apr 1979 (MMl)
19, Union Co., 7 May 1977 (SBC)
1, Union Co. CA, 20 May 1972 (VK)

AUTUMN—Because Lincoln's do not sing in fall, fewer are reported then. They regularly are found in habitat patches where other sparrow species are numerous, though they do not seem to directly associate with the other birds. The termination of fall migration may depend on weather; in warm winters, some late fall migrants may linger and attempt to overwinter.

8, Fountain Bluff, Jackson Co., 4 Oct 1993 (CS)
9, West Frankfort, Franklin Co., 21 Oct 1993 (LS)
2, Harrisburg, Saline Co., 23 Nov 1989 (WDR)

WINTER—May regularly attempt to overwinter, especially in the southern Floodplains, but the pattern is somewhat obscured by the numerous reports from Christmas Bird Counts, most of which are plagued by identification problems. Observers should use great care when identifying winter Lincoln's.

1, near Wolf Lake, Union Co., 22 Dec 1994 (WDR, TRR)
1, Alexander Co., 29 Dec 1977 (BP)
1, Rudement, Saline Co., 14 Jan 1992 (JD)
1, Pomona, 6 Feb 1971 (VK)
1, Crab Orchard NWR, 12 and 26 Feb 1983 (JCR)

DOCUMENTATION: Specimen—ad. female, near Cobden, Union Co., 15 May 1968 (WGG 2223).

FIELD GUIDES: G=342; N=406; P=284.

Swamp Sparrow *Melospiza georgiana*

Late September–Early May

STATUS AND ABUNDANCE: Common migrant and winter resident.

HABITAT: Marshes, wet weedy fields, and woodland thickets.

RECORDS AND REMARKS: Medium-sized reddish-brown sparrows with a fairly long tail, "Swampies" have a distinctive metallic chip note and readily respond to spishing noises; these two habits greatly increase the conspicuousness of this common species. They also sing a fairly musical trill, primarily from mid-March through their departure in early or mid-May.

AUTUMN—First arrivals typically appear during the last week of September or first few days of October. Migration probably peaks during late October and November, but few high counts are available. Distinguishing migrants from winter residents is problematic because of the presence of the large winter population.

1, Crab Orchard NWR, 21 Sep 1989 (WDR)

WINTER—Sometimes very numerous in wet fields, especially in the southern Floodplains and in western sections of the Shawnee Hills; much less abundant, though still common, in the northern Floodplains and the Till Plain. Along with Song Sparrows and other species that prefer wet habitats during winter, Swampies will sometimes visit bird feeders for millet.

654, Union Co. CBC, 22 Dec 1994

430, Horseshoe Lake CBC, 29 Dec 1976

187, Crab Orchard NWR CBC, 4 Jan 1976

SPRING—Northward migration is obscured by the large winter population, but large numbers sometimes occur in optimal habitat during March and April. Very few birds linger past 10 May.

100, Crab Orchard NWR, 28 Mar 1987 (WDR)

2, s.e. Saline Co., 10 May 1986 (SO)

2, Crab Orchard NWR, 17 May 1983 (JCR)

DOCUMENTATION: Specimen—male, Crab Orchard NWR, Williamson Co., 2 Feb 1961 (SIU A-1202).

FIELD GUIDES: G=342; N=406; P=280.

White-throated Sparrow *Zonotrichia albicollis*

Late September–Early May

STATUS AND ABUNDANCE: Common migrant and winter resident.

HABITAT: Brushy fields and woods, hedgerows, and residential areas.

RECORDS AND REMARKS: One of the most numerous winter sparrows. Large noisy flocks sometimes congregate in hedgerows to form nocturnal roosts. They regularly associate with other sparrow and finch species in weedy fields and brushy tangles along woodland edge. During spring, in particular, they often forage and sing in woodlands, making a morning echo with their beautiful, whistled song. Regular visitors to bird feeders, they especially come for millet that is spread on the ground near a brush pile or conifer tree that can be used for cover.

AUTUMN—Typical first arrival dates are near 20 September, but the first big pulse of migrants is routinely associated with the first cold front in early October. The large winter population obscures the peak and termination of fall migration.

1, Crab Orchard NWR, 12 Sep 1987 (WDR)

WINTER—Most high counts come from Christmas Bird Counts. Typical daily counts by single observers, however, range from twenty to seventy-five birds. Populations are highest in the Shawnee Hills and the Floodplains and lowest in the Till Plain. Highest densities can be found in hedgerows adjacent to grain crops, such as sorghum, that are left unharvested.

1,473, Horseshoe Lake CBC, 18 Dec 1984

1,087, Union Co. CBC, 19 Dec 1984

1,100, Crab Orchard NWR CBC, 15 Dec 1984

350, Union Co. CA, 2 Jan 1976 (BP)

SPRING—Because of the winter population, the beginning of spring migration is difficult to detect, but it may begin as early as mid- or late February in warm springs. An increase in song activity in March and April increases the conspicuousness of these birds. Most have departed by the end of the first week of May.

1, s.e. Saline Co., 9 May 1987 (SO)

male, Pomona, 26 May 1986 (TF, WDR)

male, Trail of Tears SF, 7 June 1990 (SKR)

DOCUMENTATION: Specimen—ad. male, LaRue Pine Hills, Union Co., 3 May 1956 (SIU A-306).

FIELD GUIDES: G=340; N=404; P=278.

White-crowned Sparrow *Zonotrichia leucophrys*
Early October–Early May

STATUS AND ABUNDANCE: Fairly common migrant and winter resident.

HABITAT: Woodland edge, brushy fields, and hedgerows (especially multiflora rose).

RECORDS AND REMARKS: Closely resembles the White-throated Sparrow, but has a peaked head, pink bill, and clear gray breast and throat, which lacks black mustache streaks. Immatures have rusty crown stripes that border buffy crown patches, instead of the black-and-white pattern of adults. White-crowns sometimes come to feeders for millet. Two subspecies have been reported from the region: *Z. l. leucophrys,* the eastern race, has black lores and is the predominant form in the region; whereas *Z. l. gambelii,* from the western United States and Canada, has white lores and is very rare (though it is easily overlooked). An adult Gambel's White-crowned Sparrow was at Wayne Fitzgerrell SP, Franklin Co., on 21 December 1990 (WDR).

AUTUMN—Arrives with the first cold front in the first week of October, occasionally earlier. Surprisingly, no high counts have been published for fall migration, but typical daily counts range from five to twenty-five birds, with occasional concentrations of up to fifty or more birds.
1, Crab Orchard NWR, 3 Oct 1987 (SO)

WINTER—Forms flocks with other species of sparrows, especially White-throats, though it is not unusual to find pure flocks in multiflora hedgerows.
270, Crab Orchard NWR CBC, 17 Dec 1983
194, Cypress Creek NWR CBC, 21 Dec 1994
305, Horseshoe Lake CBC, 2 Jan 1987
116, Union Co. CBC, 2 Jan 1976

SPRING—The large winter population makes detection of spring arrivals problematic. The bulk of migration appears to occur much later for White-crowns than for other sparrow species, however, being concentrated in the last half of April and early May. A few regularly linger past the middle of May.
3, Williamson Co., 9 May 1987 (SBC)

1, Cache, Alexander Co., 27 May 1989 (EW)
1, Kinkaid Lake, Jackson Co., 28 May 1983 (JCR)

DOCUMENTATION: Specimen—female, Carbondale, Jackson Co., 30 Dec 1960 (SIU A-1135).

FIELD GUIDES: G=340; N=404; P=278.

Harris' Sparrow *Zonotrichia querula*

Late September–Early May

STATUS AND ABUNDANCE: Rare migrant and winter resident.

HABITAT: Brushy fields and woods; multiflora rose hedgerows.

RECORDS AND REMARKS: Most records of this sparrow of the Great Plains come from the winter season; surprisingly few have been encountered during migration. They often associate with White-crowned Sparrows in multiflora hedgerows. There are apparently no records from the eastern counties.

AUTUMN—There are few fall records; theoretically, Harris' should arrive in late September and depart by mid-November. The reason for the paucity of fall records is unclear, but the species may simply be overlooked.

1, Carbondale, 22 Oct 1988 (BD)

WINTER—Most sightings are of one to three birds visiting feeders or associating with White-crowned Sparrows in hedgerows. Although the birds appear to overwinter in at least some years, most of the reports are of birds that were observed over a period of only a few days. This pattern may occur simply because most birds have been discovered during Christmas Bird Counts.

3, Union Co. CA, 19 Dec 1971, 2 of which were banded on 8 Jan 1972 (VK)
1, Horseshoe Lake CBC, 30 Dec 1974
1, Union Co. CA, 3–5 Jan 1987 (RC, WDR)
3, Crab Orchard NWR CBC, 4 Jan 1976
1, Carbondale, 14 Jan 1976 (BP)
imm., Union Co. CA, 24–25 Jan 1973 (VK)
2, Carbondale, all winter 1972–1973 (DH)

SPRING—The spring migration pulse is very late; it begins by mid-April (perhaps earlier) and extends into May.

ad., Oakwood Bottoms, Jackson Co., 8 May 1971 (VK, DH)
1, Carbondale, 13 May 1972 (DH)
DOCUMENTATION: Specimen—female, 2 miles n. of Cobden, Union Co., 18 Mar 1967 (SIU A-1677).
FIELD GUIDES: G=340; N=404; P=278.

Dark-eyed Junco *Junco hyemalis*
Early October–Mid-April

STATUS AND ABUNDANCE: Common migrant and winter resident. Very rare summer visitor.

HABITAT: Nearly any weedy or brushy area. Also numerous at feeders in residential areas.

RECORDS AND REMARKS: One of the most numerous winter birds, at times even abundant. Flocks of ten to two hundred birds are commonplace. They seem to occupy nearly any available weed patch or woodland edge. The plumage is highly variable. In the predominant subspecies, *J. h. hyemalis*, the "Slate-colored" Junco, the males are a very dark, slaty gray, whereas females and immatures are much paler, sometimes even appearing to be brown. At least two other subspecies have been reported in the region. *J. h. montanus*, the "Oregon" Junco, is regularly reported, but it poses a difficult identification problem because intergrades between this form and the more common *J. h. hyemalis* closely resemble female and immature Oregons. Consequently, most reports should be regarded with caution unless of adult males. Oregons probably occur as very rare migrants and winter residents. *J. h. aikeni*, the "White-winged" Junco, has been reported at least once (Carbon Lake, Jackson Co., 15 Dec 1948, [RB]), but specimen evidence is needed; it is not unusual for Slate-colored Juncos to show some traces of white wing bars. Finally, *J. h. shufeldti*, the "Gray-headed" Junco, has been reported once from Mt. Vernon (7 May 1983 [FG]).
AUTUMN—The first juncos typically arrive behind the first cold front in October, and they are widespread by late October. Because of the winter population, the end of fall migration is difficult to discern, but populations appear to level off by late November or early December.

1, Carbondale, 4 Oct 1986 (WDR)

WINTER—Most high counts come from Christmas Bird Counts. Daily counts by single observers usually range from forty to one hundred birds. Juncos are frequent visitors to feeders, where they will take millet, cracked corn, sunflower seed, and occasionally suet.

1,305, Union Co. CBC, 19 Dec 1984

1,726, Horseshoe Lake CBC, 20 Dec 1983

2,623, Crab Orchard NWR CBC, 4 Jan 1976

"Oregon" male, Pankeyville, Saline Co., Feb 1987 (SIU AP-146; KP)

"Oregon" female, s.e. Jackson Co., 19 Feb 1989 (WDR)

SPRING—Northward migration may begin as early as late February, because numbers seem to increase during March. Most birds have departed by the end of March, but stragglers routinely linger into the first three weeks of April, but rarely later.

1, Ozark, Johnson Co., 24 Apr 1989 (TF)

1, Alexander Co., 7 May 1977 (SBC)

SUMMER—ad. collected, near Elizabethtown, Hardin Co., 9 June 1881 (Forbes 1881)

DOCUMENTATION: Specimen—male, Giant City SP, Jackson Co., 20 Jan 1982 (SIU A-1823

FIELD GUIDES: G=339; N=402; P=266.

Lapland Longspur *Calcarius lapponicus*

Early November–Late March

STATUS AND ABUNDANCE: Uncommon migrant and winter resident in the Floodplains and the Till Plain. Rare migrant in the Shawnee Hills.

HABITAT: Large, fallow agricultural fields.

RECORDS AND REMARKS: This sparrowlike species often associates with flocks of Horned Larks and forages with them for seeds strewn across barren agricultural fields. Longspurs can be difficult to see, but their distinctive call, which resembles the sound made when a person runs a finger along the tines of a comb, alerts the observer to their presence.

AUTUMN—Single individuals flying overhead uttering their distinctive flight call are typically the first fall arrivals encountered. Although some may occasionally appear in October, most migrants do not begin arriving until November or December.

1, Rend Lake, 27 Oct 1985 (LH)
1, Carbondale, 6 Nov 1988 (WDR)
16, Crab Orchard NWR, 21 Nov 1989 (WDR)
WINTER—Numbers vary widely from year to year and seem to depend in large part on the amount of snow cover. Heavy snowfall concentrates birds along roadsides, where they are more visible and hence easier to count.
48, Crab Orchard NWR CBC, 15 Dec 1984
818, Horseshoe Lake CBC, 18 Dec 1984
1,200, Murphysboro, Jackson Co., 23 Dec 1951 (RB, JWH)
5,000, w. Jackson Co., 8 Jan 1995 (BD, TF, JD)
100, Baldwin Lake, Randolph Co., 23 Jan 1983 (RG, SRu)
200, Olive Branch, Alexander Co., 28 Jan 1975 (RS, HDB)
160, Perry Co., 15 Feb 1986 (WDR)
SPRING—The spring retreat northward is inconspicuous. Most birds move back north as soon as the snow melts. A few are recorded each year into late March, but late departure dates vary from year to year.
70, Rend Lake, Jefferson Co., 4 Mar 1988 (TF)

DOCUMENTATION: Provisional acceptance.

FIELD GUIDES: G=344; N=410; P=264.

Smith's Longspur *Calcarius pictus*

Early March–Early April
November

STATUS AND ABUNDANCE: Very rare spring migrant.

HABITAT: Large short-grass fields and fallow agricultural areas.

RECORDS AND REMARKS: An elusive species that may very well be more common than the few records indicate. Small single-species groups tend to forage in the middle of extensive fields, so they can be easily overlooked. They seem to have a preference for patches of short vegetation that have been flattened by being submerged under ephemeral pools of rainwater. Because there are so few records, the timing of migrational passage through the region is not well known.

The primary migration route is through the Great Plains, so they should be somewhat more numerous in the western counties.

SPRING—There are more records for spring than for fall, as is the case for the entire state (Bohlen 1989).

9, Nason, Rend Lake, Jefferson Co., 10 Feb 1991 (WDR, TF, BD)

6, Perry Co., 6–10 Mar 1986 (TF, RBu)

1, Rend Lake, Jefferson Co., 20 Mar 1976 (BP)

3, near Perks, Pulaski Co., 8 Apr 1992 (TF, JD)

AUTUMN—2, Valmeyer, Randolph Co., 14 Nov 1971 (Bohlen 1978)

DOCUMENTATION: Written description—6, Perry Co., 6–10 Mar 1986.

FIELD GUIDES: G=344; N=410; P=264.

Snow Bunting *Plectrophenax nivalis*

Late November–Early February

STATUS AND ABUNDANCE: Rare winter resident.

HABITAT: Large agricultural fields, pastures, and extensive rocky shorelines of lakes.

RECORDS AND REMARKS: A species of the arctic, Snow Buntings occur in southern Illinois only irregularly. A few can sometimes be found during severe winters, especially when heavy snow forces many birds up along roadsides. Small flocks of buntings may associate with Horned Larks and Lapland Longspurs, but they form single-species flocks just as commonly. Few buntings winter south of Illinois, so the first fall arrivals and the last spring departures are likely to be birds that overwintered in or near southern Illinois.

AUTUMN—7, Rend Lake, Franklin Co., 30 Nov 1975 (BP)

WINTER—2, Rend Lake, Jefferson Co., 29 Nov 1987-early Jan 1988 (TF, m.ob.)

4, Crab Orchard NWR CBC, 15 Dec 1984

1, Horseshoe Lake CBC, 29 Dec 1976

1, Union Co. CBC, 2 Jan 1976

1, w. Jackson Co., 8 Jan 1995 (BD)

SPRING—5, Carbondale, 7 Feb 1982 (MMl)

DOCUMENTATION: Provisional acceptance.

FIELD GUIDES: G=344; N=412; P=266.

Subfamily Icterinae: Icterines

Bobolink Dolichonyx oryzivorus
Late April–Late May
Late August–Early October

STATUS AND ABUNDANCE: Uncommon spring migrant. Rare fall migrant. Very rare winter visitor.

HABITAT: Large weedy fields, especially those with clover, alfalfa, and mustards.

RECORDS AND REMARKS: Bobolinks have a distinct preference for clover and alfalfa fields. A field covered with singing males is a spectacular sight. Perhaps partly because of their lovely song, Bobolinks are much more conspicuous during spring; they are probably numerically more common as well. Very few are detected during fall migration; most often a few flybys are heard calling during September. There are no summer records, and consequently there is no evidence of breeding in the region. There are two winter records, however; the 1983 record was a bird that visited a suburban feeder. SPRING—The first Bobolinks are usually noted during the last week of April. Numbers peak during the first week of May and then decline quickly until 20 May, after which only a few straggle behind.
120, Union Co., 12 Apr 1987 (TF)
male, near Perks, Pulaski Co., 17–18 Apr 1992 (TF, WDR)
183, Alexander Co., 5 May 1984 (TF, KR)
123, Massac Co., 5 May 1984 (WDR)
AUTUMN—Migration extends primarily from late August through late September. Numbers do not seem to peak at any particular time, and in general Bobolinks are very difficult to find.
1, Carbondale, 27 Sep 1970 (VK)
4 in a milo field, Gorham, Jackson Co., 2 Oct 1993 (TF)
WINTER—1, Crab Orchard NWR, 6 Dec 1953 (Smith and Parmalee 1955:51)
1, Carterville, Williamson Co., 26 Jan 1983 (TE)

DOCUMENTATION: Specimen—ad. male, Carbondale, Jackson Co., 5 May 1966 (SIU A-1579).

FIELD GUIDES: G=296; N=418; P=256.

Red-winged Blackbird *Agelaius phoeniceus*

STATUS AND ABUNDANCE: Common year-round resident.

HABITAT: Marshes, weedy fields, roadsides, and agricultural lands.

RECORDS AND REMARKS: Truly one of the most abundant bird species in the region, Red-wings form huge roosts from autumn through early spring that may number up to or even exceed a million birds. Many of these roosts are located in the marshes and woodlots on strip-mined land in the Till Plain, where some of the largest gatherings congregate in *Phragmites*. After the first warm spell of the year, which is often in late January, male Red-wings begin to set up territories in marshes and along roadsides. Many of the roosts are still active at this time and may remain active until mid-April or so, when the last birds depart on migration. The first nests are built during late March, but the peak of nesting activity is in May and June. Surprisingly, very few Red-wings are parasitized by cowbirds in southern Illinois, but they are sometimes heavily parasitized in other sections of their range. Flocks of juveniles begin forming by late July and August, and adults join in soon thereafter. Red-wings associate with other blackbird species while foraging and at their roosts.
WINTER—1,000,000, Crab Orchard NWR CBC, 27 Dec 1956
930,000, Horseshoe Lake CBC, 29 Dec 1976
3,250, Union Co. CBC, 30 Dec 1987

DOCUMENTATION: Specimen—ad. male, Crab Orchard NWR, Williamson Co., 15 Feb 1956 (SIU A-278).

FIELD GUIDES: G=298; N=420; P=252.

Eastern Meadowlark *Sturnella magna*

STATUS AND ABUNDANCE: Common year-round resident.

HABITAT: Weedy fields, large mown grassy fields (such as airports), and agricultural lands.

RECORDS AND REMARKS: A familiar bird on fence posts and electrical wires in rural sections of the region. Two subspecies have been reported; of 358 specimens, Hamilton and Klimstra (1985) identified 115 as *S. m. magna*, 175 as *S. m. argutula,* and the remainder as intergrades between the two subspecies. Migration definitely occurs, but the large breeding and wintering populations obscure the patterns.

SPRING—In warm winters, northward movements may begin during January, but a mid- to late February initiation is more typical. Because of breeding population, it is difficult to discern either peak migration or late departure dates.

SUMMER—Nests have been discovered from April through July, but there are little quantitative data available. Because the nests are placed on the ground and are usually covered over the top with grasses, they require tremendous effort to locate; most nests are found by luck when a female flushes off eggs. Spring Bird Counts census the breeding population.

266, Union Co., 4 May 1991 (SBC)

AUTUMN—Fall migration is inconspicuous. Some larger flocks, which may be composed of migrants, are seen in October and November.

WINTER—Most winter counts come from Christmas Bird Counts. Groups of ten to forty or more birds are routinely encountered during winter. Populations seem to be higher in the southern Floodplains and the Shawnee Hills than in the Till Plain and the northern Floodplains. Flocks sometimes gather in grain fields, where they feed on waste corn, milo, and sunflower seeds.

331, Crab Orchard NWR CBC, 28 Dec 1970
256, Union Co. CBC, 30 Dec 1973
270, Horseshoe Lake CBC, 2 Jan 1987

DOCUMENTATION: Specimen—ad. male, near Cobden, Union Co., 3 Feb 1983 (SIU A-1876).

FIELD GUIDES: G=296; N=418; P=256.

Western Meadowlark *Sturnella neglecta*

Early November–Mid-May

STATUS AND ABUNDANCE: Rare migrant and winter resident.

HABITAT: Weedy fields, large mown grassy fields (such as airports), and agricultural fields.

RECORDS AND REMARKS: If not for their distinctive song and call, most Westerns would be passed by as Eastern Meadowlarks. The two species are very difficult to differentiate by sight alone, though it is possible. Westerns tend to be noticeably paler, with less yellow on the underparts but more on the face.

AUTUMN—Little is known about their fall movements, probably because most birds are silent during this season. Migrants may arrive during October, but there are apparently no records yet. Very few Westerns winter south of Illinois, so most that are seen here during fall probably winter here or to the east.

1, Carbondale, 8 Nov 1970 (VK)

WINTER—Most winter records are from Christmas Bird Counts, when observers tend to take more time to scrutinize every bird they see, which suggests that Westerns may be more numerous than current information indicates. Sometimes Westerns associate with flocks of Easterns, so each bird in meadowlark flocks should be carefully identified.

2, Alexander Co., 21 Dec 1983 (RG, JE)

3, Crab Orchard NWR CBC, 28 Dec 1970

1, Horseshoe Lake CBC, 28 Dec 1979

1, Union Co. CA, 2 Jan 1976 (BP)

1, n.w. Union Co., 6 Jan 1973 (VK, MH et al.)

SPRING—Singing and spring movements begin soon after the first warming spell of the year and extend well into May. Most birds, however, have departed by the end of March.

5 singing, near Mermet, Massac Co., 28 Jan 1989 (WDR)

male, Somerset Township, Jackson Co., 15 Feb 1975 (BP)

1, Crab Orchard NWR, 17 Feb 1951 (JWH, RB)

1, Carbondale, 28 Feb 1982 (SO)

1, Crab Orchard NWR, 2 Mar 1985 (SO)

1, s. of Murphysboro, 4 Mar 1950 (JWH)

1, s.e. Saline Co., 20 Mar 1994 (JD)

3, Willard, Alexander Co., and 2, Cypress Creek NWR, 21 Mar 1993 (TF, JD)

1, Lovett's Pond, Jackson Co., 18 Apr 1993 (TF)

1, Baldwin Lake, 16 May 1981 (RK)

DOCUMENTATION: Written description—3, Willard, Alexander Co., 21 Mar 1993.

FIELD GUIDES: G=296; N=418; P=256.

Yellow-headed Blackbird
Xanthocephalus xanthocephalus

STATUS AND ABUNDANCE: Very rare migrant and winter visitor.

HABITAT: Usually found with other blackbirds foraging in agricultural fields, marshes, or at feeders.

RECORDS AND REMARKS: A conspicuous bird that is hard to miss, yet it is undoubtedly overlooked to some extent; there may be some that regularly overwinter amid the roosts of millions of other blackbirds in the strip mines of Perry, Williamson, Franklin, and Jefferson Cos. There are very few fall sightings; most records are from winter and spring.
AUTUMN—imm., Carbondale, 25 Sep 1990 (BD)
male, Royalton, Franklin Co., 3 Nov 1993 (LS)
WINTER—male, near Colp, Williamson Co., 20 Dec 1986 (LN et al.)
male, Rudement, Saline Co., 21–22 Dec 1989 (JD et al.)
1, Alexander Co., 20 Jan 1992 (TF, JD, DKa, CW)
pair, Carterville, Williamson Co., 12–14 Feb 1982 (WDR)
SPRING—pair, Harrisburg, Saline Co., 29 Mar–13 Apr 1992 (GSm, JD)
male, Ozark, Johnson Co., 18 Apr 1990 (TF)
2, Randolph Co., 6 May 1972 (MMo)
1, Grand Tower, Jackson Co., 14 May 1972 (DB)
male, LaRue Pine Hills, 29 May 1979 (WDR)

DOCUMENTATION: Photograph—male, Rudement, Saline Co., 21–22 Dec 1982 (SIU AP-uncatalogued).

FIELD GUIDES: G=298; N=420; P=252.

Rusty Blackbird *Euphagus carolinus*
Late October–Mid-April

STATUS AND ABUNDANCE: Uncommon migrant and winter resident.

HABITAT: Agricultural fields, woodland edge, and bottomland forest.

RECORDS AND REMARKS: Although this blackbird often associates with other blackbird species in fields and at roosts, it can also be found foraging along the margins of wooded creeks or lakes, where it flips over wet leaves to expose food items. The females have yellowish irises, which helps separate them from the dark-eyed female Brewer's Blackbird, which is similar in appearance. Rusties also have a curved culmen, which can be seen at close range. The call is characteristic once learned and can be used to pick Rusties out of mixed-species flocks of blackbirds as they fly over; it sounds very much like a rusty hinge squeaking.

AUTUMN—Most first fall arrivals are not detected until late October or even early November. They are easily overlooked if mixed in with other blackbirds in a flying flock. Numbers remain fairly steady throughout the fall and winter.

WINTER—Most high counts come from Christmas Bird Counts, when observers take more time to inspect every blackbird flock. It is not unusual, however, to encounter pure flocks of three to one hundred Rusties on a regular basis.

6,750, Horseshoe Lake CBC, 18 Dec 1985
431, Mermet Lake CBC, 21 Dec 1965
2,500, Alexander Co., 29 Dec 1977 (BP)
687, Union Co. CBC, 2 Jan 1976
5,000, Crab Orchard NWR CBC, 4 Jan 1976

SPRING—Northward migration probably begins as early as the first warm spell of the year, in late January or early February, and is well underway by late February. Numbers slowly dwindle throughout spring; most birds have departed by early April.

500, Oakwood Bottoms, Jackson Co., 16 Feb 1975 (BP)
hundreds roosting in marsh, Vienna, Johnson Co., 5 Mar 1974 (VK, HDB)
1, near Renshaw, Pope Co., 25 Apr 1973 (VK, HDB)

DOCUMENTATION: Specimen—male, 3 miles e. of Carbondale, in Williamson Co., 3 Dec 1958 (SIU A-665).

FIELD GUIDES: G=298; N=422; P=254.

Brewer's Blackbird *Euphagus cyanocephalus*

Late October–Mid-December
Mid-March–Mid-April

STATUS AND ABUNDANCE: Occasional migrant in the Floodplains. Rare migrant in the Shawnee Hills and the Till Plain. Rare winter resident.

HABITAT: Agricultural fields and pastures; also forages on waste grain at livestock feedlots with other blackbirds, and sometimes comes to bird feeders.

RECORDS AND REMARKS: Numbers encountered vary widely from year to year, probably depending on prevailing winds, because this species is from western North America. A few can usually be found each year with some searching of appropriate habitats. Difficulty distinguishing these blackbirds from Rusties obscures determination of their true status and abundance. Typically, Brewer's forage in small groups (of less than a dozen birds) in very open areas, such as plowed fields. They sometimes associate with large blackbird flocks, but they seem to prefer staying with their own kind.

AUTUMN—Populations seem to be lower in fall than in spring, but more work needs to be done to determine if this observation is true. Observers should use care to make thoroughly described sight records. The first fall arrivals appear in late October or early November. A few are found throughout November and early December, but fewer are found after mid-December.

female, Carbondale, 28 Oct 1940 (SIU specimen)

2, Union Co. CA, 17 Nov 1973 (VK)

1, Rend Lake, Jefferson Co., 29 Nov 1987 (TF)

WINTER—Some Brewer's undoubtedly winter in the region each year and are simply overlooked because they are mixed in with thousands of other blackbirds at roosts. When heavy snowfall covers the ground, Brewer's will sometimes come to feeders for cracked corn or millet.

3, Horseshoe Lake CBC, 21 Dec 1982

2 females, Nason, Jefferson Co., 21 Dec 1990 (WDR)

2, Union Co. CBC, 23 Dec 1981

male, Ozark, Johnson Co., 25 Dec 1990 (TF)

1, Horseshoe Lake CBC, 2 Jan 1987

2, Alexander Co., 20 Jan 1992 (TF, JD, DKa, CW)

SPRING—Migrational movements may begin during February but seem to vary from year to year. Brewer's are reliably encountered each spring after mid-March; most birds have departed by 15 April.

The agricultural land bordering the Big Muddy River and Mississippi River levees in Jackson and Union Cos. are good places to
find Brewer's.

4, Union Co., 15 Mar 1986 (TF, WDR)
10, Union Co., 19 Mar 1976 (BP)
9, Jackson Co., 25 Mar 1984 (JCR)
2, s.w. Jackson Co., 4 Apr 1988 (WDR)

DOCUMENTATION: Specimen—female, Carbondale, Jackson Co.,
28 Oct 1940 (SIU A-66).

FIELD GUIDES: G=298; N=422; P=254.

Great-tailed Grackle *Quiscalus mexicanus*

STATUS AND ABUNDANCE: Very rare visitor.

RECORDS AND REMARKS: There is one record. An adult female was
observed in a corn-stubble field north of Cutler, Perry Co., on 23
February 1994 (TF, CS). This species is expanding its range northward in the Great Plains and could occur more frequently as a vagrant. Females differ distinctly from the much smaller Common
Grackle, but males are superficially similar. This grackle's very large
body and bill size and its long, remarkably keeled tail are key fieldmarks.

DOCUMENTATION: Written description—1994 record.

FIELD GUIDES: G=282; N=424; P=254.

Common Grackle *Quiscalus quiscula*

STATUS AND ABUNDANCE: Common year-round resident.

HABITAT: Agricultural lands, suburbs, parks, hedgerows, and
marshes.

RECORDS AND REMARKS: A truly abundant bird that is difficult to
miss on nearly any day of the year. Grackles form large flocks after
breeding, and they forage and roost together throughout the winter
and well into spring. They even nest together, in conifers, forming
loose colonies; sometimes a half dozen or more pairs will nest in a
single tree. They are rarely parasitized by cowbirds; when a cowbird

does slip in an egg, the egg is quickly removed by the adult grackles. Nests have been found from April through June. The large flocks of grackles that consume waste grain and insects can sometimes do damage to standing farm crops as well. They frequently associate with other blackbirds, especially Red-winged Blackbirds. Grackles are quite migratory, but their year-round abundance and wide-ranging daily movements make delineation of migration periods difficult. Northward movements seem to begin in late February, however, and extend well into March. Fall migration is even more difficult to detect, because so many grackles are associated with large roosts at that time. Roosting birds radiate out into the surrounding lands to forage during the day, and then they return at dusk to the roosts. They travel many miles in a day, so it is difficult to distinguish between local movements and long-distance migration.

WINTER—750,000, Crab Orchard NWR CBC, 27 Dec 1956
615,000, Horseshoe Lake CBC, 29 Dec 1976
60,000, Union Co. CBC, 31 Dec 1987

DOCUMENTATION: Specimen—ad. male, Crab Orchard NWR, Williamson Co., 26 Nov 1957 (SIU A-288).

FIELD GUIDES: G=300; N=424; P=254.

Brown-headed Cowbird *Molothrus ater*

STATUS AND ABUNDANCE: Common year-round resident.

HABITAT: Agricultural lands, especially pastures; also, forest, forest edge, and residential areas, particularly near feeders.

RECORDS AND REMARKS: Southern Illinois is infamous for its large populations of cowbirds. Cowbirds are obligate brood parasites; that is, they do not build their own nests, nor do they care for their young. Instead, they deposit their egg in the nest of another bird similar in size and let that bird incubate the egg and raise the young cowbird. To make matters worse for the parasitized songbird, cowbirds often remove one or more of the host's eggs before depositing their own egg into the host nest, to make room for the cowbird egg. In addition to losing some of their eggs because the cowbird has removed them, hosts also may lose their young because the

Wood Thrush nest with three thrush eggs and two cowbird eggs, Pine Hills, Union Co., 4 June 1991

cowbird egg hatches first and the cowbird nestling grows quickly by successfully competing with the host young for food from the un-suspecting parent songbirds.

In some sections of the United States, cowbirds do not parasitize songbirds that breed inside forests, but southern Illinois forest birds are heavily parasitized. The combination of highly fragmented for-est, abundant pastureland (where cowbirds prefer to forage), and close proximity to the wintering grounds in the Gulf States is thought to contribute to the overabundance of cowbirds in the re-gion. Cowbirds are quite migratory, but there are some in the region all year. Spring migrational movements begin in late January or early February and continue at least into early April. Fall migration seems to occur from September through November.

Despite their negative impacts on songbird populations, cowbirds are protected by law, and it is illegal to kill them without a special permit. In some areas of the country where parasitism is a problem, cowbird extermination programs have been instituted; they seem to work quite well. Bohlen (1989) gave a list of sixty-one bird species parasitized by cowbirds in Illinois, to which can be added the Carolina Wren, North-ern Mockingbird, Cedar Waxwing, Northern Parula, Yellow-throated Warbler, Pine Warbler, Cerulean Warbler, Blue Grosbeak, Lark Spar-row, and Northern Oriole—for a total of at least seventy-one species!

WINTER—Cowbirds associate with other blackbird species at large roosts and when foraging for waste grain in agricultural fields. They can be strangely absent from some areas of the Shawnee Hills during winter.
75,000, Horseshoe Lake CBC, 29 Dec 1976
50,000, Crab Orchard NWR CBC, 31 Dec 1958
650, Union Co. CBC, 30 Dec 1977

DOCUMENTATION: Specimen—male, Crab Orchard NWR, Williamson Co., 4 Feb 1959 (SIU A-647).

FIELD GUIDES: G=300; N=422; P=252.

Orchard Oriole *Icterus spurius*
Late April–Late August

STATUS AND ABUNDANCE: Fairly common migrant and summer resident. Very rare winter visitor.

HABITAT: Deciduous woodland edge, old fields with fairly large scattered trees, large trees along streams, and hedgerows.

RECORDS AND REMARKS: Regional populations of this small oriole species vary from year to year. Especially during spring migration, they can be very local. The males take more than one year to reach adult plumage; immature males have plumages that are intermediate between adult males and adult females, though they tend to be more yellow-green overall, like the females.
SPRING—Small groups of migrant orioles can be found in flowering trees, where they forage on nectar and insects. Soon after their arrival, these groups break up, and the birds form breeding territories.
1, Wamble Mountain, Saline Co., 14 Apr 1992 (TF, JD)
142, Union Co., 4 May 1991 (SBC)
SUMMER—Frequently parasitized by cowbirds, these orioles build their hanging, cuplike nests out of green grasses; the nests turn brown as the grass dries out. Nests have been found from early May through late June.
AUTUMN—Fall migration begins very early, possibly in June. Numbers of orioles decline conspicuously past 15 July. A few linger into August, but most birds depart much earlier. During late June

and July, small groups of two to six orioles are sometimes encountered, especially in shrubby old field habitats.
1 imm. or female, Rend Lake, Jefferson Co., 26 Aug 1994 (TF)
WINTER—ad. male, near Cobden, Union Co., 23 Nov–16 Dec 1975 (TM)

DOCUMENTATION: Specimen—ad. female, 2 miles n. of Cobden, Union Co., 7 May 1966 (SIU A-1380).

FIELD GUIDES: G=302; N=426; P=258.

Northern Oriole *Icterus galbula*

Mid-April–Mid-September

STATUS AND ABUNDANCE: Common migrant and summer resident. Very rare winter visitor.

HABITAT: Bottomland deciduous woods, especially where tall cottonwoods and elms are present.

RECORDS AND REMARKS: The "Baltimore" Oriole is the subspecies of this striking black-and-orange songster found in southern Illinois. There are two reports of the western subspecies, "Bullock's" Oriole, from the region: 2 males, Horseshoe Lake CA, 8 May 1965 (WS); and a female, Fort Kaskaskia SP, Randolph Co., 3 May 1986 (RG). Because both were sightings by single observers, Goetz and Robinson (1988) consider the status of Bullock's hypothetical.
SPRING—The distinctive song of this oriole alerts the observer to the first spring arrivals, which usually appear by 15 April. Numbers of migrants peak in late April and early May, but the large breeding population obscures the pattern.
1, Saline Co., 10 Apr 1987 (KP)
82, Union Co., 4 May 1991 (SBC)
38, Massac Co., 10 May 1986 (SBC)
SUMMER—Orioles build hanging nests that they place near the tips of long, thin, drooping branches, usually far away from the trunk of the tree. They are very rarely parasitized successfully by cowbirds, because they recognize and reject cowbird eggs from their nests. Few quantitative data are available on the nesting success within the region, but active nests have been discovered from early

May through early July. Sometimes orioles will come to feeders for sugar water or oranges.

AUTUMN—Fall migration begins very early. Groups of orioles are often encountered in late July and throughout August. Most orioles have departed by 10 September, though a few may linger later.

1, Rend Lake, Jefferson Co., 7 Sep 1988 (TF)

WINTER—imm. male at feeder, Carbondale, winter 1972–1973 (VK)

DOCUMENTATION: Specimen—ad. male, 4 miles s. of Carbondale, Jackson Co., 29 Apr 1975 (SIU A-2057).

FIELD GUIDES: G=304; N=426; P=258.

Family Fringillidae: Finches

[Pine Grosbeak *Pinicola enucleator*]

STATUS AND ABUNDANCE: Hypothetical.

RECORDS AND REMARKS: There is only one record, for which documentary details were apparently not preserved: 2, Crab Orchard NWR CBC, 30 Dec 1972. This species is native to boreal forests in northern North America and coniferous forests in western and northeastern North America. During severe winters, some wander south into Illinois, where they feed on tree seeds and fruits.

FIELD GUIDES: G=316; N=436; P=270.

Purple Finch *Carpodacus purpureus*

Mid-October–Early May

STATUS AND ABUNDANCE: Common migrant and winter resident. Very rare summer visitor.

HABITAT: Woodlands, residential areas near feeders, and hedgerows.

RECORDS AND REMARKS: Regional populations of this small, chunky finch vary from year to year. They sometimes form flocks of up to two hundred individuals, but they are usually found in groups of less than ten or so birds. Their distinctive flight call, a faint *tick* uttered at regular intervals, can be heard on calm days. They are fond of feeders that offer sunflower or thistle seeds. In forests, they feed on seeds of sycamore, ash, sweet gum, and tulip poplar trees. The males take more than one year to attain their purplish plumage, so many of the brown, streaked birds are actually subadult males.

AUTUMN—Detection of first fall arrivals varies tremendously from year to year. Most often the first birds arrive in mid-October. Because of the winter population, it is difficult to determine departure dates or peak migration periods.

1, Ozark, Johnson Co., 21 Sep 1993 (TF)

1, Little Grassy Lake, Jackson Co., 2 Oct 1976 (BP)

190, Little Grassy Lake, Jackson Co., 9 Nov 1975 (BP)

WINTER—Regular visitors to feeders, where they associate with Pine Siskins and American Goldfinches.

88, Crab Orchard NWR CBC, 4 Jan 1976

72, Union Co. CBC, 3 Jan 1987

60, s.e. Jackson Co., Jan and Feb 1987 (WDR)

SPRING—The beginning of northward migration is difficult to discern in most years, but numbers peak reliably in March and April. A few linger into May, but most birds have departed by mid-April.

150, Ozark, Johnson Co., 25 Feb 1994 (TF)

128, Rudement, Saline Co., 29 Mar 1990 (JD)

1, Mermet Lake CA, 10 May 1986 (WDR)

SUMMER—1 in female/imm. plumage, Ozark, Johnson Co., as late as 28 June 1992 (TF)

DOCUMENTATION: Specimen—ad. female, 2 miles n. of Cobden, Union Co., 30 Mar 1966 (SIU A-1678).

FIELD GUIDES: G=316; N=440; P=270.

House Finch *Carpodacus mexicanus*

STATUS AND ABUNDANCE: Locally common year-round resident.

HABITAT: Towns with coniferous shrubbery. Very local in rural hedgerows and around homesteads.

RECORDS AND REMARKS: This native North American species was introduced from the West Coast to New York about 1940. Since then the eastern population has increased dramatically and expanded its range westward into the Great Plains. House Finches first reached southern Illinois in 1971, but they were not numerous until about 1983 or 1984. The first arrived in Carbondale in spring 1982 (SO). They are most numerous in towns, but as the population increases, they begin to move out into rural areas as well. Fifty or more birds regularly visit a rural feeder near Rudement, Saline Co., each winter (JD). There are definite periods of migration, but little is known about the extent of these movements. The peak movements occur in March and November, when birds often appear at bird feeders in rural areas. They may have some sort of post-breeding movement as well, because Scott K. Robinson and I have routinely heard them calling as they flew over the extensively forested tracts of Union Co. during June and July. They also migrate nocturnally (TF).

Nesting activity begins in late February, as males begin singing vigorously and pairs stake out territories. The earliest reported nest with eggs was found on 22 March (1990, Carbondale), but undoubtedly some have eggs earlier. Nests are placed in conifers from one to fifteen meters above the ground; in light fixtures, potted plants, or under eaves of houses; or even in bird boxes. There are no reports of cowbird parasitism.

House Finches will readily visit bird feeders for sunflower or thistle seed, and they may even be very aggressive patrons and chase away other species. It has been suggested that they outcompete House Sparrows for nest sites, but there is no good evidence to support the idea. Some recent records from Christmas Bird Counts include 708, Union Co. CBC, 22 Dec 1994; 263 Horseshoe Lake CBC, 20 Dec 1994; and 92, Rend Lake CBC, 19 Dec 1993.

The first regional record was a female at Mt. Vernon, Jefferson Co., mid-Nov–late Dec 1971 (*IAB* 160:20–21).

DOCUMENTATION: Photograph—female, Carbondale, Jackson Co., 27 May 1985 (SIU AP-68).

FIELD GUIDES: G=316; N=440; P=270.

Red Crossbill *Loxia curvirostra*

Late October–Early April

STATUS AND ABUNDANCE: Rare migrant and winter resident.

HABITAT: Cone-bearing coniferous trees.

RECORDS AND REMARKS: An irruptive species that does not occur in most years; a few are detected in moderate flight years, but most are found during major invasions into the Midwest. They travel in tight flocks, uttering distinctive *kip* call notes, and forage by extracting seeds from evergreen cones. No one has determined which subspecies have been collected in the region. Only a few wander south of Illinois for the winter, so most of the birds encountered during late fall and early spring are probably wintering.

AUTUMN—1, Carbondale, 24 Oct–14 Nov 1981 (MMl, SO)
4, Little Grassy Lake, Jackson Co., 2 Nov 1975 (BP)
1 female found dead, Crab Orchard NWR, 1 Dec 1954 (Brewer 1958)
WINTER—Sometimes visit feeders for sunflower or thistle seeds.
16, Crab Orchard NWR CBC, 15 Dec 1984
6, Union Co. CBC, 19 Dec 1984
5, Crab Orchard NWR, 20 Dec 1981–18 Jan 1982 (MMl, m.ob.)
14, Crab Orchard NWR CBC, 4 Jan 1976
4, Pounds Hollow, Gallatin Co., 9 Feb 1988 (WDR)
SPRING—35, Crab Orchard NWR, 10 Mar 1973 (VK)
1, Devil's Kitchen Lake, Williamson Co., 10 Apr 1988 (WDR)
2, Crab Orchard NWR, 3 May 1976 (BP)

DOCUMENTATION: Specimen—ad. male, 2 miles n. of Cobden, Union Co., 14 Nov 1966 (SIU A-1405).

FIELD GUIDES: G=322; N=436; P=268.

White-winged Crossbill *Loxia leucoptera*

Mid-November–Early March

STATUS AND ABUNDANCE: Very rare migrant and winter resident.

HABITAT: Cone-bearing coniferous trees, especially hemlocks.

RECORDS AND REMARKS: An irruptive migrant that reaches southern Illinois only in major flight years. Most sightings are of individuals or small flocks foraging in hemlocks, sweet gums, or other small-coned coniferous trees. Although they sometimes associate with Red Crossbills, they usually remain in separate flocks. Most regional records are from December through early February.

AUTUMN—1, Little Grassy Lake, Jackson Co., 9 Nov 1975 (BP)
WINTER—7, Crab Orchard NWR, 7 Dec 1975 (BP)
1, Little Grassy Lake, 1 Jan 1976 (BP)
6, Trails of Tears SF, Union Co., 2 Jan 1976 (PB)
5, 2 miles n. of Cobden, Union Co., 7 Feb 1966 (WGG)
SPRING—1, Carbondale, 3 Mar 1974 (TM)
DOCUMENTATION: Specimen—male, 2 miles n. of Cobden, Union
Co., 1 Feb 1966 (SIU A-1406).
FIELD GUIDES: G=322; N=436; P=268.

Common Redpoll *Carduelis flammea*

STATUS AND ABUNDANCE: Very rare winter resident.

HABITAT: Weedy fields and residential areas with feeders.

RECORDS AND REMARKS: Erratic visitors from extreme northern
North America, redpolls reach southern Illinois only in major flight
years. They may be found mixed in with flocks of siskins or
goldfinches visiting feeders for sunflower of thistle seed. They also
have been found in weedy fields. Some recent reports of redpolls
may have been of misidentified male House Finches, which redpolls
resemble.
1 at feeder, Carbondale, Jan and Feb 1981 (HD)
1 at feeder, Murphysboro, 15–25 Jan 1982 (DTe)
2, s.e. Jackson Co., Feb 1982 (WDR)
1, Jackson Co., 20 Feb 1976 (BP)
DOCUMENTATION: Provisional acceptance.
FIELD GUIDES: G=318; N=438; P=270.

Pine Siskin *Carduelis pinus*

Late October–Early May

STATUS AND ABUNDANCE: Fairly common to common migrant and
winter resident.

HABITAT: Woodland edge, weedy fields, sunflower plantations, and
residential areas with feeders.

RECORDS AND REMARKS: Numbers vary widely from year to year.

At least a few occur every year, but they can be very scarce at times. They often associate with flocks of goldfinches, so they can easily be overlooked, but their distinctive voices should alert observers to their presence. Indeed, many sightings are made by hearing a flock of siskins calling as they fly overhead. In addition to taking thistle and sunflower seeds at feeders, siskins commonly eat seeds from sweet-gum balls.

AUTUMN—Most siskins do not arrive until well into October, but occasionally some are detected earlier. Because of the winter population, fall departure dates are difficult to determine.

1, Rend Lake, Jefferson Co., 24 Sep 1989 (WDR)

WINTER—Large flocks may visit feeders or be found in sunflower fields with goldfinches. During winter, siskins seem to be more numerous in the Shawnee Hills than in the other divisions.

474, Union Co. CBC, 19 Dec 1985

SPRING—The start of spring migration is obscured by the wintering birds but seems to begin by late March. Peak numbers occur in April, and most birds have departed by early May. A few linger into late May or later in some springs.

150, Harrisburg, Saline Co., 10 Apr 1987 (JD)

102, Saline Co., 5 May 1990 (SBC)

1, Pomona, 25 May 1985 (VK)

1, Cairo, Alexander Co., 26 May 1988 (WDR)

1, Trail of Tears SF, Union Co., 7 June 1981 (MMl)

DOCUMENTATION: Specimen—imm. female, 2 miles n. of Cobden, Union Co., 6 Nov 1969 (WGG 2321).

FIELD GUIDES: G=320; N=434; P=272.

American Goldfinch *Carduelis tristis*

STATUS AND ABUNDANCE: Common year-round resident.

HABITAT: Shrubby fields, residential areas with feeders, sunflower plantations, and woodland edge.

RECORDS AND REMARKS: Nomadic flocks of goldfinches wander through the region during fall, winter, and spring; the pattern and destination of their movements is difficult to decipher. For instance, one goldfinch banded at a feeder during winter in Carbondale was recovered the next spring in Montreal, Canada (SS). Goldfinches are most sedentary during late summer, when they are breeding; but at other times of the year, they seem to be constantly on the move. SUMMER—Few nesting data are available for the region, partially because they nest so late in summer. Nest initiation begins in mid- to late June, and young may still be in the nest during September. Nests are usually placed in a vertical fork of a branch on a small tree; the nests are well built, and they are lined with thistledown. Goldfinches are sometimes parasitized by cowbirds, but the impact has not been quantified. They may largely escape parasitism because they nest well after the peak of the cowbird nesting season.

AUTUMN—Little is known about the fall migration, because goldfinches are so common during both summer and winter. Flocks are encountered during September, however, so migration may begin by then.

WINTER—Winter flocks regularly visit feeders for sunflower and thistle seed, sometimes in large numbers. At a feeder near Carbondale where no more than seventy-five birds were seen at the feeder on a given day, nearly two hundred were banded during the winter of 1982–1983 (WDR). Most high counts come from organized counts, such as the Christmas Bird Counts; the largest counts are made where fields of sunflower plants are present.

945, Union Co. CBC, 31 Dec 1987
769, Union Co. CBC, 19 Dec 1985
546, Horseshoe Lake CBC, 30 Dec 1987

SPRING—The beginning of spring migration is obscured by the winter population. Northward movements probably begin by mid-April, however, and perhaps much earlier. Adult male goldfinches acquire full breeding plumage by early April and begin singing vigorously then, usually from the tops of trees, even in very extensive forest. Because the breeding season begins so late, it is quite possible that spring migration extends well into May or even into early June.

50, Jonesboro, 18 Apr 1992 (TF, WDR)

DOCUMENTATION: Specimen—ad. male, Belknap, Johnson Co., 19 Feb 1961 (SIU A-1195).

FIELD GUIDES: G=320; N=434; P=272.

Evening Grosbeak *Coccothraustes vespertinus*

Early November–Early May

STATUS AND ABUNDANCE: Uncommon migrant and winter resident. Very rare summer visitor.

HABITAT: Woods, often near box elder and sycamore trees, and feeders with sunflower seed.

RECORDS AND REMARKS: An erratic migrant from the boreal forest of northern North America; in some years they are numerous, but in others very few can be found. Often form sizable flocks that visit feeders for sunflower seeds; they also eat box elder and maple seeds. The noisy flocks are easily detected during the morning, but they are difficult to find by midday, apparently because they wander off to a quiet spot in the woods to roost. Oddly, the bulk of the records from southern Illinois are from the southeastern counties.

AUTUMN—Fall flocks usually do not arrive until November. The extent of fall migration is unclear, because most birds sighted during fall are at feeders, and they tend to stay into winter.

50, Harrisburg, Saline Co., 2 Nov 1985 (JD)
45, Jackson Co., 9 Nov 1975 (BP)
40, near Rudement, Saline Co., 15 Nov 1993 (CCu)
22, Pounds Hollow, Gallatin Co., 17 Nov 1993 (TF)
15, Crab Orchard NWR, 20 Nov 1985 (TF)

WINTER—When large flocks visit feeders they dominate the activity and consume huge amounts of seed. Although large flocks are not uncommon during years when many grosbeaks are present in the region, most sightings are of one to ten birds.

100, Golconda, Pope Co., Jan and Feb 1984 (RGr)
39, s.w. Williamson Co., 1 Jan 1987 (WDR)
58, Crab Orchard NWR CBC, 4 Jan 1976
200 at 2 feeders, Saline Co., 17 Jan 1987 (JD, KP)

SPRING—Northward migration begins at least by late March, but probably much earlier. Even in years when few were present during winter, a few are generally encountered during spring migration, as single individuals or perhaps in pairs, often in the first week of May.

22, Carbondale, 26 Mar 1976 (BP)
77, Saline Co., 25 Apr 1986 (JD, KP)

4, Harrisburg, Saline Co., 10 May 1987 (JD)
2, Carbondale, 12 May 1984 (TF)
SUMMER—1 photographed, New Burnside, Johnson Co., 7 June
1991 (DC)
1, Dutch Creek, Union Co., 14 June 1991 (SKR)
DOCUMENTATION: Specimen—ad. male, Carbondale, Jackson Co.,
7 Apr 1984 (SIU, uncatalogued).
FIELD GUIDES: G=310; N=442; P=272.

Family Ploceidae: Weavers

House Sparrow *Passer domesticus*
STATUS AND ABUNDANCE: Common year-round resident.

HABITAT: Nearly any human-inhabited area, but especially farms
and towns.

RECORDS AND REMARKS: Originally introduced to New York in 1852.
The year of the first appearance of the species in southern Illinois is
not known, but it was somewhere around the 1880s. About the only
place one cannot find this sparrow is deep in the forest; they avoid all
but the forest edge. House Sparrows usurp nest boxes and outcompete
Cliff Swallows, bluebirds, and martins for nesting sites, partially because they begin breeding so early in the year. One way to keep House
Sparrows out of boxes or martin houses is to keep the holes plugged
until the bluebirds and martins have returned. Nests of House Sparrows have been found from February through October, and there are
probably some that try to breed in the other three months. Nest building has been seen at least as early as 16 February (1990, Carbondale),
and fledglings have been seen at least as early as 19 March (1949,
Murphysboro). Will (1973) studied them in McLeansboro, Hamilton
Co., and found 275 adults and 130 nests on his one-hundred-acre
study plot. Most observers, however, neglect counting this species, except during organized counts, like Christmas Bird Counts.
1,570, Union Co. CBC, 22 Dec 1982
1,430, Horseshoe Lake CBC, 2 Jan 1987
592, Crab Orchard NWR CBC, 28 Dec 1970

DOCUMENTATION: Specimen—ad. male, Carbondale, Jackson Co., 20 Feb 1961 (SIU A-1141).
FIELD GUIDES: G=296; N=432; P=262.

[Eurasian Tree Sparrow *Passer montanus*]

STATUS AND ABUNDANCE: Hypothetical.

RECORDS AND REMARKS: Bohlen (1989) lists a record from Modoc, Randolph Co., but no substantiating details have been preserved. These sparrows were introduced from Germany to St. Louis in 1870 (Flieg 1971) and spread into Illinois by the early 1900s. They are now well established in central Illinois and seem to be slowly spreading northeastward, but not south toward southern Illinois.

FIELD GUIDES: G=296; N=432; P=262.

Part Two

A Southern Illinois
Site Guide

Included here are directions to twenty-six of the traditionally best birding spots in southern Illinois. The accounts are arranged from northern to southern regions. Each account includes information on what birds to expect to find at that site and what rarities have been found there. Maps accompany some of the site accounts to help readers find some of the better birding spots. Hopefully these accounts illustrate the unique aspects of each site in a fashion that will encourage readers to visit them and enjoy the scenery and the birds.

Baldwin Lake, Randolph and St. Clair Counties

Baldwin Lake is the most reliable site in the region for finding Ross' Geese. They have been found here annually since at least 1983. The first birds arrive each year at about the same time as Snow Geese, with whom they always seem to associate. One or more seem to winter at the lake, too. Other unusual species recorded here include Red Phalarope, American White Pelican, Sandhill Crane, and Greater White-fronted Goose.

A good time to check the lake is in January. Because of the warm water discharge from the power plant on the site, the lake does not freeze; excellent numbers of common waterfowl and a few lingering species (such as Green-winged Teal, American Coot, and Common Loon) are often present during January. Recently, large numbers of Horned Grebes have spent portions of January on the lake as well; an occasional Eared Grebe has been viewed with the Horned Grebes, too. One important drawback to visiting in January, however, is that on very cold days, steam rising from the lake substantially limits viewing conditions. Windy days can often be somewhat better, but even then conditions are difficult. If you want to spend a lot of time looking for waterfowl, you may not want to rush to get to the site at dawn; all good viewing sites are on the west side of the lake, which means you will be staring into the sun until nine or ten o'clock.

Baldwin is best during winter, but good numbers of waterbirds (e.g., terns) stop there during migration, too. Summer is virtually worthless. Dozens of fishing boats cruise around the lake in summer, and there is very little good shorebird habitat at that time. But one way to find unusual birds is to check familiar sites at "odd" times of the year.

Probably the easiest way to reach the lake is to take Route 154 to the town of Baldwin. There, a sign will direct you to turn north on county road 2250E. Drive approximately 3.8 miles, and then turn west on county road 100N. You can see the power plant off to the northwest as soon as you leave Baldwin, and there is a sign for the wildlife area at your turn onto 100N. The main entrance is on the northwestern corner of the lake, which is about 1.5 miles after you turn onto 100N.

Randolph County Conservation Area, Randolph County

Rolling hills covered in oak and hickory forest are the rule in the Randolph County Conservation Area. A moderate-sized lake was built in the early 1960s but seems to attract only the common waterfowl species. Occasionally, a Common Loon or an Osprey will stop during migration, but the waterbirds are not the attractive feature of this area. Woodland birding can be quite good, especially during migration. In addition to the forest, there are also extensive hedgerows and a few food plots. Blue Grosbeaks, Grasshopper Sparrows, and Lark Sparrows occur in the farmland just outside the site boundaries.

Access this site from Chester. Take county road DD north four miles from Route 3 in Chester. There are signs in Chester, but the road is somewhat tricky; if you keep heading due north, your problems should be minimal.

Pyramid State Park, Perry County

Pyramid State Park is an old strip mine that has been allowed to revegetate. The mounds of overburden, now covered in scrubby vegetation and small trees, are separated by numerous small, narrow lakes. The park has been relatively unexplored ornithologically. There is good habitat for Blue-winged Warblers and Yellow-breasted Chats, and you may even see an occasional Prairie Warbler. Lark

Sparrows breed in the area nearby, so a few pairs could occur within the park, too. The lakes are unlikely to produce many birds, because most of them are narrow and deep and have steep banks, but some of the more tolerant species may sometimes occur here.

The park is located 4.5 miles south of Pinckneyville off of Route 127. Inquire at the park office for a map of the many trails available.

Rend Lake, Franklin and Jefferson Counties

Rend Lake is the largest reservoir in southern Illinois, covering over nineteen thousand acres (see map 4). In 1965, construction of the 1.5-mile-long dam began, and it was finished by 1970. The dam backs up the Big Muddy River to create the large, shallow lake. Most of the land around the lake is publicly owned and is used for recreational purposes as well as wildlife management. The area is excellent for birds because of the wide variety of habitats present. There are bottomland forests to the south below the dam and to the north along the Big Muddy River and Casey Fork; extensive plots of second-growth forest all around the lake; many acres of weedy fields and agricultural land; scattered, small pine plantations; the open water of the lake itself; and extensive mudflats.

The mudflats draw most birders to Rend Lake, because the flats attract such a high diversity of shorebird species. To date, the only species of shorebirds that have been seen in the state of Illinois but have *not yet* been found at Rend Lake are Sharp-tailed Sandpiper, Purple Sandpiper, Long-billed Curlew, Snowy Plover, and Wilson's Plover; these are some very rare species. Rend Lake attracted the state's first record for Curlew Sandpiper and is the best place in downstate Illinois to find Buff-breasted Sandpipers. In all, at least thirty-six species of shorebird have been found at Rend Lake. It is also a great place to find gulls, terns, herons, and ducks. Laughing Gull has become almost regular here, especially in fall, and Rend Lake is probably the best place in southern Illinois to find Common Terns. Least Terns are sometimes found here in August and September.

There are many great places to look for waterbirds and shorebirds at Rend Lake; I highlight the best here. For diving ducks and deep-

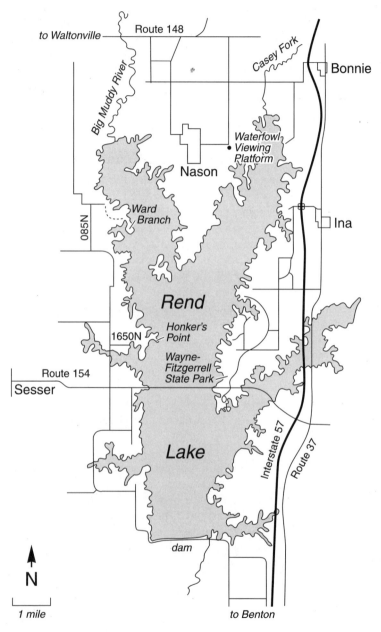

to Waltonville — Route 148

Casey Fork

Bonnie

Big Muddy River

Waterfowl
Viewing
Platform

Nason

085N

Ward
Branch

Ina

Rend

Honker's
Point

1650N

Wayne-
Fitzgerrell
State Park

Route 154

Sesser

Lake

Interstate 57

Route 37

dam

N

1 mile

to Benton

Map 4. Rend Lake

water birds, be sure to check the dam and the Route 154 causeway that passes through the center of the lake. These two sites give you views of the majority of the lake. You can also get good views of the northeast arm of the lake by going into Wayne-Fitzgerrell State Park (off of Route 154), following the road north through the park as far as it will take you, and walking out to the lake shore to scope the water. Shorebirding can be rather unpredictable. If the water level is high, there may not be very many birds, but if it has been dry recently, the mudflats may be exposed and covered with birds. In good shorebird conditions, there is hardly a time during the year when there are not at least a few shorebirds present. The first Killdeer begin arriving during late January or February, and there are birds there through the first severe weather in December, at which time the last Least Sandpipers, Dunlins, and Killdeer depart.

Historically, the best place to find a diversity of species and to have a good shot at rarities has been Ward Branch. It is located on the west side of the northwest arm of the lake. To get there from Interstate 57 take the Sesser exit (77) and head west to the lake along Route 154. After you cross the lake, look for your second right turn (Road 800E), which is just past a barn that usually has lots of sparrows, starlings, and doves around it. Turn north here and follow the road four miles until you cross some railroad tracks. Turn right immediately after the tracks (Road 085N). As you continue north, you will see a pond on your left surrounded by *Phragmites*. This site has been a good place to find Least Bittern from May through October and has turned up a few Marsh Wrens during December. Soon you will cross another set of railroad tracks and then the road will come to a T-intersection. Turn right here and follow the road to a parking lot. At the lot, you will see a gated gravel road that heads south. Walk this road out to the mudflats. You will definitely want to take your scope, because the mudflat is huge. It is a long walk out to the flat, but it is well worth it. The best time to visit is from July to November, when the water level is reliably low enough to attract shorebirds, terns, and gulls.

Another place to look for shorebirds is at Honker's Point, a peninsula of sand that sticks out in the lake at the base of the northwest arm on the west shore. It is accessible by taking the same road (800E) off of Route 154 that you take to get to Ward Branch. Take a right turn at Road 1650N (1 mile after you leave Route 154) and follow the road until you come to a gate. You can park in the lot here and walk along the gated road out to Honker's Point. The birding here is a bit unpredictable, and it is a long walk for sometimes very little reward. Some good birds that have been found here include Piping Plovers and Laughing Gulls. Sanderlings are fairly regular here, too.

The third good place to look for shorebirds is the waterfowl viewing platform near Nason. From Interstate 57, take the Sesser exit (77) and go east on Route 154 for about half a mile, until it intersects with Route 37. Turn left (north) onto Route 37 and follow it through the town of Ina and into the town of Bonnie. Once in Bonnie, look for a billboard on your left that says "Bonnie Camp." Turn left (west) here and follow this blacktop road over the interstate, past the camp, and to the lake. The point at which the blacktop crosses the lake can be an excellent place to find waders and ducks. A heron colony is located nearby. Continue across the lake and through an area of private agricultural fields. Take the first blacktop road on the left after leaving the causeway. Follow this road straight for a couple of miles. It will soon turn sharply to the right. Here you will see a parking lot and the waterfowl viewing platform. When the water level is high, the birds are often very close to the platform. During late fall and early spring, there are often thousands of Canada Geese and hundreds of Snow Geese present here. This site is a good place to search for Ross' Goose, too. Other good birds found mixed in with the Canadas here include Sandhill Cranes and Greater White-fronted Geese. When the water level is lower, the birds may be quite far away. Aside from Ward Branch, this site is the best place for shorebirds.

For land birding, check the forest below the dam for Red-headed Woodpeckers, Brown Creepers, Pileated Woodpeckers, and Barred Owls during winter; and for warblers and vireos during spring and summer. There are plenty of grassy fields and hedgerows to search in Wayne-Fitzgerrell State Park. The park is a great place to find raptors, and there are even a few Ring-necked Pheasants there.

Rend Lake is best for its shorebirds and waterbirds, so take some time to search the water and the flats thoroughly to see what you may find. A bird checklist for the lake is available at the Wayne-Fitzgerrell State Park office, the rest area off of Interstate 57, and the Army Corps of Engineers office on the west side of the main dam.

Hamilton County Conservation Area, Hamilton County

Located 5.5 miles east of McLeansboro off of Route 14, the Hamilton County Conservation Area is dominated by young, scrubby woodland. Apparently, much of the site is abandoned farmland that is slowly maturing from dense patches of young trees covered in vines and bushes to mature, upland, oak and hickory woods. The prevalence of edge habitats makes the fall migration, in particular, a good time to see birds here. The moderate-sized lake sometimes hosts Wood Ducks, Common Goldeneyes, Pied-billed Grebes, and some of the more common divers, such as Ring-necked Ducks. Many finches and sparrows often frequent the edges of the area, because of the waste grain available in the bordering crops. Not much is known about the birding here, but the mix of habitats suggests that it could be a good site for viewing a wide variety of species.

Lake Murphysboro State Park, Jackson County

The 900-acre Lake Murphysboro State Park includes a 145-acre lake and an extensive parklike woods. The woodlands and shrubby areas in the park have been reliable sites for Chuck-will's-widow. Many forest birds are common here. A few Pine Warblers can be found here as well. The lake sometimes attracts waterfowl, but there is often a fair amount of boat traffic. Nevertheless, small flocks of scaup and goldeneye are regular occurrences, and loons are even occasionally found here.

The park is located about one mile west of Murphysboro off of Route 149. There are plenty of nice sites for camping and picnics.

Pomona and Cave Creek Valley, Jackson County

The tiny town of Pomona lies just south of one of the nicest floodplain forests in the region. Cave Creek is a meandering mud-bottomed stream that flows through forest composed primarily of box elder, sycamore, silver maple, and other lowland tree species. The understory is well developed at times and is where you are most likely to find Swainson's Warbler, a state endangered species, and the species that draws so many birders to Cave Creek Valley. There are other nice attractions, too. The extensive forest is home to the region's largest population of Cerulean Warblers and American Redstarts; there are easily more than one hundred breeding territories of Cerulean Warblers scattered along the length of Cave Creek. American Redstarts are even more abundant. In addition, this site is a good place to find Hooded Warblers, Louisiana Waterthrushes, Red-shouldered and Broad-winged Hawks, Wild Turkey, and Mississippi Kites.

Pomona is easy to reach, and there are many trails and little-used roads to walk. Coming from the north, follow Route 127 south from Murphysboro about 9.5 miles to the Pomona road, which is well marked. From the south, take 127 north from Jonesboro about 12 miles. Turn west off of 127 and head down the hill to Pomona. The road comes to a T-intersection. On your right is the Pomona General Store, which has great ice cream, so be sure to stop by on your way out. Turn right (north) at the general store. Bear to the right at the first fork and continue straight north. Within about a mile, you will come to a bridge. Just before the bridge, there is a pull-off on the right where you can park. The area around the bridge is excellent for birding, especially during spring and early summer. From the pull-off, you can follow a dirt trail toward the east that will take you around a pine-covered ridge and into the bottomland forest. Pine Warblers sometimes nest on the ridge, as well as Cooper's Hawks, Yellow-throated Warblers, and Chipping Sparrows. The clearing at the base of the ridge is where Mississippi Kites have been seen most regularly. Back in the forest, you should find plenty of Cerulean Warblers and American Redstarts.

Another good walk to bird is the old railroad bed, which has now been converted into a narrow gravel road. From the bridge, walk north and take your first right. This is the old railroad bed. Birding can be excellent from this road. The road is basically straight for about a half mile and then bends to the left. At the bend, there is a wildlife opening on the south side. If you follow the trail along the edge of the opening and back into the forest behind it, you will come to a pond. Osprey and even Double-crested Cormorants have been seen here. Just to the south of the pond is a stand of enormous trees, where there is usually a cluster of Cerulean Warbler territories present each summer. Back on the old railroad bed, you will notice that the road is closed several hundred yards past the wildlife opening. You can continue walking the road if you wish, but the birding farther along is not much different from that around the pond.

One other good place to look for birds is at the Natural Bridge. From the bridge where you parked, drive north past the old railroad bed turn-off and follow the gravel road up the hill until it dead-ends at a picnic area. This upland forest is good for migrant warblers, vireos, thrushes, and tanagers. Worm-eating Warblers breed here and can be found reliably in good numbers.

There is really no reliable location for Swainson's Warblers anymore. Formerly, a pair was always present near the first bridge, but it has not been there in recent years. The best way to find them is to talk with the local birders or just spend lots of time looking and listening. Be sure to keep in mind, however, that there are very few around and that they should not be harassed with playbacks of their songs just so that someone can add them to their "list." It is important that we all respect the potential for negative effects of this kind of activity. If you are lucky enough to find a Swainson's, please take the time to fill out a documentation form and send it to the Avian Ecology Program, Illinois Department of Conservation, Springfield, IL, 62701. This will help the appropriate agencies monitor the status of this endangered species.

Carbondale, Jackson County

Two sites in the Carbondale area have been especially good for birding (see map 5). The first is Evergreen Park, which includes Carbondale Reservoir. The lake is one of the best places in the region to find Ruddy Duck, Redhead, Canvasback, and American Coot. These species are not particularly difficult to locate at other sites, but they pack into Carbondale Reservoir in surprising numbers. The lake teems with activity from October through March as long as there is open water. The best times to find a lot of ducks are October through early December and February through late March. The park is located south of Carbondale on Reservoir Road between State Route 51 and McLafferty Lane. From downtown Carbondale, take Route 51 south past the SIU Arena to Pleasant

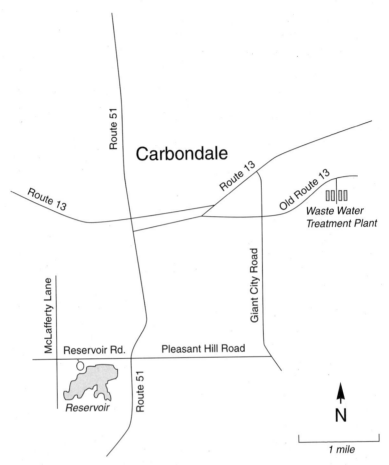

Map 5. The Carbondale area

Hill/Reservoir Road (at the first stoplight after you pass by the arena). Turn right (west) onto Reservoir Road. You will see the levee for the lake almost immediately, but the entrances to the park are about three-fourths of a mile farther west. When you are in the park, be sure to check the pine stand on the north-central part of the lake for Pine Warblers, Red-breasted Nuthatches, and Pine Siskins.

The other place to visit in Carbondale is the Waste Water Treatment Plant east of town. From the intersection of Old Route 13 and Giant City Road, take Old Route 13 east about two miles to the sewage ponds (the site is well marked with a green-and-white sign). The ponds were excellent for waterfowl during the mid- and late 1980s but seem to have become less productive recently. This site was always the place to find lots of birds from October through April, even when every other site was frozen. In spring 1987, the ponds were drained and the mudflats attracted hundreds of shorebirds. The two west ponds have been the best, but the small east ponds also have been good; the east ponds tend to attract shorebirds, and the ducks prefer the west ponds. This site has been a good place to find Greater Scaup and scoters. Other good birds found here and in the brushy fields nearby include Peregrine Falcons, Harris' Sparrows, Yellow-headed Blackbirds, Least Terns, White-rumped Sandpipers, and Merlins.

Crab Orchard National Wildlife Refuge, Williamson County

The Crab Orchard National Wildlife Refuge is one of the most frequently visited birding sites in southern Illinois (see map 6). It includes three lakes: Crab Orchard, Little Grassy, and Devil's Kitchen. Crab Orchard Lake, by far the largest of the three, is the best for birds. Some of the rarities found here include Iceland, Glaucous, Great Black-backed, Thayer's, Little, Sabine's, Laughing, and Common Black-headed Gulls; Black-legged Kittiwake; Pomarine Jaeger; Red Phalarope; *Plegadis* ibis; Red-throated Loon; Western and Red-necked Grebes; Brant; Rock Wren; and Townsend's Solitaire. In addition, Crab Orchard is an excellent place to find large concentrations of Ring-billed and Bonaparte's Gulls, Common Loons, Horned Grebes, and most waterfowl species.

The refuge caters primarily to industry and agriculture and puts secondary emphasis on wildlife management, so much of the refuge property is not open to public access. Nevertheless, some good birding spots remain open. The best times to visit the refuge are during spring and fall migrations and winter. The summer birding can be good, too, but there is so much boat traffic on the lakes that you

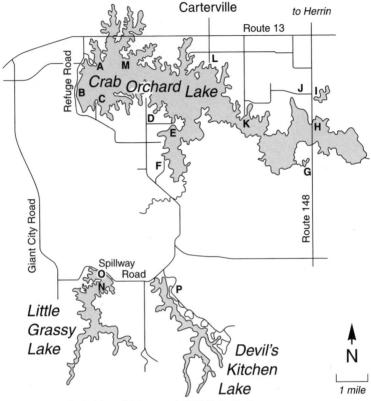

Map 6. Crab Orchard National Wildlife Refuge

have little chance of finding waterbirds. There are numerous places
to search for birds along your drive around the refuge; the sites I
outline here have traditionally been the best.

A good place to start birding is along Refuge Road. The road is
about 2.2 miles east of the stoplight at the intersection of Route 13
and Giant City Road on the east edge of Carbondale (there is a
McDonald's on the corner). Refuge Road heads south from Route
13 toward Crab Orchard Lake. The first good place to stop is Lookout Point (site A on map 6); take the third left after you turn onto
Refuge Road. For most of the year, this road is gated off, but you

can park at the entrance and walk to the lake. The birding along the road is usually good for Pine Warblers and Red-breasted Nuthatches. Follow the road all the way to the beach and scope the lake for birds. This site is especially good when the lake begins to freeze over during winter, because the birds tend to keep an area of water open just off Lookout Point. There are sometimes hundreds of birds crowded into this opening.

Continuing south along Refuge Road, you will soon reach the dam. There is a parking area on the north side (site B). This site also offers an excellent view of the deep part of the lake. Be sure to check the rock riprap for birds, too; Rock Wren has been found here.

Continue south again along Refuge Road to get to the next stop at Dogwood Lane (site C). After going through a very sharp curve, take your second left turn. This long, straight gravel road dead-ends at the lake. This site is probably the best vantage point for viewing birds that are out in the middle of the lake. Unfortunately, the turnaround at the end of the road is also the meeting place of undesirable sorts of company, so use caution.

After leaving Dogwood Lane, Refuge Road heads straight through a section of pine woods and then enters a long S-curve through open fields before straightening again. Just as you enter another sharp curve after the second long straight section of road, take the gravel road on your left. This road leads to the north end of Grassy Bay. Immediately after you exit Refuge Road, you will have a choice of turning left or continuing straight; both roads lead to good viewing places. The better sites for land birding, however, can be reached by taking the left road. Follow this gravel road north until it turns sharply to the right. An old road that continues north is gated off here. This old road (site D) is an excellent place to walk for birds. Wild Turkeys are fairly common along the road. Eventually the road becomes just a footpath, which leads out to the lake. The land birding back along the gravel road is also good. If you continue driving east after the road turns to the right, you will come to a peninsula (site E). Here, there are places to view the lake to the north and Grassy Bay to the south.

Another place to view Grassy Bay can be reached by traveling further south along Refuge Road. After a long straight stretch of road through agricultural fields, Refuge Road curves to the left and enters the woods again. Take the first left turn off of Refuge Road back to the south end of Grassy Bay (site F). The birding along this road can be excellent. During winter, this site is a good place to find Brown Thrasher, Hermit Thrush, Fox Sparrow, Purple Finch, and Cedar Waxwings. A Bald Eagle nest is located almost due east across from the parking lot at the end of this road.

The next stop along this tour of Crab Orchard Lake is the waterfowl viewing platform along Route 148 (site G). To get there from Grassy Bay, follow Refuge Road south until you come to a three-way intersection. Turn left here (if you continue straight, you will soon arrive at Devil's Kitchen Lake). Follow this road east until it intersects with Route 148. Turn left (north) and follow Route 148 about 2.8 miles to the waterfowl viewing platform. This site is one of the best places on the refuge to view the Canada Goose. It is also a good place to view Snow Goose, Northern Shoveler, and Redhead. Among the rarities found here are American Avocet, Tundra Swan, Golden Eagle, Greater White-fronted Goose, and Ross' Goose.

Continuing north along Route 148, you will soon cross the Route 148 causeway over the eastern portion of the lake. This area is excellent for viewing waterfowl, especially during fall, when hundreds of Hooded Mergansers can be found here. The parking lot on the north side of the lake (site H) is a good place to stop and scope the lake.

Continue north 0.9 miles to the refuge visitor center (site I). You can pick up a list of birds here. Go west across Route 148 here and take the blacktop road into the refuge. There are several good birding places along this road. The Chamness Town School Trail (site J) can be fairly good for woodland birds. Follow the blacktop until you come to a T-intersection. Turn left here and follow the road until you come to another T-intersection. Turn left again. This road ends at the lake, at the Wolf Creek Causeway (site K), which has turned up some very good birds in the past. It is an excellent place to see Bald Eagles, mergansers, and gulls. Scoters have been found here, and a Brant was found here once.

Another good place to check is Carterville Beach (site L). To get there from Wolf Creek Causeway, head north until you come to a four-way intersection; turn left at the intersection and proceed about one mile until you arrive at another four-way intersection. At this point, turn left toward the beach. This road is usually closed, but the walk is good for birding. There is an excellent place to view the lake at the end of this road. This area has turned up Willets, Sabine's Gulls, good numbers of terns, and Eared Grebes.

Head north from Carterville Beach to Route 13 to get to the final stop on our tour of Crab Orchard Lake. Take Route 13 west 2.2 miles to the Crab Orchard Campground (site M), which is also called Pirate's Cove. Take a left turn into the campground here (you pass by a boat dock first). Be sure to stop at the campground office and ask permission to enter the area and look for birds. You may be denied; they have not been very friendly to birders recently. If you are allowed to enter, head straight south to the lake and scope for birds. Another excellent viewing place is on the west side of the campground. After leaving the office, take your first right. Follow this road as far out on the peninsula as you can go. You will reach a dead end at a boat ramp. Some good birds have been found from this campground, including Common Black-headed, Glaucous, Thayer's, and Great Black-backed Gulls.

Also included in the Crab Orchard National Wildlife Refuge are Devil's Kitchen Lake and Little Grassy Lake. These lakes can be reached by going south from the three-way intersection between Grassy Bay and Route 148 or by taking Giant City Road south from Carbondale about seven miles and then turning left on Spillway Road. The boat dock/campground at Little Grassy Lake (site N) can be a surprisingly good place for land birds. Breeding densities of common birds are remarkably high there. The entrance is located on the Jackson and Williamson county line off of Spillway Road. Follow Spillway Road across the dam of Little Grassy Lake. There is a parking area on the dam at the spillway (site O), from which you can view the lake for birds. The lake is very deep here (about one hundred feet), so there are not usually very many birds, but Forster's Terns, Common Loons, and Pied-billed Grebes are fairly regular.

The entrance to Devil's Kitchen Lake is located off of Spillway Road between Little Grassy and the three-way intersection. It is well marked, but the lake is not usually visible from Spillway Road except during winter. There are many roads along the shores of Devil's Kitchen that are good for birds. To get to these roads, turn off of Spillway Road and head down to the dam of Devil's Kitchen Lake. There are sometimes a few waterfowl on the lake, but more often there are no birds. Follow the road over the dam and down into a deep valley. After you cross a bridge and ascend a fairly steep hill, you will see a road on your right. This is the first of many loop roads (site P) that are worth driving or walking to view land birds. None of the loop roads is particularly better than any other, so have fun exploring. In winter, sapsuckers and Red-breasted Nuthatches occur in the woods along most of the loop roads.

One important note: like many national wildlife refuges, Crab Orchard National Wildlife Refuge now requires that visitors pay a user fee. Annual or daily and weekend rates are available. You must purchase a sticker or risk being fined by the refuge police. Stickers are available at the refuge visitor center on Route 148 or at any of the three campgrounds.

Pine Hills, Union County

The LaRue Pine Hills Ecological Area is one of the finest forests remaining in southern Illinois (see map 7). Between the upland forest and the swamp, this site has the highest plant diversity of any place in Illinois. Along with this floral diversity comes a wide variety of birds as well. Excellent numbers of forest birds breed here and stop here during migration. The waterbirds are not as noticeable, in large part because they inhabit a rather inaccessible swamp.

There are three convenient ways to access the forests in Pine Hills. The easiest way to get to them is to take Route 3 into northwest Union County. The southern entrance can be reached by turning east in the town of Wolf Lake and going about 0.6 miles to a gravel road that heads north into the forest. This road leads immediately into upland forest, where you should be able to find many thrushes, warblers, vireos, and other songbirds during migration. During the breeding season, there are numerous Wood Thrushes, Scarlet Tanagers, Worm-eating Warblers, Kentucky Warblers, and Red-eyed Vireos all along this road. About 0.7 miles from the entrance, you will come to the primitive campground. There are many pine trees here, and this site is a fairly good place to find Pine Warblers in early spring. There are always a few Yellow-

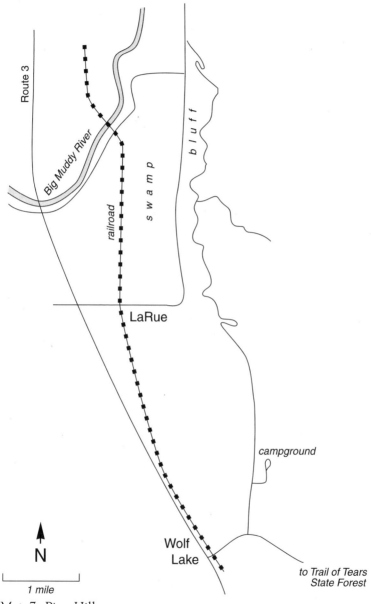

Route 3

Big Muddy River

railroad

s w a m p

b l u f f

LaRue

campground

N

Wolf
Lake

to Trail of Tears
State Forest

1 mile

Map 7. Pine Hills

throated Warblers here during summer, as well as Chipping Sparrows and an Orchard Oriole or two. Red-breasted Nuthatches and
Yellow-bellied Sapsuckers can be found here during winter. As you
continue north along the road, you should have no trouble finding plenty of Acadian Flycatchers, Northern Parulas, and Yellow-
throated Vireos during summer. Pileated Woodpeckers, Carolina
Chickadees, White-breasted Nuthatches, and Tufted Titmice are
conspicuous here during winter. Wild Turkeys can be found here
during any season, too.

The road starts to climb steeply and goes through a switchback
about three miles from the Wolf Lake blacktop. Once it crests the
hill, you will notice that the forest is a bit shorter and somewhat
more open. The road follows the ridge for more than four miles.
All along this ridge, there are many good places to stop and search
for birds. There are several nice picnic areas and scenic overlooks
where you can look out over the swamp and the Mississippi River
floodplain. During spring migration, the birding along the ridge can
be great. Migrant warblers, vireos, thrushes, and tanagers can be
extremely common. During summer, Eastern Wood Pewees, Summer Tanagers, and Yellow-throated Vireos are common.

After about four miles, the road begins to descend again and goes
through another switchback before coming to a T-intersection.
Turn left (south) here and you will soon come to the Big Muddy
River levee. If you follow the road on the levee, you will parallel
the river and eventually reach Route 3. If you cross over the levee,
you will be on the road that runs between Pine Hills Bluff and the
swamp. There is a nice picnic area next to a small pond right after
you cross the levee. This is a good place to find American Coot,
Pied-billed Grebe, Turkey Vulture, Great Blue Heron, and lots of
Red-winged Blackbirds. It is a good idea to walk much of the road
below the bluff. This forest is impressive, and the birding can be
very good along here. It is also a good place to find reptiles and
amphibians; the road is closed at certain times of the year to allow
the reptiles to migrate unharmed between the swamp, where they
breed, and the bluff, where they spend the winter. The road is good
for finding all species of forest birds, and Prothonotary Warblers are
very common here from April through August. If you proceed
south along the road, you will eventually come to a point where

the road turns back to the west. From here it goes back out to Route 3. The two access roads that intersect with Route 3 are located about 4 and 5.5 miles north of Wolf Lake.

Trail of Tears State Forest, Union County

Trail of Tears State Forest, a predominantly upland forest, is located in west-central Union County between Routes 3, 146, and 127. A blacktop road runs through the forest and intersects Route 127 about one mile north of the intersection of Routes 127 and 146. The blacktop road intersects Route 3 at Wolf Lake. There are many excellent places to look for birds in the forest. There are two gravel roads that form one-way loops, one on the south of the blacktop and one on the north. The south loop begins at the picnic area on the western edge of the site. Follow the gravel road through the picnic area and up onto the ridge road. As you drive along this narrow road, you will notice numerous trails blocked off with metal gates; most of these are numbered. These trails are great places to walk and look for forest birds. Most of the trails dead-end after about half a mile, so you will have to retrace your steps if you want to stay on the trails. You may want to drop down into one of the ravines and walk back to the road along one of the streams instead, because the bird communities in the ravines differ from those on the ridges.

Some of the better trails to walk are numbers 3, 4, 8, and 10. Numbers 3 and 4 are mature forest; 8 and 10 go through forest that was cut in the early 1990s. The cut forest usually has higher numbers of Hooded Warblers, Carolina Wrens, and Rufous-sided Towhees. The uncut forest has more Wood Thrushes. These forests were studied extensively by ornithologists from the Illinois Natural History Survey from 1990 through 1993. When you go past trail number 15, you will start down a steep a hill that ends at the blacktop road. You can cross here and start up the north loop road. The situation is similar to that on the south loop road, but there are fewer trails to walk.

This forest is an excellent place to visit during spring migration, when warblers, vireos, thrushes, and tanagers can be extremely

common. Trail of Tears may have southern Illinois's highest concentration of breeding Worm-eating Warblers. Hooded Warblers
and Ovenbirds are common here, too, but they are rather patchily
distributed. There are a few small pine plantations along the main
blacktop road that have attracted Pine Warblers, Red-breasted Nuthatches, and White-winged Crossbills in the past.

Saline County Conservation Area, Saline County

A mature upland forest surrounds much of the man-made, 105-
acre, Glen O. Jones Lake in the Saline County Conservation Area.
The forest is excellent for passerines, especially during migration.
A foot trail circles the lake and wanders through some of the best
stretches of woods. The second-growth habitats near the park entrance are also very good for finding passerines, especially Indigo
Bunting and White-eyed Vireo. The lake attracts a surprising variety of waterbirds despite the boat traffic and the lake's depth, perhaps because it is one of the few bodies of water in the area. Common Loon, Pied-billed Grebe, Lesser Scaup, Ring-necked Duck,
Common Goldeneye, Canvasback, Common Merganser, and Osprey have all been seen here.

To get to the park, take Route 13 east from Harrisburg to Route
142. Follow it south 1.1 miles to Walnut Street in Equality. Turn
right (southwest) and follow this road south for almost 2 miles until
you must turn to the right. Continue west for about 2 more miles
until you see your first left turn. Take this south about half a mile
to the park entrance.

Oakwood Bottoms, Grand Tower, and
Fountain Bluff, Southwest Jackson County

The Big Muddy River and the Mississippi River floodplains meet in
southwest Jackson County (see map 8). This rich area offers a wide
variety of habitats and, hence, a diversity of birds. Rarities found
here include Fulvous Whistling-Duck, *Plegadis* ibis, White Ibis,
Black-necked Stilt, and Golden Eagle. In addition, Least Terns nest
nearby on sandbars in the Mississippi River, so they are sometimes
encountered as they fly up and down the Mississippi and when they

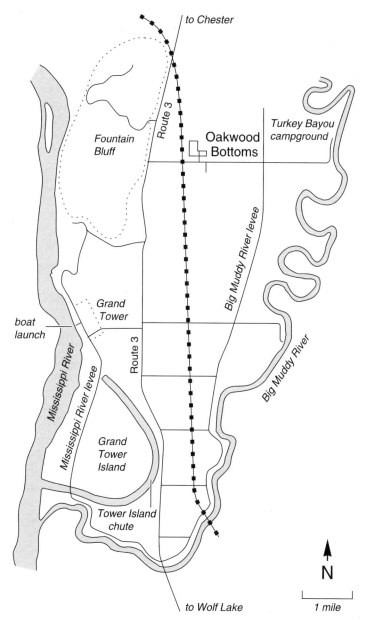

to Chester

Route 3

Fountain
Bluff

Oakwood
Bottoms

Turkey Bayou
campground

Big Muddy River levee

Grand
Tower

boat
launch

Route 3

Mississippi River

Mississippi River levee

Big Muddy River

Grand
Tower
Island

Tower Island
chute

to Wolf Lake

N

1 mile

Map 8. Oakwood Bottoms, Grand Tower, and Fountain Bluff

venture inland to forage in the flooded agricultural fields. This site is undoubtedly the best place in southern Illinois to find Yellow-crowned Night-Herons, and Fish Crows are common here as well. During wet years, many of the agricultural fields become flooded, and hundreds of waterfowl, shorebirds, and herons flock here to forage.

A good place to begin the day's birding is at Oakwood Bottoms, which can be reached from Route 3. The entrance is 3.4 miles north of Grand Tower or about 6 miles south of the intersection of Routes 149 and 3. As you enter the site, you will cross a busy railroad track, and then you will come to a picnic area and pond on your left. The pond is often a good place to find coots, grebes, a few waterfowl, or swallows. Marshy areas on the south side of the pond have attracted at least three species of rail recently. In the woods next to the parking area is a boardwalk that leads a short way into the oak forest. The birding is sometimes good along this walk, especially during spring.

Continuing east along the blacktop road, you will soon come to a pair of abandoned sites; at the very next gravel road, pull off and park (do not block the gate). This site is a good place to find Yellow-crowned Night-Herons. Walk south along this road until you come to the first ditch (about one hundred yards); scan this ditch for night herons and other birds. If you do not find any herons here, wander around the roads and levees back in this area and search any open water you can find; the herons are here, they are just hard to find sometimes. This area is also good for Red-shouldered Hawks, Barred Owls, Wild Turkeys, Willow Flycatchers, and Yellow Warblers.

Back at the blacktop road, you may wish to walk along the road itself and look for birds. There are numerous small trails that lead into the woods and offer good opportunities to find forest birds. When you continue driving eastward, you will cross the Big Muddy River levee and head toward the Turkey Bayou Campground and the Big Muddy River. The birding along the road and at the campground can be very good.

To get to the good wader habitats, you should get on the Big Muddy levee and follow it south. For the first few miles, you will pass through woodland, but eventually you come to the agricultural fields. Check any and every flooded field for birds; this area is an excellent place to find rarities. If the year is dry, however, you will be hard-pressed to find much of interest. The levee eventually meets Route 3; you can either continue across the highway and follow the levee to Grand Tower or turn right (north) and take Route 3 about five miles to Grand Tower. There are usually several excellent sloughs along the levee west of Route 3, which constitute the best place to find Vesper Sparrows and Brewer's Blackbirds. From late March through late April, Vesper Sparrows can be found in small groups right on the levee itself, and Brewer's Blackbirds forage in the agricultural fields.

An excellent place to view the Mississippi River is at the Grand Tower boat launch. The entrance to the launch is across from the post office. Just follow the main road into Grand Tower and then up over the Mississippi River levee and down to the boat launch. This is a good place to sit and watch for Least Terns, Fish Crows, and migrating cormorants or waterfowl.

Another good birding spot in southwestern Jackson County is Fountain Bluff, a large Ozarkian uplift that the mighty Mississippi left unscathed. It is an island of upland forest in the Mississippi's wide, flat floodplain. The area is excellent for woodland birds, including Pileated Woodpeckers, Worm-eating Warblers, thrushes, and other migrant vireos and warblers. The entrance is 0.75 miles north of the Oakwood Bottoms turn on Route 3. The first stretch of road is along a small valley, and the land here is privately owned, but once the road begins to climb into the hills, the land is public property. There is a beautiful view of the Mississippi River at the top of the bluff.

Giant City State Park, Jackson and Union Counties

Giant City State Park (see map 9) is named for one of the impressive sandstone bluff formations within the park boundaries. There are numerous trails that wind through, around, over, and even under many of the rock formations. The oak and hickory forests in the park are especially good for spring migrants and summer breeding passerines. Wild Turkeys, Broad-winged Hawks, and Cooper's Hawks are also regularly found here. The park is filled with excellent trails to walk and bird. The lodge has a nice restaurant, where

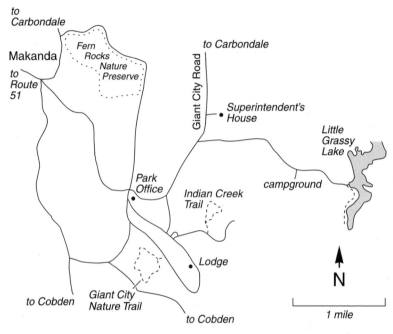

Map 9. Giant City State Park

you can get something to eat and pick up a map and a bird check-list for the park. There are also cabins and camping available if you want to spend the night.

Some of the best places to look for birds are the Fern Rocks Na-ture Preserve on the north side of the park, the road to the family campground and Little Grassy Lake, and the shrubby fields near the site superintendent's residence. The nature preserve is good for Winter Wrens, Ruby-crowned Kinglets, and Hermit Thrushes in late fall and winter. Many Eastern Phoebes nest along the bluffs during spring and summer. If you park at the northern-most shelter and walk across the road to the nature preserve, you will find a trail that takes you along the base of a very tall bluff near a nice stream; this trail is excellent to walk for birds. It is also a great place to find wildflowers, especially in early and mid-May.

The road to the campground is less heavily traveled by cars than the other roads in the park, so the birding is better. Walking sections of the road can turn up turkeys, Northern Parulas, Kentucky Warblers, Louisiana Waterthrushes, and tanagers during the breeding season. During migration you can find just about anything here. An especially good spot is at the end of this road, where it dead-ends at Little Grassy Lake. A dirt road continues to the southeast from the lake and wanders through some young woods; this area is a great place to find flycatchers, vireos, thrushes, and warblers.

There are many other good places to check in the park, but one that you should definitely plan to search is the area of shrubby fields near the superintendent's house. This area is the most reliable place to find Prairie Warbler, Blue Grosbeak, Field Sparrow, and lots of White-eyed Vireos. Bell's Vireo has also been recorded here. This site is also a reliable place for finding lots of ticks. The deer population is very high here, so there are plenty of ticks, too. If you are driving through the park at night, be sure to drive carefully; it is difficult to pass through the park without finding a deer somewhere along your way.

To get to Giant City, you may follow Giant City Road south from Route 13 in Carbondale for about 11.5 miles, or you may take Route 51 to the Makanda turn (between Anna and Carbondale), turn east and wind through the hills into Makanda, follow the main road to the north after it crosses the railroad, and then turn right (east) at the park sign, into the north part of the park.

Ferne Clyffe State Park, Johnson County

Ferne Clyffe State Park is better known for its scenic beauty than for its birds, but the birding can be quite good. There are many trails that lead through picturesque wooded valleys and along fern-covered sandstone bluffs. Ephemeral streams run all through the park. The woodland birding is excellent during spring and fall. During summer, Ferne Clyffe is a good place to find Broad-winged Hawks, Louisiana Waterthrushes, Acadian Flycatchers, Summer Tanagers, and Prairie Warblers. The Deer Ridge Campground has been a reliable site for Chuck-will's-widows. During winter, Ferne Clyffe is one of the better places to find Ruby-crowned Kinglets, Yellow-rumped Warblers, Winter Wrens, and Hermit Thrushes. Be sure to stop and check the lake, too; it caters to flocks of migrant waterfowl and even to an occasional loon or Osprey. The railroad tracks just outside the park entrance often have several Blue Grosbeak territories. Bachman's Sparrow once occurred here, but the habitat has matured so much that it seems unlikely that the species will be found here again.

Ferne Clyffe is located in Johnson County, just south of Goreville. It is most easily reached by taking the Goreville exit off of I-24 and following the signs for the park; the route is well marked.

Dixon Springs State Park, Pope County

Known for its clear spring water, Dixon Springs State Park is also home to nesting Black Vultures. The vultures breed in cavities in the bluffs and can be viewed in and near the park at almost any time of year. The woods in the park are excellent for birds during migration. During the breeding season, Summer Tanagers, Pileated Woodpeckers, and Eastern Phoebes are common. Occasionally, a Black-and-white Warbler may summer here. Broad-winged Hawks have bred here as well.

The park is located in Pope County, about ten miles west of Golconda on Route 146, and just east of the intersection of Routes 145 and 146. There are many camping and picnicking sites available.

Cave-in-Rock State Park, Hardin County

Cave-in-Rock is a fifty-five-foot-wide cave located in a picturesque limestone bluff overlooking the Ohio River. The cave was a frequent resting place for weary eighteenth-century travelers headed to the Great Plains, but it became the haunt of dangerous pirates in the late 1700s. Travelers were lured into the cave and then robbed and murdered. By the mid-1800s, most criminal activities had been discouraged. In 1929, the area became state property, and it is now maintained as a public park.

The view of the Ohio River from the blufftops is excellent. Migrating Red-headed Woodpeckers, Blue Jays, and raptors follow the bluff southwestward during the fall. Sometimes flocks of gulls, terns, and waterfowl can be seen migrating along the river, too. There are several trails through woodland atop the bluffs, along which Yellow-throated Warblers, Summer Tanagers, and occasional Cerulean Warblers can be found. Audubon found the region's first Sharp-shinned Hawk nest on a bluff ledge here in about 1820.

The area is located in Hardin County and is best accessed from State Route 1. Picnicking and camping sites are plentiful.

Union County Conservation Area, Union County

Western Union County is one of the best birding areas in southern Illinois (see map 10). The wide, flat floodplain of the Mississippi River meets the Ozark Hills in a fashion of impressive contrast. A wide range of habitats—including swamps, lakes, bottomland forest, upland forest, agricultural fields, and the river—occurs within a relatively small area. Consequently, the diversity of birds that can be found here is quite high.

The Union County Conservation Area is maintained primarily as a waterfowl refuge, with management emphasis on Canada Geese. Access to much of the area is restricted, but good birding is always available. Spring and winter are the most exciting times to visit. During spring, be sure to look for songbirds in the extensive bottomland forest along the north section of Refuge Drive. Pileated and Red-headed Woodpeckers are very common in these woods. As you travel further south along Refuge Drive, check the ditch that parallels the east side of the road for Wood Ducks and herons; cottonmouths are also fairly common in the ditch. The road soon turns west into the agricultural fields managed as foraging areas for geese. Scan any wet area for shorebirds and waterfowl. When the geese are present, it is well worth scanning through them (sometimes the flocks are huge), because other rare species associate with them. A few Snow Geese can usually be found, and this area is a good place to find Greater White-fronted Geese as well. Brant, Ross' Geese, and Barnacle Geese have all been seen here, too. During winter, Refuge Drive is a good place to see raptors, especially Bald Eagles and Red-shouldered Hawks. In April and early May, Upland Sandpipers and Bobolinks frequent the site.

Another excellent birding route at the Union County Conservation Area is the drive along the periphery of the refuge. About 2.3 miles east of Ware, Route 146 crosses the Clear Creek levee. Drive south onto the levee; sometimes the road is in bad shape, but most

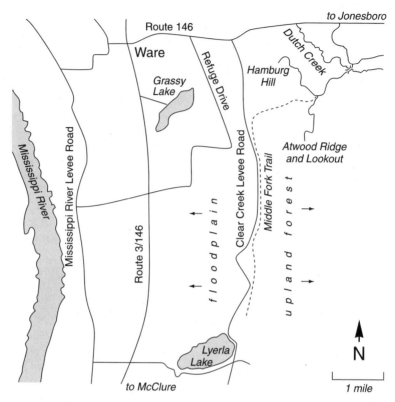

Map 10. Union County Conservation Area and Atwood Ridge

street cars can pass over the few rough spots. Drive the levee slowly and check all bodies of water for shorebirds and waterfowl. One of the best spots for shorebirds is a flooded section at the south end of the first field you pass on the right. The levee passes through riparian woods and swamps, so it is beneficial to stop occasionally and walk along the woodland edge; American Redstarts and Pro-thonotary Warblers are especially common here. Fish Crows and Red-shouldered Hawks are reliably found here, as are Mississippi Kites. The kites are present from May through August, and you can often get very good looks at them here, because they perch on dead snags high in the cottonwood trees that line the levee. If you are here at midday, scan high in the sky for soaring kites. Toward the southern end of the levee, you will come to a cluster of swampy ponds. Scan these for waterfowl, herons, terns, and Osprey. A Purple Gallinule was found along here one year. At the southern end of the levee is Lyerla Lake. It is extensive enough to attract some of the diving ducks in good numbers; cormorants are also regular visitors. During winter, Lyerla Lake is an excellent place to find Bald Eagles. It is not unusual to find a dozen or more eagles perched in the forest edge along the shore of the lake.

When you come to the first blacktop road crossing the levee (at Lyerla Lake), turn right (west) and follow the road back to Route 3/146. Here, you can either turn north on Route 3/146 or cross it and go to the Mississippi River levee. The Mississippi River levee takes you north. There can be good shorebird habitat in the agricultural fields along the levee, as well as opportunities to find Northern Harriers coursing over the fields or Vesper Sparrows along the levee itself. During some winters, large concentrations of Horned Larks and Lapland Longspurs use the agricultural fields. Among the rarities discovered here are Western Meadowlarks and Prairie Falcons. There are several opportunities to get off the levee and return to Route 3; the second turn will take you back to Ware.

The last place to check on this peripheral tour of the Union County Conservation Area is Grassy Lake. The turn is located 0.9 miles south of Ware along Route 3. It is on the east and is rather inconspicuous, so it can be easily missed. The road is usually open from March to October but gated off at other times. Grassy Lake is the best lake for waterfowl, so it is usually worth the walk if the road is closed. When the road is open, you can drive right to the lake. Check this lake even in the heat of the summer; it seems to have an unusual number of straggling waterfowl species.

Atwood Ridge, Union County

The upland forest of Atwood Ridge may be the best spring woodland birding spot in the state or perhaps even in the Midwest. The concentrations of warblers, vireos, thrushes, and other passerines here in late April and early May is sometimes staggering. The trees seem to drip with birds during fallouts. Finding thirty species of warblers here in a day is fairly commonplace.

To get to Atwood, turn south off of Route 146 between Jonesboro and Ware onto the road at the historical marker (about four miles east of Ware and four miles west of Jonesboro). The road forks immediately, so turn right. Follow this around the base of a wooded hill for a couple miles and then take your first right. You should cross a concrete bridge over Dutch Creek as you continue south. The road soon turns west and fords a shallow creek before it turns back south and starts up a long hill. When the road levels off, you should be at a fork in the road, which is called the Middlefork. Park here and begin birding; this site is one of the best areas to find warblers and vireos. You can walk south or west along the gravel roads or southwest down a dirt trail between the two forks. The trail takes you down into a bottomland forest about a mile from the parking area. For the best birding, walk the west fork of the gravel road. It winds around for a mile or so before dead-ending at a clearcut at Hamburg Hill. Be sure to check the edges of the clearcut for Mourning Warbler and Connecticut Warbler during May. At the parking area at Hamburg Hill, a dirt trail leads to the south into some excellent forest; Hooded and Cerulean Warblers breed here. The trail has several spurs that dead-end at wildlife openings, so you cannot get lost as long as you backtrack.

There are plenty of other good birding sites on Atwood, too. The whole road is worth walking. If you drive to the end of the south fork, the road will end on top of Atwood Lookout (where the trees are so tall that there is not much of a view anymore). A dirt trail starts here and follows the ridge south before branching into a complex of trails. The birding can be good along here, but the area is often very windy. Atwood Ridge is a wonderful place to explore for forest birds, especially during spring.

Heron Pond and Little Black Slough, Johnson County

One of the most amazing places in southern Illinois is the cypress and tupelo swamp along the Cache River in Johnson County. The Little Black Slough State Natural Area and Heron Pond Nature Preserve include a rather large tract of mature swamp and bottomland forest (see map 11). In many places, the trees stand well over one hundred feet tall and have diameters of several feet.

Besides the scenery, the birds are impressive as well. Swainson's Warbler has nested here and could potentially still breed here,

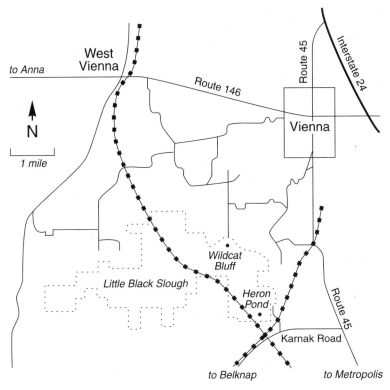

Map 11. Heron Pond and Little Black Slough

though there have been no records since the 1970s. A traditional heron colony is home to many pairs of Great Blue Herons and a few pairs of Great Egrets. Purple Gallinules have been spotted here in early May. The main attraction to the area, however, is the exceptional abundance of spring migrants and summer breeders. Prothonotary Warblers, Northern Parulas, Scarlet Tanagers, Yellow-throated Vireos, Cerulean Warblers, Acadian Flycatchers, Barred Owls, Red-shouldered Hawks, Pileated Woodpeckers, and Yellow-throated Warblers are all very common.

There are essentially two access points to this mostly inaccessible site. The first, and most famous, is Heron Pond. Take Route 45 south from Vienna about 5 miles to Karnak Road (blacktop) and turn right (west). Follow the blacktop about 1.5 miles to the first righthand gravel road; if you get to the railroad tracks, you have gone too far. Along the blacktop, be sure to check the high-tension power poles for vultures. Both Black and Turkey Vultures often roost on the poles. At the gravel road, turn right and follow the signs from there to the Heron Pond parking lot. At the lot, you will see the trail entrance that leads back to the pond.

Along the trail is some excellent bottomland forest that surrounds the Cache River. Here you may find lots of warblers, gnatcatchers, vireos, and thrushes, but you may strain your neck trying to see the warblers. The trail borders the river and then comes to a wooden boardwalk that leads out into the cypress swamp called Heron Pond. Yellow-throated Warblers should be a sure bet here in spring and summer. During winter, there should be Brown Creepers and, perhaps, a Yellow-bellied Sapsucker around. If you are adventurous, you can keep walking around the edge of Heron Pond past the boardwalk to continue birding, but the trail essentially deadends within a few hundred meters. During the spring and summer, watch your step for snakes; cottonmouths are common here, as are many other species of snakes; the rich diversity of amphibians and reptiles attracts many herpetologists to visit here.

The other access point is at Wildcat Bluff. To get there from Heron Pond, go back to Karnak Road and return to Route 45. Turn left (north) and go about 1.6 miles to a set of double bridges. Take the first left turn immediately after crossing the second bridge. This gravel road winds around for about 0.8 miles and then turns to the north. Keep following it north for about a mile, to the first road on the left. Turn here and follow this road west until it comes to a T-intersection. Turn left again and proceed south until you reach a dead end at a parking lot; this site is Wildcat Bluff.

There is not much to see here at the parking lot, but if you look to the west, you should see a narrow dirt road. This road heads down along the top of the bluff and eventually descends to the Cache River and the surrounding forest. The birding can be very good along this road, especially during migration. Once it descends into the floodplain, the birding is unpredictable. During early summer, when the breeders are present, it is usually very good. Acadian Flycatchers are incredibly common here. The walk to the swamp from the top of Wildcat Bluff is very long. The stretch of road to get to the floodplain is about one mile, and then there is a trail a couple of miles long that circles an island in the center of the slough, Boss Island. If you want to see the whole area, give yourself some time.

Following the road down to the floodplain is straightforward. The road ends on the bluff, but where the road ends, a trail heads south down to the floodplain. This trail leads down to the river, which can be impassable if the water level is too high. If the water is low, there is a concrete crossing that you can walk across to get out to Boss Island. A trail from the river to and around Boss Island is usually maintained, so it is not easy to get lost. Out on the island, you may find a few pairs of Blue-winged Warblers, Prairie Warblers, or Mississippi Kites. There are a couple of pine stands on the west edge of the island that have turned up Pine Warblers during spring and summer and Long-eared Owls and Northern Saw-whet Owls during winter. If you happen not to see many birds on your trip to Heron Pond and Little Black Slough, however, you probably will not be disappointed, because the scenery is absolutely beautiful.

Cypress Creek National Wildlife Refuge and Frank Bellrose Waterfowl Reserve, Pulaski County

A newly created area for waterfowl management in Pulaski County is the Ducks Unlimited Tract, otherwise known as the Bellrose Reserve (see map 12). An extensive area of shallow ponds and sloughs attracts many waterfowl, herons, and shorebirds. Some good rarities have been found here, including Glossy Ibis and Scissor-tailed Flycatcher.

The tract is located between Ullin and Perks, along the Cache River. The best birding spots require a long walk in from the gate at the entrance to the tract, but they are often worth the effort. To get to the area, take the Ullin exit off of Interstate 57 and head east on the Shawnee College Road. You should go to the refuge office at the Shawnee Community College first before going to the reserve, because it is necessary to get permission to enter; the refuge office may also be able to loan you a key so that you can avoid the long walk past the gate. The college is located about 6.5 miles from the interstate; when you get there, ask for directions to the Cypress Creek National Wildlife Refuge office.

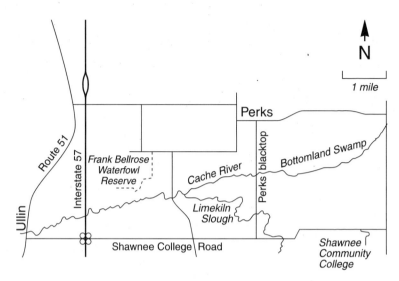

Map 12. Cypress Creek National Wildlife Refuge and Frank Bellrose Waterfowl Reserve

From the college, head back west toward the interstate and take your first through road to the right (north), the Perks blacktop. Follow this road north 3 miles to Perks and turn left. Proceed west through town, and when the road begins to make a sharp turn to the right, bear left. The road soon turns sharply to the left, heads due south for about 0.7 miles, and then turns back to the west. Follow it about 2.7 miles until you come to the second side road on the left; there should be a sign here for the Frank Bellrose Waterfowl Reserve, which is the Ducks Unlimited Tract. If the gate is open, you can probably drive down, but if not, and if you were unable to get a key, you will have to walk.

The first impoundment you come to near some buildings has been good for waterfowl and shorebirds. You can get to some additional good areas by following the dirt road west along the north edge of this first pond and then south to a wooden bridge. Cross the bridge and follow the dirt road to some additional impoundments. The wet areas eventually reach the interstate. Probably the best time to visit this area is in April and May; September and October may be good, too. If the water is open, this site can be a good place for lots of waterfowl during winter as well.

Mermet Lake Conservation Area, Massac County

Mermet Lake Conservation Area (see map 13) is located in western Massac County and contains an old cypress and tupelo swamp reminiscent of the days when the ocean's waves nearly reached "Illinois's" shores. The cypress swamp is preserved in a 2,580-acre refuge created especially for migrant waterfowl. The 450-acre Mermet Lake was created in 1962 as a water source for flooding the surrounding bottomland woods each autumn for ducks and hunters. Mermet Lake's shallowness and its many snags provide ample feeding and roosting sites for herons, cormorants, Osprey, and swallows. The east side of the lake is covered in an extensive cattail and lotus marsh. There is an extensive oak and sweet gum woodland on the west side of the lake and a drier oak and poplar woods to the south. Open fields and hedgerows are present to the east of the lake.

To most birders, Mermet Lake is known for its Purple Gallinules. Gallinules have bred here in the past and may still occur regularly today. The best way to locate the gallinules is to listen for them. They tend to frequent the cattail and lotus transition zone and can be quite difficult to see when they are skulking around beneath the large lotus leaves. May and June are the best times to search the marsh for Purple Gallinules. Also present during May and June are Least Bitterns, which breed here. They tend to utilize the large areas of cattails at the north edge of the marsh. The bitterns respond well to recordings of their calls, especially if played at dawn. Other species recorded at Mermet Lake in the past include Anhinga, Laughing Gull, Yellow-crowned Night-Heron, Snowy Egret, King Rail, Least Tern, Swainson's Warbler, and American White Pelican. Of course, the typical southern Illinois species—such as Red-shouldered Hawk, Barred Owl, Chuck-will's-widow, Pileated Woodpecker, Fish Crow, Acadian Flycatcher, Kentucky Warbler, and Summer Tanager—can usually be found here in the appropriate season.

The best time to visit Mermet is in the spring. The sheer number

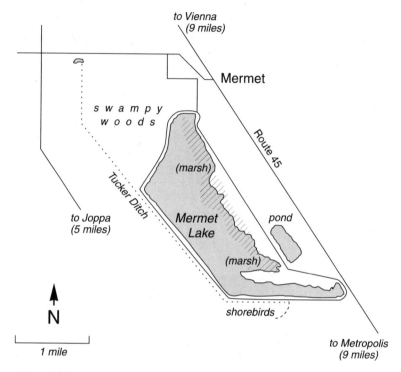

to Vienna
(9 miles)

Mermet

*s w a m p y
w o o d s*

Route 45

(marsh)

Tucker Ditch

to Joppa
(5 miles)

**Mermet
Lake**

pond

(marsh)

N

shorebirds

1 mile

to Metropolis
(9 miles)

Map 13. Mermet Lake Conservation Area

of warblers, swallows, flycatchers, and herons can be quite impressive as one walks the levee around the lake. Another exciting time to visit is fall, when the lake water is used to flood the surrounding woods for duck hunting. The water level of the lake drops as much as three to four feet, exposing extensive mudflats that are utilized by shorebirds. If one is not enticed to Mermet by the possibility of seeing great birds, however, viewing the remnant cypress swamp itself is well worth the visit.

To access Mermet Lake, take the Vienna exit off of Interstate 24 and follow Route 45 south thirteen miles to the town of Mermet. If you are approaching from the south, take the Metropolis exit and follow Route 45 north to Mermet. There is an entrance to the lake in the town of Mermet, and it is well marked.

Fort Massac State Park, Massac County

At Fort Massac State Park, towering cottonwood and sycamore trees line the shores of the Ohio River, providing habitat for Northern Orioles, Pileated Woodpeckers, Yellow-throated Warblers, and Red-headed Woodpeckers. Fish Crows nest in the park, and Mississippi Kites can sometimes be seen flying along the shoreline as well. During spring migration, this site is an excellent place to find Yellow-bellied Flycatchers, Philadelphia Vireos, and Cerulean Warblers. It is not unusual to find twenty-five or more species of warblers here in a single day in early to mid-May. A pair of Swainson's Warblers were found in dense woodland in the eastern portion of the park in 1982.

There are three good access points into the park (see map 14). The two western entrances off of Route 45 in Metropolis lead you to the fort itself and to the picnic and camping areas. The birding in the western portions of the park can be good, but human traffic is sometimes heavy, especially on the weekends, and the area is just too manicured to be really good for birds. The mowed areas around the fort can, however, be good for Chipping Sparrows. It is also well worth the time to stroll through the fort and look out over the Ohio River for passing herons, terns, gulls, and swallows. A nice interpretive center provides plenty of information on the history of the fort and its occupation by French, British, and American troops. Interestingly, the site was probably first used by European explorers as early as 1654.

The best birding route on the west side of the park starts at the fort. Follow the road nearest the river east to the boat ramp. Check here for terns and other waterbirds. Proceed east, always following the roads that keep you near the river. You should soon come to a stretch of road that parallels Massac Creek; sometimes this road is gated off during high water. It is well worth walking along this road, where Yellow-bellied Flycatchers have been found regularly. If you follow this road far enough, you will come to a wooden bridge over Massac Creek that is usually gated off. Walk east across the bridge. Warblers and thrushes are common here in spring.

Access to the east side of the park is by foot only. Follow Route 45 east from Metropolis across Interstate 24. Just over half a mile east of Interstate 24, turn south onto a blacktop road. Follow that

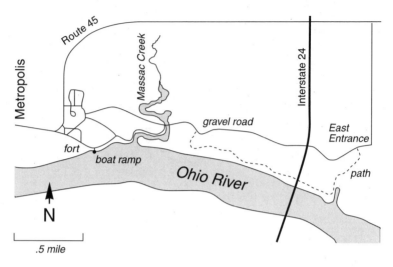

Map 14. Fort Massac State Park

road until it dead-ends at the park's east entrance. You can walk
the gravel road west all the way back to Massac Creek and find
good birding all along the route. Wilson's and Golden-winged Warblers can be found here regularly. Just west of the Interstate 24 over-
pass, there is a patch of shrubby second growth that has been home
to a pair of Prairie Warblers since at least 1977. The best birding
route on the east side of the park, however, is along a grass path
that parallels the river. From the parking area at the east gate, walk
about two hundred yards west along the gravel road. A wide grassy
road turns off to the south. If you follow this path, it will eventually
take you to the base of Interstate 24. In the past, there has been a
large Cliff Swallow colony on the iron beams supporting the interstate.

Smithland Lock and Dam, Pope County

Smithland, along the Ohio River, is an underappreciated site for
birding. Probably the main reason it has been overlooked is that it
is located in the extreme southeastern corner of the state. Also, if

a good waterbird is discovered there, it will inevitably be on the "Kentucky side," because Illinois owns virtually none of the river at the current time. Politicocentric views aside, some excellent birds have been reported from the river just below the dam. These include Lesser Black-backed Gulls, Glaucous Gulls, Thayer's Gulls, Laughing Gulls, Black Scoters, and Surf Scoters. Good numbers of terns (Forster's and Black, especially) and Bonaparte's Gulls occur there during migration. During summer, an occasional Least Tern has been spotted. During winter, there are always lots of Ring-billed Gulls and a few Herring Gulls. Unfortunately, the river is renowned for its almost schizophrenic birding; on some days the river is full of birds, whereas on others it is difficult to find anything of interest.

Fortunately, the waterbirds are not the only draw. The mown fields along the drive to the dam are one of the few places in southeastern Illinois to find Grasshopper Sparrows. Willow Flycatchers occur in the dense willow thickets during summer, and Bell's Vireo has even been recorded there. There is a very large colony of Cliff Swallows that nest on the dam. You may also want to check the pines along the road to the dam for Yellow-rumped Warbler, Red-breasted Nuthatch, Yellow-bellied Sapsucker, and Hermit Thrush during winter and for Pine Warbler in spring and summer.

To get to Smithland from the north, take the main blacktop south from the four-way stop at the Golconda post office for about seventeen miles. A sign for the lock and dam is positioned on the crest of a hill, where you turn to the east to access the site. To get to Smithland from the west, take the Unionville blacktop (400N) east from just north of Brookport until you get to New Liberty. Turn northwest and follow the blacktop about three miles to the Smithland entrance.

Horseshoe Lake Conservation Area, Alexander County

An oxbow lake of the Mississippi River, Horseshoe Lake is now a shallow, cypress and tupelo swamp (see map 15). It is regionally famous for attracting huge numbers of wintering Canada Geese; Olive Branch, the nearby town, claims to be the Canada Goose capital of the world. Winter flocks of geese sometimes exceed 150,000

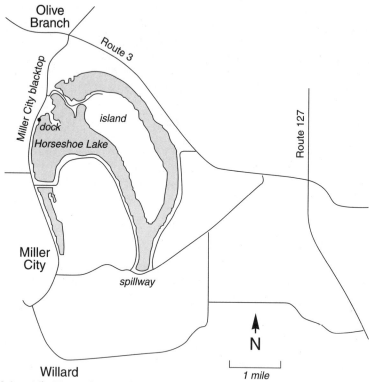

Map 15. Horseshoe Lake Conservation Area

birds. Often quite a few ducks and even a swan or two winter here, too. Bald Eagles are regular winter visitors, and a pair has bred here for years. A few rare finds have been turned up at Horseshoe Lake, including Cinnamon Teal, Purple Gallinule, and Wood Stork. Golden Eagles are found here every winter.

Probably the best tactic for birding Horseshoe is to drive and stop as you go around the lake. Go south on the Miller City blacktop from Olive Branch, which is located on Route 3 between Cairo and Thebes. The blacktop borders the west side of the lake after about a mile of passing through private property. When the lake first comes up to the edge of the road, you should see a small dock. Check the lake here for birds; this site has been a good place for

Pied-billed Grebes and Tundra Swans. Proceeding south, scan the lake any time you can get a look through the cypress trees to open water. You might try stopping and walking along the road to find songbirds, too; there should be plenty of Northern Mockingbirds and Eastern Bluebirds, and there may be a Loggerhead Shrike or two.

About 1.5 miles after the dock, there is a blacktop road to the left that crosses a causeway over one arm of the lake and then turns to the left and goes around the inside of the lake. Driving this road can be good for finding a wide variety of birds. There is an open field on one side of the road, and the lake is on the other. Check the field for Northern Harriers, American Pipits, Horned Larks, and meadowlarks. The road eventually comes to the south end of Horseshoe. If you turn left, you will cross the spillway. The parking lot here is a good place to view the lake; this part of the lake is traditionally the best place to find diving ducks.

If you turn left after leaving the parking lot, you can continue straight out to Route 3 or turn left immediately and drive along the eastern edge of the lake. Both routes pass through some nice forest that might be worth checking for birds. If you turn right from the parking lot, this road will take you back to the Miller City blacktop. If you are here in fall or winter, be sure to look through all the flocks of Canada Geese for Greater White-fronted, Snow, and Ross' Geese; Brant is even a possibility. Between May and early September, there may even be a chance of finding a Least Tern. Fish Crows are a sure bet between March and October.

Willard Area, Southern Alexander County

The extreme southern tip of the state in southern Alexander County can be an excellent place to find unusual birds (see map 16). In particular, the agricultural lands and river bottoms south of Horseshoe Lake near Willard have turned up such rarities as Prairie Falcon, Anhinga, White Ibis, Swainson's Hawk, and Magnificent Frigatebird. Some species that are rare elsewhere can be found here routinely such as Least Tern, Mississippi Kite, and Fish Crow. An additional attraction is the large concentration of herons that forage in the sloughs and flooded fields throughout the area during late

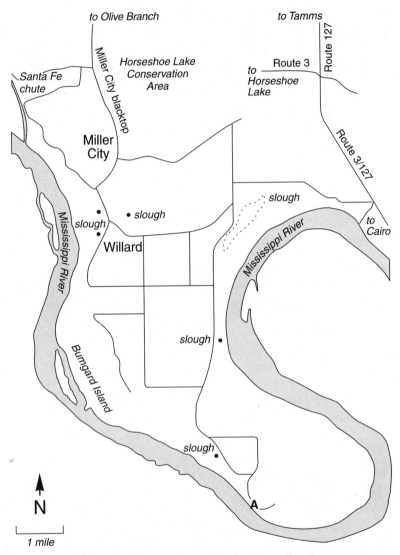

to Olive Branch

to Tamms

Route 127

Santa Fe chute

Miller City blacktop

Horseshoe Lake Conservation Area

Route 3

to Horseshoe Lake

Route 3/127

Miller City

Mississippi River

slough

slough

slough

to Cairo

Willard

Mississippi River

slough

Bumgard Island

slough

A

N

1 mile

Map 16. Willard and extreme southern Alexander County

summer and early fall. Some of southern Illinois's largest concentrations of Little Blue Herons and Snowy and Cattle Egrets have been seen here. Huge flocks of swallows occur here from July through early October as well.

Like many of the really good birding sites, however, Willard is either boom or bust. The quality of birding depends directly on the availability of pools of water and mudflats in the slight depressions in the agricultural fields. In dry years, it can be difficult to find even a single heron or shorebird.

The area can be reached most easily by taking Route 3 to Olive Branch and then turning south toward Horseshoe Lake Conservation Area and Miller City; this turn is located next to a small convenience store just west of where an old railroad bed crosses Route 3. Follow the Miller City blacktop south about three miles to Miller City; this road takes you along the western edge of Horseshoe Lake, which can be a worthwhile birding area as well. Continue south after Miller City for approximately one mile. (Note: the Flood of 1993 washed away some of the roads described from this point on; after repair, they may not follow exactly the same paths as the following account describes.) Here, the road forks; both directions lead to good birding sites. The right fork will lead you north to Santa Fe Chute, which can be good for finding Least Terns, Snowy Egrets, and a few shorebirds during summer and fall; there is usually a Bank Swallow colony here as well. At other seasons, the water level in the chute is often very high, and the birding then is poor. A search of the nearby woods and agricultural fields, however, may be profitable; five species of blackbird were seen here in one day in January 1992.

The left fork takes you to more productive birding areas. Beginning immediately after you turn south, you should see small sloughs along the roadside edge where depressions in the agricultural fields have filled with water. Check all of these sloughs carefully for shorebirds and herons. These sloughs are the main birding attractions. The locations of some of the best sloughs have been marked on map 16. These sites are ephemeral, so there may be no sign of water at some of them. In addition, farmers actively drain these sloughs, so many will not have water except in very wet years. The best strategy is to take some time and wander all the roads looking for signs of water. Be sure to scan plowed, dry fields occasionally as well for Lesser Golden-Plovers, especially during spring.

One place you should definitely visit is near the very southern tip of this part of the county. At site A on map 16, the road meets the levee that separates the Mississippi River from the floodplain. Park here and walk up onto the levee; a small trail will take you down the other side into some woods and out onto the shores of the river. This is an excellent place to sit and watch for passing Mississippi Kites and migrating herons; Anhinga, Swainson's Hawk, and Magnificent Frigatebird have all been seen from here.

Your best chance to see Least Tern is to check Santa Fe Chute between late May and late August; July seems to be best. The terns nest on sandbars in the river and fly into the chute and into the many sloughs south of Willard to forage. They tend to fly around a lot, visiting many different areas, so persistence is your key to success.

Cairo, Alexander County

There are a few birding areas around Cairo similar to those near Willard. From the intersection of Interstate 57 and Route 3, go northwest along Route 3 a few hundred yards to the Dairy Queen. Turn west and follow the road up onto the levee behind the Dairy Queen. Turn left and go south down the levee. After you pass under Interstate 57, you will come to agricultural fields that are sometimes flooded and have herons and other waders. These sites are not as good as those south of Willard, but they sometimes have many birds.

Another interesting place to visit in Cairo is Fort Defiance State Park. Follow Route 3 through Cairo; just before you get on the bridge to go to Missouri, you should see a sign for the park on your left. The birding is only fair in the park, but the spectacle of the Ohio and Mississippi Rivers merging is very impressive. If you spend some time here, you may see Least Terns, migrating herons, and waterfowl.

Other Recommended Sites

There are innumerable places to go birding in southern Illinois. Any woodlot, field, roadside hedgerow, or lake should be home to some interesting birds. It would take an entire book to detail all the exciting localities to visit. Some additional sites that could be quite well worth exploring include Fort Kaskaskia State Park in Randolph County, Lake of Egypt in Williamson and Johnson Counties, Kinkaid Lake in Jackson County, the floodplain around East Cape Girardeau in Alexander County, the Wabash River floodplain in White and Gallatin Counties, the immediate vicinity of Harrisburg in Saline County, Pounds Hollow in Gallatin County, Garden of the Gods in Saline County, and the Bell Smith Springs/Lusk Creek area in Pope County. Be encouraged to explore new areas!

Literature Cited
Index of Common Names
Index of Scientific Names

Literature Cited

Albano, D. J. 1992. Nesting mortality of Carolina Chickadees breeding in natural cavities. *Condor* 94:371–382.

American Ornithologists' Union. 1983. *Check-list of North American birds*. Sixth edition. Allen Press, Lawrence, Kansas.

———. 1985. Thirty-fifth supplement to the A. O. U. *Check-list of North American birds*. *Auk* 102:682.

Ammann, G. A. 1939. Swainson's Warbler in Illinois. *Wilson Bulletin* 51:185–186.

Anderson, R. 1964. Observations from southern Illinois. *Audubon Bulletin* 129:18.

———. 1971. Bird survey. *Bluebird* 38:2–4.

Appleby, R. H., S. C. Madge, and K. Mullarny. 1986. Identification of divers in immature and winter plumages. *British Birds* 76:365–391.

Audubon, J. J. 1831. Ornithological biography. Volume 1. Adam and Charles Black, Edinburgh.

———. 1835. Ornithological biography. Volume 3. Adam and Charles Black, Edinburgh.

———. 1838. *The birds of America*. Volume 4. London.

———. 1868. *The life and adventures of John James Audubon, the naturalist*. Edited by Robert Buchanan. Sampson Low, Son, and Marston, London.

———. 1929. *Journal of John James Audubon*. Edited by Howard Corning. Club of Odd Volumes, Boston.

———. 1942. Audubon's "Journal up the Mississippi." Edited by J. F. McDermott. *Journal of the Illinois State Historical Society* 35:148–173.

Baker, F. C. 1937. An Illinois record for the Little Brown Crane. *Auk* 54:388.

Bartsch, P. 1922. Some tern notes. *Auk* 39:101.

Bellrose, F. C. 1944. Bald Eagles nesting in Illinois. *Auk* 61:467–468.

Bennett, E. V. 1952. Checklist of birds of southern Illinois. Southern Illinois University, Carbondale. Mimeographed. 19 pp.

———. 1957. Nesting birds of the shoreline and islands of Crab Orchard Lake, Illinois. *Transactions of the Illinois State Academy of Science* 50:259–264.

Bent, A. C. 1925. Life histories of North American wildfowl. U.S. National Museum Bulletin 130.

Birkenholz, D. E. 1958. Notes on a wintering flock of Long-eared Owls. *Transactions of the Illinois State Academy of Science* 51:83–86.

Black, C. T. 1941. Ecological and economic relations of the crow, with special reference to Illinois. Ph.D. diss., University of Illinois, Urbana.

Blake, J. G., and J. R. Karr. 1984. Species composition of bird communities and the conservation benefit of large versus small forests. *Biological Conservation* 30:173–187.

Bohlen, H. D. 1978. *An annotated check-list of the birds of Illinois.* Illinois State Museum Popular Science Series, vol. 9.

———. 1986. The status of the Ferruginous Hawk in Illinois. *Illinois Birds and Birding* 2:40–41.

———. 1989. *The birds of Illinois.* Indiana University Press, Bloomington.

Breitburg, E. 1990. The faunal assemblage. In *Archaeological excavations at the Petitt Site (11-Ax-253), Alexander County, Illinois,* (P. A. Webb, ed.). Center for Archaeological Investigations, Research Paper Number 58. Southern Illinois University, Carbondale.

Brewer, R. 1954. Nesting of the Least Tern in Illinois. *Wilson Bulletin* 66:223.

———. 1955. Size of home range in eight bird species in a southern Illinois swamp-thicket. *Wilson Bulletin* 67:140–141.

———. 1958. Some corrections to "A distributional checklist of the birds of Illinois." *Audubon Bulletin* 106:9.

———. 1963. Ecological and reproductive relationships of Black-capped and Carolina Chickadees. *Auk* 80:9–47.

Brittingham, M. C., and S. A. Temple. 1983. Have cowbirds caused forest songbirds to decline? *BioScience* 33:31–35.

Brooks, M. 1938. Bachman's Sparrow in the north-central portion of its range. *Wilson Bulletin* 50:86–109.

Cahn, A. R., and A. S. Hyde. 1929. Easter birds of Little Egypt. *Wilson Bulletin* 41:31–38.

Calhoun, J. C., and J. K. Garver. 1974. *The Wild Turkey in Illinois.* Illinois Department of Conservation, Springfield.

Carson, M. P. 1926. The Wood Ibis in Jefferson County, Illinois. *Bird-Lore* 28:195–196.

Clark, W. S., and B. K. Wheeler. 1987. *A field guide to hawks of North America.* Houghton Mifflin, Boston.

Coale, H. K. 1915. The present status of the Trumpeter Swan. *Auk* 32:82–90.

Comfort, J. E. 1961. The St. Louis area. *Bluebird* 28:17.

Conley, C. L. 1926. Purple Martin in winter. *Audubon Bulletin* 17:26.

Cooke, W. W. 1888. *Report on bird migration in the Mississippi Valley in the years 1884 and 1885.* U.S. Department of Agriculture, Division of Economic Ornithology and Mammalogy, Bulletin 2.

Cory, C. B. 1909. The birds of Illinois and Wisconsin. Field Museum of Natural History Publication 131, Zoological Series, volume 9.

Danley, R. F. 1994. Rufous Hummingbird: Illinois' second record. *Meadowlark* 3:43–44.

DeNeal, J. 1993. Jefferson County's first Black-necked Stilt. *Meadowlark* 2:62.

Eddleman, W. R. 1978. Selection and management of Swainson's Warbler habitat. Master's thesis, University of Missouri, Columbia.

Eddleman, W. R., K. E. Evans, and W. H. Elder. 1980. Habitat characteristics and management of Swainson's Warbler in southern Illinois. *Wildlife Society Bulletin* 8:228–233.

Ehrlich, R. M. 1990. Nest site habitat of Cooper's Hawks (*Accipiter cooperii*) in southern Illinois. Master's thesis, Southern Illinois University, Carbondale.

Enderson, J. H. 1960. A population study of the Sparrow Hawk in east-central Illinois. *Wilson Bulletin* 72:222–231.

Findley, C. H. 1949. Trip to Horseshoe Lake. *Bluebird* 16.

Fink, T. 1993a. Curve-billed Thrasher: First Illinois record. *Meadowlark* 2:87–89.

———. 1993b. Glossy Ibis in Pulaski County. *Meadowlark* 2:138.

———. 1994. Breeding evidence for Black-necked Stilt in Jackson County. *Meadowlark* 3:18.

Fink, T., and W. D. Robinson. 1992. Spring record of Sprague's Pipit from southern Illinois. *Meadowlark* 1:139–140.

Flieg, G. M. 1971. The European Tree Sparrow in the Western Hemisphere: Its range, distribution, life history. *Audubon Bulletin* 157:2–10.

Ford, E. R. 1956. Birds of the Chicago region. *Chicago Academy of Sciences Special Publication* 12:1–117.

Frey, D. A. 1975. A Siberian-born Snow Goose in southern Illinois. *Illinois Audubon Bulletin* 172:6.

Ganier, A. F. 1937. The Reelfoot cranetown. *Migrant* 8:42–43.

Gault, B. T. 1922. *Checklist of the birds of Illinois.* Illinois Audubon Society, Chicago.

Gelman, B. 1993. Painted Bunting: First confirmed state record. *Meadowlark* 2:127–128.

George, W. G. 1968. Check list of birds of southern Illinois, 1968. Southern Illinois University, Carbondale. Mimeographed. 28 pp.

———. 1969. The current status of certain bird species in southern Illinois. *Audubon Bulletin* 150:12–15.

———. 1971. Vanished and endangered birds of Illinois: A new "black list" and "red list." *Audubon Bulletin* 158:2–11.

———. 1972. Age determination of Hairy and Downy Woodpeckers in eastern North America. *Bird-Banding* 43:128–135.

Goetz, R. E. 1983. Spring identification of Laughing Gulls and Franklin's Gulls. *Illinois Audubon Bulletin* 204:33–36.

Goetz, R. E., and J. C. Robinson. 1988. First report of the Illinois Ornithological Records Committee. *Illinois Birds and Birding* 4:57–63.

Gower, C. 1933. Horse-shoe Lake. *Audubon Bulletin* 23:31–33.

Graber, J. W., R. R. Graber, and E. L. Kirk. 1977. Illinois Birds: Picidae. *Illinois Natural History Survey Biological Notes* 102.

———. 1978. Illinois Birds: Ciconiiformes. *Illinois Natural History Survey Biological Notes* 109.

———. 1979. Illinois Birds: Sylviidae. *Illinois Natural History Survey Biological Notes* 110.

———. 1983. Illinois Birds: Wood Warblers. *Illinois Natural History Survey Biological Notes* 118.

————. 1985. Illinois Birds: Vireonidae. *Illinois Natural History Survey Biological Notes* 124.

————. 1987. Illinois Birds: Corvidae. *Illinois Natural History Survey Biological Notes* 126.

Graber, R. R. 1957. Sprague's Pipit and Le Conte's Sparrow in Illinois. *Audubon Bulletin* 102:5–7.

Graber, R. R., and J. W. Graber. 1963. A comparative study of bird populations in Illinois, 1906–1909 and 1956–1958. *Illinois Natural History Survey Bulletin* 28:383–528.

Graber, R. R., J. W. Graber, and E. L. Kirk. 1971. Illinois Birds: Turdidae. *Illinois Natural History Survey Biological Notes* 75.

————. 1972. Illinois Birds: Hirundinidae. *Illinois Natural History Survey Biological Notes* 80.

————. 1973. Illinois Birds: Laniidae. *Illinois Natural History Survey Biological Notes* 83.

————. 1974. Illinois Birds: Tyrannidae. *Illinois Natural History Survey Biological Notes* 86.

Grant, P. J. 1986. *Gulls: A guide to identification.* Buteo Books, Vermillion, South Dakota.

Grier, J. W., J. B. Elder, F. J. Gramlich, N. F. Green, J. V. Kussman, J. E. Mathisen, and J. P. Mattsson. 1983. *Northern states Bald Eagle recovery plan.* U.S. Fish and Wildlife Service, Denver.

Gross, A. O. 1908. Swainson's Warbler (*Helinaia swainsoni*). *Auk* 25:225.

Hahn, P. 1963. *Where is that vanished bird?* University of Toronto Press, Toronto.

Hamilton, J. D., and W. D. Klimstra. 1985. Taxonomy of southern Illinois meadowlarks. *Transactions of the Illinois State Academy of Science* 78:223–240.

Hanson, H. C., and C. W. Kossack. 1963. The Mourning Dove in Illinois. *Department of Conservation Technical Bulletin* 2:1–133.

Hardin, M. E., J. W. Hardin, and W. D. Klimstra. 1977. Observations of nesting Mississippi Kites in southern Illinois. *Transactions of the Illinois State Academy of Science* 70:341–348.

Hardy, J. W. 1955. Records of Swainson's Warbler in southern Illinois. *Wilson Bulletin* 67:60.

————. 1957. The Least Tern in the Mississippi Valley. *Publication of the Museum of the Michigan State University* 1:1–60.

Harris, L. D. 1984. *The fragmented forest.* University of Chicago Press, Chicago.

Hayman, P., J. Marchant, and T. Prater. 1986. *Shorebirds: An identification guide to the waders of the world.* Houghton Mifflin, Boston.

Howell, A. H. 1910. Breeding records from southern Illinois. *Auk* 27:216.

Hussel, D. J. T. 1980. The timing of fall migration and molt in Least Flycatchers. *Journal of Field Ornithology* 51:65–71.

Hutto, R. L., S. M. Pletschet, and P. Hendricks. 1986. A fixed-radius point count method for nonbreeding and breeding season use. *Auk* 103:593–602.

Johnsgard, P. A. 1983. *The Hummingbirds of North America.* Smithsonian Institution Press, Washington, D.C.

Johnston, R. F., and J. W. Hardy. 1962. Behavior of the Purple Martin. *Wilson Bulletin* 74:243–262.

Kaufman, K. 1990. *A field guide to advanced birding: Birding challenges and how to approach them.* Houghton Mifflin, Boston.

Kleen, V. M. 1972. Black-headed Grosbeaks in Illinois. *Audubon Bulletin* 163:20–21.

———. 1973a. The density and territory size of breeding Prothonotary Warblers (*Protonotaria citrea*) in southern Illinois. Master's thesis, Southern Illinois University, Carbondale.

———. 1973b. A winter record for the Indigo Bunting in Illinois. *Illinois Audubon Bulletin* 166:30–31.

———. 1976. Middlewestern prairie region. *American Birds* 30:724–728.

———. 1987. Illinois heron colony surveys: 1987 report. *Illinois Birds and Birding* 3:79–82.

Kleen, V. M., and L. Bush. 1972. Checklist of birds of southern Illinois. Southern Illinois University, Carbondale. Mimeographed. 20 pp.

Kleen, V. M., and J. Schwegman. 1993. First Fish Crow nest in Illinois. *Meadowlark* 2:15.

Lehman, P. 1983. Point: Some thoughts on Thayer's Gull and *Sterna* terns. *Birding* 15:107–108.

Long, J. L. 1981. *Introduced birds of the world.* Universe Books, New York.

Lunk, W. A. 1952. Notes on variation in the Carolina Chickadee. *Wilson Bulletin* 64:7–21.

Madding, R., and J. Bell. 1975. Third state record: Fulvous Tree Duck. *Illinois Audubon Bulletin* 172:5.

Madge, S., and H. Burn. 1988. *Waterfowl: An identification guide to the ducks, geese, and swans of the world.* Houghton Mifflin, Boston.

Mayfield, H. F. 1965. The Brown-headed Cowbird with old and new hosts. *Living Bird* 4:13–28.

McKee, J., and C. McKee. 1994. Scissor-tailed Flycatcher in Pulaski County. *Meadowlark* 3:19–20.

Mengel, R. M. 1965. The Birds of Kentucky. *Ornithological Monographs* Number 3.

Mohlenbrock, R. H. 1986. *Guide to the vascular flora of Illinois.* Southern Illinois University Press, Carbondale.

Monroe, B. L., Jr., A. L. Stamm, and B. L. Palmer-Ball, Jr. 1988. *Annotated checklist of the birds of Kentucky.* Kentucky Ornithological Society, Louisville.

Montgomery, R. A., and J. Rice. 1967. Observation of Brant in southern Illinois. *Wilson Bulletin* 79:242.

National Geographic Society. 1983. *Field guide to the birds of North America.* First edition. Washington, D.C.

———. 1987. *Field guide to the birds of North America.* Second edition. Washington, D.C.

Nelson, E. W. 1877. Notes upon birds observed in southern Illinois, between July 17 and September 4, 1875. *Bulletin of the Essex Institute* 9:32–65.

Nolan, V., Jr. 1978. The ecology of the Prairie Warbler *(Dendroica discolor)*. *Ornithological Monographs* Number 8.

Parmalee, P. W. 1967. Additional noteworthy records of birds from archaeological sites. *Wilson Bulletin* 79:155–162.

Payne, R. B. 1977. The ecology of brood parasitism in birds. *Annual Review of Ecology and Systematics* 8:1–28.

Peale, T. R. 1946–1947. The journal of Titian Ramsey Peale, pioneer naturalist. *Missouri Historical Review* 41:147–163, 266–284.

Peterjohn, B. G., and M. D. Morrison. 1977. Sight record of a Curlew Sandpiper in southern Illinois. *Illinois Audubon Bulletin* 180:29–30.

Peterson, R. T. 1980. *A field guide to the birds: A completely new guide to all the birds of eastern and central North America*. Houghton Mifflin, Boston.

Pratt, H. D. 1976. Field identification of White-faced and Glossy Ibises. *Birding* 8:1–5.

Pulliam, H. R. 1988. Sources, sinks, and population regulation. *American Naturalist* 132:652–661.

Quay, W. B. 1989. Timing of sperm releases and inseminations in resident emberizids: A comparative study. *Condor* 91:941–961.

Ridgway, R. 1873. The prairie birds of southern Illinois. *American Naturalist* 7:197–203.

———. 1874. The lower Wabash Valley, considered in its relation to the faunal districts of the eastern region of North America; with a synopsis of its avian fauna. *Proceedings of the Boston Society of Natural History* 16:303–332.

———. 1878. Notes on birds observed at Mt. Carmel, southern Illinois, in the spring of 1878. *Bulletin of the Nuttall Ornithological Club* 3:162–166.

———. 1881. A revised catalogue of the birds ascertained to occur in Illinois. *Illinois State Laboratory of Natural History Bulletin* 4:163–208.

———. 1887. List of birds found breeding within corporate limits of Mt. Carmel, Illinois. *Ridgway Ornithological Club Bulletin* 2:26–35.

———. 1889. *The ornithology of Illinois*. Part 1, volume 1. State Laboratory of Natural History, Springfield.

———. 1895. *The ornithology of Illinois*. Part 1, volume 2. State Laboratory of Natural History, Springfield.

———. 1914. Bird life in southern Illinois. *Bird-Lore* 16:409–420.

———. 1915. Bird life in southern Illinois. *Bird-Lore* 17:191–198.

Robbins, C. S., B. Bruun, H. S. Zim, and A. Singer. 1966. *A guide to field identification: Birds of North America*. First edition. Golden Press, New York.

———. 1983. *A guide to field identification: Birds of North America*. Second edition. Golden Press, New York.

Robbins, C. S., D. K. Dawson, and B. A. Dowell. 1989. *Habitat area requirements of breeding forest birds of the Middle Atlantic States*. Wildlife Monographs Number 103.

Robinson, J. C. 1985. Recent nesting attempts of Bald Eagles in Illinois. *Illinois Birds and Birding* 1:4–7.

———. 1990. *An annotated checklist of the birds of Tennessee*. University of Tennessee Press, Knoxville.

Robinson, J. C., and R. E. Goetz. 1988. Introductory report of the Illinois Ornithological Records Committee. *Illinois Birds and Birding* 4:1–6.

Robinson, W. D. 1988. Bird finding—Mermet Lake Conservation Area. *Illinois Birds and Birding* 4:94.

———. 1989. Cliff Swallow colonies in southern Illinois. *Illinois Birds and Birding* 5:10–12.

———. 1990. Louisiana Waterthrush foraging behavior and microhabitat selection in southern Illinois. Master's thesis, Southern Illinois University, Carbondale.

———. 1991a. Illinois specimens in the Southern Illinois University bird collection. *Illinois Birds and Birding* 7:68–70.

———. 1991b. Southward breeding range extension by Rose-breasted Grosbeaks. *Illinois Birds and Birding* 7:3–4.

Robinson, W. D., and S. K. Robinson. 1992. Late spring migration and extralimital summer records of migrant birds in the Illinois Ozarks. *Transactions of the Illinois State Academy of Science* 85:221–225.

Rothstein, S. I. 1982. Success and failures in avian egg and nestling recognition with comments on the utility of optimality reasoning. *American Zoologist* 22:547–560.

Sauer, J. R., and S. Droege. 1992. Geographic patterns in population trends of Neotropical migrants in North America. Pages 26–42 in *Ecology and conservation of Neotropical migrant landbirds* (J. M. Hagan III and D. W. Johnston, eds.). Smithsonian Institution Press, Washington, D.C.

Schorger, A. W. 1955. *The Passenger Pigeon: Its natural history and extinction*. University of Wisconsin Press, Madison.

———. 1973. *The Passenger Pigeon: Its natural history and extinction*. Revised edition. University of Oklahoma Press, Norman.

Schwegman, J. E., G. D. Fell, M. Hutchison, G. Paulson, W. M. Shepherd, and J. White. 1973. *Comprehensive plan for the Illinois nature preserves system. Part II—The Natural Divisions of Illinois*. Illinois Nature Preserves Commission, Springfield.

Shy, E. 1984. Habitat shift and geographical variation in North American tanagers (Thraupinae: *Piranga*). *Oecologia* 63:281–285.

Smart, G. 1960. Ross' Goose taken at Horseshoe Lake, Illinois. *Wilson Bulletin* 72:288–289.

Smith, H. R., and P. W. Parmalee. 1955. A distribution checklist of the birds of Illinois. Illinois State Museum Popular Science Series, volume 4.

Soule, M. E., and B. A. Wilcox. 1980. *Conservation biology: An evolutionary-ecological perspective*. Sinauer Associates, Sunderland, Massachusetts.

Spitzkeit, J. W., and T. C. Tacha. 1986. Subspecific composition of Canada Geese wintering in southern Illinois. *Transactions of the Illinois State Academy of Science* 79:171–174.

Staff. 1981. Nesting eagles at Crab Orchard National Wildlife Refuge. *Illinois Audubon Bulletin* 199:18–21.

Terborgh, J. W. 1989. *Where have all the birds gone?* Princeton University Press, Princeton.

Thwaites, R. G. 1906. *Early western travels.* Volume 22. Arthur H. Clark Co., Cleveland, Ohio.

Tobish, T. 1986. Separation of Barrow's and Common Goldeneyes in all plumages. *Birding* 18:17–27.

Verner, J. 1985. Assessment of counting techniques. *Current Ornithology* 2:247–302.

Waldbauer, G. P., and J. Hays. 1965. Breeding of the Purple Gallinule in Illinois. *Auk* 81:227.

Whitcomb, R. F., C. S. Robbins, J. F. Lynch, B. L. Whitcomb, K. Klimkiewicz, and D. Bystrak. 1981. Effects of forest fragmentation on avifauna of the eastern deciduous forest. Pages 125–205 in *Forest island dynamics in man-dominated landscapes* (R. Burgess and D. M. Sharpe, eds.). Springer-Verlag, New York.

Widmann, O. 1895. Swainson's Warbler an inhabitant of the swampy woods of southeastern Missouri. *Auk* 12:112–117.

———. 1898. The great roosts on Gabberet Island, opposite north St. Louis, Missouri. *Auk* 15:22–27.

———. 1907. A preliminary catalog of the birds of Missouri. *Transactions of the Academy of Science of St. Louis* 171:1–288.

Wilcove, D. S. 1985. Nest predation in forest tracts and the decline of migratory songbirds. *Ecology* 66:1211–1214.

Wilds, C. A., and M. Newlon. 1983. The identification of dowitchers. *Birding* 15:151–166.

Will, R. L. 1973. Breeding success, numbers, and movement of House Sparrows at McLeansboro, Illinois. *Ornithological Monographs* 14:60–78.

Wright, A. H. 1911. Other early records of the Passenger Pigeon. *Auk* 28:427–449.

———. 1912. Early records of the Carolina Paroquet. *Auk* 29:343–363.

Index of Common Names

Duck
  American Black, 43, 44
  Ring-necked, 53, 371, 384
  Ruddy, 66, 373
  Wood, 40, 371, 391
  Dunlin, 130, 369

Eagle
  Bald, 74, 86, 378, 391, 393, 404
  Golden, 86, 378, 384, 404
Egret
  American, 18
  Cattle, 23, 407
  Common, 18
  Great, 18, 395
  Reddish, 23
  Snowy, 20, 399, 407
Eider, King, 56

Falcon
  Peregrine, 90, 375
  Prairie, 91, 393, 405
Finch
  House, 354, 357
  Purple, 353, 378
Flicker
  Northern, 186
  Red-shafted, 186
  Yellow-shafted, 186
Flycatcher
  Acadian, 192, 382, 389, 391, 396,
    399
  Alder, 193, 194
  Ash-throated, 199
  Great Crested, 189, 198
  Least, 195
  Olive-sided, 188
  Scissor-tailed, 200, 397
  Traill's, 193
  Vermilion, 198
  Willow, xxi, 193, 194, 386, 403
  Yellow-bellied, 191, 401
Frigatebird, Magnificent, 14, 405, 408

Gadwall, 48
Gallinule, Purple, 99, 393, 395, 399,
  404

Gnatcatcher, Blue-gray, 229
Godwit
  Hudsonian, 119
  Marbled, 120
Goldeneye
  Barrow's, 61
  Common, 57, 60, 371, 384
Golden-Plover
  American, 105
  Lesser, 104
  Pacific, 105
Goldfinch, American, 358
Goose
  Bar-headed, 35
  Barnacle, 39, 391
  Canada, 32, 34, 36, 38, 39, 87,
    370, 378, 391, 403, 405
  Egyptian, 31
  Greater White-fronted, 34, 365,
    370, 378, 391, 405
  Ross', 37, 365, 370, 378, 391,
    405
  Snow, 34, 36, 37, 39, 365, 370,
    378, 391, 405
Goshawk, Northern, 80
Grackle
  Common, 348
  Great-tailed, 348
Grebe
  Clark's, 10
  Eared, 7, 9, 365, 379
  Horned, 7, 9, 365, 375
  Pied-billed, xx, 5, 371, 379, 382,
    384, 405
  Red-necked, 8, 375
  Western, 10, 375
Grosbeak
  Black-headed, 308
  Blue, 310, 350, 366, 389, 390
  Evening, 360
  Pine, 353
  Rose-breasted, 305, 308
Ground-Dove, Common, 162
Grouse, Ruffed, 93
Gull
  Bonaparte's, 144, 145, 375, 403
  California, 147

Index of Scientific Names

W. Douglas Robinson was born and raised in southern Illinois. His interest in birds began at the age of ten and has led him to study birds in Costa Rica, Brazil, and Panama, as well as in southern Illinois. He received his bachelor's and master's degrees in zoology from Southern Illinois University at Carbondale and has published more than twenty-five articles on birds. He is now a doctoral candidate at the University of Illinois at Urbana, where he studies the ecology of tropical bird communities.